Cross-Cultural Management Revisited

Cross-Cultural Management Revisited

A Qualitative Approach

PHILIPPE D'IRIBARNE, SYLVIE CHEVRIER,
ALAIN HENRY, JEAN-PIERRE SEGAL, AND
GENEVIÈVE TRÉGUER-FELTEN

OXFORD
UNIVERSITY PRESS

OXFORD
UNIVERSITY PRESS

Great Clarendon Street, Oxford, OX2 6DP,
United Kingdom

Oxford University Press is a department of the University of Oxford.
It furthers the University's objective of excellence in research, scholarship,
and education by publishing worldwide. Oxford is a registered trade mark of
Oxford University Press in the UK and in certain other countries

First Edition published in 2020

Published in the United States of America by Oxford University Press
198 Madison Avenue, New York, NY 10016, United States of America

British Library Cataloguing in Publication Data
Data available

Library of Congress Control Number: 2019957837

ISBN 978–0–19–885747–1

DOI: 10.1093/oso/9780198857471.001.0001

Contents

Acknowledgements

The authors of this book would like to thank all those whose contribution proved to be a milestone in the accomplishment of their end goal.

First and foremost, our Gestion & Société colleagues who accompanied the lengthy process that led to the completion of this book. Among those, Anda Djoehana and Emmanuelle Sauvage who took part in the seminar in which it was given its final architecture; Catou Faust, Eléonore Mandel, Morgan Marchand, Maya Putois, Sébastien Regnault, Yasmine Saleh, and Helà Yousfi who, whenever they could make themselves available, attended the meetings in which the first versions of our chapters were discussed and enriched; may they all find here our sincere thanks. We would like to also thank our colleagues Christoph Barmeyer, from Universität Passau, Sophie Caratini from Université de Tours, and Jean-Pierre Dupuis from HEC Montréal, who commented on more advanced versions of some of our chapters. We are very grateful to them all for their contribution to our work.

Translating our chapters—initially written in French—into English constituted a great challenge which could never have been achieved without the help of the many English native speakers who proofread and amended the versions that we had produced. Thank you so much to Betty Beeler, Hayley Harris, Annette Herholdt, Kathleen Larsen-Dupuis, Mathilde Segal, Hugo Sicurani, Susanne Tietze, Niamh Tixier, Mary Vigier, Luisa Weintzierl, and Gail Wood for the time that they managed to give to that task. Some other chapters were handed over to our translator, Sam O'Connell, whom we also wish to thank for the quality of the work delivered.

This book also results from the numerous exchanges that we have had over the years—and still have today—with colleagues working on similar themes, specifically, GEM&L (Research Association on Management & Language) members and all the attendees of the 'Management and Culture' seminars organized by ATLAS-AFMI (French speaking Association on International Management). Similarly, the tracks on cultures in organizations at EURAM (European Academy of Management) and EGOS (European Group for Organizational Studies) were extremely worthy loci for discussing our topics. So many of our colleagues have contributed to the widening and deepening of our thinking that we could never mention them all. May they find in this collective mention the expression of our sincere thanks for their comments and criticisms.

Many years of teaching and doctoral supervision have led us to present our theoretical and methodological choices as clearly as we could. Our teaching within the Master's Degree in Intercultural Management at Paris-Dauphine University has made us share the rich international experiences of students from very diverse backgrounds. Last but not least, supervising our doctoral students—some of whom have now become our colleagues—has allowed us to broaden the geographical scope of our work and contributed to nourishing the dynamics of our research. The authors would like to pay tribute to all their former doctoral students: Cristina Carzozi, Moussa Elias Farakhan Diomande, Anda Djoehana Wiradikarta, Mingming Duan, Catherine Faust (Morel), Serge Alain Godong Bend, Liece Khalfaoui, Fang Li, Eleonore Mandel, Morgan Marchand, Anne Morel-Lab, Viet Long Nguyen, Aneta Orlinska (Hamza), Sébastien Regnault, Emmanuelle Sauvage, Michaël Viegas Pires, and Hèla Yousfi. Their research fields were located all over the world, and their results have substantially contributed to the progress of our research, with each field providing new insights into the issues discussed within our team.

The research on which this book is based owes much to the companies and organizations that have supported and funded our research over these three decades. We would particularly like to mention l'Agence Française de Développement, Air France–KLM, Belgacom, Chanel, Danone, EDF, le Gouvernement de la Nouvelle Calédonie, the French NGO GRET, Lafarge, Orange, Peugeot S.A., Pechiney, RATP, Renault, SNCF, SNECMA, STMicroelectronics, and Total Group. Without the access to the field that these companies and organizations granted us, we would never have been able to build and implement the contextualized approach that characterizes our research in cross-cultural management. We are therefore very grateful to all those who, in these companies, have trusted us and given us access to the field and, in particular, to Geoffroy Bouvet, Yves Bucas-Français, Pierre Garcia, Christian Herrault, and Georges-Yves Kervern.

Finally, we would like to thank Université Paris-Est Marne-la-Vallée and the Vietnamese company BECAMEX, whose support made it possible to finance the translation of some of the chapters in this book.

We cannot end these acknowledgements without thanking Geert Hofstede for his decisive encouragements and international promotion of our first book and Alain d'Iribarne for his instrumental role in the launching of our research group. Last but not least, we wish to pay our deepest respects to Tatjana Globokar, who contributed to our first co-edited book, *Cultures et Mondialisation*. Her memory is still vivid today.

List of Tables and Boxes

Tables

Boxes

List of Abbreviations

AFD	Agence Française de Développement
B2B	Business to Business (Communication)
CCDA	Cross-Cultural Discourse Analysis
CCL	Common Corporate Language
CDC	Commonwealth Development Corporation
CEO	Chief Operating Officer
COSCO	China Ocean Shipping Company
CRM	Customer Relationship Management
CSR	Corporate Social Responsibility
DB	Deutsche Bahn (German national train company)
EGOS	European Group for Organizational Studies
ELF	English as a Lingua Franca
ENEO	Energy of Cameroon
EURAM	European Academy of Management
GE	General Electric
GLOBE	Project of Survey on leadership: Global Leadership and Organizational Behavior Effectiveness
HR	Human Resources
HRM	Human Resources Management
ILO	International Labour Organization
JIT	Just in time
KPI	Key Performance Indicator
MBO	Management by Objectives
MNE	Multi National Enterprise
MP	Member of Parliament
NGO	Non-Governmental Organization
RNET	Régie Nationale des Eaux du Togo
SME	Small to Medium Enterprise
SNCF	Société Nationale des Chemins de Fer Français (French national train company)
SONEL	Société Nationale d'Électricité du Cameroun
TQM	Total Quality Management
UAW	United Automobile Workers
UGTT	Tunisian General Labour Union (*Union Générale Tunisienne du Travail*)
WWF	World Wildlife Fund

Introduction

The Need for a New Approach to Culture in Organizations

We are experiencing a rather curious situation today. Globalization is in full swing. International cooperation actions are more and more frequent. An increasing number of agents, who were socialized in different worlds, experience first-hand the difficulties that need to be overcome in such situations. Yet management practices are being homogenized all over the world. The elites in emerging countries are falling over themselves to follow the expensive training given by Western universities. Attempts to achieve a global standardization of management practices have probably never been stretched so far in multinational companies. However, the dissemination of the best practices of a management claiming to be universal is confronted with the irreducible resistance of the diversity of cultures. This resistance remains poorly understood. The most common representation of cultural differences taught in universities and in training seminars for companies disregards the analysis of concrete realities, thus failing to shed light on what is actually taking place in these encounters. Understanding this constitutes a major intellectual and practical challenge for researchers who focus on both *culture* and *management*. Based on extensive empirical data, this publication aims to provide a response to this, through a renewed conception of the link between these two terms.

A Denial of Reality

Are we really seeing a convergence of managerial practices around the world, based on a reference model, built in the Western world and especially in the USA, a model which companies worldwide would appear to be clinging to under the combined pressure of consultants, certifying bodies, and their clients? Observing the realities in the field reported in this publication leads us to believe that this is not at all the case. Considerable transformations have, admittedly, taken place in management methods due to the development of information and communication technologies. The apparent homogenization of practices is, however, misleading. The uses made of these methods at local level very often diverge from the

Cross-Cultural Management Revisited: A Qualitative Approach. Philippe d'Iribarne, Sylvie Chevrier, Alain Henry, Jean-Pierre Segal, and Geneviève Tréguer-Felten, Oxford University Press (2020).
DOI: 10.1093/oso/9780198857471.001.0001

original version of the model: the latter is largely reinterpreted and adjusted to the social and cultural requirements of the context in which it is implemented. This phenomenon does not only concern companies in developing countries where managers themselves easily admit that quite some patience is required to make oneself understood by locals and convince them to change their ways of organizing themselves. As we will have the opportunity to show, it equally concerns companies in advanced countries on every continent.

Furthermore, do we really believe that employees involved in international projects always manage to clearly communicate, thanks to the combined virtues of English as a Lingua Franca (ELF) and of an English managerial vocabulary learnt at university or on the job? Observing how these teams function and unveiling the extent of the misunderstandings which need to be managed on a daily basis lead us to abandon the utopia of a world that has become homogeneous, in which 'international' management has succeeded in erasing the identities and cultural differences of the old world.

Why Revisit the Theories Concerning Culture?

The present situation in terms of cultural analysis is profoundly unsatisfactory. International companies have not adopted analytical tools enabling them to address the problems they frequently face. This seriously affects the relevance and, ultimately, the effectiveness of the management in a context of application which is now increasingly intercultural.

The reality of the functioning of subsidiaries of international companies is generally not known by headquarters which, most of the time, only receive accounting information and operational management ratios which ignore the human and social realities of local organization. Local managers, who are responsible for both implementing the managerial methods received from headquarters and building local legitimacy, are hard-pressed to combine these two objectives. They lack elements to understand the underlying reasons for both their local successes and failures, or semi-failures. Without analysing to what extent their initiatives have meant something to those they have to manage, it is impossible for them to build and capitalize on the lessons learned from their experience and pass them on to their successors. Knowledge management is today desperately poor on this cultural dimension.

Reflection on experience is especially limited as the management methods and tools proposed by manuals and consultants are presented as bringing a technical rationality of universal value. The conditions in which these methods were originally defined, the meanings given to them by their first user, the successive adjustments and fine tuning that accompanied their development locally, have all been kept quiet. The final product, which is firstly destined to be exported to other organizations, then, if it meets with success, to other countries and other continents, has been presented as universal. Yet, the transfer is not always simple. Misunderstandings are frequent. Local reinterpretations and hybridization are common. However, there is never any mention of these 'managerial impurities', which are considered as heresies needing to be covered with the cloak of charity.

Admittedly, a vast body of research is attempting to understand cultural differences through quantitative methods. This approach makes it possible in a short time to produce statistical data that give a feeling of objectivity. They provide a first layer of awareness of the existence of differences between countries. But we shall see that the data obtained hardly help build in practice at local level management methods tailored to each field of management and to each context. By reproducing, ad infinitum, an approach whose benefits have been largely exhausted, the discipline risks losing its credibility.

The authors of this publication share the conviction that there is a need for an extensive renewal of the analysis of the interactions between cultures and management. This renewal involves analysing qualitative data collected by the researchers from the field, a too-often neglected approach to-date. It also involves the use of a new approach to national cultures adapted to the analysis of management issues. It requires going beyond the unproductive debate which exists today between two opposing streams. On the one hand, a 'main stream' in intercultural management continues to pursue the chimera of confining the national culture of a country to figures that take no account of organizational contexts and culturally-structured social relations. On the other hand, 'anticulturalists' enclosed in universalist paradigms—whether power relations in organizations or the impact of technological changes on working relationships are concerned—refuse to acknowledge the diversity of behaviours around the world and their impact on the functioning of organizations.

The purpose of this publication is to plunge into the hidden realities of the adaptation of management procedures deemed universal to the diversity of cultures and seek to understand their determinants. It confers on this adaptation a status and legitimacy that the all too theoretical and disembodied universe of management tends to deny.

Why have the differences between what is prescribed and what is real not fed more into the analysis of situations where cultures come into play? Practical reasons can be put forward, which provide a first level of analysis: headquarters are poorly informed about how subsidiaries actually function, expression of the difficulties encountered is generally restrained. Very few international companies are willing to critically examine this. Most prefer to stick to a diplomatic avoidance for fear of worsening the problems. Beyond these practical reasons, a fundamental question concerns the generally accepted distinction between the management of people—a field where the relevance of a cultural analysis is not contested—on the one hand, and all the other management procedures, such as deciding, controlling, planning, on the other hand. For the latter, the so-called 'human factor' is considered by experts as 'off topic'. We simply have to comply with such unavoidable technical rationality. However, this separation is inappropriate. It leads to two attitudes which are equally questionable: either giving too much credit to the rationality of international standards and the effectiveness of best practices, and ignoring the impact of the cultural issues associated with their implementation, or essentializing the individuals belonging to a given area, claiming that their 'culture' authorizes, or does not authorize, them to effectively appropriate the methods that are held up as a reference today.

Our Approach

Our approach is based on a set of empirical data collected over the past thirty years from a large sample of companies of different sizes and industries in about fifty countries around the world. These data were collected by members of a research team, Gestion & Société, in close collaboration with multinational companies concerned with better exploiting the potential of the cultures with which they were dealing. They covered all management issues—not just HR issues—and constituted a considerable amount of concrete experience, both in economically developed and emerging countries, where the culture shock is often spectacular.

Our observations pointed to differences between the meanings that individuals, throughout the world, conferred on the daily situations arising from companies' operations, such as being subject to the authority of a superior, responding to requests made by a client, or even having the proper execution of one's work monitored. These are all social relationships that individuals approach differently from one country to another, be they men or women, engineers or labourers, generations X, Y, or Z, IBM employees, or members of a small company in which everyone knows everyone else.

These empirical foundations led to an in-depth review of existing theoretical approaches to account for the nationwide significant features we had observed. Our approach will be presented in detail in Chapter 3. It falls within the scope of interpretative approaches to culture, which consider the latter as a filter through which people understand reality and give it meaning. However, it was necessary to innovate relative to what these interpretative approaches—which feed into cultural studies—usually are. In general, the field of cultural studies adopts an interactionist vision which takes culture as a social construct constantly being redefined, the result of a continual negotiation between protagonists. They consider small communities, constantly reinventing their practices, their norms, and even their values, according to the requirements of their environment, in which the postulate of the co-construction of culture by actors may apply. But they avoid considering what one can find to be common in one country, despite great individual diversity. We have here a new sociological object which has not aroused their interest, maybe especially because national cultures have been assimilated in a controversial way to folkloric constructions mobilized for rather disturbing nationalist purposes. As a result, their impact on the legitimacy of forms of management has been largely ignored.

To account for these traits that we observed at national level and finally to theorize them, d'Iribarne (2014) proposes to split the analysis in two.

A first level corresponds to the existence of positive or negative reference images of ways of living and working together which structure a universe of meaning. What is experienced resonates with these images. Not only do they impact the way experience makes sense, but they also colour it with the emotions that they carry in the collective universes of meaning. In the life of organizations, great efforts are made, with varying degrees of success, to make daily reality look like the positive images and to fight against what evokes negative images. A second and deeper level refers to the existence, within each society, of a specific type of concerns, of fears, associated with situations that generate feelings of malaise, anxiety, situations which evoke a peril, a threat, which it is essential to ward off. The meaning taken on by situations (and, consequently, the reactions to them) is governed by a framework of interpretation which leads to a keen interest being given to what evokes either the type of serious threat, or the ways of salvation that make it possible to escape from it. However different they may be by their social position as by the interests they defend, individuals belonging to the same society share the manner in which they structure their understanding of social situations.

It is because culture brings very strong and very deep feelings into play that acting in a culturally inappropriate manner is likely to provoke extreme reactions. What seems to go without saying in one place can, elsewhere, provoke indignation and revolt. These representations have a powerful influence on both the processes to legitimize authority and on the conditions on which confidence and cooperation between stakeholders is built. Intercultural situations highlight them via the analysis of what happens when they meet. But such situations are merely the tip of the iceberg. National cultures have an effect on management on a much larger scale and in fact concern all organizations. This is particularly true when managers seek to introduce forms of management which clash with the local representations of what could be called 'virtuous authority'. Such situations, which are to be seen in every country in the world, generate active or passive forms of resistance that are sources of collective inefficiency. Other forms of management, in tune with local conceptions of a legitimate exercise of virtuous authority, can put an end to these resistances in a spectacular manner.

We have taken up the main chapters of classic textbooks on management, the same ones which almost always ignore the cultural contexts from which the solutions given as models have emerged. We felt that it was essential to break with this overshadowing of the context and show readers how culture, as we understand it, has an impact on all the acts of management of companies, including those which are described as the technical part of management.

The conviction which guides us is that these methods—generally presented as being inspired by a universal rationale of effectiveness—are ALSO deep-rooted cultural productions. We have endeavoured to show in what way, in each field, the international standards taught in business schools and recommended by consultants convey a particular culturally-rooted conception of on-going social relations. Our concern for not separating these two technical and relational dimensions from any managerial practice has led us to adopt this thematic breakdown.

A Publication Informed by our Research Results

This publication is based on the experience of longstanding research conducted by the authors. In each chapter, we chose the examples which were the most instructional. We show how economic, technological, and social transformations, which have a dramatic effect on the lives of companies today, coexist with a cultural continuity in the way in which local employees identify problems and build their response to these new issues. Having started this research in 1982, we have observed a considerable cultural continuity on a scale of several decades in the countries where we made several distant observations over time.

Most 'modernizers' consider what they call 'cultural burdens' as factors that generate inefficiency and resistance to the changes that they would like to drive. In fact, cultural continuity is in no way incompatible with the success of change. Taking account of this is, instead, an essential ingredient of this success: it allows the desired transformations to find a positive meaning in employees' cultural references. Welcome changes are those which manage, beyond the inevitable conflicts of power and interests, to be perceived by those who implement them as better than the status quo.

To highlight the cross-cutting nature of the influence of culture on management practices, we granted two countries, the USA and France, a special place in this book. We show how their management practices, whatever the areas of management considered—leadership, control, or customer relations—systematically incorporate representations that are consistent with their own visions of social relations. The choice of the USA was obvious because of its international influence—not to say its hegemony—in the field of management. Choosing France is justified by the easy access to research sites thanks to the support we received from French international companies who counted on this research to implement a more effective management of their foreign subsidiaries. Moreover, France, like the United States, is part of the large Western cultural area. Including both makes it possible to avoid simplifications involving such contrasts as, for example, that of 'Westerners' and 'Asians', without measuring the extent to which the various components of these large groups can, alongside common characteristics which give reasons to bring them together, have major cultural differences within them.

A Prominent Place to the Formulations of Stakeholders

While sociological analyses of organizations (Morgan, 1988) generally seek to identify conflicts of power and interest—seen as a universal property of organizations—we seek to clarify the way in which the corresponding issues take on a particular form in a given cultural context. Admittedly, at a high level of abstraction, any organization is a place with a complex combination of internal conflicts and cooperation requirements. However, we show that the specific content of these issues, far from being a universal expression of a 'human nature', depends on cultural references which specify the local conception of 'virtuous authority' or a 'legitimate' form of reconciling interests. The detailed analysis of the stakeholders' comments, with input from international comparisons, gives access to the originality of each of these references and highlights the influence that cultures have on management much better than 'average' scores of attitudes and behaviours can.

The field survey gathers the comments made by the local respondents. The way they use their language, the images and associations that it inspires or those they select among the possibilities that it offers—images that may vary considerably between cultures associated with one and the same language—allow access to the universes of meaning in which people make sense of their daily realities. The abundant use of the verbatim collected in our surveys is never intended to summarize the wide variety of opinions expressed by stakeholders. It aims to highlight the categories in which they express judgements, which are, furthermore, very diverse depending on many factors, including their position in the organization.

To shed as much light as possible on the universe of meaning of which these verbatim testify, we paid great attention to their translation. Despite the need to transpose them into another universe of meaning—that of native English speakers, but also respecting those of English-as-a-lingua-franca speakers, or ELF (see Chapter 10)—we often opted for literal translations so as to remain as faithful as possible to the speakers' categories. Whenever the distance with the nearest English words appeared too important, we mentioned the original language terms—for example, the French term *métier* (profession) occasionally encountered in its original version in Anglo American literature. As the book was originally written in French, we also paid great attention to the difficulties associated with translating the authors' spontaneous use of expressions related to their French culture. All the quotations mentioned in this book which are not associated with a reference are taken from our transcriptions or translated transcriptions of the interviews from field studies. As we ensured the anonymity to all our respondents, we will not provide their name or date in association with their quotes. Their position or role in the organization only are mentioned when necessary. We use three ellipsis dots in brackets to indicate that a small section of text has been removed to facilitate readability and provide clarifying pieces of information in square brackets.

Organization of the Publication

The publication comprises four parts.

The first part lays the foundations of our approach, starting by placing readers before the realities of the field which inspired it (d'Iribarne et al., 1998). The first chapter takes the example of Management by objectives (MBO) to highlight the embeddedness of 'American-style' management in the political and cultural world of the country which conceived it, the United States of America. That management model is held up as a reference all over the world, although it reflects a local conception of management which is far from being shared in a universal manner. Chapter 2 illustrates the deviations undergone by MBO in Tunisia, France, and Vietnam. How can these deviations be accounted for? What conception of culture should be used to account for this? This is the purpose of Chapter 3 which, with input from our empirical research, presents the theoretical framework that inspired both our previous research and the writing of this book.

The second part of the publication proposes to revisit the main fields of management in the light of a cultural perspective. It shows how national cultures come into play, both in the way of raising problems and in the way appropriate responses can be provided. We see how features of the social world in which stakeholders are immersed, whether they are 'at home' and 'with each other' or, on the contrary and increasingly often, 'elsewhere' and with 'others' have to be taken into consideration. These features regulate the relationships that employees have with their boss, their hierarchy, their colleagues, their clients, and, more generally, all the stakeholders of the organization.

This second part comprises six chapters. Chapter 4 addresses leadership, based on a comparative analysis of the recommendations given to future managers in the United States, Germany, and France. It shows how far these two European countries are from the charismatic approach to leadership advocated by Americans. Chapter 5 deals with the use of formalized operating procedures. Examples from Cameroon, France, and the United States illustrate how, from one culture to another, identical procedures give rise to very different reactions, in each case related to specific human and social issues. Chapter 6 addresses decision making. First, the analysis of a Franco-Dutch case highlights the contrast in decision-making between a process of accommodation between people with different views and interests and an intellectual process in search of "what is best", according to general criteria shared by all participants in the decision. Then, examples from Cameroon and from Jordan illustrate the very dissimilar attempts that are made in different cultures to mitigate the destructive effects of the resentment felt by those disadvantaged by decisions made. Chapter 7 deals with industrial relations between management and trade unions. It highlights how, from one country to another, very different conditions must be put in place to ensure effective dialogue between them. It shows that the regulation of their relationships is dependent upon the local representations of what it means to exercise power fairly. Customer relations are addressed in Chapter 8. It focuses on the different readings of the relationship between sellers and their customers. Three examples, in China, France, and Côte d'Ivoire, illustrate how these relationships take on a meaning that is dependent on the forms of social relations involved. Chapter 9 addresses issues of corporate ethics and social responsibility: it points to the dissimilar roles in society that are assigned to companies in France and in the United States. It tackles corruption issues by analysing an Argentine case, and focuses on what distinguishes cultures in which an ethic of respect for principles prevails from those in which an ethic of fidelity takes precedence. In each case, we highlight the local deviations of (reputed) international management standards and propose an interpretation that integrates the local meanings of the considered management practices.

The third part addresses the situations of interactions which are more and more frequent in organizations in today's increasing internationalization of business life. Chapter 10 points to and analyses the pitfalls linked to the use of a so-called common language which each correspondent understands using their own cultural references. More generally, it addresses the risks related to the transposition of messages from one language to another. Chapter 11, which is devoted to the corporate communications of international companies, shows how national specificities inspire the very way in which they introduce themselves to international audiences. Chapter 12 addresses the challenges of multicultural teams. It specifically highlights the consequences of diverging conceptions of social relations on interactions in the workplace, whether they involve the exercise of authority or the settlement of conflicts.

The fourth and last part aims to propose possible avenues for improving the taking into account of this cultural dimension, in particular in the context of emerging countries. The difficulty of effectively taking this dimension into account, when cultural references remain implicit, is illustrated in the erratic history of the national electricity company of Cameroon narrated in Chapter 13. Chapter 14 analyses both failed and successful transfers of management methods and tools in contexts that are culturally different from those in which they were initially forged, and recommends culturally-informed transfers. Chapter 15 deals with the various avenues to improve multicultural teams' efficiency. Finally, Chapter 16 aims to familiarize readers with the data collection and analysis method used by the authors. It aims to encourage researchers to extend the approach we have developed to new national contexts and new management issues.

Who is this Publication Intended For?

This publication is intended for all those—prescribers, practitioners, or theorists—who, in their professional practice, wish to renew their views on the interactions between national cultures and management.

It is naturally intended for academics, our colleagues, whether they belong to the intercultural management community or teach contextualized management practices drawing attention to their cultural roots. We feel that an awareness of the original context of theories and management practices given as examples everywhere is a major teaching objective. This monograph will be of interest for graduate students who have already been introduced to cross-cultural management and who wish to explore the subject further.

It is also intended for consultants and trainers in cross-cultural management. It is important for those working on international cooperation to be aware of the cultural roots of the tools they are using, and which they all too often believe to be 'neutral'. We would like to contribute to a renewal of cross-cultural management teaching. We urge consultants and trainers to give up attributing simple sets of attitudes and behaviours to employees in a given country. They should not merely present them as more collectivist, more hierarchical, or more bureaucratic than those of another country. They should open their audiences to the subtleties of cultures, and stop taking as the only reference a Western world given as an example of what it is necessary to be and to do in order to be efficient.

Last but not least, the book is intended for those who work in cultural environments differing from their own. Our aim is to help them to analyse the complex situations that they encounter as well as make the most of the potential of local contexts.

PART I

UNIVERSAL MANAGEMENT UTOPIA

1
The Cultural Roots of American Management

The concept of management by objectives (MBO) was born in the United States in the middle of the twentieth century. Since then, it has been so successful worldwide that it is associated in many minds with the very idea of 'modern' management, together with other American practices—such as lean management (Womack & al., 1997) or reengineering (Champy & al., 1995)—that have also become managerial standards. MBO can be considered a major component, if not the core, of the American idea of effective and acceptable management. From its inception, the principles on which it is based have not been seriously challenged and MBO continues to inspire business practice, despite the significant changes that have taken place since then in both the American economy and in US society in general.

Peter Drucker (1998), who codified the practice, considered that the implementation of the model needed to adjust only marginally to the context in which it is applied:

> Whether you are managing a software company, a hospital, a bank or a Boy Scout organization, the differences apply to only about 10% of your work. This 10% is determined by the organization's specific mission, its specific culture, its specific history and its specific vocabulary. (Peter Drucker, 1998)

Drucker did not anticipate the future transfer of his model to businesses outside his own country, nor the subsequent impact on it of the cultural diversity to be found in the world outside the US. Today, evidence of different versions of MBO are routinely to be found in the daily life of a large number of organizations in many different countries, where its origins are often ignored. However, MBO was not born 'anywhere' and the people experiencing it in the workplace were not 'anybody'. Those who developed it and those who subsequently applied and experienced it were part of a specific society that had its own views on the right way to better organize labour relations. It was out of this very specific national vision of their world that the creators of MBO identified problematic situations which needed to be addressed. When they were thinking about ways and means to

Cross-Cultural Management Revisited: A Qualitative Approach. Philippe d'Iribarne, Sylvie Chevrier, Alain Henry, Jean-Pierre Segal, and Geneviève Tréguer-Felten, Oxford University Press (2020).
DOI: 10.1093/oso/9780198857471.001.0001

better mobilize the energies of a workforce, they had American employees in mind, not Chinese, Peruvian, or Russian employees. How could responses adapted to their expectations have been elaborated without taking into account the singularity of these employees' fears and aspirations? Similarly, how could effective and acceptable solutions emerge if local employees' points of views remain unheeded?

The purpose of this chapter is to re-establish the original link between the philosophy underlying the design of MBO on the one hand, and the cultural environment in which it came about, on the other. Generally speaking, academic work has focused more on the hegemony of these tools (Birkinshaw, 2013) than on their original inspiration. Re-establishing the link between MBO and the prevailing culture of the United States of America at the time of its inception will shed light on the reasons why MBO has been so successful there, and why its implementation in businesses in countries outside the US has not always achieved the expected result.

This chapter is divided into two sections. The first is devoted to explaining the link between MBO—this hard core of 'American-style' management—and associated cultural references that have been widely shared by Americans for generations. The second part highlights the ethos underpinning the American cultural roots of MBO, before demonstrating that they are not universal but cultural, using situations in which Americans are employed in foreign companies operating in the USA. The mutual misunderstandings generated by this meeting of different cultures sheds light on the singularity of the American expectations that MBO satisfies so well, but also on the poor knowledge that foreign managers have of the cultural drivers behind those expectations.

1.1 A Cultural Inspiration that Spans Generations

This section aims to show how the concept of a fair and just exercise of power that inspired the creators of the MBO concept was retained through the following decades, despite important demographic, economic, technological, and social changes taking place in American society. First, we will show the extent to which the founding fathers of MBO were sensitive to the aspirations of American workers of their time. Second, the interviews of ordinary employees, performed two generations later in an ordinary Maryland factory, will indicate the lasting nature of these aspirations and point to the cultural benchmarks within which they are embedded. Finally, we will see that these same attitudes still prevail in today's workers, even those working for American companies deemed to be the most innovative and revolutionary in terms of management practice.

1.1.1 At the Roots of Management by Objectives

It is difficult to determine an exact date for the first formulation of the idea of MBO. Practice most likely preceded the theory that later formalized it. It all began with General Electric (GE). GE's decision-makers were, like many other executives before them, confronted with the need to improve the functioning of an organization whose growth and business diversification was making it increasingly difficult to manage. Their response, in the form of a coordinated decentralization of missions and responsibilities—previously concentrated at the top level of the organization—was successful.

The new system succeeded in providing line managers with the guarantees required for them to assume the risks associated with delegation, while at the same time offering their subordinates the guarantees they needed to accept their new responsibilities. The balance thus found was based from the outset on a shared representation of the relationship between employees (analogous to suppliers) providing their work to superiors (analogous to customers). It was up to managers to clarify orders given and requests made, and up to subordinates to say if they were able to 'deliver' the expected results. A frank and open dialogue between the parties was seen to be the necessary tool to enable them to come to an agreement. A contractual agreement, negotiated person-to-person, clearly setting down the commitments made by each party, was considered necessary to build the trust and cooperation required for them to work effectively together.

The GE manual (1956: 73) was distributed in the early 1950s to its managers. The originators of MBO and in particular, Peter Drucker himself, were closely involved in its drafting. The manual itself is particularly interesting from the perspective of its championing of co-operation and mutual understanding rather than coercion. Instead of proposing techniques or recipes, it presents a commercial interpretation of the working relationship between employees, based on the main principles of American democracy—that is, the acknowledgement of each citizen's lawful right to remain in control of the choices that affect his or her destiny. From the beginning, the distancing from an authoritatively unilateral command style is clearly stated:

> Delegation is much more than simply a one-way channel through which instructions are issued downward from a higher authority. To be effective, it must be a two-way understanding between a man and his manager.
>
> (General Electric Manual, 1956)

Of particular interest is the latter sentence contrasting *one-way channel instructions* with *two-way understanding* and explicitly introducing the idea that an employee, even under the hierarchical authority of his superior, remains a man—a man, with his own will and with whom an agreement must be reached.

Regardless of the hierarchical level within the company of the persons concerned or the extent of their responsibilities, or of the various technical requirements needed to fulfil tasks, the manual further states that the delegation process must meet the same social requirements:

> The details of responsibilities and relationships, of authorities, and of accountabilities, change from component to component, from position to position, and from level to level in the organization structure. But the process of delegation itself is fundamentally the same in the kind of agreement and understanding that should exist between each man and the manager to whom he reports. This process for arriving at an agreement and understanding is independent of the differences in scope, degree, and consequence, which vary from position to position. (General Electric Manual, 1956)

The accountability expected from employees is presented as an expression of a voluntary choice, rather than a constraint:

> When a man accepts a particular job or position, he agrees to perform this work and team work and to be accountable to his manager for such performance. This is a voluntary acceptance of responsibility and accountability on the part of the man when he accepts and, for as long as he continues to hold his particular position in the organization structure, he thus makes himself accountable for all the work and team work so defined as long as he holds that particular position.
> (General Electric Manual, 1956)

MBO is thus presented as a tool for coordination that respects the autonomy of individual volition, and not as an instrument of control for establishing a form of domination by the one who commands over the one who obeys. A mature and adult person does not need to be supervised in the same way as a child would.

> One does not need to be 'controlled' or 'commanded' if one knows what is to be done and why, if one knows, from continual measurement of results, whether the work is getting done as planned and on schedule, or if not, why not.
> (General Electric Manual, 1956)

Anyone who, in good faith, has not found grounds for agreement with his manager must accept the consequences by withdrawing with dignity:

> Minor differences of opinion between a man and his manager are normal, inconsequential, and to be expected where both are men of good mind, of

> creative capacity and of good purpose. Of course, if an issue of fundamental principle is involved, the man can either ask to have his recommendation referred to higher authority; or he can, if he considers that serious, elect to avoid following the desired course by removing himself from the situation entirely. (General Electric Manual, 1956)

An employee does not cease being a man, the manual explicitly says—and this is an interesting statement when we consider that this was not written by the leader of an anti-capitalist organization but by consultants closely working with the company's CEO.

> If after fair discussion, the man does not succeed in persuading his manager, and if he strongly believes that his position is so right that he cannot go along with his manager's decision, he should seek a new job and a new manager with whom he can work in harmony. (General Electric Manual, 1956)

Just as a supplier will inform his customer that he is unable to satisfy his request, the employee may inform his manager that he does not feel up to the task requested and refuse the contract offered—and in this way, the familiar figure of the American citizen free to negotiate the use and value of his work emerges. He is depicted as a man free to make his own choices, ready to confront the hardships and demands of life and to forge his own destiny, provided that he is given the power to decide for himself. This reference to the figure of the free man evoked by the words *man*, *voluntary*, and *accepting*—the epitome of the American vision of the universal requirement of respect for people—implies that the rights due to each employee as a citizen must be respected, including at work.

Have all GE managers ever since faithfully applied these principles of particularly high moral inspiration? Possibly not, and presumably not all of them. Nevertheless, as we will now show, it is true that American subordinates both past and present, have expected—but not necessarily received—such treatment.

1.1.2 A Plant in Maryland in the Mid-1980s

We will now see what American employees themselves say when asked about the way in which the relations with their superiors are organized and regulated. We will use data collected in the mid-1980s in an aluminium plant in Maryland[1]. They illustrate the unique way in which local actors analyse their working relationships, and we will measure their analysis against other responses in the following chapter. As will be seen, their responses are consistent with the logic that inspired the architects of objective-based management forty years earlier.

A large number of sociological surveys launched in companies take the following question as their starting point: 'Could you tell me what your job is?' In countries such as Germany or France, researchers will most certainly hear their interviewees highlight what their profession and function are. German employees will be happy to speak about the tasks for which they are responsible and for which they have been prepared by the organization employing them. They will not feel the need to introduce the figure of their superior in order to explain what their work consists of. Their French counterparts will not act differently, preferring, as will be seen in the next chapter, to present themselves as independent and autonomous people, rather than as individuals working under someone else's authority. Within an American company, however, the answers are different.

When asked to explain their jobs, American employees, whoever they are and whatever their position in the company hierarchy, usually begin by explaining to whom they report. 'I'm a maintenance mechanic on the pot line', said one worker. 'I work for a foreman who tells me every morning what my daily task is'. 'My title', says his immediate supervisor, 'is "maintenance supervisor" in the carbon plant maintenance structure. I report to the general foreman who himself reports to the superintendent for the maintenance department'. This *for whom* has at least two meanings: on the one hand, it refers to the person to whom the employee reports hierarchically and from whom he receives his instructions; on the other hand, it refers to the special relationship connecting subordinates to their superiors. As part of this relationship, subordinates are expected to achieve the objectives assigned by their superiors, while the latter are in turn expected to ensure that workers are given the right conditions to carry out their duties.

Everyone must be able to make a fully-informed commitment to the objectives set by the next level in the company hierarchy. Managers' authority to formulate their requests is not contested, as long as they are clearly stated. Neither is their authority to control. According to a head of department:

> There are supervisors who like it when the head of department goes to the factory to see what is happening. It's mainly if they feel they're doing a good job...morally, it's good...workers in general appreciate supervisors, foremen... Everyone, I think, likes to know where they stand, what their responsibilities are, and what their results are.

Everyone must equally be forewarned of the criteria according to which their performance will be measured and judged. The provision of quantified performance indicators—even though they do not always fully reflect the quality of the work done—is considered legitimate, both for the person who controls and for the person whose work is controlled. The director of the plant maintenance department explains:

> I'm trying to reduce the activity in maintenance to a quantifiable measure. Everyone must also be regularly informed in order to know where they stand in the accomplishment of the mission entrusted to them. I think it is important to share it with the people. I am convinced that a well-informed person tends to operate better than a person that doesn't know.

The appraisal procedure is presented in the guide distributed to each employee. It emphasizes its role in maintaining a balanced relationship between supervisors and their employees, even if it is not an egalitarian relationship. As such, it is entirely in keeping with the way in which the procedure was introduced in the GE manual some forty years earlier.

> Performance appraisal is an integral part in the development of an individual. Supervisors should conduct performance review at regular intervals with all employees. This review involves the discussion of the position's current objectives as well as the future ones. It provides an opportunity for both the supervisor and the employee to resolve possible misconception concerning what is expected and how it should be achieved. (General Electric Manual, 1956)

The principles of autonomy and accountability, on which the originators of MBO placed great emphasis, are taken on by many of those involved. 'I don't like being told how to do it. Just tell me what you want and I'll try to get it for you', says a general foreman. 'My boss shares this philosophy and we have worked well together'.

One of his colleagues associates this autonomy with a form of control over his own destiny:

> Most people, the American people, don't like to be told how to do this job, what I do first and what I do second. Most of the people feel they have to be somewhat of a master of their own destiny by determining how they accomplish their job. As long as their goals are accomplished, the boss should be happy with that.

It may seem surprising that an American foreman should connect the way in which he chooses to perform his daily work with his aspiration to *control his own destiny*. However, it is not insignificant. It makes a clear distinction between being allowed to freely mobilize one's own skills and competencies on the one hand, and being subjected to a strict organizational discipline and closely controlled in one's actions on the other—as may be happening elsewhere in other companies.

Many other remarks made by the employees in that factory resonated, not only with the technical principles that guided the designers of MBO, but also with their general American ethos of respect and consideration for others.

The symbolic equality of the members of the production-line is expressed in various ways. Managers must keep their door open and remain accessible to their subordinates. Whatever the functional and statutory differences between the two protagonists, each of them is owed the same respect. 'From my experience,' says a supervisor in the Maintenance Department of the metallurgical plant, 'it's a nation where anybody, you know, who needs to talk to somebody higher, normally they have the option to come up and talk to him'.

In addition, in this perspective, it is acceptable for subordinates to express disagreement with their superiors: 'We don't want people to be yes people', says the director of the department, 'if the people truly think this is not proper, we think we should hear about it'. Superiors will have the last word, in the name of the personal responsibility they assume: 'I'm sorry, I know you disagreed, I understand why, but this is how it is going to be'. But by listening to their subordinate, they will have shown respect—as Americans view it.

Such a 'Russian doll' conception of the hierarchical lines of authority—where subordinates are entitled to consider that they help their superiors to cope with the pressure to which they are all submitted by those further up the hierarchy—also contributes to the symbolic equality of their working environment. Subordinates depend just as much on their superiors, who set their tasks, as superiors depend on them to carry them out. It is the sum of the clearly individualized contributions of each individual that produces the expected collective result. A foreman explains:

> The goals my boss has have got to go down to the personnel who accomplish the goals. He defines who should accomplish what goal, and we have to try to shoulder some of the responsibilities and some of the pressure.

As will be seen, the fundamentals of American management practice as it was in the 1980s are still relevant in many companies operating today.

1.1.3 Managerial Innovations Confirming Cultural Continuity

Several generations have come and gone since Drucker first formulated his theory of MBO. In this time, the educational level of many employees has improved significantly. New information-processing tools have revolutionized the organization of the workplace. The service sector now occupies a large proportion of the workforce. Authority relations have undergone profound changes everywhere, in families, at school, and within companies. Managerial methods have followed one another, praising successively, for efficiency sake, the merits of a unifying corporate culture, of corporate loyalty, or of new management software-packages that measure individual and collective performance from every angle.

Despite all the changes that have taken place in recent years, the ultimate vision of good social relations in the workplace inherent in the concept of objective-based management appears to have lost none of its relevance. The new possibilities offered by technology have been used to strengthen exchanges between managers and their employees in order to clarify, now in near-real time, what is expected from each and every employee. And all these changes have taken place in remarkable compliance with the founding principles of MBO. The need for explicit and clear instructions and well-defined areas of responsibility, as well as the requirement to objectify performance measurement criteria, are both still in force. Far from breaking with the old ways of working, these changes are keeping pace with them or even reproducing them.

Viewed from this perspective, it is evident that MBO is not simply a technical management tool, aimed at controlling the smooth running of the company by means of statistical reporting, but also, an intrinsically connected system capable of responding to the human imperatives forged by the local culture. Three contemporary examples of related practices in companies in very different sectors will serve to illustrate this point. The first, Accenture, is a world-renowned consulting firm employing young, highly qualified, and mobile staff. The second example is a logistics company, the majority of whose employees are drivers, while the third, the ubiquitous Google, embodies the model of corporate management practice that has been designed anew for the twenty-first-century digital age.

The consulting firm Accenture were recently proud to announce the abolition of the ritual annual performance review. The procedure was deemed too time-consuming and, above all, took place too infrequently to meet the mutual expectations of the two participants. Did this mean that the explicit formalization of objectives was to be discontinued? Not at all. The change was instituted in response to a perceived need to increase the number of such exchanges between superiors and subordinates in order to be ever more 'agile' in adapting to fluctuations in market conditions. If either thought that a change or adjustment of direction was required, the other one would fare better if he or she were immediately informed. Loyalty thus required that any modification in the terms of the contract between them be made explicit. Under these changeable conditions, doing away with the formal annual, semi-annual, or even quarterly review meeting seemed preferable. Instead, more flexible and frequent means of communication between superior and subordinate were instituted, which meant that each was kept on the same wavelength at all times.

The guiding principle of MBO remains the same, that is, ensuring that everyone knows what they are in charge of, understands clearly what is expected of them, and, as a result, is able to act independently. The American managerial response to the demands for greater autonomy made by the recent generations of workers has not led to a reduction in the frequency of exchanges between managers and employees. On the contrary, it has led to an increase in that frequency. According to a company manager[2]:

> Millennials make up 70 percent of Accenture's workforce—with Gen Z not far behind—and they tell us they want flexibility in how they work and immediate feedback about how they are doing. If we put them in the decades-old, traditional box of rear-view performance management, we will lose them, and rightfully so. After all, who wants to wait for an annual cycle for feedback, when, in fact performance happens every day?

Generations have succeeded one another, but the fundamentals appear to have remained constant. An employee responding to the requests of his manager is as concerned as ever his or her predecessors were to know if the work for which he is paid, once done, will meet the expectations of the person he considers to be his client—his superior. New technologies offer new opportunities to facilitate and accelerate communications between a manager and his team, but they do not change the purpose of their content.

> No longer will we fill out time-consuming assessment forms that focus on the past. It's not what we need, and it's not how the millennial generation wants to be recognized. The focus is on the future and how—through frequent, timely and individualized coaching discussions—people can improve their performance, develop professionally and achieve their career aspirations.

Our second example, a major American company in the transport sector, has a meritocratic credo which has as its basis that, no matter what an employee's title or function is, recognition will depend on results. 'Your stature, compensation, and standing within the firm, are not based on the title you hold, but are dependent upon the contributions you make'. The firm affirms its willingness to be honest and transparent in displaying the objectives assigned to everyone, in measuring their performance, and in indicating its impact on the reward granted:

> We are constantly challenged to make sure people understand what *their reporting lines are*, how *their goals* and bonus is [sic] going to be determined *at the end of the year* and that sort of things. (emphasis added)

These principles also state: 'The company firmly believes in the virtues of constructive controversy: systematically agreeing with each other and never challenging things does not make a healthy organization. We have to support constructive dissatisfaction'. Clearly the MBO fundamentals conceived two generations earlier are still being practiced there.

Our final example is that of Google, whose managerial practices have inspired the numerous high-tech start-ups that surf on the wave of global digital communication. Google's corporate image is that of a company which focuses on keeping its bright new recruits satisfied with their jobs, and doing its utmost to retain them. With this in mind, the company strives to offer its employees a pleasant, even fun, environment to limit to a minimum the weight of the bureaucratic constraints that constrain creativity, and to select and train managers who are expected to put themselves entirely at the service of the collective performance of their team. At the same time, as explained in a video by Vice President Liane Horsey[3], Google intends to recruit people 'who really want to work on shared goals, shared products, and shared things'. With this objective in mind, in order to encourage innovation, great importance is attached to teamwork and interdepartmental cooperation.

One would imagine that within such an enterprise, which celebrates informality, openness, and vertical and horizontal cooperation, the procedures for the individual evaluation of contributions would also have been thoroughly revised and distanced from the formalism inherent in MBO. Interestingly, this is not the case. Celebrating collective efficiency clearly does not exempt the company from its duty to carefully measure and reward everyone's performance. See what a Google vice-president said as she was interviewed:

> Everybody, the vast majority of people in the organization, have quarterly goals. So, they are supposed to sit down with their manager and maybe with their team and say: 'Right, this is what I think I can do this quarter; does it sound right?' Let's work out the measures around that. (ibid.)

'All good ideas are good to take', she says, starting with those of the employees themselves, but also those of individuals in the group in which they work, and thus ideas coming from different sources, and in particular not only those of the supervisor for whom they work, are aired and listened to. At the same time, the effectiveness of these good ideas should be measurable, thus retaining the fundamentals of the individual evaluation system.

> Each quarter will be reviewed and we take it *very seriously*. We are all performance related and cultured. So, the manager will review how the individual has done, sit down with the individual and they will have a long conversation together and the manager will calibrate how they feel about the whole team. We do take this process *very, very seriously*, and it does impact compensation, as you would expect. (emphasis added)

The idea that employees can themselves formulate what they consider to be the objectives that will enable them to best serve their organization is not new. This formula existed at GE in the 1940s (Greenwood, 1981) in the form of 'letters to the management' that senior managers could send to executives to propose their own action plans.

Superiors are the ones who, in one-on-one sessions with their subordinates, review the way in which the commitments made by them individually have been fulfilled.

> We believe that people are grown-ups and adults and that they do the right things. (. . .) I never look at their sick leaves or at what time they come in and at what time they leave. *I do look at their output; that's what I am interested in.* Why should I have to bother them? You know, they are grown-ups. *They have to make decisions for themselves.* (emphasis added)

Google's unconventional approach to the traditional performance review, adapted in order to try and make working conditions for young, innovative employees move conducive to 'thinking outside the box' as it were, confirmed the conventional expectation—even in this much later generation of employees—of the evaluation of their performance against clearly set goals.

1.2 The Deep Roots of American Management

The cultural continuity that we have uncovered has its origins in the very beginnings of American democracy. Labour historians have traced this vision of the employment relationship even further, back to the beginnings of the Industrial Revolution in England—already in full swing at the time of the creation of the American Constitution in the late 1780s. In his analyses of the representations of work in the nineteenth century, Biernacki (1995) shows how, at that time, work was seen as a commodity, the value of which was determined by the market. This portrayal of the employer–employee relationship was adopted by English economists. To them, an individual selling his or her labour could be regarded as a supplier, while the employer buying his work could be seen as a customer.

Tocqueville (2002), in his role as early-nineteenth-century observer in an America that was still largely rural, postulated a theory of the democratic and egalitarian relationship between employer and employee that was being created, based on the democratic ideals of the young nation. The way he describes the relationships between what he called the 'servant' and the 'master', sheds light on how these working relationships were perceived even quite early on in American history:

> In democracies servants are not only equal amongst themselves, but it may be said that they are in some sort the equals of their masters. This requires explanation in order to be rightly understood. At any moment a servant may

> become a master, and he aspires to rise to that condition: the servant is therefore not a different man from the master. Why then has the former a right to command, and what compels the latter to obey? The free and temporary consent of both their wills. Neither of them is by nature inferior to the other; they only become so for a time by covenant. Within the terms of this covenant, the one is a servant, the other a master; beyond it they are two citizens of the commonwealth - two men (ibid.: 545).

These historical references shed light on the depth of the cultural roots of American corporate management. They show the place occupied by the English understanding of labour relations between a supplier and a customer in which both parties, manager and employee, must specify in full detail the service expected by the former from the latter. They illustrate clearly the local American norm of respect for the subordinate, a very important ethos in all American companies. Even in situations of profound disagreement about the quality of the work provided by a subordinate, the superior will always remain careful to separate the criticism that he can legitimately make of the work provided from the required respect for the failing employee as an individual. In this tradition, those who work for others are regarded as fully deserving the consideration and rights owed to any free citizen. As Tocqueville points out, you can consider yourself on an equal social footing with those for whom you work even if you are temporarily submitting to their discipline.

This requirement to treat workers as citizens enjoying equal rights has not always been respected in modern companies, as has been amply demonstrated in American literature and films. But the idea has never disappeared, to the point of inspiring the authors of the best-selling *In Search of Excellence* to choose the following poignant extract from a poem distributed in a leaflet by the UAW (union of automobile workers):

> What is it that instantaneously makes
> a child out of a man?
> Moments before, he was a father, a husband,
> an owner of a property,
> a voter, a lover, an adult.
> When he spoke at least some listened.
> Salesmen courted his favor.
> Insurance men appealed to his family responsibility
> and by chance the church sought his help.
> But that was before he shuffled past the guard,
> climbed the steps,
> hung up his coat and
> took his place along the line.
>
> (Peters & Waterman, 1982: 235–6)

The text depicts a production-line worker taking up his post at the factory and moving, from the moment he crosses the threshold, from the position of a free and respected adult in the outer world, to that of a subordinate, subject to the authority of others.

Each of the examples that we have used so far has involved Americans working with, or for, other Americans. They have allowed us to demonstrate the unchanged cultural continuity between the values that inspired the inventors of MBO in the 1940s—to which the employees of an ordinary Maryland factory continue to refer even in the early 1980s—and those that are still to be found today in the leading companies of the Internet and digital age.

To close this first chapter, we will briefly examine the way in which Americans working in US-based subsidiaries of foreign companies collaborate with managers from cultures other than their own, who may not be sensitive to the same cultural norms. The descriptions we give of these situations will strengthen the thesis that we defend here, namely that management, as Americans conceive it, is not a technique for simply meeting the requirements of rationality and efficiency. The model is deeply imbued with the ethos to which Americans refer when they make judgements about what is fair or unfair, normal or shocking, or, indeed, in the way they exercise hierarchical authority in organizations.

1.2.1 Supposedly Universal Characteristics Put to the Test

When American employees are managed by foreign managers, it is not uncommon for the American subordinates to complain that their expectations of 'normal' labour relations are not being met. Analysing their reactions to such situations can cast interesting light on the cultural embeddedness of their managerial references.

Two such examples will be given. The first one is based on the experience of two American vice presidents employed in the local US branch of a Japanese bank (Ouchi, 1981), and the second, on our own investigation of the afore-mentioned Maryland plant, which, at the time, had a French managing director. In each case we will first examine the point of view of the American employees, before moving to that of their foreign managers. In both cases, we will see that a good way to understand and monitor the adherence to a particular way of doing things consists in observing what happens when it is not respected.

In the subsidiary of a Japanese bank based in the USA, Ouchi (ibid.: 33–35) interviewed the two locally-recruited vice presidents as well as the Japanese president in situ, in order to determine what their experience of working together was. All three responded positively and expressed the high level of esteem they had for one another, but when probed further, they expressed their difficulties concerning the notion of objectives.

To the Americans, the Japanese president simply could not understand the concept: 'These Japanese don't understand objectives and it drives us nuts!' While a wealth of data was available to quantify the results of their actions, they could not get their boss to formalize the targets to be achieved. How could they know, they complained, whether or not they had performed well?

> We have a non-stop running battle with the president. We simply cannot get him to specify a performance target for us. We have all the necessary reports and numbers, but we can't get specific targets from him. He won't tell us how large a dollar-increase in loan volume, or what percent decrease in operating costs he expects us to achieve over the next month, quarter, or even year. How can we know whether we're performing well without specific targets to shoot for?

Things were just as clear in the mind of the Japanese president, who thought exactly the opposite: 'These Americans just don't seem to be able to understand objectives.' We are not in the presence of a simple semantic quarrel between foreigners about the 'true meaning' of a given expression. The stakes are much higher. This is a profound divergence of opinion on a central management issue. Under what conditions will employees feel that they are being well treated by their employer? Under what conditions will an employer consider that he has succeeded in obtaining from its employees a commitment in line with his expectations? As we have seen, the Americans and their Japanese president did not come up with the same solutions in response to these two questions.

What the Americans wanted to be told at regular intervals was where they stood with their employer, and especially with their boss. Were they performing well? Were there any criticisms to be made about them? How could they get the answers to these questions if their boss didn't think it necessary to provide them with clear objectives against which their performance could be measured? This omission on the part of the Japanese manager annoyed them considerably (*it drives us nuts!*). The lack of formal rules for individual objectives, and—very importantly for the vice-presidents—the rewards associated with achieving them, fuelled their psychological discomfort and mistrust.

Similar misunderstandings emerged between some Americans and their French boss. A French engineer, sent over by the French parent company, was managing the afore-mentioned Maryland plant at the time of our research. Managing American employees was as new to him as it was for them to be managed by a non-American.

He was suddenly confronted with employees who attached great importance to the negotiation of a detailed roadmap, and who expected to be judged on the objectives set for them by their superior. An American head of department directly reporting to him complained:

> We've been working together for a year. You changed my goals; your predecessor was very happy because all you told me that I was doing well, that's what your

> predecessor wanted me to do. Now, what you tell me to do in addition, no one before you told me.

The objection raised by this employee is fully consistent with the representations that Americans share of what a fair exercise of hierarchical authority is. For this American head of department, his new manager was quite within his rights in drawing his attention to new aspects of his work that could be improved in such and such a way. He was well aware that the instructions he had received from the former managing director could, potentially, be modified. To him, though, they should first have been discussed with him by his manager, thus allowing him to express his own opinion, and giving him the opportunity to explain any difficulties he foresaw or indeed to request the additional material or assistance he deemed necessary to satisfy his boss' requirements. While he considered that the boss was entitled to modify the criteria for assessing his subsequent performance, he felt that he was not entitled to modify the requirements for his past performance.

Such misunderstandings are not trivial.

1.2.2 Management is Embedded in Culture

Neither the Japanese president nor the French director were really convinced of the validity of the requests made to them by their American subordinates for clear statements of goals and objectives. We highlight this important point which testifies to the distances that these Japanese and French executives do not hesitate to take from a management model that enjoys solid international prestige.

The Japanese president regretted to be unable to make his American vice-presidents understand what he expected from them:

> If only I could get these Americans to understand our philosophy of banking. To understand what the business means to us—how we feel we should deal with our customers and our employees. What our relationship should be to the local communities we serve. How we should deal with our competitors, and what our role should be in the world at large. If they could get that under their skin, then they could figure out for themselves what an appropriate objective would be for any situation, no matter how unusual or new, and I would never have to tell them, never have to give them a target.

Similarly, in the eyes of the French director, a worthy manager must be able to find out by himself what will allow his unit to function as well as possible. It was not for his manager to tell him.

> There are some obvious objectives; making your service work well is one; engineers in France, the way I see it, tend to create their own value system by saying to themselves: 'Well, it's obvious, I have to run my own thing'.

He therefore considered that it was not for him to tell his subordinates what to do. 'I refuse,' he said, 'to take responsibility for them, to set goals for them, because that is really the foundation [of their work]'. For him, identifying and a fortiori making a hierarchy of tasks that were to be monitored was the role of the engineer himself, not that of the managing director. He considered that he was playing his role correctly when he refused to enter into an exercise that, for him, was simplistic: it would be futile to identify and a fortiori prioritize among the many elements that needed to be done those that required particular vigilance. Locked in his own certainties, he did not interpret the requests to explain what he expected as a means for his American subordinates to help him to fulfil his personal objectives, but rather as a way for them to free themselves from an essential part of what they were responsible for—in the sense that he, himself, understood it.

> People would like to have a goal, a record from me: this is what you have to do, and we'll check at the end of the year. So that is a sort of a way to protect themselves. People tend to hide behind the objectives that are convenient for them and that they have negotiated.

He was slightly sceptical about the way in which any of his subordinates came to him for approval, including and especially when they had met the objectives that he had set for them. 'There is a "pleasing the boss" aspect,' he said, 'which is much more developed, I think, than in France'.

If the Japanese president and the French director were not really convinced of the validity of the requests addressed to them by their American colleagues, it was first and foremost because they themselves had other references that were no less rooted in cultural traditions than those of the Americans, but in different ones. And if this is true for France or Japan, it is equally true for other countries, as will be shown in the following chapter.

1.3 Conclusion

This chapter has shown the spectacular ability of American management practice to maintain its core principles over long periods of time, despite the major transformations that have taken place in society and the economy in recent decades. Considering the way workers in American companies speak about their jobs—be they employees or managers, of yesteryear, or of today—leads us to conclude that the shared social representations of the decent way to deal with interpersonal relationships influenced—and continues to influence—the way in which the practical rules organizing their cooperation in the workplace came to be codified and validated. MBO has often been the subject of criticism, including from American experts themselves. American companies are aware of the risk of seeing the borders of responsibility, to which they are so attached, become the borders of disempowerment, allowing actors to lose interest in issues that go beyond their own perimeter. They do not underestimate the reductionist role that statistics play when they are used to quantify the quality of an individual's or a team's performance. However, the reason why they still favour an MBO approach is because of its underlying basis of shared social representations. Emphasizing the cultural roots of American-style MBO in no way diminishes the recognized merits of the tool for rationalizing modes of delegation and control. However, our emphasis on this entrenchment of MBO in American culture inevitably leads to the question of the universality of its application (Hofstede, 1991) in terms of company management, and is one of the key topics examined throughout this book.

Notes

1. This factory, which is mentioned several times in this book, was the site of an in-depth sociological investigation the results of which were extensively published in La logique de l'honneur (d'Iribarne 1989).
2. http://www.careerpaths.it/10-accenture-saying-goodbye-annual-performance-reviews/ (accessed on 1 November 2017)
3. Best Practice HR Tips from Liane Hornsey, Google VP, *Operation Meet The Boss*, YouTube, 23 November 2012. https://www.youtube.com/watch?v=FRsJbpppvEU (accessed on 29 November 2019)

2

American Management Put to the Test

American management is widely taught in business schools, used by multinational firms in an attempt to homogenize management practices in their subsidiaries, recommended by consultants, and is now present on the five continents. Management by objectives (MBO), in particular, is often presented as the universal cure-all to treat these organizational pathologies, which are often mentioned in emerging countries, such as hyper-centralization, the disempowerment of middle managers, and the lack of involvement of employees. This international presence makes it possible to examine what actually happens when this model is put to the test. How will it be received by local actors? What improvements are credited to it? What misunderstandings or reserves does its implementation raise? What modifications, where relevant, are made locally to make it more acceptable and allow it to better meet its goals?

The objective of this chapter, relying on three examples based on our field research, is to show how MBO, each time it travels beyond its original context, is subject to local reinterpretations. It is through other benchmarks that local stakeholders interpret this new object which this tool represents for them. The virtues they find in it or the fears it inspires in them play a crucial role in how they receive and use it. What happens subsequently depends on the capacity of the company to take into account these interpretations which will largely determine its acceptability and, ultimately, its effectiveness. Our first two examples, one in a Tunisian firm, the other in a French one, correspond to situations where MBO has succeeded in establishing itself permanently while being substantially modified by a combination with local practices to make it more acceptable. The third example is to be found in a Vietnamese company. It corresponds to a failure that led the promoters of this attempt at 'modernization' to give up a management system that local managers did not take on board. Beyond these clear differences, which reflect the great diversity of local situations to be considered, the same phenomenon can be seen: the cultural roots specific to MBO, as we have described in the previous chapter, are no longer there. Other consistencies will need to be found between the cultural benchmarks that guide local stakeholders and the logics guiding the forms of management that are implemented locally. Otherwise there is a risk of seeing the transfer of the method fail.

The objective of this chapter is to report on these encounters between the MBO and other cultures from two points of view.

Cross-Cultural Management Revisited: A Qualitative Approach. Philippe d'Iribarne, Sylvie Chevrier, Alain Henry, Jean-Pierre Segal, and Geneviève Tréguer-Felten, Oxford University Press (2020).
DOI: 10.1093/oso/9780198857471.001.0001

On the one hand, it involves showing the diversity of the interpretations that are made, from one country to another, of each of the key notions of MBO: what does an objective mean? Is it essential to quantify its level of achievement? For managers, is relying on 'as-objective-as-possible' criteria measuring and rewarding the merits of each member of a work team sufficient to dispel suspicions of favouritism and permanently maintain the internal cohesion of their work teams?

On the other hand, it involves putting this variety of interpretations in relation to the variety of uses which are made locally of MBO. We will see, by using three very different examples, how the various reinterpretations of this system lead to a wide range of conducts from the implementation of local versions able to find positive echoes in local cultural benchmarks to outright abandonment.

2.1 The Successful Modernization of a Tunisian Conglomerate

Poulina Group was set up in 1967 by a local entrepreneur and has since experienced continuous development and great economic success which have led it to being regarded as a flagship of the Tunisian economy. The research (Yousfi, 2014) we are using was conducted when the group already had over 6,000 employees. Poulina already benefited from a sterling reputation, in particular for the rigour and effectiveness of its management. The objective of the survey conducted was to analyse how employees received the management practices established by the founder.

Yousfi particularly focused on an element of the management system directly inspired by MBO. It involved creating an evaluation system for individual performance called '*mise à mille*' (target 1,000). The practical guide distributed in the company specified: 'What is the purpose of the "*mise à mille*"? To fully understand its purpose: the "*mise à mille*" is closely linked to the job description. It clarifies what is required of each employee and provides a contractual basis for the objectives for a specified period (generally a year)'. The ideal score of 1,000 points corresponded to a maximum bonus.

The presentation of the system on the company's website made explicit reference to the American model: 'We have recently developed a system which we have called "*mise à mille*" which directly links evaluations, the achievement of objectives and results to the remuneration of directors and employees. These systems have, among other things, the objective of an evaluation in the group based on the merit and competence of the employee and not on seniority or age'.

Thanks to this tool, Poulina intended to take a distance from traditional family practices which, at the time, remained widely present in Tunisian SMEs: 'The "*mise à mille*"', stated the guide published by the company, 'specifies predefined rules of the game able to dispel any subjectivity and any jealousy or misplaced competition'. The executives interviewed assumed this modern stance which was clearly far removed from the traditional paternalism: 'The strong point of Poulina', says an executive, 'is that it has neutralised the excesses of a family system. The watchwords here are rigour and discipline. Here, we manage figures, not feelings... The *"mise à mille"* commits people because they sign the paper, if not, otherwise, they do not assume responsibility. There is no paternalism'.

2.1.1 Mixed Initial Reactions

How did local employees receive the use of these methods?

The company's executives stressed the American inspiration of the management practices established in their company which, in their view, were synonyms of efficiency and modernism: 'We are simply in the processes of adopting the American management system which makes each person responsible so that they see where the objectives are'.

The approach was also accepted—or at least its principles—by the employees who were satisfied with the clarification of rules and the new style of management: 'There are people who are pleased to have appraisals because they can say (to the boss): "I know on what bases you appraised me. You give me the elements which I accept, I play the game".' This transparency of rules made it possible to dispel the spectre of favouritism which, in Tunisia, is often associated with the clan dimension that the traditional functioning of family-run companies could take. As managers were regarded as fallible human beings like their subordinates, the latter appreciated the fact that their superiors' judgements were supported by objectified facts that could not be contested.

However, the employees were very soon concerned about the impact which the score given to them had on their bonus. For example, there were penalties likely to reduce the score in the event of repeated lateness. This focus on respect for rules opened the way to a normative interpretation of the *'mise à mille'* returning to the strictly disciplinary practices that were common in other companies. There was consequently some criticism from workers who saw the *'mise à mille'* as a system that could block their salary. Some employees were thus ironical, playing on words: 'It's a way to block our salaries', said a workman, 'if our objectives are not achieved! It's clearly a way of exploiting us'. 'The "mise *à mille*"', said another, 'is a "*mise* à pied" (layoff)!', playing on the word '*mise*'.

These reinterpretations and the resulting misunderstandings did not escape the attention of the local management: 'The *"mise à mille"*', regretted an executive, 'is not a remuneration system, it is a system of MBO and people find that hard to understand'. He was also vigilant over the risks of division between team members that could occur due to an excessive individualization of performance measurement: 'Employees', says this manager, 'pass the buck because they are afraid that their *"mise à mille"* will fall and their bonus will be reduced'.

2.1.2 An Adaptation of Practices to the Local Context

The survey showed that there had been a significant amount of adjustments made locally to the original model, some of them from the outset, others to take account of the expectations expressed by the local employees. This local adaptation in particular reflected the concern of protecting employees from an overly direct dependence on their hierarchy. This was the very spirit of the notion of objective conceived in the original version of the MBO which was modified.

The annual appraisal interview was no longer treated as a direct discussion of the objectives set by the superior for his subordinate. The '*mise à mille*' no longer aimed to formalize their mutual commitment in a transparent and democratic manner. It did, admittedly, involve clarifying the obligations of the subordinate with regard to the company that employed him: 'The "*mise à mille*" appeared . . . as a means to convert the company's overall strategy into operational sub-objectives'. But it above all involved bringing about a soul-searching with each employee, reminding them of their duties, as mentioned in the guide published by the company: 'to know your strong points and your weak points and to be accordingly self-critical'. It also involved giving each employee an objective measurement of the way in which they had fulfilled their duties.

Employees were inclined to believe that they were no longer asked to execute the orders of their superior to please him but rather to fulfil a moral duty. Indeed, the '*mise à mille*' was understood as a sort of reminder to everyone of their moral duties with regard to their employer: 'The "*mise à mille*"', specifies the guide published by the company, 'is a moral contract supporting the company's objectives and aligning one's professional objectives with those of the company'. It is not allegiance to the boss which the '*mise à mille*' aims to reward; it is the moral exemplarity of conduct: 'The "*mise à mille*" means', explains an executive, 'that if you fulfil your duty, your boss rewards you.' The employee himself also seems to agree. 'Everyone knows what they owe the company', says a worker, 'and what is their rightful due.' The superior does not feel he has a role as a mentor or educator. It is up to each employee to do their own soul-searching to correct their shortcomings where necessary. 'Muslims', the founder points out to explain the success of the procedure, 'do not have an intermediary with God, there is no hierarchy, they feel uncomfortable with a boss who checks behind them. With a procedure, they check themselves.'

At Poulina, the implementation of the '*mise à mille*' was combined with guarantees reducing the direct dependence of employees with regard to their direct superior. They had the possibility of appealing to the higher level in the event of disagreement with the evaluation received. The possibility of appealing to the authority of headquarters averts the risks of dependence with regard to a despotic boss in the subsidiaries: 'The good thing', says an employee, 'about dictator managers, is that they know there are the recourses to headquarters. They cannot abuse.'

A central aspect of the local manager's role was to guarantee the internal unity and cohesion of the groups he was managing. Special attention had been paid to preventing internal jealousies, clan groupings, which tend to threaten the overall cohesion. 'One of my jobs is to ensure there are no groupings, it's not official, it's very informal. If I see there are people grouping against a person, I step in.'

To promote mutual assistance and limit the impact that the highly meritocratic direction given to the appraisal system could have, attention was paid to mitigate its effects which could be potentially divisive in the work teams. The bonuses accompanying the score obtained on the '*mise à mille*' could be distributed locally on a collective basis, including between client services and suppliers. 'In certain subsidiaries', said an executive, 'we set common objectives, not to penalise but to help each other, for example, between maintenance and production.' Without losing sight of the importance of their role, certain managers interviewed adopted a deliberately modest attitude and refused to separate their own merit from that of their team. They considered the score they obtained on the '*mise a mille*' as being more or less equal to the sum of those of their team members.

2.1.3 A Resonance with Local Benchmarks: Honour and Equality

These local reinterpretations of a system based on a model from elsewhere thereby allowed this model to find positive resonances with the cultural benchmarks through which local stakeholders interpreted them. As Yousfi (2005: 63) writes: 'This management system allows employees to work in a context that more or less coincides with the ideal they have of good working relations.'

Ideal working relations, explained the founder of the company, would have been a situation of complete independence with regard to the hierarchy: 'Working for others is considered as unworthy in Tunisia (. . .). As soon as a person starts to succeed professionally, their family and friends encourage them to work on their own account. The term "*zoufri*", which means "thug" in Arabic, has its origin in the French word "*ouvrier*" (worker).'

The theme of equality is also omnipresent in the statements. 'This system', explains an executive, 'by fighting against the risk of arbitrary action by the authority, allows them to be treated on an equal footing'. 'We are managed by a law which applies to everyone without exception, including myself', says the founder.

In this context, getting everyone to accept a management system devised in an American world where the employee willingly accepts the fact of working for his manager was not self-evident. But the modifications made to the system compared to its original design and the interpretation given to it had avoided having to establish this American form of subordination, while protecting against the most common abuses in hierarchical relations in Tunisia.

The restrictive nature for all of the management rules protected subordinates from a dependence experienced as being unworthy with regard to their hierarchy. If it meant obeying, it was better to have to do so by following rules that were imposed on everyone than to bow to the will of a superior. 'We prefer', said an employee, 'to submit to the procedure than to a boss who dictates to us what we must do depending on his mood.'

The focus on individual responsibility could also fuel a feeling of pride in the local cultural benchmarks. 'We feel that we are responsible, because we are not acting in the shadow of someone'. 'I am not an employee', said a respondent, 'I am practically a boss with all the rights because only my abilities limit me.'

We measure here what separates this interpretation of working relations from the American commercial one. The first is impregnated with the local conception of an honour that needs to be defended and shows concern, in this respect, about remaining unduly in the shadow of one's manager. The second interpretation addresses employees who do not mind working 'for' their managers, provided that they are protected by all the guarantees deemed necessary.

Finally, the example of Poulina which, at the level of countries in the South, is far from being an isolated case (Iribarne, 2003), provides us with two lessons: on the one hand, it shows the existence of deep local reinterpretations of the 'American-style' management model when it travels and lands in a different cultural context. On the other hand, it shows that the local application of this model can be effective, provided that those who implement it have found the means to modify it by ensuring that it has a positive resonance with the categories of judgement of local staff.

2.2 The Hoped Renaissance of the Parisian Metro

The setting of our second example is the Parisian metro. Here again, the intention of the managers was to establish MBO to support a major decentralization of the organization based on the principles of New Public Management. While certain aspects of the changes introduced won over the employees of the Parisian metro, who were generally unsatisfied with the former state of the organization, others provoked strong reactions. They were related to the interpretation that French employees have of working relations and their links with their superior, an understanding which guided their interpretation of the changes proposed to them.

In the early 1990s, the organization of the Parisian metro experienced a real revolution. Based on the example of other networks, particularly the London network, the new managers established an unprecedented decentralization of the organization. Each line would now be headed by a manager with a new autonomy and new means to meet the objectives that the general management was to set for him or her. The daily management of general staff had until then been handled by an undifferentiated group of supervisors. From now on, each employee would know his or her manager and would be assessed on the quality of his or her work and conduct. The company had called on the French office of a world-renowned American consultancy firm, presenting itself as an expert in change management. Their consultants organized workshops in each unit to convince employees of the benefits of what they presented as the prerequisite for an enchanted renaissance of a company drowsing in its old routine. They developed their arguments on the basis of what they had been taught in their corporate university where, once recruited, they had been trained in American approaches to change management.

Their message was clear. Instead of the anonymity and lack of recognition which they attributed to the old company culture, new person-to-person relations needed to be built between each employee and a manager who should '*know him and recognize*' him, according to the terms of a brochure widely distributed internally. Contrary to the bureaucratic anonymity which characterized the old world, where only employees who had infringed the rules were noticed by the hierarchy in order to be sanctioned, a new world was announced in which everyone would accede to an individual recognition associated with a responsibility based on clear, measurable, and shared objectives.

2.2.1 Mixed Reactions from Employees

To measure the degree of support that their message encountered among the staff, the consultancy firm carried out a survey by questionnaire which benefited from a high response rate. The modernizers could not fail to be pleased by the particularly high rate (80%) of positive responses or very positive responses to the question: 'I want to be set objectives in my work'. However, the responses to another proposal of the questionnaire were such as to temper their enthusiasm: 'It is the role of my line manager to set my objectives' only obtained 30% of support.

Employees felt it was very helpful to have objectives that give both sense and meaning to their work. They would not have been satisfied with an activity with no prospects. However, almost as many of them rejected the idea that their immediate superior was the person the best placed to tell them what they had to do. They did not see themselves under any circumstances working 'for their manager', which would seem normal to American subordinates.

The prospect offered of personalizing relations with the line manager did not generate any great enthusiasm, either among the employees or their management. The use of the expression 'endure a professional interview' was common, in particular at the base of the organization where the exercise created unease and concerns among those who felt helpless in a face-to-face situation with their manager. Part of the management was itself reluctant to conduct such appraisals, fearing that they might aggravate their relations with some of their subordinates without really motivating them more.

Many of the general staff admitted that they found it hard to identify their direct hierarchy with the model of the charismatic manager who 'knows and recognises' his (or her) employees. *'Donnez-nous des cadres qui soient des vrais* cadres (give us real executives)', joked one of them playing on words, *'pas des* cadres *posés au mur'* (not frames put on the wall), the word *'cadre'* meaning both 'executive' and 'frame' in French.

2.2.2 An Original Interpretation of Working Relations

How to interpret this resistance from French employees to engage in this modernizing approach whereas they all aspired to seeing their organization change? American employees consider it 'normal' to work 'for' their manager. Their French counterparts do not see things in the same way.

The autonomy demanded by French employees is different from the one Americans are attached to. The latter want to have an autonomy of execution to meet the expectations of their line manager. The French aspire, as far as possible, to be able to define the content of their work themselves, using the professional standards of their *'métier'* (profession)[1] (see Chapter 3 pp. 64–65). It is the idea they have of their mission and their profession, rather than the desire to be seen in a good light by their superior, which motivates their involvement. They even consider as servile and self-serving the intentions of those who are overzealous in meeting the expectations of their hierarchy. Most of them will only accept that they work 'with' a manager and some will continue to commit themselves to their work despite their bad opinion of their line manager.

According to them (see Table 2.1), the criteria used by the organization to measure if the objectives set for the units have been achieved cannot alone account

Table 2.1 How Parisian Metro's agents see the reforms: an internal survey

	We reward	We should reward
The achievement of objectives	65%	5%
The quality of work	11%	54%
The efforts made	6%	35%
Don't know	18%	6%

for either the expertise or commitment of employees. In their opinion, the most deserving employee is the one who knows how to handle complex and sensitive situations which only occur when there is an operating incident. It is also the one who will take the time necessary to handle the situation entrusted to him from A to Z. More generally, employees consider that the professional standards specific to their profession are better benchmarks to evaluate their work than the judgement made about them by their immediate superior. This way of considering both the content of work and the way of measuring its quality based on professional standards quite logically leads to questioning the legitimacy of the line managers to impose their priorities and define the related performance indicators.

The reluctance to accord such a role to the superior was even greater in the Parisian metro as the vast majority of the management staff was from the base, having been promoted to these functions not because they had shown recognized professional excellence but to reward them for having behaved as expected.

The reservations on the part of both the superiors and the subordinates with regard to the 'American-style' formalization of objectives become clear: the former may think—as our French director of the American factory in the previous chapter—that it is not up to them to 'spoon-feed' their subordinates, who are perfectly capable of knowing what they have to do themselves; the latter, inevitably, could interpret such a formalization as a demonstration of mistrust towards them, as a patronizing interference or, worse still, as reflecting a determination to subjugate their employees to their wills, by abusing their hierarchical power.

The introduction of MBO, which strengthened a hierarchical dependence—which had until then been avoided—was unlikely to contribute to facilitating the cooperation and confidence between the superior and the subordinates. The superior was either dealing with a subordinate who deserved to be considered as a 'real professional'; it was therefore not only pointless but also inappropriate to dictate his or her conduct; or explaining his or her expectations to a subordinate whose lack of qualifications put him or her in a position of weakness which was highly likely to seem too direct and thereby humiliating, or too indirect and thereby hypocritical. Other forms of communication, more informal and, if possible, more 'comradely', would contribute much more to building a trusting relationship which, in the most favourable cases, could even be regarded by the two protagonists as a form of complicity.

2.2.3 Possible Accommodations

These reservations led the Parisian metro to substantially modify its initial projects. Instead of an individual performance measurement, collective performance indicators were established in each unit, measured by an independent and stated body.

The principle of an annual meeting between each employee and a representative of the hierarchy was maintained. But it was decided that it would no longer be the immediate superior of each employee who would conduct this interview. It would now be the HR manager of each unit. This modified the very spirit of the interview. It no longer involved reviewing objectives set a year before, as this aspect, which is essential for Americans, had been abandoned. It only involved reviewing the relations between each employee and the organization. The discussion was therefore about training, mobility, and career plans and, only in difficult cases, rectifying attitudes and conduct with regard to users or the hierarchy.

This adaptation to the French context has been made in many other French organizations. Without being converted to the idea that it was right and fitting to 'enter into a contract' with their immediate superior following a frank and amicable discussion, the French employees gradually accepted the idea of the organization proposing annual meetings with their superior to usefully take stock of how the past year had gone and discuss the prospects offered for the coming months. The performance review is therefore addressed as a cross between the self-assessment that employees make of their strong points and their weak points and the assessment made by their line managers.

This type of meeting has become widespread in France[2] over the past decades. In most large companies, HR departments have made the number of these meetings and the percentage of employees concerned an indicator measuring the effectiveness of efforts to widely implement a managerial practice that was almost non-existent two generations earlier. Recently, the French labour code[3] has obliged companies to organize individual professional interviews at least once every two years, reviewing the professional expectations of employees and the skills that need to be developed to allow them to both advance in their careers and develop useful skills for the company.

These reinterpretations of MBO have allowed its dissemination in companies in forms that have been more or less extensively modified depending on the positions held, the hierarchical level of employees, and the size of the company. Consequently, commercial professions have not encountered great difficulties in moving towards the model, which is in many respects in line with existing practices to measure the level of achievement of sales targets. Receiving objectives from one's superior for which one is periodically accountable has gradually been integrated into the social representations of executive status in contemporary France, which has contributed to normalizing it. However, the surveys conducted among executives have shown that the latter, who for a long time took pride in the full confidence of their managers, suffered from seeing the evaluation of their work reduced to a sum of statistical indicators (Dupuy, 2005).

Our next example is singular in that it leads to a failure where the first two had ultimately managed to come up with accommodations.

2.3 A Vietnamese Start-up

Data-Viet[4] is a start-up set up in the early 2000s by a young Franco-Vietnamese engineer wishing to contribute to Vietnam's development. The company's clients are mainly large French companies which subcontract part of their activity to it for data and image programming and processing. At the time of the survey, which was carried out in 2010, it employed a hundred or so people mainly recruited from the foreign language departments of local universities. These young Vietnamese people were managed by other Vietnamese people who were barely older than them, supervised by a handful of young expatriate French engineers. Like the new Vietnamese generation, these recruits were largely informed about the realities of the contemporary world and some of them had been able to follow training abroad. At Data-Viet, these employees benefited from a large degree of freedom in the performance of their tasks and the management of their working hours. At the time, this was not very common in Vietnamese companies and was really appreciated by Data-Viet's young employees. The founder of the company wanted to promote a relaxed and liberal working atmosphere, in line with the expectations of this young labour force. This atypical CEO was a great admirer of IT companies on the West Coast of the USA and also wanted to follow their example in the management of his company. This, as we will see, proved to be much more difficult than planned.

As the company grew, an ever-increasing number of demands from all the departments were made to senior management. Faced with his personal time being constantly taken up, the CEO decided to introduce a new management tool, called PROGRESS,[5] which was directly inspired by American management standards. This system took up the principles of MBO. Every manager had to set four to six objectives for each of their employees to be achieved in the next six months, which were to be reviewed every six months. The performance achieved was assessed on a scale of one to five ranging from Outstanding (1) to Insufficient (5). If the performance, measured on the basis of a set of indicators fixed in advance, was considered insufficient, an improvement plan was established for eight weeks, after which employees could be dismissed if they did not meet the expectations of their manager. The objective was both to mobilize employees and increase accountability at all levels of the company and, in particular, for the local Vietnamese management. The CEO was counting on this middle management to obtain more from his teams, to focus more on the development of the skills of their team members and to focus more on the future development of their careers. He was convinced that PROGRESS, which he had himself experienced when he worked for a large company in Europe, was the appropriate way of encouraging them to do it.

2.3.1 The Local Reactions to a New Procedure

The survey (Segal, 2010) was conducted one year after the launch of this new programme. Its findings gave cause for concern. The Vietnamese staff expressed their lack of understanding of the purpose of PROGRESS and a deep scepticism over its effectiveness. It revealed the sense of unease felt by the middle management with regard to this new tool. A supervisor, questioned about PROGRESS, replied that by accepting the interview, he himself hoped to obtain additional information about it. Most supervisors did not know how to respond to the instructions received and wondered what objectives they could possibly set for their employees. In response to a question concerning the objectives, a team manager provided a response which, at first sight, appeared to reflect a total incomprehension: 'He gives his colleagues objectives', translated the interpreter, 'This employee must make a report at the end of each week. Everyone must attend the meeting. In six months, everyone must have learned a now process'. A closer reading showed us how the notion of objectives upheld by PROGRESS was here reinterpreted within Vietnamese benchmarks in which the supervisor's main role was to ensure the strict application of the proper working methods. It was not by mistake or by chance that submitting a report at a fixed date and attending the meeting daily were mentioned. These were all rituals (fixed date, daily) considered as ensuring collective effectiveness. It could be said metaphorically that these local managers had chosen to translate the message received 'in the original language' (Western) into the target language (Vietnamese) so that their team members could understand it, even if it meant reformulating it and distorting the original spirit.

The Vietnamese managers were supposed to take advantage of PROGRESS to encourage their employees to project themselves into a controlled future with ambition and voluntarism. Yet our Vietnamese employees were much more sensitive than the Americans, with a sometimes unpredictable character in terms of the future and a fugitive character in terms of the opportunities of what this future could offer. They had a much more unstable vision of the world (Jullien,1997) and doubted that it was possible—as the Americans may hope to do—to direct it by setting objectives in advance. Their idea was that it was better to seize and channel the successive movements of this changing world to make the best strategic use possible. Consequently, MBO, which was set in a vision of a different world, did not really convince them.

The survey showed the difficulty which this local management had in assuming the role imagined for them by their CEO. They were admittedly not opposed to the idea of having regular discussions with each member of their team—which they already did before—in order to verify that their instructions had been clearly understood and accepted. However, in their minds, the aim of these meetings was not to set challenges for everyone but rather to ensure their support to obtain greater collective efficiency. A supervisor described his own practice: 'Always, before setting the objectives for my members of staff, I always need the collaboration of each employee. If I set objectives that are considered too high by these employees, then we modify them. Oh yes, then! We need to have a discussion to achieve this goal!'

These middle managers considered that their role was firstly to give clear instructions to subsequently help their team members to accomplish the tasks requested. They thought that in this way they would ensure the collective effectiveness which, for them, was central to their position. They thought that it was not by setting ambitious medium-term objectives that one was the most demanding. In their opinion, there was practically no interest in evaluating their team members, six months later, on the basis of abstract criteria established a long time in advance. 'We don't think we need objectives. Those we set in June for six months, in December, they're no longer relevant when we see each other again. It's 100% different from the reality'. It was better to be direct and practical: 'There are people who don't like PROGRESS,' a supervisor said, 'They find that it's an inconvenience. I don't see the use. 80% of satisfied customers, or win two bid invitations out of three, I don't know, but it doesn't interest me.'

These managers were also not very comfortable with the obligation, which was new for them, of rating their employees. It was not because they were unwilling to be strict with regard to subordinates who broke the rules. On the contrary, many of them felt that the local discipline was too lax at Data-Viet. They believed more in strict adherence to rules than in the incentive effects of rating. 'Our CEO must be stricter with people', said his Vietnamese personal secretary, 'If they work well, they can have rewards. If they don't work well, they have to be punished. It's very important to me'. It is the rating exercise itself which they were not happy about. In their opinion, it would have been better to reward the continuous respect of rules and discipline than the achievement of objectives in the American sense of the term. Consequently, they did not believe in the effectiveness of the new system. 'I find that we have a very good management here,' said one of them diplomatically, 'but what I want is to always have a more concrete and more precise plan envisaged.'

The employees of Data-Viet were not more convinced. Like their supervisor, they doubted that PROGRESS was the right answer to the disorderly functioning of their young company. 'I want you to propose us a method to improve the organisation,' one of our respondents told us, 'otherwise I don't believe we can develop like that.' The idea of individual responsibility—which the Americans associate with MBO—did not really mean anything to them. They felt that managers could certainly delegate tasks, but they remained the first to be responsible for their achievements. 'It's the manager who gives us objectives,' said an employee, 'but if there is a problem, there will certainly be a good discussion with him to have the right solution.' They were therefore not looking for a direct negotiation with their manager concerning objectives which they would personally commit to achieving. The CEO observed this with regret: 'The employees, today, they expect their manager to set objectives for them. This is not at all smart to negotiate your salary, it would be better for them to be proactive.'

For lack of understanding the logic on which PROGRESS was based, the Vietnamese employees of Data-Viet focused on the concrete effects related to its application. They were particularly concerned about the impact of this new system on their bonus and on their career advancement in the company. Employees were concerned about this evaluation, despite the fact that it had a limited impact on the distribution of bonuses. They wondered about the way in which supervisors would evaluate them: how would these new judgement criteria—the logic of which remained difficult for them to grasp—be combined with the previous criteria based on the quality of the interpersonal relationship established by their supervisor with them?[6] 'I don't think the bonus system is fair, I don't understand how it's calculated. It's something very broad which doesn't really give details of the work we do and it can also depend on the relations between the staff and the manager.'

2.3.2 A Conflict with Local Interpretations of Managerial Roles

It was therefore extremely difficult for PROGRESS to take on meaning in the local conceptions that the various local employees had not only of the content of their role but also of the complementarity between these roles. How can such reluctance towards PROGRESS be explained? The Vietnamese, unlike Americans, do not consider the hierarchical link between the superior and the subordinate as a relationship between equals ideally regulated by a balanced contract. For them, the link with their superior is of another nature (Nguyen, 2015). Whether they were in a position of manager or in a position of employee, the introduction of MBO in Data-Viet put them in an uncomfortable position.

Vietnamese superiors consider that they have been given two roles which, considered from a Western perspective, may seem difficult to reconcile. In the Vietnamese reality, these two roles are considered as complementary.

On the one hand, superiors are the guardians of order and discipline, readily adopting a moral posture which could appear, with other cultural benchmarks, as rigid and authoritarian. 'There should be a better distinction between what is right and wrong', said a team manager, 'There is, of course, the bonus for the best employees. But for someone who does wrong there should surely be punishment.' This moral posture is combined with a mission to educate one's subordinates that aims to show them the right way to improve themselves (Henry, 2011). A Vietnamese manager of a local subsidiary of an international company evokes the memory of a prominent director he knew: 'Mr. B. had a very strong impact on young Vietnamese managers. He looked after them, helped them, and ensured their development. The relations with them were not only professional.' A good superior is indeed regarded as someone who guides and teaches.

On the other hand, superiors must also embody a benevolent authority, watching over their employees in a paternal way. Each employee expects this type of support. 'He takes time to explain', said an employee about the CEO of Data-Viet who, in this respect at least, knew how to be appreciated. 'It's here that I can learn things I can't learn elsewhere.' In addition to the demanding roles expected of them, generous managers know how to give affection to the relations with their subordinates. This is what an employee explained: 'In our country, for the Vietnamese, it's important: we want a boss, he's kind, he's sincere, he works, and thinks about us.'

The Vietnamese employees also develop a double interpretation of their integration into the company which could seem disconcerting seen through the prism of another culture.

On the one hand, they are willing to become attached to the manager in proportions that surprise Western expatriates, as one of them said to us: 'The manager, they idolise him; they respect him, even more if he is foreign. There is also the respect for age, the respect for the elder, what we find in pupils' attitudes towards the teacher.' The unexpected departure of a manager (they are highly sought after on the local labour market) can cause a real trauma in his former team. 'Here, when the manager leaves, the cult of the manager causes tears', pointed out the founder of Data-Viet. The Vietnamese employees rely tremendously on their managers to give their groups an effective organization by providing it with a 'good system'. They hope that their leaders will facilitate their success, in particular thanks to their social networks. For them, the leaders' role is firstly to provide effective solutions to ensure the success of these small 'families' that they manage.

On the other hand, each of these Vietnamese employees is at the same time—outside the company—part of a family and a social network whose fortune he intends to contribute to. To do so, it is important for him or her to remain in permanent movement so that they can develop their skills, materially secure their families, and increase their reputation. Their current company is only a means to achieve this. Only a particular social link with one's managers, combining affection and interest, commits one to remaining by their side. The same ambivalence applies to relations with the work group. The Vietnamese consider themselves as stakeholders of a work group in which they are willing to make a strong investment. But this in no way prevents them from leaving this group if there are better opportunities elsewhere. Consequently, the staff turnover level is particularly high in Vietnam. The way in which the employees of Data-Viet envisage their professional careers does not fit well with the approach that PROGRESS would like to initiate by encouraging them to plan their career development in the company.

2.3.3 The Reasons for Abandonment

Three years later, PROGRESS, which had gradually fallen into disuse, was officially abandoned, much to the chagrin of our entrepreneur. He later accepted the fact that he had not managed to convince his employees of the merits of his initiative. He understood rather late that the middle managers of Data-Viet had merely applied PROGRESS in a 'ceremonial'[7] manner (Henry, 2011), while at the same time maintaining their own way of leading their teams. They therefore made sure that the objectives they set were not too difficult to achieve and that the ratings they gave were encouraging. It is no accident that the Vietnamese managers of Data-Viet were particularly benevolent in the evaluations given to their team members, which the CEO did not appreciate, as he considered they were not playing the expected game: 'It's Disneyland here, we only have strong points'. By mitigating the severity of their judgement, these Vietnamese managers especially wanted to encourage them and to leave open the possibility of obtaining from them continuous improvement, in line with the dynamic vision they have of their role. They also aimed to preserve a form of equality in the brotherhood within their teams by ensuring they did not create too many differences in the remunerations of their subordinates. 'In our Business Unit', says a supervisor, 'we try to give homogeneous bonuses without too much difference, it's something that we will not really shout from the rooftops, as salaries remain relatively taboo.'

Their employees, for their part, were especially concerned about the impact of this measure on their bonus which, fortunately they thought, was only very moderately affected.[8] This is precisely the criticism expressed by a Vietnamese employee with regard to her peers. She was at the same time pinpointing what she saw as a consequence of the shortcomings of a management that was too young and not experienced enough: 'We don't see the soul at work of the other staff members. What we do, it's simply what's necessary. We don't do our best. No one in the Business Units plays the role of teacher.'

It would be very excessive to attribute to PROGRESS alone all the responsibility for the difficulties encountered by the management of Data-Viet at the time of the survey. But this example clearly shows the limits of importing an approach in an environment in which working relations are structured in a very different manner than those in the USA. The Vietnamese of Data-Viet were just as disoriented by the logic guiding PROGRESS as the two American vice presidents (in the example given in Chapter 1, pp. 26–27) were disturbed by the refusal of the chairman of their Japanese bank to set them quantified objectives. In the cultural benchmarks of American employees, the approach on which PROGRESS was based takes on a value of transparency and equity. It offers the possibility of building direct person-to-person relations that are confident and balanced between supervisors and the supervised. It contributes to putting each individual, whether they are supervisors or supervised (and many are both at the same time), face-to-face with their responsibilities and promises to balance the contributions and retributions. The Vietnamese see hierarchical relations differently. It is for this very reason that the managers and employees of Data-Viet did not see the interest of reproducing a system like PROGRESS which, although it claimed to rebalance the rights and duties of each party concerned, never managed to have a positive meaning in their own benchmarks.

2.4 Conclusion

MBO was initially devised by its founders as a tool intended to both organize the distribution of functions and strengthen the confidence and cooperation between the superior and subordinate. As we have shown in Chapter 1 (pp. 29–30), the coherence between these two aspects is permitted by the vision of the relations of authority that prevail in the American world. Its transfer outside its original cultural universe leads to a break in this coherence to the extent that it fuels mistrust and paralysis instead of the confidence needed to support an effective action. It is only by taking some distance with regard to certain requirements set out in the original version of the model that this confidence and this effectiveness can be found in other cultural contexts.

The dissemination of MBO, which is today seen in an increasing number of countries, does not necessarily herald a standardization of management practices. Each of the three examples presented shows this in their own way. Yet some people still think that this standardization is still to come, that the process is underway, and that learning processes, accelerated by a training effort, will end up producing their effects (Lunnan & Traavik, 2009). For this, they could trust large international companies which send consultants and trainers to their distant subsidiaries to spread the word and seek to obtain a more rigorous application of the model.

The fact that the recontextualization (Brannen, 2004) of MBO takes, as we show, each time different paths is a strong argument against the proponents of the hypothesis of the future convergence of management practices. Each cultural area develops a particular reinterpretation of MBO based on the specificities of its understanding of social working relations. The Tunisians sway between several interpretations: some are favourable when it involves celebrating the equality of all before a transparent procedure and, by giving responsibility, nurturing professional honour, others less so, if the implementation of the procedure creates jealousy and divisions in work groups. The French find it hard to see the added value related to setting detailed objectives, considering that the requirements of the profession, which are assumed to be largely internalized by everyone, are a better compass. The Vietnamese, who expect clear instructions and help from their supervisor, would prefer to receive a detailed action plan (which can be revised if necessary) than objectives to be achieved in a longer term. In their diversity, these reinterpretations therefore demonstrate the plurality of readings that cultures in the world give to work situations and the profound impact that they can have through these readings on the functioning of organizations and their regulation.

In each society, the content of the social roles assumed by the superior and the subordinate is envisaged in a singular way, as can be the ways of acting to ensure an acceptable balance can be found between the rights and duties of each of the protagonists in hierarchical relations. This is even reflected in the vocabulary used to designate these protagonists. The Americans, stressing the responsibility of leadership of the person who exercises authority, speak about managers and employees. The French, sensitive to the differences of positions, speak about the superior and his subordinates. The Germans, stressing a common belonging, prefer the terms *Vorgesetzter* (literally, the person placed in front) and *Mitarbeiter* (literally, the person who works with). The Japanese use a variety of terms corresponding to the subtle distinctions between employees at each level of their internal hierarchy.

Culture fuels the representations that local stakeholders have of the right ways of organizing their cooperation. Unlike the visions generally accepted in the world of managers, the impact of cultures does not materialize in a form of attachment to practices, competing with the American model, as archaic as they are ineffective and which it would be a question of combating. In many situations, pre-existing hierarchical practices are far from enjoying consensus among local employees. Yet this will not prevent them from judging the merits of the new forms of management that are proposed to them by their own cultural benchmarks.

Whenever management practices are transferred out of their original cultural context, they are subject to local reinterpretation (Primecz et al., 2014). To report on these processes, management sciences must mobilize other social sciences (Chanlat, 2018; Dupuis, 2013) and innovate. This is precisely what our approach, which is presented in Chapter 3, intends to do.

Notes

1. The word '*métier*', which French surveys very often refer to, has a particular depth due to the role given to it in the independence strategies of stakeholders and the place it takes in the construction of their identity. *Métier* can be used for any activity in a much broader way than the American '*profession*' can. This makes its translation difficult into the

language of another country where belonging to a profession is not loaded with such issues in the same proportions.

2. This development is important although it only concerns, according to a 2014 estimate by a major Human Resources consulting firm, 75% of executives and only 35% of workers. Source: CEGOS, 2014.
3. Article L6315-1.
4. The company's name was modified.
5. We decided to modify the programme's name.
6. Similar fears are seen in all countries where this logic of relations, which governs the external social organization, is presumed to pervade the sphere of the organization (see Chapters 5 and 13 about Cameroon).
7. The Vietnamese translation sets stakeholders in family symbols. It sketches, between the lines, a coherent scene: the affirmation of wills disappearing behind roles; the social unity shown through ceremonials; the moral values dictated as natural laws which must be complied with; the world constantly changed by its own movement; the moral oath to deploy favourable processes in it, to ward off harmful movements and resolve difficult situations; the horror immediately felt when one departs from the roles and rituals and, conversely, the implicit link posed between the fact of observing rites and economic effectiveness. (Henry, 2011: 55, 56, 58, and 59).
8. *A fortiori* in proportion to another bonus, distributed once a year, through which each Vietnamese company upholds its prestige by demonstrating its good health and its generosity towards its staff.

3
Theorizing National Cultures

The vision of humanity as being composed of peoples who differ by their customs and languages already existed in ancient times. Aeschylus (1981: 6–7) contrasts the Greeks' attachment to freedom with the Persians' acceptance of servitude. The Bible, in its first pages, differentiates between 'of such as dwell in tents, and of such as have cattle', 'of all such as handle the harp and organ', and 'of every artificer in brass and iron' (Jones, 1966: Genesis 4: 20–22). This perception of the diversity of the world has been constantly fuelled by tales of travellers expressing surprise at the mores encountered in other lands. To account for this, the notion of culture has been developed under various names, for example the soul of peoples, the spirit of nations, national character. When the term is used, it is always, in one way or another, about what is shared by the members of a group but not by humanity as a whole, about something which has been passed on and which will, in turn, be passed on more or less faithfully. However, beyond this common vision, many uncertainties remain. How can a culture be characterized? Through behaviour, ideas, doctrines, values, psychological traits, attitudes? If it is all of these at once, what links can there be between these various dimensions? To what extent does culture have an influence on those whose existence it guides? Social sciences have provided many answers over time and continue to do so.

In our research, we regularly come across ways of getting organized, managing, deciding, treating clients, that differ greatly from one country to another. Unable to find in literature a theory that would serve to interpret satisfactorily what we were observing, we had to innovate. The purpose of this chapter is to present the approach that we finally arrived at and which underpins this whole book.

Firstly, we will specify why it was necessary to innovate. In the field of management, two main strands are currently concerned with cultures: one, originating from social psychology, uses attitude scales to characterize national cultures; the other, which is sociological and anthropological, considers small groups—an organization, a profession, a service—and tends to reject the notion of national culture. We shall see that the first strand ignores the complexity of cultures and that the second one is too quick to consider that a common culture cannot exist in pluralistic societies which are also marked by history. Furthermore, we shall see that sources of inspiration are to be found in the approaches to cultures that coexist in social sciences, but that innovative work is still required.

Cross-Cultural Management Revisited: A Qualitative Approach. Philippe d'Iribarne, Sylvie Chevrier, Alain Henry, Jean-Pierre Segal, and Geneviève Tréguer-Felten, Oxford University Press (2020).
DOI: 10.1093/oso/9780198857471.001.0001

A second section will be devoted to the approach that we have finally built, as we were striving to describe what we had observed. We were led to identify two layers in a culture. We shall firstly present these two layers in a general manner and subsequently take the USA and France as examples illustrating them.

A first layer corresponds to the existence of a specific way of giving meaning to situations and events, of interpreting successes and failures, of experiencing power relations, of deciphering the intentions of others on the basis of how they act, of attributing an origin to conflicts, and of imagining ways in which to overcome them. Great figures, either real or mythical, associated with histories and characters, conveying hopes and fears, sources of enthusiasm and indignation, structure a representation of the world. Existence takes on meaning by echoing this representation. The corresponding universe of meaning concerns the life of organizations. It includes images of ways of living and working together that are perceived as being desirable or, on the contrary, unacceptable. These images carry specific conceptions of authority, of duty, processes to arbitrate between opposing views, and conceptions on the basis of which the situation experienced takes on meaning.

A deeper layer comes from the existence, in each society, of a specific type of concern: fears associated with situations which give rise to feelings of unease or anxiety; situations which evoke a peril, a threat, which it is essential to ward off. The diversity of cultures is related to the fact that what is feared and from which one seeks to be free *via* the organization of social life varies significantly from one society to another.

Plunging into the universe of each culture, focusing on its wealth and its complexity, shows the extent to which it is unrealistic to seek to grasp it in a few words. A real intellectual engagement is necessary, such as that required to learn a language. And this is the only way for managers to be able to make the best use of the potential of each culture.

3.1 Why Innovate?

In this first part, we will begin by discussing the two main strands in the approach to cultures that currently coexist in management literature. We will go on to review the main families of approaches to culture which are more generally found in the social sciences and in interaction with which we gradually built our approach, while at the same time confronting them with our field research.

Concerning the role played by national cultures in management, we shall see that the literature is principally divided between two main strands. One fully accepts the notion of national culture and seeks to characterize each culture by using attitude scales. The other is very reserved, not to say hostile, in terms of the idea of national culture, while taking an interpretative approach to highlight cultures concerning much smaller groups, such as corporate, professional, social class cultures, etc. We shall see that neither of these approaches can account for what we have observed. We shall subsequently discuss the multitude of approaches to cultures that coexist outside the field of management. We shall see that the interpretative approach which currently dominates ethnological approaches appeared particularly fruitful, but that we had to innovate also by drawing on other approaches, in order to adapt it to national cultures.

3.1.1 National Cultures and Management: the Attitude Scales Approach

When it comes to how organizations and management function, the dominant trend for gaining an understanding of national cultures draws on social psychology and not on ethnology. It uses attitude scales (Boyacigiller, N. A, et al., 2004: 99–167). This approach leads to each culture being characterized by a small number of figures. For instance, Hofstede (1980, 2001) whose research is held up as a reference in this field, for a long time used four attitude scales: power distance, individualism *versus* collectivism, uncertainty avoidance, masculinity *versus* femininity; prior to adding a fifth: long-term orientation *versus* short-term orientation, and then a sixth: indulgence *versus* restraint. Several reasons account for the importance given to an approach which seems strange to an ethnologist (Chapman, 1996). As for managers, thanks to the use of statistical processing, they have the reassuring impression that they master the complexity of a culture in an objective and scientific manner. It is in keeping with the importance that management gives to statistical indicators. In the academic field, this approach has the great merit of allowing publications to be produced based on a tried-and-tested methodology, without there being the need to make an in-depth analysis of how organizations function—with the difficulties to access the field and analyse material which this involves. The results of surveys based on questionnaires conducted in several countries simply need to be correlated concerning the most diverse data, with the scores obtained for a few attitude scales. But anyone wishing to understand the life of organizations and seeking to adapt management as well as possible to the diversity of cultures cannot rely on these scales.

What does stating that a country has a certain score on a given attitude scale, for example, individualism, mean? Would this indicate a defined attitude to be found, identical in all ways, in all situations? Or conversely does it mean that this score relates to the attitudes which are specific to the dimensions of corporate life that concern the questions used? In social psychology—the disciplinary field under which the construction of attitude scales falls—specialists agree that the scores obtained do not correspond to a property to be found in all forms of behaviour. For example, according to Triandis (1995: 2),

> In recent years social psychologists have made numerous attempts to measure tendencies toward individualism and collectivism, and in doing so they discovered considerable complexity in what should be included in these constructs. They have also theorised about the causes and consequences of people's behaving in individualistic and collectivist ways and discovered that people are typically both individualists and collectivists. (Triandis, 1995)

Various authors who studied a specific culture, examined in more detail how, in each of them, and in particular in Asian countries, ways of being that can be described as individualistic coexisted with other ways of being that are usually described as collectivistic. For instance, Kim (1994: 36) wrote: 'Sinha and Tripathi (1994) have coined the term coexistence to describe a model that allows diverse, even contradictory, elements to coexist within a culture and within a person.'

So, depending on how one observes, the same culture can take on very different perspectives and various researches can attribute very different positions to the same country. The USA and France can be taken as an example of this, by comparing the results of Hofstede's research with those, also widely quoted, conducted by Schwartz (1994) in thirty-eight countries. The latter, based on a questionnaire concerning fifty-six values, defines seven dimensions, four of which are correlated with the individualism dimension of Hofstede, three positively (Affective Autonomy, Intellectual Autonomy, and Egalitarian Commitment), one negatively (Conservatism). The USA, the most individualistic country on the Hofstede scale, is much less so on the scale of Schwartz (particularly eleventh in Affective Autonomy, eighteenth in Intellectual Autonomy). In contrast, France, which is only tenth on Hofstede's scale of individualism, is first here in Affective Autonomy, second in Intellectual Autonomy. France, which is less individualistic than the USA according to Hofstede, is more so according to Schwartz. The same phenomenon can be found in the 'power distance' dimension: the USA, which is less hierarchical than France for Hofstede, is more so for Schwartz.[1]

As was seen concerning the decentralization and control issues, and as we shall see again throughout this publication, anyone who manages a company needs to take carefully into account this complexity. When one seeks to set up a management tool, in whatever field, whether it involves relationships with clients, decision-making, industrial relations, or any other aspect of management, there is a need to know how those who will implement it will react to this specific tool. It is not sufficient to know whether they are generally a little or very individualistic, a little or very hierarchical. It is necessary to have a clear understanding of the various forms that individualism, respect for authority, etc., take in a given aspect of existence.

Furthermore, very different attitudes, which tend to prevail in various areas of social life, are likely to coexist within the same country. For example, in Mexico, there is usually a great hierarchical distance in companies, but it coexists with egalitarian relations between brothers and between cousins (d'Iribarne, 2007a). When attitudes that are not conducive to good productive efficiency tend to prevail in companies, the role of management seeking efficiency is not to consider that it can do nothing about it, which is encouraged by the attitude scales approach. On the contrary, as we shall see in Chapter 14, it needs to set out to import attitudes into the company which, while they are not common in it, exist in other sectors of social life. By doing so, it can set up more efficient forms of management which diverge from the most common practices. It is consequently essential to take into account the diversity of attitudes coexisting within the same culture.

In addition, a crucial aspect of intercultural relations lies in the way in which those who have received their references from different cultures mutually decipher their actions (a point which will be developed in Chapter 10). This deciphering is often governed by visions of foreigners that are full of stereotypes, combined with a belittling vision of the other, which fuels an atmosphere of mistrust. Consequently, it is highly likely that the use of attitude scores will obstruct rather than support good cooperation. We came across this type of situation when analysing the failure of the attempted alliance between Renault and Volvo (a point which will be developed in Chapter 12). The staff of Volvo involved in the attempt received intercultural training based on the use of attitude scales, a training course which led them to consider France as a very hierarchical country. They interpreted the ways of acting at Renault by trusting this representation, which led them to largely overestimate the power of superiors while ignoring the role played by dedication to the profession at all levels of hierarchy. Seeking to understand people's specific ways of managing their relations with others—rather than viewing them through a lens which labels them as more this or more that, with all the value judgements attached—increases the ability to adapt to them in a constructive manner.

Managers cannot but benefit from an approach revealing the meaning for those who experience them of situations brought about by management tools use and the encounter with other cultures.

3.1.2 The Notion of National Culture Called into Question

While in the field of management, the dominant approach to national cultures uses attitude scales, other strands focus on qualitative approaches to cultures, but by moving away from national cultures. Although they use the same term 'culture', they in fact associate this word with other sociological objects than the one the expression 'national culture' refers to.

One approach, which is widely held up as a reference, presents a culture as a repertoire of possible actions, a sort of toolkit within which each actor could draw on each time they need to choose a direction (Swidler, 1986). This approach tends to consider each field of action separately. For example, it would encourage considering a repertoire of possible ways of going about convincing a client, another repertoire of ways of going about proceeding with a recruitment, etc. But the very idea of a culture concerning simultaneously all the areas of life of an organization, such as more broadly social life, then disappears.

The interpretative approach which dominates contemporary anthropology is also used. It is the meaning given to the world in which we live that is the focus of attention. In this respect, the approach we were led to adopt fits in with this strand (Geertz, 1973). However, whether it is a question of management or of other aspects of social life, this strand focuses on smaller objects than a national set. Thousands of research studies have focused, and still focus, on cultures that are specific to a professional group, a particular organization, a business sector. But the very notion of national culture concerning the various aspects of social life is largely called into question. It is widely accused of corresponding to an approach pejoratively described as 'culturalist', an approach which supposedly considers individuals as 'cultural dopes', by neglecting their ability to act in a creative manner (Garfinkel, 1973).

This mistrust is understandable. The notion of shared culture is not an issue when one thinks of what unites, in a so-called 'traditional' world, a relatively small community, such as those which anthropologists usually consider. But in societies marked by history, considering a culture as something which has some permanence is a legitimate question, and speaking of a shared culture is not self-evident when one changes scale and considers a country taken as a whole. Two arguments come into play when one considers culture as giving meaning. Firstly, meaning is not only received but produced. In addition, society is divided into social groups which often give different meanings to the same situation.

A significant strand of research has highlighted the role played by actors in the construction of meaning and has consequently emphasized the evolutionary aspect of cultures. For example, for Berger & Luckmann (1989: 47–48), in an encounter 'the two typificatory schemes enter into an ongoing "negotiation" in the face-to-face situation'. This perpetual negotiation of meanings does not spare the field of organizations. For Weick, 'people (. . .) persistently rework their categories and refine them, differentiate them, update them, and replace them' (Eisenberg, 2006: 1701). Yet, if everything is negotiated at all times locally, it is unclear what national aspects could remain (Soderberg & Holden, 2002; Staber, 2006). For Staber (ibid.: 192), referring to Giddens (1984):

> Culture-based understandings are not a static, pre-existing condition that can be seen as exerting a simple causal influence on action. They are themselves fundamentally constructed phenomena that arose and are sustained or adjusted through social interaction. The resulting meaning systems are the outcome of individual agency and patterned social interaction. (Staber, 2006)

When representations are used which give a prominent place to action and to actors (agency), the essentially local nature of the action makes something like national cultures difficult to conceive.

Admittedly, some are quick to point out that the construction of meaning by actors does not come about from nothing. It is then a question of 'raw materials of sense making', 'institutionalized roles, templates for action, scripts, schemas, logics' (Weber & Glynn, 2006). The effects of institutions, such as 'the institution of employment', are then highlighted and analysed. But it is then a question of specific institutions, guiding perceptions and behaviours in a particular field where specific actors act such as—to take two areas which have been subject to in-depth investigations—the regulation of railways in the UK, the USA, and France (Dobbin, 1994), or the institutions governing labour relations in the UK and Germany (Biernacki, 1995). What we see here is not related to the specificities of national cultures taken as a whole and the consideration of such specificities is even rejected.

Furthermore, within the same society, one comes across rival definitions of the reality and, even if there are dominant definitions, they coexist with deviant definitions, possibly with the creation of counter societies (Berger & Luckman, 1966: 147, 149, 168, 173). For example, for Willis, 'Culture is (...) the very material of our daily lives, the bricks and mortar of our most commonplace understandings, feelings and responses', but for him, culture is not something common at the level of a nation. It is related, he states, to the specific position held in society: 'The direct experiences of production are worked through and over in the praxis of different cultural discourses' (Willis, 1979, in Alexander & Seidman, 1990: 183–184). A sharp criticism sometimes leads to accusing the notion of national culture of concealing the phenomena of domination behind a so-called unanimity and of hiding forms of power behind what is supposedly self-evident. For example, for Alvesson, managers play a major role 'in the shaping and reshaping of meanings and ideas held by the people they interact with', but the elaboration of the meaning is subject to conflict. There are also forms of counter-cultures, carrying another vision which allows the dominated to liberate themselves. The issue is to 'counteract the taken-for-granted beliefs and values' (Alvesson, 2002: 11, 44, 69, 121).

This attention given to the constructed character of universes of meaning and to the many ways of giving meaning within the same society suggests that it is only legitimate to speak of culture at a much smaller level than a country: a workshop, a sports club, or at most a company. Indeed, it can be assumed that while one is on this level, at any given time, one finds sorts of shared meanings, associated with a set of shared values and behaviours. These meanings remain local and transitional.

However, the value of these arguments should not be overestimated. In fact, the unquestionable existence of differing interpretations does not mean that the specific ways of interpreting of the various actors belonging to the same society do not have anything in common. The sociological tradition refers to what is common while manifesting itself in very different ways. Montesquieu (1748) speaks of 'the general spirit (...) of a nation' and Weber (1992: 105) of 'the national character (...) of peoples'. Geertz (1983: 195), for his part, refers to the existence of 'a horde of hyper-particular, hyper-concrete manifestations of hyper-general, hyper-abstract form; a world of avatars'. These terms *spirit, character, avatar* express the idea that something stable remains within a changing reality. But they do not guide towards a clear understanding of what it is about.

In countries, such as the USA, the Netherlands, Cameroon, Vietnam, or France, where we have conducted research in fields which are very diverse in many respects, we did not fail to find a certain 'family resemblance' (Wittgenstein, 1953: 64). Right from the start of our research, it certainly did become apparent that within a given country, and even within a given company, diversity is the rule. There is no homogeneity of forms of organization (d'Iribarne, 1989). For example, observing life in an American factory, we were able to note the extent to which the procedures implemented for the management of employees differ from those which are used for the management of hourly workers. We were also able to note, by observing a French factory, the coexistence of very diverse ways of exercising authority with, for example, considerable differences between the way in which this exercise was carried out in the manufacturing services and the way in which it was carried out in the maintenance services. However, when we analysed our observation data, we were able to bring to light, within both factories, conceptions of a good way of living and working together that were common across departments. In addition, when we continued our research, we were able to see that well beyond these factories, these conceptions mark the countries where the latter are established. We were gradually able to generalize these observations and arrive at a conception of culture which accounts for both the diversity and unity within each cultural universe.

A crucial point in understanding national cultures lies in the difficulties associated with the use of the same word 'culture' to describe sociological entities of a very different nature. A socially situated 'culture', specific to an organization, a social group, a particular field of action, is one thing. It involves a sociological entity in which social strategies, identity struggles, and permanent creativeness are to be found. A national 'culture', common to those who have very diverse social situations, can only be a very different sociological entity. To understand its nature, we must resist the temptation to start with the image of a 'culture' that can be formed, based on the observation of small communities.

3.1.3 A Wide Variety of Approaches in Social Sciences and Beyond

In our search for a conception of cultures to account for our observation data, we came across the fact that a number of political philosophy, sociology, ethnology, social psychology, and linguistic approaches, emerged over time to account for the diversity of ways of being and acting (Wuthnow, 1987; Alexander & Seidman, 1990; Alexander, 2005). We felt that they did not fully answer the questions that we were asking, although they did have certain aspects which we considered informative.

One way of distinguishing between peoples is to seek to bring to light the main conceptions of existence which fuel the various ways of organizing public life. For example, Montesquieu looks at 'human passions' which 'set in motion' the government (Montesquieu, 1748, part I, book III). He sees in virtue the 'spring' of the republican government, in honour that of the monarchical government, and in fear that of the despotic government. This attention given to the main ways of existing is also found with Weber (1978, ch.10), who, for his part, pays particular attention to the doctrines of salvation carried by religions. He contrasts ascetism in the world, which is conducive to rational activity, with the withdrawal from the world of contemplative mystics, which turns away from it.

Another orientation, which is also ancient, focuses on the role of language. For example, for Humboldt (2000: 57, 101), languages 'form or mostly indicate the difference in national character', due to the fact that their diversity 'is a diversity of visions of the world'. This idea was especially developed by Sapir and Whorf (hence the so-called 'Sapir-Whorf' hypothesis):

> We dissect nature along lines laid down by our native languages. The categories and types that we isolate from the world of phenomena we do not find there because they stare every observer in the face; on the contrary, the world is presented in a kaleidoscopic flux of impressions which has to be organized by our minds – and this means largely by the linguistic systems in our minds.
>
> (Whorf, 1956: 213)

The input from psychoanalysis marked the American cultural anthropology of the mid-twentieth century, from Abraham Kardiner and Ralph Linton to Ruth Benedict and Margaret Mead. It led to a culture being characterized by a type of personality. Consequently, the opposition between balanced and peaceful 'Apollonian' personalities and impassioned and violent 'Dionysian' personalities was highlighted, and the Oceanic societies were celebrated as being peaceful and tolerant, in contrast to American society. Great interest was taken in the way in which education forms the personality.

Another strand focuses on questions of identity. There is reference to 'imagined communities' (Anderson, 1983), to the ideological work which allows everyone to invent a specificity for themselves (Hobsbawm & Ranger, 1983). Much attention is then given to national myths, national heroes, and national emblems. The way in which national history is reconstructed, with the aim of fuelling a feeling of national pride, is subject to critical interpretation.

The vision of culture that dominates contemporary anthropology is, for its part, intrinsically linked to the bringing to light of the universe of meaning (Geertz, 1973).

These different approaches have, to varying degrees, allowed us to understand what we had observed. Consequently, we shall see in this chapter that Montesquieu's analyses have helped us give meaning to what we have observed in France or again, in Chapter 9, p. 176, that a comparison between the ways of referring to the same situation in various languages has sometimes been informative. As we shall see, our approach is largely inherited from an interpretative vision. It was through the contact with these various strands, tested by our field research, that it gradually took shape (d'Iribarne, 2012a).

3.2 An Interpretative Approach Adapted to the Complexity of Modern Societies

In this second part, we will begin with a general presentation of the approach to national cultures which we have developed. We will subsequently give two illustrations concerning the USA and France. As it appears necessary to understand the general approach in order to grasp the illustrations clearly, and as the reverse is also true, the reader should first of all simply take a quick look at the general approach, then move on to the illustrations, before coming back to the general approach.

3.2.1 Ideal Images and Structuring Fears

In the research that we have conducted all over the world, we have paid great attention to the way in which what people experience on a daily basis—hierarchical relations, cooperation between services, relations with clients—takes on meaning for them. This led us to look at the self-evidences on which their judgement is based and the categories they use when they describe their daily reality. By doing so, we were led to identify two categories of phenomena which correspond to two levels of analysis.

A first category corresponds to the existence, in each universe of meaning, of positive or negative reference images with which what is experienced resonates. Not only do these images impact the way experience makes sense, but they also colour it with the emotions that they carry. In these images, we find major events and great figures, either purely mythical or raised to the level of myths beyond their historical materiality: for instance, in China, the image of the good emperor devoted to his people; in Jordan, the image of the perfect community of the early stages of Islam; in Cameroon, the image of the clairvoyant able to thwart the misdeeds of witches; etc. Some images particularly concern the life of organizations: the vision of ways of living and working together which are aspired to or rejected; particular conceptions of a legitimate authority, of the autonomy which subordinates must benefit from, of professional duty, of arbitration processes between opposing views; etc. Each chapter in this book will lead to certain traits of such visions being highlighted in the countries which will be mentioned.

In the life of organizations, great efforts are made, with varying success, to make everyday reality look like images of life-in-society which stand as a reference. Whether or not what they experience is in tune with or deviates from them, these images are present in the background in the comments made by those who talk about their experience, to express their satisfaction, or to complain about it. While the latter are generally unable to explain this background, it is a sort of implicit self-evidence for them. As the investigations continue and as new fields are explored; as we compare what we have been able to observe in various areas of social life; as we link daily behaviours and institutional constructions; as we look at political ideas; these differentiated visions of a good way of living and working together appear in an increasingly clear, rich, and precise manner.

These images, and the affects which are related to them, are underpinned by the existence, within each society, of a specific type of concern and fear, associated with situations which generate feelings of unease, anxiety, or even abandonment; situations which evoke a peril, a threat, which it is essential to ward off. The existence of an area of experience which gives rise to disorder, concern, anxiety, influences the way in which events, situations, are experienced. The meaning they take on—and consequently the reactions to them—is marked by a framework of interpreting which leads to a special focus on what evokes either the type of major threat or the ways of salvation allowing to escape from it. It is because culture thereby brings into play very strong and very deep feelings that acting in a culturally inappropriate manner is likely to provoke passionate reactions, and that what appears to go without saying in one place can provoke indignation and revolt in another place. We will see that many aspects of the life of organizations are concerned: the exercise of authority, judgements made about peoples' actions, decision-making, etc.

The presence of such a specific area of concern is well known in certain societies which openly retain links with a so-called 'traditional' past. For example, it is particularly visible in Indian society, where it concerns contacts with what is impure. 'India', notes Luc de Heusch (1981), 'offers us (...) the strange and dramatic spectacle of a universe where the metaphorical delirium of soiling reigns supreme over thinking, invests all the prohibitions, all the classifications.' Our research has shown that societies reputed to be not very 'modern' do not have a monopoly on the existence of a specific area of fears. It exists, even if it is not immediately perceptible, in so-called 'modern' societies, as we shall see for the USA and France. The diversity of cultures is related to the fact that the fears and ways to dispel them vary significantly from one society to another, while being marked, in each of them, by a strong continuity over time.

The opposition between this peril and the ways of salvation that make it possible to escape from it may be represented by referring to a sort of scene of peril and salvation within which events and situations take on meaning, depending on whether they are on the good or the bad side. This scene provides a framework of common meaning, which is both unconscious and remarkably stable throughout history. The fact of being constantly exposed to it, of adopting it oneself as well as one's counterparts, when one puts forward an argument or even simply when one recounts events and describes situations, means that such a perspective is fully part of the workings of the mind. New situations, new events, are interpreted, as well as what is familiar, by adopting this perspective.

The desire to escape from situations where the peril feared by all materializes is a fundamental driving force for action, for the daily action of everyone, or for the collective construction of institutions. Individuals, social, and political currents which everything may otherwise oppose, share the corresponding framework of interpretation as a sort of undiscussed self-evidence. This framework is present when it fosters the acceptance of routines. It is also present when it structures the way in which revolutionaries legitimize their action.

Actors receive this framework of meaning without being aware of it and do not have any control over it. In contrast, it is indeed based on the markers it provides that actors interpret a situation more or less favourably, depending on whether it evokes what is the subject of fear or, on the contrary, what makes it possible to escape from it. Actors seek to influence this interpretation, while at the same time applying themselves to transforming institutions and practices. They seek to associate positive images with what they want to justify and negative ones with what they want to denounce. Consequently, the sense they make out of a given situation is the subject of differences of interpretation and conflicts, and evolves throughout history.

Understood at these two levels, culture—ideal images of a good and bad way of living together and a central fear—does not only correspond to a vision of the world, but also to an emotional relationship to the latter, to a whole way of fearing and hoping.

What do these cultures become in a globalized world? Do they disappear in a great mixing of identities and values? In fact, the force of the affects attached to the founding fears makes the cultural foundations particularly resistant to external influences. This does not, however, prevent their manifestations from having a great plasticity, as we shall see with many examples.

The inventory of cultures, and in particular the founding fears that are specific to each of them, is a huge task, the bulk of which still has to be conducted. The various chapters in this publication report on what we have been able to bring to light in the countries that we are discussing. The contrasting examples of the USA and France give a clear understanding of the nature of the phenomena in question and of their role in questions of management.

3.2.2 To Be Free of the Will of Others in the USA

In American society, the fundamental fear is to find oneself at the mercy of the actions of others. To escape from this fear, it is necessary to remain the master of one's own destiny. One comes across this fear when one observes any aspect of social life.

A particularly striking depiction of this—and one especially significant as this text is a major point of reference in the USA—is to be found in *The Federalist*, written at the time when the nation adopted a constitution (Hamilton et al., 1992). A look at the short chapter which concerns the structure of the Union's institutions (number 51) shows that the sentiment of a peril—evoked by the terms *insecure, insecurity, danger, attack*—is omnipresent. Faced with this peril, the will to protect oneself is affirmed continuously. It is a question of defending oneself (*defence, self-defence, precautions, guarded against, resist, counteract, protect*), by implementing appropriate means (*armed, sentinel*). It involves reaching a situation whereby one is safe (*preservation, safe, security, secure*). What is thus feared? The term *encroachment*, which is repeated several times (*encroachments of the others, dangerous encroachments*), clearly shows what it involves. According to the dictionary (Webster's), 'encroach' means 'to trespass or intrude (on or upon the rights, property, etc. of another)'. It is against this encroachment, with which ideas of dependence, oppress, submit are associated, that one needs to protect oneself. The establishment of a system of checks and balances is seen as the main means of defence.

The central role of the reference to property, and the intimate association, in the USA, between the notion of liberty and that of property, are associated with the preeminent nature of protection against this threat. According to Foner, property 'was "interwoven" with eighteenth-century understanding of freedom' (1998: 9). For example, at the 1787 Constitutional Convention, Madison declared, 'A man has property in his opinions and the free communication of them, he has property in (. . .) the safety and liberty of his person'. This vision of peril and salvation, and the corresponding place of the reference to property, was also found in England. There, everyone was seen as being threatened in all the aspects of their existence by the action of others, and it was essential to 'preserve' what was important to them. It was the fact of having protected oneself against the vicissitudes of any foreign will—such as an owner who was the only master in his own house—which could ward off this peril of not controlling one's destiny, of being subject to the will of others. For example, for Locke (1690), 'Man (. . .) hath by Nature a Power (. . .) to preserve his Property, that is, his Life, Liberty and Estate, against the Injuries and Attempts of other Men' (§ 87); and if men create a society, it is 'for the mutual *Preservation* of their Lives, Liberties and Estates, which I call by the general name, *Property*' (§ 123).

This fear of being dependent has posed serious problems in work relations, due to the place given to dependency on a boss. How can one ensure that the relationship between a company and its employees falls within a contract between owners, or is experienced as such, despite the disparity between the positions of the parties? Part of the solution has been to consider the employee as being able to be assimilated to an owner in the traditional sense, by considering him as the owner of himself and therefore of his work (Foner, 1998: 52). It was also necessary to find practices, whether they fell within the scope of the law or of mores, which could govern work relations in such a way that they would ensure a certain equality in both parties' bargaining power (a level playing field). It is in this ideal vision of a relationship between owners averting a situation of dependency on the will of others that the place given to a contractual rationale in the formatting of the life of organization (see Chapter 1), takes on meaning.

For those who believe that a culture is marked by attitudes to be found in all aspects of social life, the contractual individualism aspect of American management will appear inconsistent with its community aspect, related, as it is, to the vision of the company as a moral community—an aspect that will be addressed in Chapter 9, pp. 173–74. But in fact, if one considers the fear of dependency, these two aspects are consistent.

In an American perspective, if one wishes to remain autonomous, protecting oneself does not only concern the control which others have over you. It also concerns bad feelings, momentary passions which, exerting their control over individuals, divert them from following their true interest. For example, *The Federalist* (§ 6) associates 'true interest' with a 'benevolent and philosophical spirit' and contrasts it with 'momentary passions and immediate interests', which are presented as being likely to exert 'an active and imperious control over human conduct', and therefore as a sort of external force likely to control the individual that they dominate. A contemporary handbook encouraging children to forgive provides a good example of this association between ethical conduct and control over the situation: 'Forgive, even if there are no excuses or reparations. (...) Do not let your life depend on the behaviour of the other' or 'By showing kindness towards an aggressor, you regain control of the situation' (Schell, 1993: 12, 34).

Yet, in an American perspective, this moral aspect has a strong community dimension. In the Protestant sects, which played a key role in the formation of American society, the community of the faithful is responsible for everyone's conduct: 'And the sect placed disciplinary power predominantly into the hands of lay persons. No spiritual authority could assume the community's joint responsibility before God' (Bellah et al., 1985: 245). This intervention by the community seems even more necessary because man is seen as being weak by nature—he is naturally 'ambitious, vindictive and rapacious' *The Federalist Papers* (Hamilton et al., 1992: 20), and he needs to be guided and supervised by the community to free himself of his evil inclinations.

3.2.3 French Society and the Fear of a Servile Attitude

In French society, the experience which above all gives rise to violently negative feelings is to bow down, out of fear or self-interest, to those who can harm you or grant you favours.

When Sieyès (1988 [1789]) passionately expressed the frustrations and thirst for revenge of the *Tiers État* (Third Estate), he brought out particularly clearly the importance given to this experience. The Third Estate, declared Sieyès, is led 'to attach himself by all kinds of contemptible actions to some magnate; he prostitutes his principles and human dignity for the possibility of claiming, in his need, the protection of a somebody' (p. 45). Besides interest, it is fear that demeans. A nation that allows itself to be 'frightened' can be described as 'vile' (p. 79). The same fear is to be found with Tocqueville although the latter, heir of a noble lineage, has a very different social position than that of Sieyès. For example, throughout *Democracy in America*, Tocqueville (1840) expresses the fear of seeing those who live in democratic societies submit, this time, to 'the tyranny of the majority'. 'The very men, who from time to time upset a throne and trample on a race of kings, *bend* more and more obsequiously to the slightest dictate of a clerk' (p. 766) (emphasis added). The most revered heroes in the history of France, such as Vercingétorix or Jeanne d'Arc, were often conquered by superior forces, but they refused to submit, whatever it cost them.

The reluctance to bow down so as to obtain favours from others still plays a central role in contemporary France. In companies, a style of relations where one has to humiliate oneself to obtain what one is seeking is hardly acceptable. One comes across complaints such as: 'Manufacturing is on its knees before maintenance'; 'The maintenance services are the kings. The manufacturing services should handle them with kid gloves' (d'Iribarne, 1989: 108, 38).

At the same time, emphasis on the duties related to the position that one has in society—duties that are consequently distinct from the will of those who can serve you or harm you—is central. The reference to the *métier* (or profession), to the man of the profession, to the grandeur of the profession, with all its representations and practices (addressed in Chapter 2, pp. 38–40), is part of this perspective. It plays a crucial role in ensuring the link between what is experienced in the everyday lives of organizations and the refusal of a manner deemed servile, that of being in a relationship with those who, in one way or another (a superior, a client), can make you benefit from some advantage provided you accept their demands.

Consequently, putting forward the profession provides a way of connecting the work accomplished in a subordinate position—under the supervision of one's boss—with a vision of independence, honour, and nobility. This is the form of autonomy that Michel Crozier (1963: 289) was referring to, in his description of the French version of bureaucratic organizations:

> Subordinates (...) will never have to bow down before the personal, humiliating will of someone; what they do, they do by their own will and, in particular, they accomplish their task outside any direct obligation. They endeavour to show that they are working, not because they are forced to, but because they choose to do so. (Crozier, 1963)

It has an impact on collective work relations. They will be addressed in Chapter 7. The labour legislation which gradually developed in France gives a major role to each individual's professional position, to the rights related to the specific place that they have in society. For many questions, recruitment, dismissal, working hours, paid leave, salaries, retirement, training, etc., a labour law, which has gradually been built, replaces the Civil Code. In all these fields, the relations between employees and their employer are only very partially governed by an agreement between the parties (be it an individual agreement or a collective one). They are marked by rights, either for employees in general or for a specific category of employees, associated with the very condition of employee. The weight of these rights is such that it is forbidden for the parties to deviate from them, even if they are in complete agreement to do so; any contractual clause by which an employee, or a group of employees, would fall back on the rights attached to their position is deemed null and void (Castel, 1995). One does, of course, sometimes seek to escape from such a conception. For example, in a general movement of abolishing privileges, the Revolution suppressed the corporations and established the freedom to be an entrepreneur and to enter into contract. But when, in the light of experience, the economic dependence hidden behind the legal equality was criticized, the way found to protect employees from the severity of a strictly contractual relationship was to build a new status (Sewell, 1983). Still today, this labour law conception is vigorously contested by proponents of an eradication of the specificities of the 'French social model', to the benefit of more strictly contractual relationships. However, translating this objection into action appears difficult.

Customer relations, which will be addressed in Chapter 8, are also concerned. Companies and their staff refer to their relations with clients using terms (*prescribe, diagnose, listen, offer, welcome*) that do not suggest the self-interested—therefore servile—submission of a simple service provider to a foreign will, but, on the contrary, the goodwill of the person who dominates the situation towards the person who calls on him. Referring to the action of 'salespeople', the English version of a CAC 40 annual report notes: 'With a thorough understanding of their customers' needs, they [our sales representatives] are able to *recommend* the most appropriate solutions' (Lafarge, 2004: 23[2]). In the French version of that same report, the sales representatives do not *recommend* but *prescribe* these solutions: *Leur connaissance intime des besoins de leurs clients leur permet de* prescrire[3] *les solutions les plus adaptées* (emphasis added). Here again, this representation influences practices, for the best—a great ability to go beyond the client's immediate desire—and for the worst—the lack of spirit of service which the French are often criticized for (d'Iribarne, 2006a).

The same reference points can be found in the manner in which business ethics are conceived in France—a question which will be addressed in Chapter 9, pp. 174–176. The latter are not seen as being the responsibility of a community which exercises tight control over its members, supervises them and punishes them, but as a matter of everyone's freedom to adopt the vision they have of their duty. It is individuals, relying on their own convictions, who are seen as supporting such conduct: 'Ethics for me are the manner in which every person perceives things and conducts themselves as best they can'; 'We have our own conscience which is sufficient' (d'Iribarne, 2002). It is only legitimate and even honourable to give in to an idea that one considers as superior, or to people who are greater 'by their virtues or talents'—to quote the sixth article of the 1789 Declaration of Human Rights[4]—than oneself, and alongside whose ideas it is honourable to stand.

3.3 Conclusion

We shall see, throughout the publication, the extent to which this approach to culture, rooted in the observation and understanding of real management situations, attentive to the meaning they take and to the affect associated with this meaning, allows for a management which makes the best use of the potentials of each culture.

Managers, faced with a staff which they seek to motivate and make innovative and cooperative, need to discover the realistic paths to change. To do so, they have much to gain from clearly understanding what, in what they are seeking to implement, is likely to give rise to resistance; what constitutes a sticking point and the adaptations which would lead to buy-in. For this purpose, they need to understand how people feel about what is proposed to them or imposed on them. They should try to figure out what mental universe, marked by what categories of analysis, what visions of good or bad, of acceptable and unacceptable, they draw on to give meaning (a mental universe within which precision in the parties' commitments makes sense in the USA; respect for the values of a profession, in France; and so on). Seeking to modify this way of giving meaning would be as unrealistic as Don Quixote's plan to conquer the windmills, whereas taking account of it makes it possible to discern how to go about ensuring that the desired changes lead to buy-in.

When one simply follows what is most commonly done in the companies of a country, there is no need to understand its culture. But it is a necessity when one seeks to have a more motivated, more innovative, more cooperative staff than is customary. It is then essential to grasp what will ensure that what is expected from them will be received positively—for example, if they are French, under what conditions being managed or meeting clients' expectations will be deemed worthy, or at least not servile.

Furthermore, when people from several cultural universes meet, experience shows that everyone has a certain idea of the culture of the other, an idea more or less fuelled by a few simplistic clichés which, often with a rather negative view (stating they are submissive, fickle, hypocritical, etc.), attribute to various peoples—Chinese, Brazilians, Russians or others—stereotyped attitudes and ways of behaving. These clichés do sometimes allow huge errors to be avoided, insofar as they have some relation with reality. But they are often a source of confusion. Not only do they not help give an understanding of why what shocks in one makes perfect sense to others, but they also foster destructive judgements. A real understanding of cultures can help towards understanding the possible share of truth held in these stereotypes and the way in which they make people blind to the wealth of what is real. This paves the way for more trusting relationships that lead to building things better together.

As we shall see throughout this publication, the people with whom managers work live in a world rich in meaning, which any manager will benefit from discovering.

Notes

1. On Hofstede's scale, where fifty-three countries are ranked from the most hierarchical to the least hierarchical, France is fifteenth, so in the first third of the most hierarchical, and the USA thirty-eighth, so in the last third. With Schwartz, there is a 'hierarchy' scale, where thirty nine countries are ranked in the same way, for which the USA is twenty-second and France thirtieth.
2. Lafarge, 2004 Annual Report, https://www.lafargeholcim.com/sites/lafargeholcim.com/files/atoms/files/05242005-press_finance_Annual_report_2004-uk.pdf (accessed 29 June 2019).
3. '*Leur connaissance intime des besoins de leurs clients leur permet de* prescrire *les solutions les plus adaptées*', https://www.lafargeholcim.com/sites/default/files/import/publication/05242005-publication_finance-Annual_report_2004_all-fr.pdf (accessed 29 June 2019).
4. https://www.conseil-constitutionnel.fr/sites/default/files/as/root/bank_mm/anglais/cst2.pdf (accessed 7 July 2019).

PART II

MANAGEMENT FUNDAMENTALS AND CULTURE

4
Leadership

Which president should lead the European Community? This was the question that the heads of the European states, meeting the day after the elections, were to discuss. According to media reports,[1] two discordant voices, those of Germany and France, were particularly vocal on the subject. Beyond defending their respective partisan and national interests—which was obviously also influencing their support to a given candidate—the representatives of these countries viewed leadership and the role of the president in a different light. The Germans wanted a candidate capable, on each issue, of forging a consensus from a multitude of points of view, generally very distant from each other but each with (some) legitimacy. They figured that a former Member of the European Parliament with long experience of debates would be particularly suitable for the position. The French view was different. A personality who, at international summits, would be able to assume a position with Head of State status and address the Chinese, the Russian, or the American president on an equal footing would be a better choice. Personal charisma and previous experience of political responsibilities at the head of a State or of a major international institution were the qualities expected of a candidate for such a position. Clearly highlighted on the political scene, these oppositions emerge in a more discreet way in the daily functioning of organizations. This chapter is devoted to the study of such differences in the way in which leadership is conceived.

All over the world, leaders are expected to be able to exert their authority, to foster employees' commitment, and to ensure the proper execution of the work they have assigned to them. Everywhere, leaders are asked to command respect, to meet the expectations associated with the role that their followers assign to them, and to be fair in recognizing their contributions. Some expectations seem quite universal. However, what is to be done to meet these expectations differs from one country to another.

The literature on management (Dickson et al., 2012) acknowledges the fact that exercising authority may be done in quite a number of forms. Various studies (Hersey et al., 2007; Howell et al., 2004) endeavour to characterize, and generally compare, the respective limitations and merits of the different leadership styles. Depending on the authors, three, four, six, sometimes even more, different styles are distinguished. Authoritative leadership is contrasted with democratic leadership, transformational leadership with transactional leadership. Adapting forms of

Cross-Cultural Management Revisited: A Qualitative Approach. Philippe d'Iribarne, Sylvie Chevrier, Alain Henry, Jean-Pierre Segal, and Geneviève Tréguer-Felten, Oxford University Press (2020).
DOI: 10.1093/oso/9780198857471.001.0001

leadership to the organizational context and the profiles—including generational profiles—of subordinates is recommended. A team of young experts in new technologies, a team of construction workers in rural areas, or of senior employees of a bank branch in a business district, will not be managed in the same way. For instance, here, attention will be paid to encouraging the best people to stay, to supporting employee motivation and presenteeism, and elsewhere to encouraging staff to change their old approaches to clients. Managers' personal profiles, as well as their way of seeing their roles and of encouraging their teams, will need to be different according to the context of their actions.

Recently, the very idea of 'leadership', which in English covers both the leadership function and the key qualities required to be a leader, has been revisited, particularly among business consultants. Effective leaders should no longer be those who know how to command but those who know how to serve the employees that they command (Spears et al., 2002). Other authors call for a radical unbundling of the idea of leadership from that of hierarchy, so that each member of the organization can become a 'leader' on a particular initiative or project (Hamel, 2007). The self-managing utopias of the 1960s are once again in vogue: horizontal organizations which, freeing employees from the constraints of hierarchy, are supposed to multiply their creativity and motivation, are being praised (Laloux, 2014). Major changes within organizations are predicted. New technologies offer new opportunities for the circulation of information, thus transforming the role of hierarchy. Human resources managers are increasingly stressing the impact that changes in families and the education system have on the management of hierarchical relationships in companies.

The requirement to align forms of leadership with the nature of the problems arising from the exercise of authority has not been addressed very much in the literature on intercultural management. The existing literature has focused on describing differences in expectations of hierarchy. It merely explains that they derive, in a very general way, from the different forms of socialization and of 'mental programming'—to use Hofstede's expression (Hofstede, 2001). The international GLOBE project (House et al., 2004), which has brought together some 200 researchers from seventy-two countries, pursues the noble ambition of highlighting the influence of cultural differences on what employees expect from their leaders. As in many comparative approaches, the research is based on the construction of a measurement tool supposed to be applied as rigorously as possible to each of the countries included in the comparison. The method is based on respondents' selecting the adjectives that they deem best to qualify leadership practices or designate the qualities that a leader should have, from a series of over twenty adjectives—such as autonomous or humane—which have been translated into each language. However, it is unlikely that respondents in different countries will put the same content behind each of the adjectives offered to them (see Chapter 10).

The interpretative approach to culture presented in the previous chapter offers another avenue for analysing the expectations expressed towards the hierarchy. As will be seen in this chapter, it consists in integrating into the analysis of the employment relationship the diversity of the readings that people from different countries make of this very special social relation. It may inspire many satisfactions, such as being recognized and 'made greater' by the esteem of one's superior. However, it can just as well inspire fears, such as those of being ignored, mistreated, or unfairly sanctioned. Leaders' expected personal attributes, attitudes, and behaviours need to be related to the content—different from one cultural area to another—of the fears and hopes that employees associate with this hierarchical relation. Indeed, employment is not only an economic relation that allows employees to earn a living, it is also a socially-structured interaction between employees and their managers, as well as their colleagues, and their clients. From one society to another, these social intercourses are experienced through different cultural benchmarks which, if given the attention they deserve, shed light on the attributes expected of the leader. These cultural frames of references also help to decipher the sense that employees make of their managers' attitudes and behaviours, and consequently what they expect from them.

This chapter will focus on three economically comparable countries, the United States, Germany, and France, and compare the way in which some of the leaders' key roles are considered. The conceptions of good leadership advocated in each of the three countries present significant differences which will be described in the first section of the chapter, before being analysed and interpreted in the second. The aim is to provide a framework for interpreting these differences that goes beyond the traditional explanations in terms of socialization. Our research suggests that a link should be established between the expectations towards holders of authority and the interpretations made of this very sensitive social relationship. From this perspective, the forms of leadership best suited to local cultures would be those that best address the fears associated with this hierarchical relationship in the stakeholders' specific frame of references.

The analysis will be based both on data collected through our own research and on widely available materials, such as recommendations on the theme 'how to be a good leader' made available on the Internet by journalists or consultants. We are aware that in the blogs that we have compared, one can find very frequent instances of blatant borrowing—but not indicated as such—from the recommendations made by American consultants. Fortunately, there are also recommendations based on in-depth experience of the country's realities that distance themselves from the particularly powerful mimicry which is so frequent in the management sphere. Each of the blogs used in our comparison aims to promote an original approach. By bringing together several of them for each country, we were able to identify a number of converging recommendations for which there were no equivalents in the other countries.

4.1 Three Contrasting Ways to be a Good Leader

In all three countries, managers are advised to strive to motivate their team members, to monitor and acknowledge the latters' work, and to build their personal credibility. These are the recommendations which will be successively considered in this first section.

4.1.1 Motivating your Team

To what extent are managers to be considered responsible for their employees' motivation? Is it not for them to find ways and means to improve their subordinates' commitment? Is it not their duty to find the words that will make the efforts they request meaningful? Such visions of leadership—according to which managers would be in charge of maintaining the motivation of their team members—seem widely accepted. However, the blogs of consultants belonging to these three countries offer recommendations that are far from converging on this topic.

The combination of leadership and team motivation is at the heart of the American approach to management. Leaders' personal responsibility is at stake in this area: lack of motivation on the part of their team members is seen as their own failure. It is up to them, personally, to ensure that their followers are duly encouraged, supported, and challenged in such a way that they finally give their best.

> A true leader should positively influence people. When employees or co-workers lose their ambitions and passions, a true leader can energise and motivate them.[2]
>
> (Caramela, 2017)

American leaders are therefore not only expected to be organisers or to function as a transmission belt between the top and bottom of the organization, they are also in charge of strengthening their followers' motivation, mobilizing their personal qualities, as well as skills in people management. A good manager is also a 'coach' who knows how to listen to each team member and identify the specific expectations of each of them in order to better help them achieve their personal goals. One needs to be encouraged, another to be accompanied, a third one to be challenged.

This investment expected of the manager is not only seen as a form of benevolence, even if this pastoral dimension also exists. It makes sense with regard to an idealized representation of the hierarchical relationship assimilated to a 'win-win' exchange: it is in the managers' interest to work 'for' the employees since they ultimately work for him or her. This view can be shared by the subordinate when the relationship is good, as is the case with the supervisor of the American factory mentioned in Chapter 1, p. 20, who reports that he 'carries on his shoulders part of the burden that weighs on those of his superior'.

Defining clear objectives for which people are held accountable, while instilling the confidence required to achieve them, is seen in the United States as the key to motivating employees. It also contributes to answering employees' desire to progress and pursue a career. A good leader, consultants say, needs to ensure that the skills of employees are developed, and that the most capable among them are entrusted with new responsibilities.

> As a leader, one should learn how to delegate the work and what to delegate. The right delegation would impact their team members' career positively and help to build their career.[3] (Lloyd, 2015)

There is no reason to fear turning the developing employee into a competitor who would aspire to usurp one's place. It is believed that the managers who train their potential successors increase the probability of being promoted themselves to higher responsibilities. This illustrates the figure of the leader dedicated to teammates and willing to help them, while at the same time reconciling professional interest and personal recognition within the community.

Instead, German managers do not consider themselves as being responsible for team members' motivation. German subordinates do not believe either that they work 'for' their leader. Thus, it is not the latter's core responsibility to 'motivate' them. Leaders are not expected to stimulate teammates. The Germans believe that the strengthening of their motivation is strongly linked to the feeling of being useful and effective within the working community. The quality of the task allocation and work sharing plays a prominent role. Ensuring this quality is a much greater responsibility for leaders than galvanizing their colleagues' energy. German managers are expected to guarantee high collective efficiency. Overall cohesion is seen as much more important than individual zeal, whose excesses could threaten the effectiveness of the community.

The organizational model underlying these recommendations supposes that the rules (of the game) have been discussed, understood, and accepted by all, that decisions concerning the work team have been shared, and that each team member is aware of, and fulfils, his or her role to serve the organization. It is up to these managers, for example, to ensure that the role distribution is in line with the expertise of team members. In this scenario, leaders fulfil an important and useful coordination role for the team.

This clarification of task division within the organization occupies a major place in the consultants' recommendations addressed to German managers. This is even the very first tip in a recent blog:[4]

> Tip #1. Assign clearly separated tasks and activities to your employees. Show what an employee is responsible for. Other employees must also be aware of this so that work within the team can proceed smoothly and conflicts over areas of responsibility are minimised. It doesn't matter if you run a large company with several thousand employees, a start-up with 15 employees or a flower shop with five employees. (Fuer-gruender)

The same view is nicely encapsulated in the comments made by a senior manager of the Berlin metro, at a time when it was undergoing restructuring, a few years after the city's reunification.

> We are building a new social structure, a new house, in harmony with the participants who will later work in it. They're already working on it. We are building the foundations and we naturally hope that the units will demonstrate autonomy in their own homes, which they are responsible for organising. They also need to know their borders. They cannot or will not do it alone.

In the eyes of German consultants, this clarification of task allocation can substantially benefit from a collegial deliberation. They recommend that this participative method be used if managers are to achieve the desired harmony and efficiency.

> Team cohesion increases when leaders ask the team for their opinion. Especially if there is a change or a new project.[5]

Managers should be mainly dedicated to removing hurdles that may demotivate those who are supposed to be committed and empowered. They emphasize stronger group cohesiveness rather than individual motivation.

> Conflicts between employees always arise when the rules of the game are unclear or roles are not clearly assigned. The advantage: in the end, it is not the boss who sets the rules but the latter emerge from the team itself. This makes them more acceptable. (Groll, 2014)

Finally, it is also up to the managers to ensure that a supportive working climate is maintained. Managers, as experienced specialists, can also help to put people in a good mood by knowing how to address their employees with benevolence and good humour:

> A friendly greeting with the name, a few short sentences and a compliment motivate an employee much more than an annual interview.[6] (Groll. 2014)

French subordinates do not consider, as Americans do, that they work 'for their boss' even if they may be sensitive to the assessment the boss makes of their contribution. They do not attach the same importance as the Germans to a strict definition of tasks. Job definitions, as they understand them, are a useful reference that helps clarify roles and assess work, but overly precise definitions are not sought because they are perceived as liable to stifle the organization. Everyone strives for a high degree of autonomy within a roughly defined area of responsibility. It is their own idea of their profession, the intention to 'do their job well', and to see their peers recognize them as true 'professionals', which drive them. The appreciation from their peers is as important as that of their manager to support their motivation. The role played by managers in maintaining or developing the motivation of their team members will not really consist in giving their subordinates additional reasons to work 'for them', as American leaders do.

Rather, they will have to identify and circumvent demotivating factors likely to reduce employee commitment. These demotivating factors abound and, unfortunately for French managers, a number of them are beyond their reach. Poor relations with clients, both internal and external, and a lack of respect and consideration on their part, can deeply weaken their subordinates' professional identity which is at the core of their engagement. The addition of less valued tasks with regard to their view of what their *métier* (profession) should be, as often occurs as part of an organizational redesign to promote more versatility, can have the same effect.

Trusting subordinates, when they have earned it, is the best way for French managers to maintain employees' motivation in the long term. Trust provides subordinates with recognition of their ability to fulfil their core responsibilities while enjoying the autonomy to which they aspire. Refusing trust sends a negative message, questioning the subordinates' professional value. In this perspective, the controls carried out by the superior are likely to be experienced as a form of surveillance coupled with a denial of recognition. This trust is all the more valuable in that it concerns the subordinate as a person and results in a delegation of responsibility that does not need to be formalized as the empowerment of the American subordinates should be (Chevrier, 2009).

The often-used metaphor of the conductor illustrates this leadership style that respects the talent of each of the soloists for the sake of common work, Music, which is perfectly honourable to serve. Serving an honourable cause can be particularly effective in strengthening individual and group motivations and egos. This flattering identification is suggested by a French blog writer for project managers:

> The project's conductor is you... You will have to make people of different profiles work together, not necessarily all of them knowing each other before the project starts but united with you towards a common objective.[7] (Cornic)

At the same time, and this is not the easiest part of their role, leaders must know how to bring together two motivation drivers, which are, for the French, the ability to do 'their' work well and contribute to the success of the shared project.

> You must be respected. You have a unifying role. You are a respectful leader of your team but who must pass on the achievement of project objectives without always opening the way to all the whims of the project team members.[8]
>
> (Perez and Samson, 2008)

If they can engage their employees in 'beautiful' and 'great' projects, enabling all those who contribute to them to grow—including those whose professional identities were previously poorly recognized—French managers can obtain from them a spectacular level of commitment to a cause (the success of the project) worth serving (Segal, 2009).

In sum, the ability to strengthen the motivation of one's employees takes very different paths in the United States, Germany, and France. Equally significant differences are to be found on a second no less important dimension of leadership: the ability to monitor and recognize one's employee's work.

4.1.2 Monitoring and Recognizing Work

The follow-up and recognition of the work required of subordinates is the second part of our comparison of recommended practices for managers in the United States, Germany, and France. Here again, the requirements addressed to managers in the three countries differ, each time referring to different conceptions of the role expected of them by their team members.

For Americans, an essential function of managers is to closely monitor the performance of their team and regularly ensure that the contributions of each of its members are in line with what is expected of them. Holding them accountable for what they have committed to is not only perfectly legitimate, but necessary.

> As a leader, you need to ensure that you and your employees are on the same page. While documenting performance and providing feedback, hold your employees accountable to adhering to the goals you set.[9] (Caramela, 2017)

Following up is considered an aspect of the role as important as asserting one's authority or maintaining the motivation of team members.

This rigour and firmness can be all the more accepted as they would have been mixed, as was seen in Chapter 1, pp. 21–22, by regular feedback from leaders to their team members. Managers are responsible for ensuring that their subordinates have correctly understood what is expected of them. But they should also allow subordinates to improve, in line with the development role which, in the Americans' view, good leaders must play.

This feedback is also an opportunity for managers to highlight everything their subordinates have done well and to thank them personally. Since their employees are expected to work 'for them', managers can consider themselves in debt to the co-workers each time they have contributed to the achievement of managers' objectives.

To be thankful is a recommendation reiterated in the do's and don'ts addressed to junior managers:

> To truly build a great culture and dynamic among your team, it's important to give your employees credit when it's due. Always, always start with a simple 'thank you'.[10] (Caramela, 2017)

'American-style' managers should not hesitate to reward more, materially or symbolically, those who have worked better than others to achieve their objectives. Where, as is the case in the Maryland plant mentioned in Chapter 1, p. 17, such an individualization of rewards was restricted by the provisions binding the company and its union (see p. 135), some managers did not hesitate to buy doughnuts and share them with their team. This practice echoed local community rituals which had strong religious connotations that easily made sense to the teammates.

Recommendations addressed to American managers reflect the original combination of two imperatives which, in other cultural contexts, may seem difficult to reconcile: on the one hand, a strong need to assert one's authority, to behave as a 'leader' by formulating assertively one's expectations and by making one's mark on the team's dynamics and; on the other hand, the requirement not to abuse this authority, by simultaneously being open, devoted, fair, and deeply grateful to the team members. This is not only a matter of balancing contributions and rewards, in accordance with the egalitarian logic of reciprocity which underlies hierarchical relationships, but also of retaining the best employees in the team. Best interests and good feelings go hand in hand.

German managers can stay at a distance because they know that they can dependably rely on employees who are supposed to be autonomous and well trained. A maintenance worker in the Berlin metro confirms this:

> My boss, it depends on how busy he is. From time to time he comes by and we talk about anything. I can't say today if he'll come, I can stay a week without seeing him.

In many activities, however, managers may be called upon to play the role of professional mentors, which leads them to focus on the proper performance of delegated tasks and, if necessary, to provide support, as do the more experienced colleagues of the person completing the apprenticeship. An employee of the same firm explains:

> Thank God, I also have more experienced, senior colleagues who can really help me. And my superior is also definitely human. We can really go to him and tell him: 'I have this or that problem'.

Ensuring the proper execution of the responsibilities with which workers have been entrusted is naturally included in German leaders' duties. It is up to them to deal, if necessary, with the discrepancies that have occurred between the observed reality and what has been collectively planned, as quickly as possible. This aspect of leadership implies a key training role which consists in monitoring and developing the skills of subordinates in their professional expertise area. This role of *Meister* (Master) is considered as one of the factors of German industrial excellence (Maurice, 1982). This educational perspective explains the emphasis in the German recommendations on the superior's supportive attitude towards the professional shortcomings detected in individual subordinates:

> Good leaders ask: 'Why did an employee make a decision of this nature?' Even if the employee is not able to give a reason, the questioning is important.[11]
>
> (Groll, 2014)

It is also up to German leaders to recognize and reward the good-quality work of subordinates. However, keeping a sense of proportion in the distribution of rewards, as in the distribution of sanctions, is recommended so as not to damage the harmony within the team by overly distinguishing the best. It is unusual for German leaders to specifically thank their subordinates, as do their American counterparts. An employee of the Berlin metro expresses his surprise at having received a very unusual letter of thanks from his supervisor (perhaps subsequent to the management training followed by the latter):

> Recently, before Christmas, we received a letter from our manager thanking us for our good work, for the work done together. This is completely new. Hearing pleasant things is pleasant. If it's said honestly, then it's good. Maybe it's to stimulate us. So that's good.

This does not deprive managers of the ability to sanction the shortcomings of team members, even if, as one head of department of the Berlin metro points out, they must keep in mind that the overall cohesion of the group remains the priority:

> Two or three times a quarter you have to write (to sanction), it is part of the chief's work but otherwise we try to work together because no job can be done alone!

Monitoring and rewarding work are not such easy tasks for French managers. As the definition of the missions entrusted to their subordinates is generally less formalized than in Germany or the USA, their follow-up is more difficult. Besides, they need to monitor the improvement of subordinates' work without giving them the feeling that the control stems from a lack of trust. French employees claim to act not 'to please their boss' but rather to have the personal satisfaction of having 'done their job' while respecting the requirements of their *métier*. At the same time, their huge need for recognition and consideration is highlighted by all the surveys conducted among French employees (Fourquet et al., 2018). Monitoring and encouraging French employees require a lot of finesse and subtlety.

The relationship between superior and subordinate is seen as easier to balance symbolically each time it is mediated by the shared values of the '*métier*', in which the two protagonists of the hierarchical relationship recognize each other equally. The superiors are seen as being fully committed to their role by claiming and defending these values.

The position of the same superiors is less comfortable outside the scope of their recognized expertise. French management consultants consider it useful to remind them that monitoring and controlling all activities are a key part of the role of a project manager, even if they consider it less attractive:

> The temptation of the young or new project manager: not to spend enough time monitoring the project, which is sometimes boring, and continue to do operational work that he or she enjoyed.[12] (Cornic)

Managers have to find the right distance between being too far from the grass roots, which may be perceived as a lack of support, and too close a presence, which will be experienced as a sign of mistrust. Their presence on the shop floor will be better accepted if they can demonstrate a sincere concern to better understand the employees, recognize the merits of the work performed, and eliminate the threat of surveillance.

Rather than being formally thanked by a fine speech, French employees appreciate more than anything else to be invested with the trust of their immediate superior, especially if he or she has solid (professional) credibility in their profession—the one in which they work. Regardless of the gaps between their respective statuses within the organization, a mutual intimate understanding can emerge, ensuring mutual trust. The best recognition therefore takes the form of a confident empowerment that requires neither the formalization nor the formal control expected of American employees.

4.1.3 Building One's Personal Credibility

Not surprisingly, Americans, Germans, and French, whose understanding of good leadership is different, also have different views on the importance to be given to the building of their managers' personal credibility and on the ways to achieve it.

American employees with a recognized 'leadership' potential will soon be promoted to managerial positions. Obviously, their technical expertise is important too, but it is not necessarily the most instrumental factor in career development. Instead, leadership occupies a prominent place in managers' appraisals; some companies even go so far as according it an importance equivalent to that given to achieving one's performance objectives. Hence the particular emphasis placed on this point in the recommendations that management consultants give to their target audience:

> Leadership skills can play a large role in career development. Often, your technical skills can only take you so far. To help you move forward in your career, you need soft skills, such as the ability to be a good leader.[13]
>
> (Yan, 2017)

How can managers achieve recognition as leaders worthy of being followed? American consultants recommend that they invest in their teams: 'People trust leaders when they know those leaders truly care about their best interests'.[14] Like captains of a sports team, leaders must know how to involve their team members through a direct connection with them:

> The first step is to develop relationships. People trust people that they know. So, take the time to know them. Get to know your people and let them get to know you. For example, find out what their hopes and dreams, goals, and career objectives are. And make sure they know the same about you. Relationships go both ways.[15] (Laraway, Radical Candor)

To obtain direct communication with their team members, managers must free themselves as much as possible from statutory distances and build a direct person-to-person relationship with those who work for them. Leaders—as Americans see them—have to engage their entire self in the construction of a strong bond with their teams in order to build their personal credibility.

Secondary importance is given to the excellence of new managers' previous accomplishments, be they educational or professional. Leadership is first and foremost a matter of personality. Personal charisma can count more than experience. A supermarket owner, for example, if he or she is recognized as a dynamic leader, can take up a management position in a totally different sector without being required to master the corresponding technical knowledge. This would be unthinkable in both Germany and France (Segal, 1987).

Americans see leadership, personality, and charisma as crucial resources for managers to energize their employees. The American vision of leadership—assimilating the leader to a hero (Deal & Kennedy, 1982: 43)—is likely to give rise in other cultural contexts to damaging misunderstandings.

> Heroes (great leaders) are driven by an ethic of creation. They inspire employees by distributing a sense of responsibility throughout the organisation. Everybody performs with tangible goals in sight. There is more tolerance for risk taking, thus greater innovation; more acceptance of the value of long-term success, thus greater persistence; more personal responsibility for how the company performs—thus a workforce that identifies personal achievement with the success of its firm. (Deal & Kennedy, 1982)

Indeed, German consultants present leadership in a different light. Unlike in the United States, building personal credibility does not seem to be a major issue that requires advice or warnings to new German leaders. One can even encounter some mistrust towards a charismatic form of authority.

> Management, in my opinion, is not a matter of charismatic leadership but of results. And for that, the management does not need to be charismatic at all.[16]
> (Battle's Blog, 2010)

Access to top-management functions in German companies is generally preceded by a solid internal career path (Barmeyer et al., 2008). This allows those who perform these functions to acquire professional expertise and excellent experience in their field. Experience and professional skills, duly validated by the organization, are the bases on which the legitimacy of managers' authority is built. The detailed knowledge of the organization they lead and the shared experience of the jobs carried out by their subordinates are seen as their best assets.

German consultants encourage 'chiefs'—an alternative way of referring to leaders—to consider themselves as part of the team for which they are responsible and not 'above' it. Chiefs should see themselves as part of their teams and work closely with their 'colleagues'.[17]

German managers have a particular responsibility but this does not prevent them from being considered as '*Mitarbeiter*', working 'with' (*mit*) the others and like all the others. First and foremost, they and their subordinates work—each of them playing their own roles—for the organization. So much the better, of course, if a rich and confident relationship is established between the managers and their teams. But the organization relies more on the quality of the training that each of the members has received or on the quality of the distribution of tasks within the work groups than on the charisma of their managers.

Conversely, French consultants' recommendations to managers give an important place to their acquiring a solid personal legitimacy, prior to taking up their duties. They insist much more than their American and German counterparts on the various qualities that managers must have already demonstrated in order to have their authority recognized as legitimate. According to a Human Resource consultant's blog:

> A legitimate manager is a person whose position is defined by a status and whose profile and behaviour are in line with the position held. A person perceived to be where he or she should be.[18] (Groll, 2014)

Knowing that their employees are liable to challenge their managers' authority, French companies ensure that they promote or recruit managers with the diplomas and experience in line with the personal status that they are to be granted. Even if they enjoy a high personal status, newcomers will nevertheless have to assert themselves. Their challenge will consist in proving themselves 'up to' (*à la hauteur*) the task assigned and the rank granted. A solid professional legitimacy is the key to French leadership.

A second requirement for French people in a hierarchical position to be recognized as legitimate at the head of their departments is their obligation to demonstrate their capacity to find the right solutions to the problems that their subordinates may encounter. Not all line managers will be able to meet this high level of requirement. Whenever they do not meet these requirements, they open the door to challenges from their subordinates, thus contradicting the images of all-powerful French leaders capable of effortlessly imposing their authority that prevail in cross-cultural management literature (Segal, 2014). Their subordinates, without necessarily confronting them head-on, rarely fail to use irony and make fun of them.

In sum, the construction of the manager's personal credibility—an element generally presented as essential in the United States to strengthen one's leadership—takes very different paths in Germany and France.

4.2 A Cultural Interpretation

The theoretical framework defined in Chapter 3 opens the way to a cultural interpretation of these differences. Various leadership profiles expected in each of our three countries can be interpreted as being inspired by the need to offer specific protections to local stakeholders against the situations that they fear most.

Their culture, as we define it, influences both the nature of the fears experienced by subordinates in a situation of hierarchical dependence and the specific ways in which they can be averted. The three research fields—the USA, Germany, and France—are democratic countries in which it is not simple to combine the role of citizen—free of one's opinions and choices—and that of subordinate. Chapter 1 pointed this out about the United States, and, as we will demonstrate, it equally applies to Germany and France. In each country, different forms of conciliation emerged over time which had a direct impact on the conceptions of acceptable leadership.

4.2.1 The United States of America

As seen in Chapter 3, pp. 62–64, their political culture leads the American people to conceive the hierarchical relationship as ideally regulated through a freely consented 'contractualization' between citizens with equal rights. This is what Tocqueville (Tocqueville, 2002: 645) described in the excerpt below, which we quote again because it is so enlightening for our purpose:

> At any moment a servant may become a master, and he aspires to rise to that condition; the servant is therefore not a different man from the master. Why, then, has the former a right to command, and what compels the latter to obey except the free and temporary consent of both their wills? Neither of them is by nature inferior to the other; they only become so for a time, by covenant. Within the terms of this covenant the one is a servant, the other a master; beyond it they are two citizens of the commonwealth, two men. (Tocqueville, 2002)

Tocqueville helped us to understand the content of the American fundamental fear underpinning work relations and, in particular, the relationship between leaders and their followers. A tyrannical leader, abusing the economic dependence in which employees are forced to be hired to earn a living, deprives them from remaining in control of their destiny, thus turning them more or less into slaves. The very terms *slavery* or *tyranny* have been and continue to be widely used by US trade union activists to refer to wage labour whenever it does not respect their rights as citizens.

How can Americans' fundamental fear of losing their fundamental rights to determine their own destinies be overcome? Turning the hierarchical relationship into a contract—epitomized in the form of MBO in the middle of the twentieth century, as seen in Chapter 1, p. 14,—is inherited from the contractual approach that was conceived to address this concern much earlier in American labour history. Its sustainability to this day, including among the new generations hired in the most high-tech companies, testifies to its perfect fit with Americans' representations of a fair exercise of authority in companies. However, this system is far from solving all the problems raised both by the motivation of employees and the effective coordination of their endeavours. It has encountered criticism, in particular with regard to the eventual disinterest in any duty outside their own perimeter that a strict delimitation of each employee's responsibilities may cause. How can one go beyond this quasi-judicial vision of labour relations and yet encourage employees to give their best? Managers' leadership skills are what Americans rely on to obtain greater loyalty and organizational efficiency—a fact that explains the predominance of the theme in management books written by American authors.

For Americans, work relations are first and foremost direct relationships between two people. These people are responsible for making direct arrangements so that they can get along well, on an explicit and fair basis. The managers' leadership skills will play a major role in the quality of this work relationship. Acting in such a way that each of their subordinates considers himself or herself fairly treated, in particular through the respect of the contract concluded with them, is an imperative obligation for leaders. But subordinates will invest all the more in their work when they find, in the way their superiors behave with them, positive reasons to do so. Superiors' leadership skills will therefore play a very important role in strengthening their subordinates' desire for cooperation.

Leaders' ability to endorse the role of community leaders is also important if they want to succeed in developing their subordinates' self-esteem and cooperative spirit. As leaders of a community, be it a work team, one department in a company, or an entire company, leaders must also epitomize the values that distinguish and unite their community. 'American-style' individualism does not equate with independence from the rules of the group to which one belongs, be it family, local community, or the whole organization. It is up to the leaders of each of these communities to give them an engaging content likely to motivate people. Faced with the centrifugal forces generated by everyone's recognized freedom to choose their destiny, leaders embody the centripetal forces that ensure the unity, strength, and sustainability of the group. In companies, they can contribute in many ways.

At the top of the organization, executives can enjoy the privilege of defining the values that each member must respect (see p. 172). At the smaller scale of a work team, it is up to the 'team leader' to create this famous 'team spirit' that will engage team members to share a common pride and help each other. This responsibility gives rise to a charismatic and pastoral dimension that permeates American managerial literature very strongly. Leaders should know how to celebrate the successes achieved, without trying to take credit for them. It is up to them to know how to symbolically thank those who have contributed. Nevertheless, as their name suggests, 'leaders' are in charge of leading their group, they are not only supposed to join in. This is why they have to give everyone the sense of pride of belonging, to convey the compelling vision that will encourage everyone to get involved in their community life.

4.2.2 Germany

In the Germanic world, the concept of liberty, dear to modern citizens—who were emancipated thanks to the Enlightenment—is associated with a particular vision of social order offering an equal membership to everyone. In this vision, everyone contributes to the elaboration of community rules and serenely enjoys the guarantees that this freely accepted vision offers. The common expression '*Alles in Ordnung*' (everything is in order) expresses this idea of the right and the good. The image embodying the opposite of this serene vision of the social world is that of isolated individuals left to their own devices in a chaotic universe giving free rein to individual impulses and the law of the strongest.

Outside the construction of this social order, the individual security and collective efficiency that can be produced by the democratic deliberations—celebrated by philosopher Habermas as the country was emerging from the dreadful Nazi era—cannot be developed or even conceived. This philosophical vision, which today nourishes the institutions of the Federal Republic, sheds light on the representations of good leadership to which German stakeholders refer. It becomes clear, when listening to them carefully, that the core responsibilities of leaders are to remove this threat of disorder, the uncertainty about the future of the organization, and the inefficiency that are bound to arise as long as the community can no longer organize itself according to proven deliberative principles. Good leaders in this world view are the ones who design an organization in line with the resources offered by the local political culture that unifies the contributions of each person towards a whole with which each person can identify.

At the time when we were conducting research on its internal management practices, Berlin's metro network was experiencing precisely the internal uncertainties and disorders that, in this cultural frame of references, corresponded to the feared situation. It is reflected in one of the unit manager's comments:

> People think it would be nice if they could discern a well-identified situation for all officers. Then they could devote all their energy, their social strength, to a

> single goal, the improvement of each part of the company, and not, as today, dissipate this energy in all directions and to all winds.

Two centuries earlier, the German philosopher Immanuel Kant (1991: 46) had illustrated the same idea through the image of the far-from-perfect tree linked to its isolation when those which grew close to each other are erect and perfect, due to their having respectively disciplined themselves:

> In the same way, trees in a forest, by seeking to deprive each other of air and sunlight, compel each other to find these by upward growth, so that they grow beautiful and straight—whereas those which put out branches at will, in freedom and in isolation from others, grow stunted, bent and twisted.
>
> (Kant, 1991)

The forms of leadership favoured by the Germans appear fully consistent with the representations of a well-ordered organization capable not only of removing the spectre of disorder but also of giving a positive and encouraging meaning to being a member of the organization. Before being superiors and subordinates, the protagonists of the hierarchical relationship are first and foremost colleagues, members of the same working community that put them in the specific relationship in which they are to cooperate—a role that the organization has prepared them for. Before being promoted, German *Vorgesetzter* have generally gone through a long internal process. Not only does it allow them to be fully aware of the content of the tasks that their subordinates have to accomplish, but also to be able to identify with them.

Not having followed this path, being unable to share a common past with their team members, ignoring the history of the working community, may seriously reduce the legitimacy of leaders. In the Berlin metro, the hiring of a director from outside the company to comply with external directives, in this case European directives on high quality transportation services, was largely criticized. A firm executive explained:

> These changes, based on European directives, have introduced considerable insecurity into the company. This makes cooperation more difficult. It's the same with employee representatives, trust has decreased. We have seen people coming in from outside who blamed everything on the former directors, people who know nothing about the company's history, who made false promises or simply perhaps fed real misunderstandings.

Obedience to superiors does not consist in submitting to them personally, but rather in rationally accepting the requirements of coordination and role articulation within the organization that brings them all together. This means that on the one hand, leaders do not need to be endowed with particular charisma to be obeyed; on the other hand, they are expected to demonstrate through their attitudes and behaviours a form of symbolic equality with their subordinates in their organization.

Similarly, in France, the cultural background has an impact on the behaviours expected of their leaders.

4.2.3 France

The content of the French fears—that is, being forced by necessity, cowardice, or self-interest to submit to an authority holder considered illegitimate—that professional situations may arouse was examined in detail in Chapter 3, pp. 64–66. A French labour sociologist whose clear-cut opinions clearly reflect the shifts in meaning between obedience and submission, remarks:

> The relationship of subordination, cornerstone of the employment contract for employees, should be questioned: characterised by the duty of obedience to one's superior, it keeps the employee in a state of archaic dependency in a society where the level of education is high and where the aspirations to perform meaningful work are real.[19] (Linhart, 2016)

The often very high tensions which, in many sectors of activity, are affecting the French professional world are obviously not unrelated to this very particular interpretation of a subordination which, in the United States as in Germany, does not fuel such concerns.

Fortunately for French employees—but also for the efficiency of their companies—the cultural benchmarks to which French employees refer open several avenues, enabling many of them and in quite varied circumstances, to avoid what they consider humiliating dependence on their hierarchy. In this respect, France is an emblematic example of a political culture's double face—that is, capable of nurturing fears but also of opening up original ways to overcome them.

Far from being belittling, serving an admirable leader will elevate. Indeed, many French employees will be emotional in referring to a line manager that they have been proud to serve or to eminent colleagues with whom they have had the pleasure of working. Accepting the arguments of leaders, who have been able to convince that the orientations they have chosen are valid, does not mean submitting to their person but bowing before overarching reason that imposes itself on all, superior as well as subordinate. Remarkably fulfilling one's professional duties will be experienced as a very honourable tribute paid to one's profession and not as a demeaning submission to a superior who does not deserve to be obeyed.

Dedication to a cause or demonstrating relentless commitment to the success of a great project can have the same effect for all those involved.

This means that, in France, a wide range of options are available to foster a positive and honourable interpretation of the work relationship, even when—as in most cases—it involves hierarchical subordination. Good leadership will not be the same everywhere; it will depend on the nature of the activity and on the personal status of both the superiors and their subordinates (d'Iribarne, 1989: 114–122). Very credible professional managers can be both fraternal and very demanding with their team members. Conversely, leaders perceived as too subservient to the higher hierarchical levels of the organization are likely to be mocked by their subordinates—who inevitably give them depreciative nicknames. Foreign observers often focus their criticism of French managers on these aspects which are in stark contrast with most of their own references, and in particular on the very visible signs in France of distance between the different statuses. The variety of professional situations to be taken into account as well as the subtleties affecting the way in which French people will adjust to one another at work make it difficult to encapsulate relations in simple patterns. External observers find it all the more difficult to understand the diversity of these subtle adjustments as their own system is based on rules and principles that are more suitable for general formalization.

4.3 Conclusion

The concepts of leadership and expectations towards leaders are two sides of the same coin. Regardless of the country, employees evidently appreciate a competent, fair, likeable, and caring leader. However, from one country to another, the interpretation of the work relations between a superior and a subordinate, and the way in which the latter's dependence on the former is acceptable, vary widely. Regardless of the country examined, this is a key dimension to understanding what is at stake between these protagonists.

The purpose of this chapter was to encourage readers to consider how the new dynamics at work may combine differently, in each and every country, with older and still vivid cultural features. These conceptions, rooted in the local culture and history, are not necessarily immutable, but it is difficult to believe that current changes in the work organization, however powerful they may be, are sufficient to eradicate the profound national differences previously observed in conceptions of a fair exercise of power. Taking an interest in the organizational dynamics at play in today's business world should not lead to neglecting the way of exercising authority in organizations embedded in national cultures and in their specific local roots.

There is every reason to believe that the progress of education, the subsequent increase in the workforce's skill level, and the potential offered by information technologies will contribute to modify the functioning of organizations and the forms taken by collaboration between the different hierarchical levels. However, saying that the new generations, be they American, German, or French, no longer work as their parents or grandparents used to—which seems highly likely—does not mean that everywhere these new generations are now working in the same way.

The implementation of these innovations is still making its way through the filter—some would say spectacles—which culture, as defined in the previous chapter, constitutes. This also applies to the transformation of the way in which a particular type of hierarchical authority is exercised in particular. The forms which exercising hierarchical authority take are certainly integrating the organizational transformations underway. Again, this does not mean that they are to converge all over the world into an ideal form inspired by the fast-moving West Coast area of the United States.

Comparing in the United States, Germany, and France, what is deemed acceptable in the exercise of hierarchical authority, and the consequently expected forms of leadership, has shown that the conditions required for an acceptable balance between manager and employee may considerably differ.

The focus of most leadership literature on the personal qualities of the leaders, and more particularly on their charisma, is perfectly in line with the American conception of leaders having to deeply engage themselves to 'assert themselves' and 'lead' their teams. Still today, this very concept inspires the leadership training programmes that multinational companies extend to their most distant subsidiaries.

The question that arises is whether it is possible to effectively train managers for the exercise of their hierarchical authority by simply giving them examples of practices from a different cultural universe from the one in which they operate.

Providing tools enabling to understand the role—as their future subordinates conceive it—that these future managers will have to take on seems essential to help them find by themselves the most appropriate means to be accepted by their subordinates and to obtain effective work from them. All too often, contemporary practices within companies are moving away from this perspective.

Notes

1. Boudet, A., 'Pourquoi Macron ne veut pas du candidat de Merkel pour la Commission européenne', *The Huffington Post*, 20 June 2019.
2. Caramela, S. 'New Manager Checklist: 6 tips for being a good leader', *Business News Daily* (26 August 2017).

3. Llyod, S. 'Managers Must Delegate Effectively to Develop Employees', https://www.shrm.org/resourcesandtools/hr-topics/organizational-and-employee-development/pages/delegateeffectively.aspx (accessed 26 September 2019).
4. '5 einfacheTippsfür die gutePersonalführung', https://www.fuer-gruender.de/wissen/unternehmen-fuehren/personal/personalfuehrung/ (accessed 26 September 2019).
5. Groll, T. 'Wie werden Sie ein guter Chef, Personalfuhrung', *Zeit Online*, published 11 November 2014: https://www.zeit.de/karriere/beruf/2014-10/mitarbeiter-fuehren-tipps-gutes-verhalten-chef (accessed 22 June 2019).
6. See endnote 5.
7. Cornic, C. http://www.blog-gestion-de-projet.com/etes-vous-un-bon-chef-de-projet/, accessed 22 June 2019.
8. Cornic, C. http://www.blog-gestion-de-projet.com/etes-vous-un-bon-chef-de-projet/; Dominique Perez and Nathalie Samson, 'S'affirmer en tant que manager', *L'Express-emploi*, 28 October 2008, (accessed 22 June 2019).
9. See endnote 2.
10. Ibid.
11. See endnote 5.
12. See endnote 7.
13. Yan, A. 'How to Improve Your Leadership Skills', *Investopedia.com*, (accessed 22 June 2019).
14. https://www.radicalcandor.com/blog/lessons-new-managers, (accessed March 2019).
15. See endnote 14.
16. https://organisationsentwicklung.me/2010/06/12/charismatische-fuhrung-ist-gut-fur-mittelmasigkeit/, (accessed 22 June 2019).
17. See endnote 5.
18. Ibid.
19. Linhart, D., Télérama, 3483, 12 October 2016, p. 24.

5

Procedures and Control

Alongside the definition of objectives, an important way to guide the action of workers consists in defining operating methods. They may be in the form of checklists, such as those that guide the crew's actions before the aircraft takes off. They will be provided in any complex operation—for example, periodic reviews of industrial installations—implying a sequence of elementary tasks, such as control operations—for example, to ensure that the product being shipped is in conformity with the customer's order—or quality procedures. Audit systems are set up to ensure that actual practices comply with the operating procedures. Considering that this management aspect deals with the materiality of things, one is greatly tempted to presume that procedures are entirely rational artefacts that escape the influence of cultures. Obviously, in cases of non-compliance with procedures, the 'human factor' will be mentioned. But whether cognitive biases or various forms of misuse are summoned, the perspective adopted remains largely universalist: general deviations are considered likely to affect any human action, in any part of the world.

However, ignoring the role of cultures is no more justified here than in any other area of management. Within an organization, those who design the operating procedures; those who implement them; and those who monitor their compliance are usually different people. As a result, relationships are established between these various actors. However, the way in which these relationships get organized, and in particular, in which the activities of those who define the operating modes and those who are responsible for their implementation combine, makes sense in specific cultural universes of meaning. And in any universe, the vision of a satisfactory way of cooperating is the reference.

The role of this cultural context is particularly clear when comparing two environments in which the use of strictly defined operating modes provokes diametrically opposed reactions: Cameroon and France. We will see that the agents experience the role assigned to each of the protagonists very differently, depending on whether one is in this or that country. The concerns that apply to this role are different.

The first section of the chapter will be devoted to a Cameroonian case, the Société Nationale d'Électricité (SONEL). We will see that the use of carefully detailed operating procedures, meant to be followed 'to the letter', is a source of enthusiasm. Just the opposite reaction to what an objective- and performance-based approach to delegation and control—the source of great concerns in this

Cross-Cultural Management Revisited: A Qualitative Approach. Philippe d'Iribarne, Sylvie Chevrier, Alain Henry, Jean-Pierre Segal, and Geneviève Tréguer-Felten, Oxford University Press (2020).
DOI: 10.1093/oso/9780198857471.001.0001

country—is likely to encounter. The fact that subordinates' concerns lie in the intentions of the superior—will the latter act as a friend or an enemy?—accounts for these contrasted reactions. Indeed, while delegation through the definition of objectives leaves the door open to this more or less anxiety-provoking question, the setting of rigorously defined and controlled procedures tends to reassure employees.

In the second part, we will see that, conversely, in France, reactions are just as sceptical towards binding operating methods as they are towards objectives set by a superior. It is because the stakes are very different from the Cameroonian ones. What is at stake is the type of autonomy claimed by those who master their '*métier*' (profession), are proud of it, and find it difficult to accept that anyone should—whatever the form that this constraint may take—tell them what to do.

5.1 From Setting Objectives to Defining Operating Procedures in Cameroon

The Société d'Électricité, whose evolution we observed over several decades (see Chapter 13, p. 257), offered a particularly noteworthy case of a positive reception of extremely detailed and restrictive operating procedures. This reception contrasted with the difficulties in implementing the classic approach to delegation and control provided by the MBO, which involved setting objectives and assessing the degree to which they had been achieved.

5.1.1 The Enthusiastic Reception of Meticulously Detailed Procedures Manuals

The development and circulation of an impressive procedures' manual, composed of a dozen binders of a few hundred pages each, was a major step in the evolution of the company's management. This manual covered all the company's activities: technical, commercial, administrative, and organizational. Each form indicated, for each task, a very complete set of elements: 'who' intervenes (which employee, which manager, etc.); 'what' he or she must do (record such information, disassemble such parts, etc.); 'how' to proceed; and 'who to transfer it to' for the realization of the next step.

An internal auditor was mandated to monitor compliance with these procedures, his role being to reveal any deviation. He, himself, was also required to apply very strictly his own procedure.

Procedures manuals are clearly not a Cameroonian singularity. They stem from some universal principles. They serve to formalize and unite individuals or collective working methods. They are used to clarify the distribution of tasks and responsibilities, foster the coordination of employees within the organization, specify and disseminate working methods, and ensure consistency of processes over time, independently of the people who carry them out. They can serve as a support for the training and dissemination of shared standards. They are a reference for control, both for self-checking (in the form of checklists) and as a support for compliance or quality audits. The written formalization of procedures, considered as a prerequisite for process reliability, is part of international quality management requirements (Henry & Monkam-Daverat, 2001).

But the manuals implemented at SONEL did not only meet these expectations: they were exceptional due to their extremely detailed and binding nature, as the example of the Complaint Recording Procedure shows (see Box 5.1).

Box 5.1 SONEL manual excerpt: complaint recording procedure

Customer relations personnel

Greet the customer in a friendly and courteous manner

Put him at ease

Record the customer's complaint in the Visitors' Log and note carefully: - First and Last Name—Address—Nature of the complaint—Name and job position of the employee responsible for dealing with the complaint—Follow-up action

Head of customer relations

Examine the complaint to determine its cause

If the problem can be solved immediately, take the necessary initiatives and complete the Visitors' Log

If no immediate solution can be found, offer the customer an appointment, taking into consideration the availability of the Group managers responsible for managing problems

Fill out the form 'Customer Visit Slip', clearly indicating: - Customer's first and last name—Address—Reason for the visit—Date set for the appointment—Group(s) assigned to solve the problem—Actual steps taken—Remarks Name and job position of the signatory employee—Signature

Transmit the complaint file to the Agency Manager, including: - Customer visit sheets—Reference documents (customer contract, installation documents, receipt slips, etc.)

Agency Manager

Check that the file transmitted by the head of customer relations is complete and sign the logbook

The particularly precise and precautionary nature of these instructions is noticeable. The user was regularly asked to *remember* or to *check*, referring to the kinds of checklists contained in the procedures. The text did not hesitate to occasionally indicate the proper behaviours expected—*greet the customer in a friendly and courteous manner*. Routine controls were systematically specified—*the manager checks that the file is complete.*

Readers may think that this precision is appropriate for low-skilled personnel in an emerging country company. However, in this particular case, this was by no means the case. The company employed well-trained staff from the sector's vocational schools and national and international universities. There must be other reasons leading to such unambiguous clarification of what is expected of each individual.

These procedures bore close resemblance to the rules in use in local associations, known as the 'tontines'. These associations—which are very popular in some parts of the country—are part of a century-old tradition and, in the present-day Cameroon, several of them have written regulations such as the tontine rulebook,[1] the excerpt of which follows (Henry et al., 1991):

> *Article [x]:* The *Cotisation* [*i.e.* the 'contribution', namely the meeting] takes place on the 25th of each month precisely at nineteen o'clock (or seven o'clock in the evening), at the coordinator's house; after 7:16 p.m. (nineteen o'clock sixteen minutes), the president's watch being the proof, the delay is consumed and recorded in a special notebook by the censor; the person who is late is to pay a fine of FCFA 5,000,[2] payable before the sale of the lots[3] (...). Any member who sends his money on time and arrives afterwards is not considered to be late or absent.
>
> *Article [y]*: When a member is hospitalised, all other members present in the locality must visit him and communicate to all other members well-founded information received on the indisposed member's health state. In the event of the death of a member or his spouse, this sad news must be brought to the knowledge of others without delay... Each member is required to attend vigils every day, to attend the laying-in and the burial in black uniform with a black tie. The member absent from the funeral may only be excused if it is accepted that he has been hindered by a case of force majeure.

The same sense of precision as before can be found in these tontine regulations: the arrival time at the meeting and the reference time for reporting lateness are specified, both indicated in figures and letters; the tasks are assigned individually—*the president, the censor*, etc. The instructions carefully describe the behaviours to be followed— for example, in the event of mourning: recalling evidences regarding information, dress code, etc.—the information must be *well-founded* and transmitted *without delay*; and finally, the procedures for conducting controls are scrupulously detailed—the recording of delays *in a special notebook*, the *president's watch being the 'proof'*, etc.

5.1.2 Consistency with Social Expectations

Far from being interpreted by the employees as an intrusive micro-management form, the company's procedures precision was welcomed. All or almost all employees considered that the content of the documents should be detailed and precise, so that everyone would know at any time what they should do. 'If my agents have got written rules that describe their jobs', explained the Human Resources director, 'this gives them greater autonomy. It will make the organisation more fluid'.

This feature, which may seem incomprehensible from a foreign viewpoint (and, as we will see, particularly from the French one), makes sense in the Cameroonian cultural context, what with the fears and aspirations that underlie social relations. Several features that are relatively minor in other contexts are here at the centre of the picture.

A first trait of this context is the constant attention given to the individual intentions and feelings that the behaviours and words can reveal. Everyone tends to subtly decipher what the persons with whom they are involved 'have behind their head'. A refusal to help, some criticism, or a punishment raises fears and suspicions about 'what motivates the person'—is it revenge, nastiness, jealousy, gratuitous willingness to harm, etc.? To escape such accusations, one must be 'kind', show 'goodwill', etc., behaviours that contrast with being 'nasty'—with its many degrees: 'a little nasty', 'very nasty', 'bad faith', etc.

A second trait concerns the ubiquitous role of 'interests'. Interests are seen as inherent to human nature. 'The goat grazes around the post', says an often-quoted Cameroonian proverb—especially about leaders and politicians—to emphasize the insatiable nature of individuals. An unusual request systematically raises concerns about the existence of an 'appetite' that 'bad faith' is meant to hide. The excessive appetites—only limited by the constraint symbolized by the post to which the goat is tethered—are the object of constant fear.

A third feature concerns the decisive role of personal ties, which are necessary to avoid negative interpretations about others' behaviours. The fact of 'knowing each other well' or of 'getting along well' has an impact on the ability to work together: 'The people who get along well outside', explains a team leader, 'work better together. When they have a problem, they chat as friends; someone you don't know, you'll approach with a lot of suspicion'. Social discourse is constantly pointing out the one who is a 'parent', 'friend', 'acquaintance' or 'brother' (a term that does not necessarily have a biological meaning). The *friend/enemy* opposition systematically underlies interpretations and is the key to acting together. Those whom we 'know well' must be 'open', in 'good faith' and should not refuse their help. They can be addressed multiple requests—to obtain useful information, material assistance, recommendation, a favour, etc. To overcome a deadlock or address an emergency in the organization, everyone systematically seeks the support of a 'friend' or 'acquaintance', for whom it will be difficult to refuse. An action is read mainly through the feelings—friendly or unfriendly—that one person has for another.

Most of the promotions or management decisions are interpreted on the basis of the direct interest of the persons concerned and of the support, visible or not, from which they have benefited. In such an interpretative context, whenever the slightest incident occurs, one wonders 'who is behind it all' and considers the person's intentions. One fears the combination of bad feelings and of a hidden agenda. 'When you think of all these skirmishes', said a director in reference to a conflict, 'you realise that there's *bad faith behind it all*, guided by personal interests'.

Such a distrustful climate opens the door to accusations of 'witchcraft' and to the numerous practices attached to it. Despite what many may have imagined, its practice has not decreased with the modernization of societies (Luneau, 2004; Geshiere, 2013). It is to be found in modern universes such as the business world (Bureau, 1979; Warnier, 1993; de Rosny, 1996; Bazin, 1998).

The widespread cliché of 'African solidarity' obliterates the constant attention on individuals, their behaviours, interests and feelings (Zadi Kessy, 1998). People have to 'eat together' and fear those who 'want to eat alone'. The mutual aid obligation, which is strong towards relatives, is not limited to the family circle, the 'village', or the 'tribe'. It applies to any friend— that is, any person with whom, as a result of previous circumstances, a personal relationship has been established. The core fear of *greedy relatives, who show a pleasant face but who invisibly seek to harm you* and, conversely, the life-saving image of *sincere friends*, are the two figures around which many situations make sense. The common discourse does not ignore these 'country's realities', even if foreign consultants and experts generally prefer to ignore them, except to incidentally mention that they are due to disappear in the end (see Chapter 14, p. 287).

These general characteristics of Cameroonian society were found within the company. A constant concern that the enforcement of bureaucratic rules would be interpreted in the interpersonal relationship register, was present throughout the interviews that were conducted. For instance, the CEO explained:

> People are afraid to assume responsibilities on the personnel and want to have reassurance by any means. (...) [The boss] is afraid of displeasing a guy

> sometimes four or five levels under them. (...) Because he thinks that the person has a high-ranking acquaintance in the Capital. It might bring trouble down on their own head or on the family, and people will say: "*That's the nasty guy who didn't want to give a good evaluation to so-and-so*, who didn't want to give a promotion, etc." These factors are real in our country. Appearing *to be kind* is very important. It's this spirit of not causing harm to anyone. I think people are afraid of their staff seeing them as *executioners*. (...) Finally, little by little, all this gets transferred to the managing director, who becomes *everyone's pet hate*.

On the one hand, fear of retaliation for decisions taken against someone is stressed. On the other hand, avoiding sanctions will give you a good reputation: 'That way they get to wear a kind of halo, concluded the CEO'.

Under such conditions, attempting to introduce an MBO was doomed. Indeed, the evaluating process tended to activate the fears associated with any action that might have a negative effect on someone. A negative evaluation is easily taken for a personal attack, a 'willingness to hit': the superior must have set objectives too high so as to trap his or her enemy. 'They say that it's the boss who prevents me from working, from working better, then afterwards, the boss might come back and hit out at me.' Conversely, the employee who receives a good assessment, based on his performance, is suspected of having had undeclared help. The door is open to subtle manoeuvres. 'To tempt us', said a director, 'they want us to evaluate the files of people from our respective tribes. You see what I mean ... I really have to examine the texts, and examine them coldly: "Okay, this guy has made a mistake." I give instructions saying: "Ok then, prepare such or such punishment".' The path is narrow: if you let yourself be convinced by the good faith of the person concerned, you are suspected of compromising in favour of a relative; if you punish him, you break with a duty of friendly understanding and you are accused of nastiness by others around you.

Unlike MBO, procedures manuals limit the risk of negative interpretations, especially if they are more precise. Those who consistently comply with them acquire a reputation that allows them, if they occasionally deviate from them, to argue in 'good faith' by pointing to the circumstances that led them to act as they did. In particular, detailed written procedures play an essential role when facing actions that have a negative impact on another person. Any criticism following control may not be interpreted as a breach of solidarity or an expression of hostile intent, because it results from complying with an explicit obligation. Those who refuse an undue request can show that they are being forced to do so. If the procedures that govern their action are violated, they are the ones who are most likely to be penalized. The more precise the procedures, the more compulsory they are, the less room for interpretation, the better they will protect from the worrying interpretations of intentions. In this context, the usefulness of procedures requiring respect 'to the letter', their extreme precision and the nature of the given instructions, etc., make sense.

An essential component of the system is the auditor. Not only must the rules be unambiguous, but their application must closely monitored and those who violate them must not be able to escape sanctions. 'That way everyone knows that if you depart from it, you'll be disciplined, and that two people behaving the same way won't receive different sanctions.' The slightest loophole would leave room for endless interpretations concerning the real intentions of whoever is required to apply the rule or is responsible for punishing those who transgress it.

A very rigid, almost ritual, respect of the rules is the warrant of 'good behaviour'. It tends to create a sense of 'harmony', a climate of friendship and trust. As demonstrated by the tontine example, this climate and the rigour of the rules are far from contrasting each other. On the contrary, they contribute to escaping the maze of suspicious interpretations.

However, although the use of such a system is in accordance with the Cameroonian interpretative context, it will not necessarily actually be used. We will see in Chapter 13 (pp. 261–65) what happened to this company over time.

5.2 French Reluctance to Use Operating Procedures Designed by Others

In France, the reactions to operating procedures that everyone is required to respect in the day-to-day running of the company are in stark contrast to those found in Cameroon. Their implementation raises a great deal of reluctance because the employees see them in a totally different light. The cultural context in which they make sense highly values the autonomy of each 'professional' whose *métier* endows them with the abilities to master the subtleties of their jobs. We will consider two different industries. We will first discuss the implementation of quality management in the automotive industry. We will then turn to a comparative analysis of the way in which compliance with procedures is perceived in French and American high-risk facilities, namely nuclear power plants.

5.2.1 The Implementation of a Quality Management in the Automotive Industry

The implementation of so-called 'total quality' management in the automotive industry led to the development of operating methods that are as perfect as possible—that is, capable of producing vehicles that do not require any refinishing when they reach the end of the production chain. The aim is to 'do it right from the very first time'. The method implies recording and analysing any malfunctioning, and subsequently searching, as early as possible, for causes and means to correct them. Any failures occurring during the final assembly of each vehicle must therefore be carefully recorded and analysed. This applies whatever the origin, be it insufficient quality of the assembly work or difficulties stemming from the design of the vehicles or the functioning of the upstream part of the production process—sheet metal work or painting. The analysis of these malfunctions is likely to lead to improving all the steps of the production process, from the design of the vehicle to its assembly.

We analysed the gap between the theoretical design of the process and its actual functioning within the assembly department of an automotive plant in northern France (Iribarne, 1997). The quality management method we were interested in was based on a so-called self-checking procedure that required operators to report the operations that they had not been able to carry out successfully. The data thus collected were scrutinized so as to identify the most frequent malfunctions and seek to correct them. As is usual in France, the corresponding system had been designed and operated according to an organizational scheme that tended to clearly differentiate the roles of 'technical services' from those of 'manufacturers'; the former defined the 'proper' ways of doing things and tried to enforce them; the latter defended themselves against the pressure that this obligation submitted them to, while affirming their ability to solve the problems that they encountered by themselves.

According to the official documents—drafted by the technical services—pressure must be exerted on the operators—that is, the 'manufacturers' side—in such a way that they comply with the operating procedures that these services prescribe. Admittedly, analysing the difficulties that operators encountered had also been planned so as to detect the imperfections that were affecting the very design of the production system (including the characteristics of the products). But what was mainly referred to were the operators' 'failures', or the imperfections that 'they had made'.

The fact that system malfunctions were primarily attributed to operators' failures seriously affected the relationship between manufacturing and technical services. To defend themselves against the pressure to which they were subjected, operators highlighted the problems that they themselves faced. Similarly, operators who had not carried the task out correctly would complain that they had had to face a defect coming from upstream—a hole obstructed by hardened mastic, a staple that had been placed obliquely; a deformed sheet that made it difficult to screw anything in; a pipe with a diameter too small for the part where it had to be plugged—or equipment that was in a bad-condition—poor functioning of the screwing machine, etc. Of course, operators were often able to 'manage' anyway—hit the putty, staple slantwise, force the screw in, cut a bit off the end of the pipe, etc. But this was not always possible. Moreover, if a problem came from upstream, ensuring that it would not happen again involved actions that went beyond the operators' scope.

These difficulties led operators to realize that the pressure put on them was illegitimate, which allowed them to justify a rather loose application of the procedures. Since the level of touch-ups was supposed to reflect the importance of operators' 'failures', there was a strong temptation to 'cope' and do 'one's job' right from the very first time. In a sort of vicious circle, this in turn justified increased pressure on operators to comply with theoretical operating procedures, which ended up in limiting operators' buy-in to the system even further. Continuous efforts were also needed to enforce procedures that encountered limited acceptance. Whenever new pressures appeared, they were effective for a time, then those subject to them adjusted, and their virtue was lost.

The vigour of the admonishments to those who were caught red-handed as they failed to report defects in the audits carried out at the end of the chain, led to the setting up within each 'Elementary Working Unit' (unit) of unofficial monitoring arrangements on each vehicle that far exceeded what was required. Those in charge of 'touch-ups', rather than only handling the problems that the operators had reported, tended to carry out systematic inspections on each vehicle. They were collectively acting so as to improve the results on which they felt that they were being judged. And other members of the unit would similarly complement their work. 'One of the touch-up guys watches', noted one operator describing the operation of his unit. Another explained: 'The instructor watches and makes some touch-ups. [As] I am the replacement for [so-and-so]; when he is around [i.e. in his own position, then] I do touch-ups, I put things back in place, I give a hand to the colleagues. I walk up the chain, I look at the engine, the inside of the car, to see if they haven't forgotten the hand brake, I look inside the car to make sure they haven't left a defect.' This continuous inspection did lead to the elimination of most of the defects that appeared on each vehicle at the end of the chain, but only due to a high level of touch-ups, which were quite costly. Besides, the monitoring itself was costly. The failure to detect these defects meant that they were left out of the scrutiny intended to improve the process and that no change would be made to improve the operating procedures.

The end result was quite different from the continuous improvement of the process—meant to achieve the 'do it right from the first time'—that was supposed to emerge from the systematic scrutiny of all the malfunction occurrences. Instead, what emerged was in the register of 'resourcefulness' and 'temporary' solutions, of irreducible differences between the theoretical operating modes designed by the technical services, and those enacted by the plant operators, with each party standing on their own positions. Of course, when the resolution of the malfunctions could be achieved internally within each unit— for example, by modifying the instructions given so that greater attention was paid by operators to a potential source of defects—substantial progress could be observed. But whenever the problems required closer cooperation between the plant and the technical services, and in particular whenever going beyond the plant boarders, the issue involved the central services (engineering, methods), progress remained unsatisfactory. Hence the process shortcomings not only remained during the entire life of a vehicle model, but were passed on from one model to the next.

What we observed was not surprising in a French context where everyone tends to accomplish their jobs according to the norms of their *métier* (profession) and criticize those who conceive those jobs in a different manner; where each profession is strongly attached to their own conceptions, their own interpretation of problems, and their ideas as to the way in which they are to be solved. Creating problem-solving approaches, information networks, etc. cannot suffice to overcome such difficulties. It is necessary to start from the existing *métiers*, ensuring coherence between the tasks carried out, the professional potentialities, the internal judgement criteria of the profession, and what is considered more or less noble.

This by no means excludes any possibility of evolution (Segal, 2009), but the path to designing and implementing change is closely linked to this context. One of the possibilities would be to involve those belonging to the specific *métier* in the evolution of the procedure. It requires transforming the relevant professions in a way that gives those who carry them the feeling of being elevated, not brought down. Another avenue consists in allowing the professionals concerned to be more aware of the impact that their work procedures will have on the production process downstream. They will also cooperate all the better, if their company is going through difficult times, and if what they are asked to accept does not appear to be simply motivated by the whim of reformers.

5.2.2 High-risk Industries

The French reluctance to follow detailed operating procedures literally is found even in high-risk industries (nuclear, aeronautics) where, because of the importance of security issues, this almost religious, strict respect is particularly required. Such respect is a major issue in France, where the idea of strict compliance with instructions received rather than smart (*intelligent*) application is not well accepted. This point is in contrast to what takes place in an American environment.

Research comparing the operation of four nuclear power plants, two in France and two in the USA (Bourrier, 1999) was enlightening in this regard.

The two American nuclear power plants involved in this research contrasted each other on the quality of cooperation between management and staff. In one, Diablo Canyon, social relations were particularly distrustful, while in the other, North Ana, good understanding prevailed. In the first case, the determination of operating procedures was the prerogative of the management, while in the second the staff contributed to it. But in either case, the operating modes displayed were strictly followed, as long as no explicit modification had been made. Worksites were 'the scene of a high degree of compliance with prescribed rules' (p. 196). There existed 'a genuine moral contract' between the participants (p. 242). Deviations from what was planned were not tolerated (p. 123). This compliance was part of a vision of labour relations whereby, for your superior, you were a sort of supplier and you had to provide the product ordered. This view was reflected in the comments made by the staff of the power plants concerned: 'normally I do this *for* them' (Foreman, North Ana, p. 112); 'you, the management, tell me what to do' (Foreman, Diablo Canyon, p. 114). Therefore, it was normal to be accountable to your supervisor for the way in which you fulfilled the contract you had signed with him or her. This included the way in which the procedures he or she had set out had been respected. People were 'accountable' to their manager.

On the French side, the relationship to formal operating procedures is quite different. As seen with MBO (see Chapter 2, p. 36), the reference is one's profession and the benchmarks it provides. The operating procedures that are supposed to be followed only seem to deserve respect if they are in harmony with these benchmarks. And to assess this coherence, everyone relies first and foremost on his or her own reasoning.

The gap between the official and the informal procedures was particularly obvious in one plant, Bugey, where few efforts had been made to modernize management. Theoretical operating procedures were openly treated with a certain distance.

> Informally, the operators and their foremen amend, supplement, and modify the procedures according to the situations they encounter. Each foreman has a personal 'small note-book', which is the basis of a 'historical-memory', where the 'real figures' are recorded. But these adjustments do not appear in the computerised historical records kept by the Preparation. Official documentation deviates from the reality on the ground and the way procedures are actually used (p. 174).

Even the aspects of the plant's operation that had been through recent reforms remained marked by this double recording. Thus 'the tasks of the "Control Officer" are largely left to his free interpretation' (p. 163) and those he assumed 'in practice' were clearly different from those he had to fulfil 'in theory' (p. 180). This did not mean that everyone's actions were governed by their own personal judgement. The benchmarks that guided their actions were not the official rules. The traditions that were specific to each of the professions dominated. 'Real numbers' are transmitted orally from the oldest to the youngest, according to learning processes that evoke those of 'companionship' (ibid.).

In Nogent, the management tried to 'break' the old operating mode. Thus, rigorous specifications defined the services of subcontractors, who played a major role in the maintenance of the plant (pp. 161, 168). Officially, consultation procedures were being put in place (p. 188). But in fact, the resistance was high. Employees' professions remained the reference. The legitimacy of the new organization was radically challenged on their behalf: 'The work I am now doing has nothing to do with my skills—*I am a* boilermaker—for me it corresponds to a breach of my employment contract, since I am not doing what I was hired for' (p. 251). The responsibilities assigned to each person took on meaning with such a benchmark and were judged by its yardstick. When the expected responsibilities did not correspond well to what they were asked—*the work I am doing now has nothing to do with my skills*—a feeling of illegitimacy developed—*it corresponds to a breach of my employment contract.* This feeling fed reactions which generated all kinds of discrepancies between the 'theoretical' functioning of the plant and its 'actual' functioning. Thus, the competition between suppliers, which in principle had become the rule, remained the exception: 'In 90% of cases', noted one buyer, 'it is without competition, they [the technicians] are afraid to work with others, and often when a new firm is called in, they do not even want to see them' (p. 188).

This reference to one's 'profession', even in fields where safety considerations are central, and the resulting distance from compliance with binding procedures, is not specific to nuclear power plants. Thus, in a hearing before the French Parliament on aviation safety, a captain, representing the pilots' union, rejected the idea of carrying out checks on alcohol levels and the consumption of illegal substances:[4] 'Checks, why not? But then you would have to control everyone, all the time. (...) You are dealing *with professionals who are highly aware of their duties* and the importance of *their mission*... For my part, I trust my fellow pilots or commercial flight attendants *to impose themselves an ethic* that will allow them to ensure this [compliance with existing regulations]' (emphasis added). The need to comply with the rules because of safety issues is not in dispute. But the idea of regular controls is seen as ignoring the 'high conscientiousness' of 'professionals'. This awareness appears here as the ultimate reference for judgement. Respect for procedures is therefore subordinated to the agents' judgements of their more or less important value.

5.2.3 Professional Skills and the Interpretation of Rules

In a French cultural context, everyone may accept to apply 'stupidly' detailed instructions if they feel that they are literally 'overwhelmed' by the situation—for example, in the event of a high-risk operation. But such an acceptation remains the exception. It is normal to draw on everyone's know-how, experience, and 'intelligence'. The 'manuals' and 'practical guides' are considered with concerns. Procedural formalization is generally seen as part of a counterproductive bureaucratic rigidity. The more hierarchical the instructions are, the more detailed they are, the more controlled they are, the more they are perceived as a denial of intelligence and a form of alienating activity. Closely controlled instructions are perceived as negating one's *métier*—along with what the word implies in terms of skills, freely accepted duties, and recognized autonomy. 'Belonging to a *métier*' presupposes a level of personal self-requirements, an ability to judge by oneself what needs to be done, and a skill that is very close to an 'art'. It is necessary to be able to 'rise above' the rules and if necessary, to 'free oneself from them'. Even the application of 'recipes' is not conceivable without a personal contribution of the person concerned. The rules and procedures are considered as having to be interpreted. Acting intelligently is almost as much a duty as it is a sort of freedom. The latitude in interpretation—difficult to explain, in particular to foreigners—results from a subtle and implicit compromise between several considerations: the traditions of the profession and/or of the service; the magnitude of the specific problem; the perceptibly theoretical nature of the rules as compared to realities; the more or less elevated status of the person in charge of the situation; the existence of a 'smart solution', etc.

Detailed procedures are perceived as more appropriate for beginners, trainees, or junior staff. Thus, a French textbook on human resources (Deguy, 1985) considers the obligation to work 'according to existing written or oral instructions' as a criterion of low qualification, the reverse applying to those highly qualified who work 'without referring to them'.

5.3 Conclusion

The examples from Cameroon and France do not only show how contrasted the reactions to the same management tool—that is, the use of accurately formalized operating procedures—can be in different cultural contexts. These examples further demonstrate that the human considerations associated with the implementation of the same tool may be very different from one context to another. In the Cameroonian context, the fear that personal relationships and favouritism may overcome impartial evaluation takes the forefront. In France, it is the humiliation involved in having to submit to the injunctions of those who work in a 'profession' other than one's own.

In management literature, these issues and the ways in which they can be addressed are generally ignored. The need to mention them is all the less apparent because these works are largely American-inspired. In an American cultural context, the standard approach to the implementation of fully formalized operating procedures has no reason to arouse enthusiasm or to be rejected. However, once you leave the United States, the existence of these human issues comes to light.

Indeed, in an American cultural context, the form of autonomy that makes sense is again of a different nature. It echoes suppliers' autonomy with respect to their customers. They are responsible for defining the product for which they have placed an order, and expected to clarify their expectations. This remains true regardless of the form that these expectations take, be they objectives to be met—as was seen in the first chapter (p. 13)—or, as in this case, respecting operating procedures designed by others. In this respect, the American context is very different from the French.

In addition, in the United States, the evaluation processes rely on a combination of appeal procedures and of a moral obligation to 'fairness'. Trust in a certain objectivity of judgement is all the greater because such a moral obligation is not only a fundamental reference but has enough weight to influence practices. This concerns both the initial assessment and the implementation of appeal procedures (d'Iribarne, 1989: 142). As a result, the well-admitted fact that these processes leave the evaluator with a significant margin of appreciation does not generate the same fears as in a Cameroonian context. And, in contrast to Cameroon, reassurance through the use of carefully defined operating procedures is not needed.

As for France, the framework of meaning that was highlighted is identical to the one that emerged when MBO implementation and leadership were considered (see Chapters 2, p. 36 and 4, p. 89): a framework centred on the particular form of autonomy that comes along with the mastering of one's profession. Those who have to cooperate with other employees, supervisors, or partners belonging to other professions, will defend this form of autonomy, be it openly or through covert forms of resistance. Whenever France is mentioned, this framework of meaning is to be found, particularly where customer relations (see Chapter 8, p. 151) or ethics (see Chapter 9, pp. 171–76) are concerned. And, throughout this book, each time we consider a new area of management in a given country, the same universe of meaning will emerge, testifying to its overwhelming influence.

Notes

1. This tontine gathered members of the urban 'elite' (business and bank executives).
2. EUR 7.60.
3. 'Before the sale of the lots', *i.e.* immediately after the monthly contributions have been paid and before the amount thus collected (the 'lot') is allocated.
4. Assemblée Nationale (2004), Rapport sur la sécurité du transport aérien de voyageurs, Tome II, Auditions, présidente Odile SAUGUES, n°1717, Parlement français, Paris.

6
Decision-making

Making decisions is a central aspect of business life. Many decisions involve a more or less vast set of individuals, services, and hierarchical levels, whether they participate in the decision-making process or are affected by its consequences. It is then a question of integrating the various points of view and anticipating what will result for those involved. This process ultimately leads to the selection and implementation of an option, even if it implies going against a set of opinions and interests. As such it involves many risks such as: being deprived of pertinent opinions; angering those who are frustrated and inducing them, once the decision has been made, to hinder its implementation or to demobilize; as well as having to bear the consequences of a bad decision. At these various stages, from the moment the decision is made to the moment its consequences are discovered, there are risks of confrontation. Of course, those who decide are not always attentive to the reactions that they are likely to provoke in those concerned. Some decision-makers want to build a consensus while others are ready to forge ahead. But even the most extreme tyrant cannot avoid taking into account the risk of being betrayed by those on whom he or she relies to establish his or her power.

In most cases, one way to limit these risks is to frame decisions with rituals. This is all the more necessary insofar as a decision is likely to be a source of conflict. These rituals play an essential role in the functioning of justice—for example, the ritual of civil or criminal proceedings—as well as in political life, for example, the ritual of elections. In their accomplishment, people of flesh and blood, with their limitations, weaknesses, and prejudices, tend to disappear behind characters of convention—for example, the magistrate or the person who, democratically elected, is considered as representing the entire population. A more or less obscure process, marked by human passions and weaknesses, is magically transformed into an achievement that tends to be seen as legitimate, authoritative, respectable, in short, as an expression of the good. Such rituals help to avoid the crossing of interests and convictions degenerating into clashes. They ensure that most decisions are more or less implemented. Additionally, thanks to these rituals, decision-makers are relatively shielded from the resentment of those affected by their decisions. Even though, in everyday life, the possible perversion of such a process is often denounced, it is generally to demand that its principles be better respected.

Cross-Cultural Management Revisited: A Qualitative Approach. Philippe d'Iribarne, Sylvie Chevrier, Alain Henry, Jean-Pierre Segal, and Geneviève Tréguer-Felten, Oxford University Press (2020).
DOI: 10.1093/oso/9780198857471.001.0001

In companies, decision theories tend to favour rational considerations relating to the organization of the material world, the efficiency of processes, the informed consideration of issues and context. Attention focuses on how best to manage the fact that the rationality of decisions is limited by the insufficient knowledge of those who take them (March & Simon, 1958). Of course, everyone is aware that many other considerations come into play, such as those relating to relationships between people; conflicts of egos; power games; fear of being set apart if one dares to oppose the dominant opinion; the desire for revenge of those whose opinions are ignored; or the arrogance of those who triumph. And, in fact, individuals take this into account when they act. But, in the world of theory, these aspects are rather considered as 'irrationality' that a concern for good management makes it imperative to overcome. The importance, even from a strict efficiency perspective, of reaching decisions that are perceived as legitimate by the actors concerned is recognized, but the ways of ensuring this legitimacy are hardly ever explored. The role of rituals in corporate life is noted, and myths and ceremonies are acknowledged (Meyer & Rowan, 1977). But this is more a sociologist's vision than a vision that inspires the design of management tools. The fact that the peace-making effect of a ritual depends on how it makes sense for those concerned remains largely underestimated or even ignored. For a ritual to work, it must appear respectable. And this is an eminently cultural interpretation.

For us to see and understand what is at stake, we shall consider two successive dimensions of the question. Based on a Franco-Dutch case, we will first examine how the selection of ideas and social interactions intertwine. To what extent must a decision appear to result from a rational elaboration to be considered legitimate? And to what extent should it be seen as resulting from an agreement between those concerned? We shall consider the difficulties inherent in the cooperation between those who give prominence to one or other of these two approaches. Then, going to Cameroon and Jordan, we shall look at the suspicions and resentment that any decision is likely to generate among those against whom it goes, whether it is likely to harm their interests or it actually rejects their ideas. We will see that, in order to overcome these suspicions and convey a sense of fairness, procedures that are aimed at monitoring the employees, or interventions of persons deemed impartial are used. We shall consider why these questions are hardly mentioned as long as we remain within Western societies. In conclusion, we shall discuss the links between the importance of the 'irrational' aspects of decisions and the need to adapt decision-making processes to cultural diversity.

6.1 Ideas and People: France and the Netherlands

Everywhere, as soon as an action involves several stakeholders, it is necessary to find a way to connect points of view and interests so as to arrive at a decision that is perceived as legitimate. This can be done in many ways. Two main families of approaches exist that can be contrasted. In the first one, everyone is entitled to defend their interests and ideas and the procedure focuses on mutual adjustment. In the other, a certain notion of what is good in itself is deemed to transcend the diversity of points of view. In the first case we have a procedural approach to the common good; in the second case a substantial approach. At the same time, within these two types of approaches, there are a set of options. The market or the 'palaver'—that is, the very constructed and ritualized meetings in use in many African societies to overcome differences in the confrontation of points of view—can be counted among the procedures; the excellence that one is seeking to achieve in one's job or, for those in power, the right behaviour track, that it is their role to preserve (d'Iribarne, 2006b) belong instead to the common good register. This is the type of cultural opposition that we encountered in the relations between French and Dutch employees within Air France-KLM[1].

6.1.1 Attachment to What is Well Thought Out in France

At Air France, we encountered a fascination with what is well thought out. This vision gets expressed in various ways, either to praise it or to criticize it[2]: 'Together we try to do *intelligent things*'; 'At Air France, we like to *study in depth* and *know a lot* before making a decision.'; or, in a Frenchman's words commenting on the way things were done in the Netherlands: 'These are not choices like we make them, they are not *thought out, structured*, or *state-of-the-art choices.*' This vision of a French approach is well perceived on the Dutch side: 'French people like to go more in details, *to really understand the difficulty*, the challenge, to understand the situation before coming up with a proposal or even before daring to discuss what you could do.'

This conception implies in-depth study before acting, in order to avoid making mistakes and being guilty of intellectual failure. 'For a route opening, launching a destination that doesn't work is a failure; it means that *we made a mistake*, that we made a bad study, that we didn't choose to open what was the best route. (...) What is expected of me is that *I do something good*, not that I make proposals with a risk of making a mistake.'

This reference to what is well thought out does not preclude listening to users. However, there is a refusal to follow them blindly. It is up to highly competent people to determine what needs to be implemented and they are entitled to enlighten those who do not have the same expertise, to make them adhere to what they have designed, or even to impose it on them. 'I listen to their requests because they are the ones who serve the customers, and it is important to have their feedback, but meeting their expectations does not mean saying "amen" to everything they ask for.' Resistance to what has been well thought out by experts seems irrational, incomprehensible. For example, an Air France representative is outraged that KLM refused to align its cash management system with that of Air France, even though the former was 'obsolete' and the latter 'up to date'. 'KLM decided in a somewhat *arbitrary way*. Treasury *professionals do not understand* why KLM did not look into it. (...) We have the same needs. *There is no reason* for us not to capitalise on the same systems.'

Being heard is difficult unless you are perceived as competent. In response to the question about her French colleagues: 'Do they listen to you?', a Dutch female employee replied: 'Actually at the beginning not at all. But I think after a year, after *I had proven myself on the content* also (...) then I was trusted and then I also had a voice in the team.'

The definition of this good way to be taken as reference can be the subject of many debates and the French even disagree among themselves as to what this good way might be.

> What is the definition of a good idea? (...) It is the ability to formulate it elegantly in a thoughtful conceptual framework, with many details etc. Finally, we all have our ego, in meetings our ideas are in competition.

In this perspective, there is a great contempt for what is described as a 'soft compromise', which ignores the reference to what is intrinsically good.

> We're in a lot of discussions. It's not just 'we both go halfway and then that's enough'. I could not bear that. There has to be a business justification behind it so that, if I really think that we shouldn't do as they say, I will not necessarily make the three steps towards them to compensate for the same three steps that they could not make. And, conversely, *if I think their idea is better than mine, I have no problem giving in to them.*

Therefore, the French argue, to put an end to debates, one has to call upon a highly competent person. He or she is generally a superior who is expected to be an expert, not just a facilitator. 'There should be an impulse from management to say: "that's it now". (...) So long as no clear, precise information has come from top management, there remains a possibility to understand differently, and this is where there is a hazy zone, different understanding, and where problems may arise.' 'An Air France manager is above all *an expert in his field* who has over time become a manager, whereas at KLM, from my experience, a manager is rather a leader who will rely on experts.'

We had already encountered such references to a relatively abstract rationality among Renault's French people when we were working on understanding the failure of the attempted alliance between Renault and Volvo (d'Iribarne, 1998)—a case that will be developed in Chapter 12 (pp. 234–39) on the functioning of multicultural teams. When such references prevail, the logical rigour of arguments is given great value, and, according to a Renault representative, the figures, seen as undisputable objective references, constitute valuable weapons in the confrontation of points of view: 'There is a debate, so you will have to prepare your weapons, *you will have to justify yourself by quantifying your positions.*' For 'surrendering' to be legitimate, one must find oneself in a situation where, faced with a decisive argument, 'one has had to face the facts'. 'To accept to change one's position', it has to be in the name of reason, by 'acknowledging that the initial assumptions were wrong'.

In practice, this reference to what is well thought out does not always hold. And it is complemented by a certain pragmatism allowing one to turn a blind eye to exceptions, with some quiet deviations from the strictly stated rule. This pragmatism comes into play downstream of the process leading from decision to action. 'For us, when there is something wrong, we go beyond that. (...) We too will be pragmatic, outside the structures, the budgets (...). We can of course adjust; to get from one point to another the paths can be varied. (...) We are not cheating, but this time it is pragmatism.'

This approach to decision-making has its merits—sometimes recognized by those who do it differently, such as this Dutchman from KLM:

> Personally, I appreciate the rigour of the French. (...) I like the rigour and the French put a lot of emphasis on the content; they really want to understand something in detail before putting it in place and that's what I appreciate very much, to have discussions a bit more, I would say, almost philosophical.

But this approach also has its drawbacks. By wanting to study and understand thoroughly, the risk is to overestimate what is really known, which some French people are well aware of.

> Air France requires a bit of fortune-telling, 'what will the situation of the country be like in 30 years and what will the traffic be with Europe, etc.?' (...) Air France (...) tends to reassure itself with very learned spreadsheets (...). What has always struck me about Air France is that the business cases are true, with no margin of uncertainty and no range of error, which is still quite fascinating. It's millions of Euros; at the end we'll earn 3.2 million Euros. What is the margin of error on this? Oh no, it's 3.2. (...) The French are going to sell us [Air-France/KLM alliance] huge Excel spreadsheets with numbers all over... and the spreadsheets say nothing except that we made a lot of assumptions in them and we hid them in Excel so it wouldn't show too much.

Those who are convinced that they are experts—as will be seen again in Chapter 11 (pp. 225–226), in the contrasting self-images that French and

Chinese companies strive to project—find it difficult to take into account the experience of those who are in the field. A situation also to be found, within Air France, in the relations between departments: 'Yes, with the French market, there is a very strong entity, it is the French market, it is the largest market. They tend to say: "what is good for France is good for the whole world", which is not necessarily true. We had difficulties with France [those in charge of the French market]: they imposed their products on us, products which were not at all saleable internationally; they also imposed processes on us that were not marketable/saleable internationally.'

The French inability to listen to the opinions of their counterparts, once they are convinced that they are right, is occasionally mentioned—as it had been by a few of the Renault people that we had previously interviewed. 'We don't know how to reassure; we don't know how to remain silent and listen to the other; we have to stop being right all the time', or 'by working on our own hypotheses, by making proposal on proposal, we were advancing according to our own point of view, and then we had difficulty listening to others'. Stating ideas, *being right, working on our hypotheses, advancing according to our point of view*, which guides action, prevails over relationships (*to reassure, remain silent, listening*), which are neglected, although this behaviour is sometimes seen as regrettable.

The difficulty in finding compromises affects social relations, as an Air France trade unionist comments:

> We also regret it, a strike is a failure because we lose money; we often have the impression that, if we do not go through this stage, nothing can happen. It is our way of operating, (...) we are not in a situation where debating is possible: we are confronted with a top management that comes up with projects; that does not allot unions enough space—unions that, as a result, behave in a somewhat irresponsible way too; since management does not give them any responsibilities, they ask for a lot.

6.1.2 Compromises Between People in Northern Europe

The cultures of northern European countries (the Scandinavian countries, the Netherlands, Belgium) differ in many respects, but they also share strong similarities. A major point is that decision-making is less perceived as the result of an intellectual process than as the result of a compromise between people. This is particularly true in the Netherlands.

The Dutch people that we met at KLM find rather strange the place given by the French to an intellectual approach in preparing decisions, and some even consider this approach as a waste of time.

> The French (...) have a very strong mind in...with lots of numbers, lots of analyses, a lot of studies. Studies, studies, studies, and after that they decide to do something. (...) For us, for the Dutch, in general, (...) our attitude is more 'act to test', and after that we adjust, we make small adjustments. But less analysis, more action.

Actually, there is no shortage of self-criticism on this point at Air France: 'I think that a terrible amount of time is wasted [at Air France] in discussions about unimportant things. Everything needs to be studied, if you want to spend €10,000 you need to go on your knees four times and get six signatures.' But this self-criticism does not lead to changes in decision-making processes.

Such an act-to-test orientation governs the way meetings are conducted by Dutch people: it is less a question of reflection and debate than of agreeing to define, in a pragmatic way, what will be done. 'I think that French people like to share ideas in a meeting. So, I think for a Dutch person it's almost philosophical: you share a lot of ideas, in order to know a lot on different topics, but in the end Dutch people want to end the meeting with actions, an action list, and a view of how to go forward.'

To be entitled to speak, it is not necessary, from a Dutch point of view, to be especially competent. All you have to do is be concerned, and no one hesitates to speak, which is in sharp contrast to what is found on the French side—a contrast that the Dutch have noticed:

> What you see, on the Air France side, is that the boss is always the one who speaks. But to be confident enough, the boss always takes his whole team of specialists, just in case there's a question for them to answer. It's a completely different practice from the Dutch setting where everybody has his own specialty and talks from his own specialty and has an opinion on that. On our side every person attending a meeting has a reason to be in a meeting, whereas on the French side, there are a lot of people who come to the meeting but most of them don't talk. For a Dutch person, it is not understandable why all those people come to a meeting when they don't say anything. Often, I hear on the French side that they are a little bit annoyed that all the Dutch people have something to say.

The superior does not need to be an expert who decides, but a facilitator who barely interferes in subjects concerning the technical competence of his subordinates, a role that surprises the French (see Chapter 4, p. 84). 'At KLM, a manager who comes from a function that has nothing to do with his current position, for example, say, commercial or operations, if he is recognised as a leader, as a manager who can lead teams, who can take along the troops, they will position him in a function in which he is really not an expert.' 'My counterpart manager at KLM (...) was in baggage or sales, he's a manager, he has a PhD in psychology. He coordinates, he makes the planning. He has no competent opinion.'

Deciding means finding compromises between those whose interests may diverge. What ensures the convergence of points of view is not the existence of an arbitrator placed above the parties, but a procedure, *vergadering* (Bony, 2007), which is the subject of religious respect. A phase of free expression of the participants' wishes—that is, everyone expressing themselves not in the name of superior ideas but of their own interest—is followed by a decision-making phase in which only the common interest and the spirit of compromise have the right to be. And the joint decision engages all members of the community, which surprises the French. '[Between them, the Dutch] When it's decided, it's decided. They have fewer scruples to say so when they do not agree with their boss in the stage of forming the decision, but actually once a decision has been taken, once they have settled between them in the interest of KLM, they go at it, they form a block.'

This spirit of compromise particularly marks social relations, and strikes are almost unknown, which is well noticed on the Dutch side, in contrast to the French situation.

> It is difficult with French unions. But I think in the Netherlands, unions are more realistic. And they are probably taken more seriously by management, because management has regular meetings with unions, very regularly. And they are kept updated on how things are going with the company, financially, operationally, partners, very confidential stuff sometimes, but they are sworn to confidentiality. So, they know what the status is, and then, when formal negotiations start and management presents some measures, then unions are never surprised, because they saw it coming.

Like the approach that values the confrontation of ideas, the one which values compromise between people has its ups and downs. On the one hand, it is favourable to social peace. On the other hand, the search for consensus may be an obstacle to taking global perspectives into account, which leads, on the French side, to critical remarks. 'The Dutch have a difficulty; they have a less synthetic approach than the French (. . .). They have great difficulty getting down to the three key messages or five key messages. It's difficult to get them to extract, at the end of the end, where they are heading.'

The Swedish approach is similar to that encountered in the Netherlands. Deciding implies building an agreement between peers, in a shared commitment to a common project. Correlatively, the leaders, in contrast to what we observe on the French side, are dedicated to a role of facilitator, of organizer. 'I avoided getting into debates about technical issues. I was dedicated to keeping the peace', says a Swedish project manager. Here again, this approach has its limits, which a French perspective tends to highlight: 'On the Volvo side, decisions are made at the grassroots level. But discussions between people at this level do not allow decisions to integrate an external view, a global perspective. The view is not "holistic" enough.'

6.1.3 A Difficulty in Understanding One Another

These differences between two ways of deciding are a source of misunderstandings. Certainly, the French and the Dutch see well, for the most part, how the other behaves, and it is striking to see how the views that they have of themselves and the way others see them converge, as long as everyone remains at what is immediately observable. But each party has a hard time grasping what meaning the other party's behaviour may have and, here, there are gross misinterpretations.

Thus, in the cooperation between French and Dutch employees within Air France-KLM, the Dutch have little understanding of the role played by expertise in enabling French superiors to settle conflicts of ideas. They tend, following their own logic, to interpret the intervention of superiors purely in the realm of relationships between people. As a result, they neglect the aspect of expertise in favour of the hierarchical dimension alone. Just as the Swedes did at Volvo, they imagine French subordinates to be much more submissive than they actually are—a quite common stereotype about French society—expressing it in such words as: 'As a manager you really need to tell Air France employees that they should do something; they wait for you to say so'; 'I think the French colleagues often dogmatically follow their leader.' They do not understand what derives from the superior character of French experts, who are convinced of their competence as individuals and only willing to give in to those that they recognize as being even more expert than they are.

The French do not understand the Dutch communitarian aspect any better than the Dutch understand the French hierarchical aspect. They fail to make the connection between the way in which the Dutch can stand together against an external partner and the liveliness of the internal debates between them. Nor do they understand why the way of acting within a community is so different from that of negotiating with a partner outside the community. 'Whereas twelve years ago we were led to believe that the Dutch practised consensus, for me now, it's not true.'

Between the French and the Swedes, mutual understanding works no better (a point to be developed in Chapter 12, pp. 234–9). Indeed, the French had difficulty understanding the role of Swedish managers. '[At Volvo] managers have very little added value; they facilitate, manage people, but do not intervene on technical issues.' And the Swedes had trouble understanding that the French could change their position once they had been convinced by rational arguments. To explain the evolving of their position over the life-span of a common project, the French put forward their own awareness of technical problems, *initial hypotheses* that *did not hold*, the fact of having *recognized* what was *bad*; all this ultimately leading to *good work*. Meanwhile, the Swedes confined themselves to questions of relationships between partners. 'When we at Volvo really came together, with our hierarchy supporting the project with the necessary data, we managed to make our will prevail.'

6.2 Overcoming Radical Mistrust

While the French and the Dutch (or the Swedes) are opposed on the way in which a good decision-making process should be conceived, they share the same major concern: how to design and implement a decision-making process that will enable effective decisions to be taken, based on a realistic consideration of the objective aspects of situations. Certainly, those who express themselves often blame their partner, on the French side, by deploring the lack of competence of the Dutch or, on the Dutch side, by criticizing the lack of listening of the French. But most of these remarks appear in debates between professionals who address issues linked to the quality of decisions. Negative feelings—that is, fear, anger, jealousy, desire for revenge, associated with a radical mistrust of people—are hardly ever mentioned. Denouncing the pursuit of strictly personal interests or an intention to harm is unheard of.

Such mistrust is expressed bluntly and systematically in many other contexts. Here, a clear question arises. How to protect those who make decisions which harm an individual or group—for example, those who sanction, refuse to place orders with a supplier or hire a job seeker, or refuse to promote a particular job-seeker—from the resentment and revenge of those who feel badly treated? And, similarly, how can managers avoid a tendency to refuse to make these difficult decisions?

A major point of cultural differentiation concerns the response to these questions: on what grounds should decisions be reached so as to be perceived as impartial by those affected by them? We shall consider what happens in Cameroon and Jordan. In Cameroon it seems difficult to trust people so that very restrictive procedures seem more promising. On the contrary, in Jordan, people rely more on arbitrations by persons perceived as endowed with an authority from God. If, in general, such mistrust is less immediately visible in the Western world, it is not because it is foreign to it. Rather, the processes that most of the time allow it to be overcome are so familiar that, in everyday life, little attention is paid to them.

6.2.1 BeingProtected from Resentment and Reprisals in Cameroon

The case of SONEL (Société d'électricité du Cameroun)—already mentioned in Chapter 5 (pp. 94–100), and to which we shall return in Chapter 13—illustrates in a particularly crude way the place of human passions in decision-making processes and the risks associated with these passions.

At the time we met SONEL, the company was extremely centralized, and this was associated, on the part of managers at various levels, with feelings of fear and an escape from responsibility. Each department head tended to refer decisions to the next level for fear of facing very negative or even violent reactions if some of their subordinates were negatively affected. 'Recently, delegations of authority have been made to directors,' noted the general manager, 'and they do not exercise it.' This is particularly true, he complained, for the implementation of the sanctions in the event of misconduct.

Caution is all the more important because—as we saw in Chapter 5 (pp. 98–99)—there is a great fear of retaliation. A sanctioned agent may 'react negatively', by counter-attacking in the visible world, 'false failures', 'small sabotages'—or even from the invisible world: 'Witchcraft,' a director remarked, 'mostly happens when people feel misjudged and they're in precarious jobs.'

Such fear of retaliation is associated with a strong focus on individual influence. Rather than say 'the Electricity Company has fired such a person', it is usual to say: 'It's Mr X who had so-and-so dismissed'. In addition, everyone is perceived as being guided by their personal interests and feelings and not by the defence of the company's interests. As a result, any decision that negatively affects someone's situation is seen as expressing the attitude of the decider towards the person who is affected. Under these conditions, it is difficult to sanction. 'They don't want a subordinate to say: "That's the nasty guy who didn't want to give a good evaluation to so-and-so, who didn't want to give a promotion, etc."', notes the general manager.

It is better to avoid punishing than to expose oneself. Controls, on the other hand, are a frequent source of tension. For instance, the agents in charge of checking subscribers' electricity meters at home complain that, often, 'dogs are released' or that 'they are threatened with a gri-gri or even a dagger'.

How can one get people to admit that decisions that harm others, or at least do not benefit them, have not been taken out of hostility or at least out of a lack of solidarity with those whose fate they affect? There are three different ways to do this.

This is a society where everyone, although they may try to escape from it, is stuck in a tight web of relationships, solidarity, friendships, enmities that make it difficult to assume, and in any case to believe in, the making of impartial decisions.

Such decisions are easier to make by someone outside the internal influences of a community: hence the role that expatriates play, which seems to be irreplaceable (Henry, 1995). It is not so much a question of passing on knowledge as of being perceived as not being part of the game of family, friendly, tribal, and other pressures. If they are consistently rigorous and carefully avoid any favouritism, this attitude can be interpreted, in their case, as somewhat strange '*White*' behaviour; difficult to understand but nevertheless credible. When it comes to supervising recruitment, resisting pressure from '*friends*', or controlling the use of financial resources, their help is invaluable.

This call to expatriates is not the only way possible. Another way is to ensure that those who make decisions that negatively affect the fate of others appear to be forced to act as they do. When you are subjected to such a constraint, you can convince your relatives and friends that if you refuse their requests, it is not because you are not loyal to them, but because you cannot do otherwise. Consequently, this constraint is not, as it would be in other countries, perceived as a deprivation of liberty, but as protection in dangerous situations. The very strict framework for decisions, as implemented by the system of procedures referred to in Chapters 5 (pp. 94–100) and 13, meets this requirement. The more binding the rules, the more they are based on 'the letter' and not 'the spirit', the less room there is for an interpretation that emphasizes personal interests and feelings of friendship or hostility towards those whose situation is affected. It is no longer individuals, inspired by their interests, friendships, and enmities, who are deemed to decide, but an impersonal system whose functioning is beyond the control of those who act as simple cogs in a machine. Processes that may lead to decisions which are biased by personal considerations can also be very extensively broken down into a set of tasks that are the responsibility of different people (Henry, 1999). As a result, no single actor has the possibility to favour or disadvantage those who are affected by the consequences of a decision—for example, in the water and electricity company of Ivory Coast, the person initiating an action must not be the one who concludes it, especially when it has a financial impact. In customer management, for example, procedures are split between several agents who do not report to the same local manager. The first superior to master the entire procedure is at the regional headquarters, in order to 'keep those in charge away from the field' and prevent them from 'being tempted to bypass the procedures'. The corresponding software, filled with double keys and cross checks, is designed like real trunk locks.

Not only must the rules be unambiguous, but their application must be closely monitored and those who violate them must not be able to escape sanctions. 'Everyone knows that if you depart from them, you'll be disciplined; and that two people behaving the same way won't receive different sanctions.' The slightest space would leave room for a number of interpretations concerning the real intentions of the person responsible for applying the rule, as well as the person responsible for punishing those who violate it. The auditors are an essential part of the decision-making system. They do not have the power to say what to do or to arbitrate between antagonistic interests. They do not decide. Their role is to reveal any deviation from the procedures governing the decision.

6.2.2 The Expectation of a Just and Firm Authority in Jordan

As we were conducting investigations within the Jordanian subsidiary of a multinational company with French roots (d'Iribarne, 2009), we encountered the aspiration to implement an impartial decision-making process. But the unrest that was being expressed was quite different from the one in Cameroon. What was at the centre of the frustrations that were expressed was the arbitrariness and contempt for those in charge. And, for decisions to become impartial, it was the firm and just authority of a holy man close to his people that was longed for.

The statement that the company's operations are marked by contempt from those in a position of power towards those in a less brilliant position was constantly present in the interviewees' discourse. Many decisions, they said, are not the result of a search for the company's good, but the expression of this contempt.

The lack of regard for lower-level managers in decision-making was denounced: 'There are strategies, parachuted, already regulated and designed, and you just have to apply, that's all.' Delegated responsibilities were not respected: 'For example, a contractor comes to me to pay his bill. So, I see what he did, I do the accounts and subtract what he didn't do. And I'm surprised to learn later that we paid him the full amount.' The procedures are manipulated: 'There is no justice, that's my feeling. If you are not in harmony with your line manager, it is difficult to have a good evaluation, despite the fact that you may have good ideas.' The allocation of resources is marked by large unequal and unjustified treatments. For those in a dominant position in offices: '*luxury*', '*privileges*', '*great advantages*', '*travel*', '*training*'; for the others who struggle in factories: the obligation to '*calculate everything*', cars '*in a lamentable state*'.

To remedy this situation, what is expected is not the establishment of countervailing authorities or binding procedures, but the advent, at the top of the company, of someone with great powers who is both fair and firm. 'It is the leader who gives protection and stability to his employees as the king who protects his people and in return the employees owe him obedience and loyalty.' 'We need a leader who is a moral example and not a manager: a leader who is both a moral example and a firm and fair decision-maker.'

The superior that people expect does not use his rank as a pretext to stand aside or free himself from the common rules: 'You have to go out in the field' and not just 'say: "Do this, this and that"'. The height of his position combines with emotional closeness. He makes the employee feel that he '*shares his sorrows and joys*', that he is '*with him body and soul*'. He accepts the existence of a rule that applies to everyone: 'You need a reference, a reference that governs you and me. Me, as a small employee, and you as a senior manager, and in the end our reference is the same.' 'I'm going to start with a new system: 1, 2, 3, 4. Its principles are justice, equality, equity between positions, between people . . . .'

Such a superior is inspired by the example of the ideal parents and, ultimately, by the Prophet.

> Leadership by example is 100% important. For me, leadership by example is similar to the son who follows his father or mother; it is exactly the same thing. How can you be an ideal mother or father if you don't behave in an exemplary way; how can you expect your son to follow you if you say things and don't apply them. '*Alkoudoua*' [meaning: being an example] is like the Prophet when he gave the example: he did everything right and then people followed his example.

'It [the company] has to recognise everyone's work. If my father preferred my brother to me, there would not be anything left to bind us.' In a religious context, the fact that all are subject to a common law, given by God, is in no way incompatible with the fact that authority may be highly personalized.

For the people we interviewed, such a vision was an ideal that contrasted with what they were experiencing on a daily basis. Should it then be considered utopian? In fact, the ideal of a virtuous authority figure inspired by the Prophet's model is not unique to Jordan. We found it in Morocco in a company where it actually inspired the life of the company (see pp. 280–285), which shows that it can inspire real life provided management's action allows it.

6.2.3 An Issue that is Largely Ignored in Western Companies

When we began our investigations in Cameroon, a source of great surprise was the fact that the concerns associated with the slightest decision were omnipresent in the words and images that people used to talk about it—the fear of being seen as a '*nasty guy*'; the '*traps*' set to push for fault; the call to witchcraft to take revenge on those who harmed you. We had never met anything like it in Western companies before, and have never met anything like it since. Would this mean that the fears, mistrust, and risks thus mentioned are absent, or practically absent, from these companies? Or that these companies have found ways of functioning which have overcome these dark aspects so well that one never talks about them? Or even that we are dealing with a taboo that prohibits mentioning these aspects?

One answer which is obvious at first sight is that over the centuries the development of bureaucratic forms of organization in the Western world has made it possible to reduce the phenomena in question to a minimum. In principle, as bureaucracy agents make a decision, they do not act as private persons guided by their interests and passions, by the friendship or enmity relations that they maintain with those they know, but *sine ira et studio* they act as representatives of an impersonal order, in accordance with the requirements of the mission entrusted to them by the organization that employs them. Moreover, it is not only a question of principles. This way of acting is common in everyday life. Whoever deviates significantly from the model will be the one to cause surprise. As a result, any newly-met person is a priori supposed to comply with the obligations of their position and trusted in that respect. But such an answer immediately leads to another question. For a long time now, bureaucratic forms of organization have been considered as a reference everywhere. Thus, the Cameroonian company where we conducted our investigations had a pile of consultants' reports that constantly recommended reforming it in that direction. Why do efforts to implement these forms meet with such little success in many parts of the world?

For bureaucratic functioning to be successfully put into practice, those who are called upon to act in accordance with its logic must be willing to comply. The emergence of 'bureaucratic personalities' (Merton, 1952) for whom respect for the rules is sacred is sometimes mentioned. But under what conditions is this emergence possible? Western societies inherited a whole history that led them to give great importance to the figure of the good man, whose sense of duty is intimately associated with fidelity to principles: for example, a moral law, a conception of honour, or a vision of what conforms to reason. It is in such a conception that the respect of impersonal rules takes on its meaning (see Chapter 9, p. 181). The place given to the figure of the good man constitutes a common core of the cultures which have prevailed in the West, even though each of them provides its own version, according to the principles it values most, be it honour, virtue, or others. Besides, this figure of the good man is largely foreign to cultures where, in one form or another, what prevails is an ethic of loyalty, centred on the particular duties that each person has towards his or her relatives and friends. When dealing with such an ethic—which marks a large part of the world—it is doubtful that bureaucratic impartiality can prevail. Therefore, to obtain decisions perceived as legitimate, other processes such as those mentioned in relation to Cameroon and Jordan must be relied on.

6.3 Conclusion

The wider the circle of countries studied, the more obvious it becomes that deciding is a source of thorny questions. Wherever specific ways to answer these questions in a manner that is consistent with the local culture abound, the trickiness of the questions raised tends to be overlooked. But, as is the case with all aspects of management, the role that cultures play appears in the spotlight each time different conceptions meet, either because people with reference points in different cultures have to cooperate, or because there is an attempt to introduce alien practices into a certain cultural context.

Decision-making may be the area in the life of organizations where the reassuring image of pure administration is the most illusory. According to this image, the aim would be to make a rational assessment—based on an objective evaluation of the situations—of the advantages and disadvantages associated with the possible options, and then to make an informed decision. Of course, confronted with a more or less uncertain future, people always make decisions with limited knowledge. It is now well known that decisions are presented as guided by an ideal of rational choice much more than they really are (March et al., 1972). Everyone is aware that it is sometimes more important, in order to build the trust of bankers and customers, to give the impression that you are rational than to actually be rational. It also happens that some considerations relating to the government of men are introduced into the design of an ideal decision-making process. It is common practice to speak of empowerment, participative management, a liberated company, with the idea that those who have been involved in a decision will be more willing to be involved in its implementation than those who have been kept out. But in doing so, we have in mind a universal-type figure and do not take into account human passions and the way in which cultures shape them.

However, as soon as an unfamiliar context is considered in which what occurs no longer appears self-evident, the perspective widens singularly. The behaviour of others, wherever they come from, suddenly seems strange. And, as soon as one digs into it, one sees to what extent deciding implies taming or even exorcizing a dangerous world. Deciding opens the door wide to human passions, to the fascination of power, fear, jealousy, to the desire for revenge. Those concerned are worried or indignant: why such an arbitration? Why was this person listened to and I wasn't; why was she rewarded and I wasn't, promoted and I wasn't? Are their opinions really worth more than mine? Why do they count and I'm not counted for anything? What do I risk if I am too frank; if I take the task that I am entrusted with too much to heart instead of protecting myself; if I disturb the powerful or those who have means of revenge; or if I simply disturb the established order? If things go wrong, who will be charged? Am I going to be a scapegoat?

In the ideal world life of organizations that seems dominant, none of these questions would need to be asked. We should not take them into account, because it would mean admitting that debasing human passions are part of the ordinary course of life; that we must make room for them instead of simply fighting them. But a fundamental lesson of field research is that believing that these passions can disappear is an illusion. And if, in the life of organizations, so many decisions seem absurd, sometimes monstrous, or an expression of the ego of those who exercise power, of their thirst for domination, of their denial of reality, of their fears, it may be precisely because there is not enough concern to put in place measures that could limit the harmful effects of all this 'irrationality'.

What companies encounter is part of everyday life all over the world. The difficult relationships between humans did not appear with the advent of modern companies. Everywhere, since the dawn of time, it has been necessary to find ways to give form to the magma of feelings and interests so that clashes are contained or that they do not render communal living or cooperation impossible. In this matter, each culture has its own recipe, linked to a way of giving meaning to difficult situations, and in particular of making the decisions that are harmful to you reasonably acceptable.

In countries where the corporate world has long been rooted, culturally appropriate approaches to decision-making have emerged over time. However, these approaches risk being destabilized by the use of 'international' tools that comply with so-called 'modern' management standards. It is prudent not to embark on such 'modernization' without thinking. At the same time, in many countries, context-specific approaches to decision-making are common in traditional institutions but finding, transposed and adapted to the world of large business, approaches that were inspired by such institutions is not yet common. Therefore, undertaking such an innovative kind of work as the one in which we participated in Cameroon—reported in Chapter 13—is essential so as to make the most of the resources offered by each culture.

Notes

1. We are very grateful to Niels Noorderhaven with whom we worked hand-in-hand on the research that materialized in a common report completed in 2017: Philippe d'Iribarne, Niels Noorderhaven: 'Relations between Air France and KLM as experienced by employees. A cultural perspective', April 2017 Report. It was produced in three versions; one French, one English, and one Dutch. The latter is accessible at: https://www.ad.nl/redactie/KLM/Rapport%20Cultureel%20perspectief%20Nederlandstalig%20AFKLM.pdf.
2. Throughout this chapter, whenever needed, italics were used for emphasis in interviewees' speech.

7
Industrial Relations

Being able to organize an effective dialogue with social partners is now widely recognized as part of good management practice. However, unlike other aspects of management, there are no deemed universal 'best practices' in this area. It is assumed that good management of industrial relations begins with the proper application of the legal framework that is specific to each country: the legal framework defines the rights and duties of the social partners. As different as local contexts may be—particularly in size and sector of activity—the same questions arise. How can a cooperative climate be established between the social partners so as to provide mutually acceptable answers to the many questions that arise from the daily functioning of an organization? Local representations of what should be a fair exercise of managerial power largely determine the acceptability of these responses. These cultural differences do not only shed light on the content of the institutional framework organizing industrial relations—they vary from one country to another—but also on the conditions required for it to function harmoniously.

The fact must be acknowledged that the comparative literature on industrial relations (Wilkinson et al., 2014) has shown little interest in this cultural perspective. This literature has focused mainly on studying the historical constructions of the institutions that regulate such relations in each country (Bamber et al., 2016). It also compares the evolution of social conflict from one country to another, as well as from one period to another, in economic, political, and social life. The conditions required for useful and mutually satisfactory cooperation to emerge between social partners at the ground level of firms, have received much less attention from cross-national researchers.

The objective of this chapter is to show how the daily functioning of industrial relations is influenced by the meanings that local actors give to the various issues discussed between social partners and to the way they hierarchize them. It is organized in two sections.

First, we will immerse ourselves in the very particular context of New Caledonia—a French territory in the Pacific—with the originality of bringing together company managers trained in Western schools and the representatives of Occanian employees in an institutional framework transplanted from metropolitan France. This unusual configuration will allow us to show how European

Cross-Cultural Management Revisited: A Qualitative Approach. Philippe d'Iribarne, Sylvie Chevrier, Alain Henry, Jean-Pierre Segal, and Geneviève Tréguer-Felten, Oxford University Press (2020).
DOI: 10.1093/oso/9780198857471.001.0001

managers' lack of cultural awareness may worsen pre-existing social tensions, whereas industrial relations may be improved by taking into consideration the local vision of how a good social dialogue should work.

In a second section, we will visit again the afore-mentioned Maryland metallurgical plant (see Chapter 1, p. 17). We will explain how the American legal framework regulating industrial relations draws its inspiration from similar culturally embedded principles to the managerial model described and analysed in Chapter 1, p. 15). Strict compliance with the legal framework is a necessary condition for building lasting cooperation between company management and employees' representatives. But it is not enough to produce truly effective social dialogue.

These two examples lead us to conclude that, in any country, an institutional model organizing industrial relations cannot work efficiently unless local stakeholders find it meaningful inside their cultural framework. This conclusion sheds light on the diversity of the existing national models and on the cultural issues linked to the transfer in this field from one country to another of so-called 'best practices'.

7.1 Building an Effective Social Dialogue in New Caledonia

New Caledonia is, in many respects, a textbook-case for analysing the impact of cultures on the regulation of labour relations (Segal, 2011). It offers the possibility of studying how Kanak employees, who have been socialized in the Oceanian world, use the opportunities offered by an institutional framework from metropolitan France not only to defend their professional interests—the stated purpose of this framework—but also to introduce into the company social ties that are similar to those to which the society around them refers.

New Caledonia is a French territory of 250,000 inhabitants located in the South Pacific. Its population is composed almost equally of Europeans—mainly from France—and Oceanians, mainly Kanak but also Wallisians. Long kept out of the labour market, Oceanians are now widely present in New Caledonian companies—generally run by Europeans—where they carry out a large part of the implementation tasks. A high level of social conflict can be observed in many of these companies where the demands and modes of action of Oceanian workers strongly confuse business leaders and, more particularly, those who have just arrived from metropolitan France (Segal, 2009).

For Oceanian employees, who have mainly lived in traditional environments, joining a company managed according to the usual French way represents a new anxiety-laden experience. Maintaining the relational links is one of the priorities of their daily social environment. However, these links tend to recede behind the importance given by Westerners to a proper performance of professional tasks.

An operator complains: 'We were never asked: "Hey! You, how are you this morning?" We were treated as though we were just numbers.'[1]

In the customary environment, young Oceanian residents are rarely left on their own: they generally move around in gangs rather than alone. The experience is also stressful because the time-discipline imposed on them in the company contrasts drastically with the daily life in their tribes. The tasks that they are in charge of in their community award them great liberty in deciding when they should be accomplished and rarely include any deadlines. The obligation to be present at fixed hours is stressful, as are the possible sanctions associated with not respecting them, in particular in the case of repeated absenteeism—one of the main concerns for local employers.

This form of insecurity accounts for the high unionization rate of the Oceanian employees who work in medium or large companies—that is, companies employing more than fifty employees on that territorial scale. This rate, which is significantly higher than in metropolitan France where unions have suffered continuous decline for several years, is clearly associated by the persons concerned with an expectation of protection in the event that they encounter difficulties after they have made errors or violated rules. Oceanian employees can choose between the several trade unions existing in the institutional framework that organizes industrial relations—almost identical to what it is in metropolitan France.

7.1.1 Surprising Trade Union Practices

Trade union pluralism, to which local employees are very much attached, is, however, of a different nature from that observed in metropolitan France. Membership of a trade union organization is, in particular among Oceanian employees, mainly motivated by a personal relationship with the local leaders. The sharing of the ideological line defended by the trade union organization plays a secondary role. Members do not hesitate to follow them if they decide to change trade union. Leaders have an undisputed authority over their members, as explained by one of the members: 'It's the highest one who speaks, the one who founded the section. Everyone follows him. We have to follow the leader's directives.' If you do not follow the line, there is no point in remaining in the union. Those who would like to challenge the leaders' decisions have no choice but to leave.

Such departures do occur; they generally involve divisions and rivalries within the workers' community. It is quite rare for a trade union to be able to have the exclusivity for representing employees within a company. There are usually two unions, sometimes more, each of them having only a handful of members. According to a well-established practice, each union submits its own set of demands which exclusively concern their members. These may include requests for salary increases, promotion to a higher qualification, or the lifting of disciplinary sanctions. Each union acts on its own without seeking to set up a common platform with the other unions, as explained by the union leader of a public transport firm (Segal, 2013, pp. 61–73): 'I told the members not to take care of them. They have their own course of action, we have ours. Their claims, honestly, I don't know them. I never asked them and he [the other leader] did the same.'

Once the demands are made, each union closely monitors the concessions made by management to rival unions and considers that it is entitled to obtain the same. Should the company's management try to satisfy the demands of one union—the one that would be considered the most accommodating—in order to get its support, it would be exposed to particularly strong reactions from the other union. As the French director of this firm explained:

> I have one of the unions on my back. Then I have the other union that thinks I made too many concessions to the first. When management gives anything to a union, it must always calculate the consequences in relation to the other (so-called) partner.

In short, many local businesses are caught up in conflicts that repeatedly paralyse their operations. Mediations organized under the aegis of local administrations generally produce only short-term armistices. And when end-of-conflict protocols are finally reached, after many hours of negotiation, they are rarely followed.

However, not all companies are affected by such a tense social climate. Some of the business leaders, who have generally been present on the territory for a long time, are able to maintain a continuous and fruitful dialogue with their trade unions. Admittedly, the material difficulties experienced by a large part of the population of Oceanian origin, due to the high cost of living in the region, give rise to repeated wage demands that not all local business leaders are ready to meet. But these economic factors are not sufficient to account for the success that some company managers achieve in building a mutually satisfactory dialogue with local unions when others cannot. These enlightened business leaders, capable of finding common ground with their Oceanian employees, seem unable to teach most other leaders. The latter, generally founders of their own companies and their sole owners, consider that these local trade union practices are unacceptable violations of both the existing legal framework and the spirit that should, in their view, inspire social dialogue.

7.1.2 Contrasting Reactions Within New Caledonian Society

As we will see, viewed from a French metropolitan perspective, these behaviours were indeed perceived as either scandalous or simply unintelligible. The blocking and intimidating practices adopted by some of the local trade unions were condemned in economic circles. Public authorities were reminded of their duty to enforce the legal rules supposed to concern everyone everywhere. In addition to this legalistic condemnation, we also heard harsh judgements about the way in which some trade union leaders in Oceania carried out their role, making personal use of their delegation hours or placing their own professional promotion at the forefront of their organizations' demands.

The leitmotif in these recriminations: 'We need unions that are real unions', was relying on conceptions nourished by cultural references—those of metropolitan France—that were far from being shared by Oceanian employees. In the French tradition, trade unionists are supposed to fulfil a noble and recognized mission within the framework of the institutionally-organized functioning of social democracy (Rosanvallon, 2011). This is why, as explains Thuderoz,[2] a French sociologist, legally recognized trade unions have a monopoly on negotiating agreements with employers and receive public financial support.

> Trade union delegates have a monopoly on collective bargaining because one of the missions of trade unionism is to improve the living and working conditions of employees. It is therefore logical that it is the trade unions that engage organisations by signing collective agreements since they are the organised expression of employees' interests. (Thuderoz, 2011)

Employee representatives receive legal protection and a working-hours discharge to allow them to serve this French-style social democracy. The nobility of their commitment lies in their struggles to obtain social progress[3] benefiting everyone. Defending the interests of their members only—as Oceanian unions do—is a major transgression in the eyes of the local MP that we interviewed:

> The unions were never fighting for collective progress. It was such a guy in such a place who was to be fired and whom they tried to save . . . and they mobilised the whole company to save him . . . an individual case that was indefensible (laughs), alcoholics driving buses, people forgetting to hand the cash register back, things that were inadmissible, unacceptable in any company.[4]

For employees stemming from a European culture many of whom worked in good spirit with their Oceanian colleagues—unconditional allegiance to trade union leaders was most surprising.

Other voices could be heard in some of the pro-independence political circles. A critical current, questioning the cultural domination exercised by Europeans, saw New Caledonian social conflicts in an entirely different light. There, social tensions were perceived as a political expression—indeed disordered but fundamentally legitimate—that joined the long and universal mobilization of indigenous peoples, such as New Caledonia Kanaks. They figured that as long as the country's economic regime would not significantly reduce the social inequalities inherited from the colonial era, New Caledonian companies would be used to express the Kanaks' social and political demands.

Contrasting each other in more than one respect, these voices converged on at least one point: neither of them attempted to grasp the meaning that Oceanian employees make, in their own cultural references, of their trade union membership or of their loyalty to the designated leader. Understanding these logics—which are so different from theirs—would have been instrumental in developing a better social dialogue with the Oceanian unions.

7.1.3 What May Account for Oceanian Employees' Behaviour?

Oceanian employees, whose common attitudes are described by European managers as usually calm and smiling, may, under certain circumstances, radically change their behaviour. What fears, if any, could account for such changes of behaviour? And what could help them put at a distance the fears that participation in a Western enterprise can occasionally inspire?

Being banished or expelled from one's community, and thereby severing the bonds that constitute one's social identity, is the highest of the sanctions that are specific to customary environments. Being dismissed, for whatever reason, from their jobs cannot but resonate with this local reference. If, moreover, the only internal justification for the sanction imposed is the strict application of what for them is an 'anonymous' and 'foreign' rule, it is likely to be interpreted in their universe of meaning as a unilateral and violent breach of the existing social bond. This bond is supposed to remain unchanged, even between whoever sanctions and the sanctioned person. Sanctioning for non-compliance is not at all foreign to the Kanak world, but it always takes into account both the personality of the offender and the social ties that bind him to the person who sanctions, as a Kanak business leader explains about one of his employees: 'I can yell at him, because I'm older than him. I yell at him, he's like a little brother to me, it's not the same as if they were older people than me.' In order not to break this link, and thereby upset the fragile balance of social relationships within the community, the sanction will generally be applied with measure. And it will take into account the history of the relationship. 'We've known the people here all our lives. We know how they behave and everything. You can already say without having seen what happened, it doesn't sound like him, and that's it!'

Oceanian employees employed in a Western-style firm have different ways of forging social ties similar to those existing outside the professional environment. The first one consists of a personalized give-and-take relationship with their employer, in particular in small companies where trade unions are generally absent, provided, of course, that the employer takes on the corresponding role. Anthropologist Godin (2009: 7) insists on the generality of this type of social link within the Kanak world:

> In the traditional Kanak world, statutory relationships (subject-chiefs, elders-cadets) are conceived and lived in a give-and-take spirit. These are person-to-person relationships that must be nurtured by mutual respect and a constant flow of reciprocal gifts (food, wealth, words, services). (Godin, 2009)

In such cases, the company has then succeeded in 'making family', in the sense that Oceania's people understand it—that is, without the pejorative nuance that the visions of a duly emancipated modern individual generally attach to the idea of paternalism.

When the company has reached a larger size, union membership can give Oceanian residents access to patterns of socialization that are similar to those offered by their customary society. It offers them protection as well as the longed-for sense of belonging. It turns out to be the best antidote to the feeling of isolation and vulnerability that comes with their being anonymous employees. This belonging, coupled with a personalized relationship with the trade union leader, accounts for the loyalty that Europeans have noticed but do not fully understand. This loyalty to the leader can be analysed as a sort of reproduction of the generic link inherent to the ordinary functioning of the social hierarchy in traditional society, as described by Godin.[5]

The shift from industrial relations to confrontation, which may suddenly occur and has generally not been anticipated by company management, can also be explained by taking into account the local conceptions of what is needed for building sustainable social cohesion. When the social bond is broken between those who were until then able to maintain peace owing to their continuous give-and-take relations, confrontation allowing neither concessions nor truces threatens to replace the ordinary regime. This is how a Kanak trade union activist explains it: 'If the exchange is rich, evolution will be rich too. On the other hand, if the exchange is poor, as you have seen here, it produces periods of conflict, periods of really hard crises.'

Where the French tradition retains the idealized figure of the utopian trade unionist fighting for social progress, the Oceanian world refers to that of the warrior to whom, in these circumstances of confrontation, the collective has entrusted the defence of its interests by force. Examined from this perspective, the union's demands appear fully consistent with the local idea of a union's vocation. Defending its members to the extreme is of paramount importance. Thus, Oceanian employees are simply projecting their own categories into an institutional framework initially created in metropolitan France from a completely different perspective.

They quickly learned how to use it so as to defend their material interests, thus partially justifying the socio-political explanation of the local social conflict. However, their joining the union also made their belonging to the company far more meaningful for them. The usual decision to put personalities endowed with strategic positions in the alliance games specific to Kanak society at the head of the local unions also made sense in local categories. A union leader explained:

> Even at the customary level, I am well positioned. The advantage I have is that my mother, she is from Païta and my father is from Boulouparis. The message gets across better and it plays a lot. I was counting on a hard core of members who would work with me. Most of us are all tribes; we are all families. I think that knowing how to talk comes to me from my father perhaps, he is a customary leader. I was always in the ceremonies, all that, in the meetings. And then it evolved into the union.

Thus, placing the professional promotion of such a personality at the top of the union's list of demands makes sense in these references; conversely, it appears particularly scandalous in the French idealized vision of the disinterested trade unionist fighting for progress.

7.1.4 Peaceful Islets in the Middle of Turbulent Areas

The formula used by many Europeans: 'A union here is not a real union!' sums up the differences between local trade unionism and the trade unionism that these Europeans had previously experienced. It is also the expression of a widespread ethnocentrism among this population, quick to compare the local realities with those of metropolitan France, perceived as the indisputable norm. Many (European) business leaders did not even attempt to adapt their practices; they dreamt of converting the Oceanian employees to their own view of a well-organized social dialogue. Others, however, managed to work in good understanding with their social partners. Their companies illustrated the possibility of producing original forms of a social dialogue regulation more in phase with natives' expectations.

What did New Caledonian companies introduce in their practices when they succeeded in creating a peaceful social climate on a long-term basis? Two very different figures coexist.

The first one was introduced when we mentioned the case of small companies whose owners adopt the protective and generous role of the Oceanian chief. Such business leaders know how to foster a continuous flow of exchanges with their employees and maintain the social ties that guarantee their involvement. One of them, who had arrived from mainland France a few decades earlier, explained the changes his behaviour had undergone.

> At first, I was of European culture. All the problems here come from the fact that we do not know this type of employee. When you are in charge of them, you start to understand. My office is always open. I am available. They have my cell phone. They even call me at night. It's mostly the Oceanian women. Usually, it is a request for time or money. It is often a request for money, loans, and advances. Depending on the profile, if they are trustworthy, help can be extensive. I try to say yes as much as I can. If I can't say yes, I have to argue. I have to justify myself. Normally, that's my job.

The second scenario concerns larger companies with several unions in which the leaders have managed to take into account local representations of the role expected of them better than others. This is the case, for example, of a company in the construction sector which employs a highly unionized workforce divided between two unions. After being for a long time both distant and the sole master on board, the company manager changed completely, not only in his management but in his own way of being. This opened the door for his employees to create the kind of relationship that they expected from him. A trade unionist explained:

> The boss, I knew him before and I don't want to speak ill of him, he has become, how we can say that, more human. Much more human. That's when you can talk to what's called the boss. Before, we met him, we never shook his hand. He was the President of the Republic, so to speak! Since then it has completely changed, he has moved much closer to us. I am able to talk to my boss, to shake his hand. He says to me, 'Hello Sir!' It was good for everyone, both for him and for us!

The greatest merit of this manager was that he had clearly identified where the sensitive areas that required to 'be discussed' were located. This *discuss* is the word that Oceanians like to use to describe their exchanging words ritual, based on the greatest possible equality, between all the stakeholders concerned by the decision that is to be approved.

Great vigilance accompanied the administration of regulatory sanctions within the firm. The boss ensured that he got approval from both unions, while accepting to partly moderate these sanctions when asked to. A peculiar routine also organized the distribution of internal promotions. Each of the two unions prepared a list that generally focused on their own members' situations and interests. The management also prepared its list in consultation with the middle management. A close discussion then ensued, at the end of which a consensus was reached at the price of mutual concessions. 'Don't give the impression that you're giving more to one than the other!', explained the director. Whether it is the distribution of sanctions or of promotions, it is always the local form of regulation of social relations that is taken into account—this local form which is neglected by the management of companies paralysed by recurrent internal conflicts. This business leader explained his position:

> Should we do all this to prevent conflicts? I think so. To do much more, I don't know... Much less, I would say: No!

This New Caledonian exploration shows how necessary it may be to take into account the judgement categories of all stakeholders so that institutional arrangements seeking to align the interests of employees and those of company management may achieve their goals. This can sometimes be difficult. Those whom the Oceanians call Europeans, or more often 'Whites', also have their own culturally rooted categories of judgement. The Kanak request to take into consideration the personality of the offender may contradict the principle—sacrosanct to Westerners—of the equality of all before the rule. Compromises made in the awarding of professional promotions can provoke violent reactions from those who shout for a pure meritocracy.

The analysis of the functioning of New Caledonian professional relations clearly shows a cultural rootedness comparable to that identified in the previous chapters for other management practices. It also reveals a spectacular ignorance of this rootedness among many practitioners and commentators alike. Political discourses, which evoke the universal nature of economic contradictions between capital and labour, participate, in the same way as managerial discourses praising the merits of transferring 'Western good practices', in a harmful form of underestimating the weight of their cultural embeddedness. New Caledonia thus makes particularly visible the phenomena of cultural rootedness encountered not only in countries reputed to be locked in the archaism of their traditions but also in so-called modern countries. It is the purpose of the next section to show this by using the example of the USA.

7.2 The American Bargaining System

Let us return to the afore-mentioned Maryland metallurgical plant (see Chapter 1, p. 17) to take a closer look at how management and local union viewed and constructed their industrial relations. This plant had experienced significant tensions in previous years. It thus offers us the opportunity to show how the trade unions and management of an American company try to agree with each other, albeit with difficulty. We will analyse the underlying representations of an acceptable social order that guided the social partners and enabled them, despite the conflicts of interests and frequent disagreements, to establish pragmatic and reasoned cooperation.

A good social dialogue is not synonymous in the United States with a benevolent cooperation in which each party is as concerned about the interests of the other as it is about its own. The parties are expected to respect each other and to apply in good faith[6] the terms of the agreement between them. The text of the law[7] defining bargaining requires reason and good faith but, at the same time, explicitly recognizing the full freedom of each of the parties to determine for themselves what they are willing, or not, to compromise on.

> To bargain collectively is the performance of the mutual obligation of the employer and the representative of the employees to meet at reasonable times and confer in good faith (...) but such obligation does not compel either to agree to a proposal or require the making of a concession.

7.2.1 A Unionized Plant in Maryland USA

This Maryland plant was a unionized American factory in which industrial relations had not always been peaceful and were still not fully consensual. The monopoly of representation acquired by the union—following a majority vote of employees—did not please the management, which had to accept cohabitation with a powerful and organized counter-power.

When asked about possible ways to improve management through closer cooperation with the union at the workers' level, the Industrial Relations manager minimized this option:[8] 'I don't know if there is an answer...', he admitted. A better understanding between supervisors and their workers would, in his opinion, be a more direct way to improve the operation of the plant: 'The only answer is just to communicate with the employees, try to work with them, trying to explain what we're trying to do.'

In his opinion, the trade union's presence in the factory deprived the management of the option to reward 'good workers' and punish 'bad ones'. He commented ironically on the impossibility for management to promote the most deserving workers: 'Here there are no good or bad workers. They are all brothers and they are all equal. You see. So, if you make one to be better than the other then you are saying one brother is better than the other.'

He also stressed the fact that sanctions imposed by the supervisors were systematically challenged through the grievance procedure provided for in the contract: 'Anytime anybody gets disciplined, right or wrong, they have a grievance.' In short, he considered the union more a source of problems than a source of solutions.

On the union side, the comments made by the union were much more positive. The local union leader of this Maryland plant was pleased with what he considered to be a satisfactory functioning of industrial relations. He attributed this situation to the good will of his counterpart but, at the same time, to the union's strength: 'I think that it basically has to do with the power of the union but it has also a lot to do with the people that you deal with on the management side.' 'I would say that the quality of the industrial relations is very good. We generally talk about problems for both sides then we both try to work them out with the minimum of problems for either side and basically come up with a compromise.'

These differences of opinions did not prevent the social partners from cooperating in a pragmatic way. Arrangements were found, in particular on points on which the contract had not made a clear decision or on situations not anticipated in its wording.

7.2.2 A Clear Separation of the Areas Under Control

So, how did the two parties of this Maryland plant reach compromise between such opposing views? A clear separation of each field of competence was the local answer given to this question. The contract clearly set out the rights of each of the parties. The union and the management both accepted this separation between management rights and union rights. In short, once a union has established itself in a company, the company plays the role of a customer who must precisely formulate its needs and the expected flexibility in how its workforce is used. The union occupies the position of exclusive supplier of this workforce at the level of hourly workers.[9]

Acting as a customer, the employer naturally intends to remain in control of determining the number of employees needed to satisfy the market demand. The employer keeps control of the production organization and rules within the company. The agreement negotiated in the Maryland plant with the union explicitly stated this:

> To the extent that is not limited or modified by the specific terms of this Agreement, Management authority and the exercise thereof shall remain exclusively in the Management (. . .) The Company may establish and post work rules, safety, and security rules and regulations, and rules of conduct, the violation of which may carry penalties. The Company reserves the right to extend, limit, curtail, or cease any or all operations.

The local union leader had no objection: 'It is their plant, they do pay our salaries, therefore they want as much say over what we're gonna do, when we're gonna do and with what, as much as they can.' In the event of cyclical recession, for example, this broad definition of the management rights allowed it, for example, to immediately begin laying off workers, whereas, in other Western countries such as France, unions are entitled to ask legal authorities to intervene and bring the workers certain guarantees, in the name of the defence of the 'social public order'.[10]

At the same time, the union has its union rights and would never give up an inch of ground in its own sphere. For instance, the union monitored the internal mobility of its members. The distribution of overtime and the possibility of setting vacation dates must comply with the negotiated rules which give a primordial role to the plant seniority. The agreement provided that in the event of layoffs, the most recently hired employees would be the ones who leave the company first. In the event of a vacant position, the agreement gave priority to the workers who, for equal qualification, had the longest service in the plant. The defence of this primacy granted to plant seniority was in this Maryland plant a non-negotiable point as the Chairman of the union stated: 'Areas of control I would have to say, at that time, and that's a major point that seniority is irrevocable. We would never give that position off'.

This clear separation of jurisdictions seemed to be acceptable to both parties. This separation in no way prevented management from directly informing their employees regarding various topics concerning their company. Many managers of other American firms are convinced of the merits of participative management and are ready to share certain decisions with their employees. The local union will never object to this management right as long as management respects their own union rights. It is meaningful within the cultural benchmarks shared by both parties in the United States.

Such a separation would certainly surprise trade unionists in Northern Europe or Germany who attach great importance to being involved in the decisions made within their company. Undoubtedly, this would anger French union representatives. Despite the fact that most French workers are not union members, union leaders consider themselves entitled by law to be the workers' voice. In their view, this obliges management to inform and consult them on the most important subjects. They demand to be formally informed first by management as representatives of an institution representing employees.

7.2.3 Industrial Relations Dealt with as Business Relations

American union leaders have another vision of their role. They lead a bargaining unit. Their role is to negotiate the agreement with the management and monitor its implementation. One of their main functions is to represent their members whenever one of them considers that he has been deprived of the rights that the provisions of the contract give him. If it were to fail to fulfil this obligation, the union could be sued by its own members. In return for the legal service provided, such as negotiating the agreement and monitoring its application, the union receives their contribution directly from the company, deducted from their wages.

They are the heirs of a very old tradition, born in England. 'Every person who sells his labour', writes Adam Smith, 'becomes in some measure a merchant', assimilating those who work for others to an independent producer and those for whom they work to their client (d'Iribarne, 2009). Not surprisingly, the growth of factories and the development of the wage system labour force have naturally disrupted this vision of the working relationship. The idealized symbolic equality that, in Tocqueville's times, was expected[11] between the independent producer and his client no longer existed. Work was still considered as a commodity but the balance of power had changed. The expression '*wage slavery*' appeared, which denounced this imbalance and the associated risks allowing employers to impose their laws and price on those who only have their labour force to sell to ensure their subsistence.

This vision of work as a commodity to be sold at best price by workers—remaining as long as possible as external to the firm they worked for—was not shared out of Britain in the early age of the industrial revolution. German workers aspired to have their word on the production organization and to be much more integrated inside a firm considered as a potential labour community (Biernacki, 1995). One century later, these workers were the first to benefit from the first social laws which partly took their demands into consideration. The obvious differences that today separate the American and German visions of industrial relations are embedded in very long national traditions.

The possibility finally granted to American workers (Vinel, 2006) to form a trade union in 1842 made it possible to restore a form of equality in wage bargaining and to find a solution to the legal dilemma represented by the conciliation of the freedom to contract and the fight against deprivations of liberty that may result, in practice, from the implementation of this principle (Foner, 1998).

The Wagner Act—which established in 1935 the present institutional framework for industrial relations in the United States—aims to promote a certain balance and justice in the negotiations between 'suppliers' and job seekers (Baremberg, 1993). Thanks to its monopoly of employee representation,[12] the union should be able to restore a more equal bargaining relationship, which itself guarantees a fairer agreement by restoring a certain balance between the bargaining powers of the two parties. Restoring balance between the parties[13] and getting out of the 'wage slavery' then appeared as a politically legitimate claim even though the dominant economic circles at the time opposed it—in the United States as in other Western countries—with all their strengths.

In this commercial vision of the employment relationship, the union appears as the tough negotiator of the value of their members' work, still regarded as a commodity that needs to be bought at a fair price. Industrial relations are mainly seen as a bargaining situation between the company, which formulates its needs, and the union, which 'sells' its members' workforce. The other issues linked to the ordinary functioning of the firm are dealt with by the two parties with the same bargaining approach, as the union chairman of the Maryland plant explained:

> We meet and generally come up with a reasonable answer for both sides because generally any questions that we come up with, the result, no matter what it is, is dollars and cents, if it's cleaning something up and make it better or whatever, it costs money to clean it up.

To reconcile these partly common and partly contradictory demands and interests, a negotiation is scheduled on a regular basis. This negotiation should be regularly reviewable to allow each of the parties involved to retain control over the commitments they make.

7.2.4 Two Similar Approaches

One can only be struck by the similarity between the way in which Americans try to find an acceptable balance in hierarchical relations, as seen in Chapter 4, and industrial relations, as seen in the Maryland plant.

Under the MBO (see Chapter 1), subordinates give their managers the right to define, within the framework of their responsibilities, the objectives assigned to them. 'Just tell me what you want and I'll get it to you', summed up, in one sentence, a foreman from the Maryland plant. It is later up to the employees to deliver the requested service. It could be said that they treat the person they work for like their internal customers, under the condition that the rules regulating their relationship have been fully clarified.

There is some similarity with the way in which management and the union understand their cooperation.

The detailed formalization of both objectives and indicators to objectively measure their achievement is at the heart of MBO. The same concern can be found in the industrial relations in the letter of the articles of agreement. This detailed formalization is considered as an essential guarantee given to each party. It explains the care taken in defining it, with a wealth of detail. Some articles of the agreement were negotiated in the Maryland plant:

> Plant Seniority length of continuous service commencing the date of first employment or re-employment following a break in continuous service with the Company; Seniority was established in alphabetical order by last names in those instances where two or more employees have been hired on the same day.

> Should any employees subsequently change their name, they would continue to maintain their position in the seniority listing as it was originally on their date of hire.

The same attention to detail governed the letter of many other articles of the convention, such as the one setting out the organization of lunch breaks:

> During the normal work day, arrangements will be made that employees can eat lunch reasonably close to the middle of the shift. The time may vary slightly. The plant will start the lunch period between the 3rd and 5th hours. Every effort will be made to apply this policy consistently in the plant. Deviations will occur only in emergency situations.

This attention to detail does not exclude that the good faith of the actors can also be called upon, in accordance with the legal definition of bargaining cited above, to admit some breaches of the rule: the text promotes the ideas of *arrangements* and *efforts*.

Finally, there is the same reference to an ideal balance between the parties so that the outcome of their negotiations can be regarded as fair, whether it is the manager and his employee or the union and the company. For the MBO practice to be fair, the 'client manager' must have specified his requests in detail and the employee—once he has verified that the conditions required to satisfy this order are met—must have freely given his consent and thus have undertaken to deliver. It is also necessary that a certain balance, a certain equality in negotiating capacity, be respected so that the agreement finally reached can sincerely satisfy both parties. The same concern can be found with regard to the negotiation of the agreement.

This equality between the parties is not guaranteed, whether it is the hierarchical relations between managers and their employees or the negotiation between employers and unions. This balance remains the common reference to which the Americans refer when judging the fairness of a situation, as the union leader of the Maryland plant said: 'I think that we have gone to an issue which is basically a 50–50 deal with in both sides, a check and balance situation. There is you know, a certain degree of fairness . . . we are at a good place here.'

7.2.5 A Shared Community Reference

The functioning of industrial relations, organized around an uncompromising use of the rights granted by the contract to each of the two parties, could give, at first sight, a negative image of cooperation between the company and the union. This first impression needs nuance. As we saw in Chapter 4 (pp. 78–79), managers could be very strict in controlling the proper execution of their requests while at the same time showing warm consideration towards their employees. Despite appearances, this combination could also be found in the functioning of industrial relations. Without these shared moral values, the operations in the Maryland plant would have been paralysed by an accumulation of time-consuming legal procedures, as explained by the union chairman:

> If you have got a guy that says: 'I don't care what they say, I'm gonna do it this way and now', they have to do what they have to do, then you have a lot of confrontations all the time. It turns itself around to where... the company fights the employees and the employees want to fight the company.

Neither management nor the union were ready to compromise on the defence of their interests simply in order to improve the quality of their cooperation. However, they clearly shared principles such as respecting their interlocutors and giving credit to good faith. This respect made it possible to obtain a certain fluidity in the settlement of situations for which the letter of the former agreement contract did not allow complex and unforeseen situations to be settled in a simple and unambiguous manner.

Managers, dissatisfied with the performance of one of their employees, can inform and even fire this employee in compliance with the company's rules. But the employee, still a member of the working community, must be respected as a person and as a citizen. The same principle applies to industrial relations. The union chairman of the Maryland plant, for example, attributed the variations in the internal social climate to the contrasting personalities of the successive CEOs of the factory:

> We had changes. I don't know how many different CEOs we had in this company that have changed the industrial relations. Over the years, we have gone [successively] from a decent CEO, [then] to no change [and later] to a bad change for us when the CEO thought the employees were animals, you know, and we had hard times because that filters down through the other people on the management side and we had a direct reflection upon the amount of grievances, then we went to a CEO who was a people-oriented person, as well as company-oriented. The CEO we have now, I will rate him as totally company, OK, but also having some awareness of the people of the plant.

The ability of local stakeholders to settle disputes between themselves amicably—for example, in the interpretation of the contract or in the treatment of situations that they had not foreseen—was the best indicator of the quality of 'social dialogue', as our union chairman perceived: 'It's not my objective, to have everything written in the book so they can't be changed, because there are certain things that have to change. How many, I don't know, but what I know is that we deal with that all the time.' Failing this, the parties accepted in the agreement to call on external arbitrators, whose remuneration would be borne by the party whose request had been rejected, a condition likely to deter procedural abuses.

By using the word 'brothers' to designate their members, as ironically mentioned by the Industrial Relations Manager, the local union was reducing the scope of the working community deliberately to 'hourly workers'.[14] Yet its message, through the religious connotation of the word *brother*, made clear references to the cherished notion of community. The American firms developing a strong corporate culture also mobilize this metaphorical vision of the company as a community asking all its members to share its values (see Chapter 9, p. 172). In this register, which competes with that of the union, it is legitimate for management—which guides the community—to praise those who have best served the community (celebrating for instance the Employee of the Month). By doing so, these companies clearly challenge the egalitarian option of the union, rarely welcome in such firms, while defending the same communitarian principle.

In a context of crisis, as the US automotive sector experienced in the 1990s with competition from Japanese manufacturers, these two approaches could be brought together in a surprising combination of corporate patriotism, assumed by both parties, and uncompromising bargaining when it came to renegotiating the agreement between the company and the union. Visitors to the Ford plants in Michigan might be greeted by a team composed of a management representative and a representative of the UAW (United Automobile Workers), who made such similar speeches that it was very difficult to know who was who. However, posters within the factory called on workers to set aside reserves to build up a war treasury to finance a possible long strike in support of the negotiation of the next agreement, where the union hoped to be able to recover the many benefits it had had to grant the employer in the previous agreement.

7.3 Conclusion

The two examples presented in this chapter show, each in its own way, the extent to which industrial relations practices and rules are as culturally embedded as other management practices.

The New Caledonian example shows the limits of transposition into a very different cultural context of an institutional framework which, in its original version, knew how to make sense of the cultural references of those who had built it (Segal, 2011). The American example shows how, in order to function effectively, the bargaining system must not deviate either from the ideal balance between the parties' negotiating powers or from each party taking into account the moral dimension that brings them together—despite their conflicting interests—in the same productive community.

The International Labour Organization defends universal principles[15] to promote the merits of social negotiation, knowing that it is far from being a reality in all countries of the world:

> From the ILO perspective, collective bargaining is an important way for workers, employers and their organizations to reach agreement on issues related to employment. Collective bargaining can be an important means for building trust. This trust can be reinforced through dialogue which continues after bargaining ends. Solutions that are built on trust and enjoy the genuine support of both sides are more likely to be respected. This is due to the sense of participation and ownership inherent in the process. As a result, unnecessary disputes, and disruptions through industrial action, can more easily be avoided.
> (ILO, 1998)

Collective bargaining will only be synonymous with trust-building—as stated in the ILO charter—if the meaning given to the collective bargaining in the local framework of references is positive. Our two examples teach us that collective bargaining does not mean the same thing in the various situations presented. It does not mean the same thing for Oceanians and Europeans in New Caledonia. The American understanding of fair industrial relations is not similar to the one given in France. In France, signing agreements when in a weak position (an option which is acceptable to American unions) would be considered as a dishonourable submission to a dominant authority holder (see chapter 3, p. 64). Calling for a one-day strike, as French trade unions often do, to express symbolic opposition to the management's plans would perplex American trade unionists. Extending the field of our comparison to other countries will confirm these findings. For example, on both sides of the Rhine, people do not have the same reading of the working situation and, consequently, the same vision of the content of a fair and constructive social dialogue. In Germany, active trade union participation is deemed a positive contribution to the building of an effective order desired by all members of the organization (see Chapter 4, p. 87). In Germany, the ILO social dialogue model is considered reasonable and acceptable. This is clearly not the case in France and those who tried to convince French unions to adopt their neighbours' practices have to date always failed.

Notes

1. 'Caroud : toute une histoire', Desbouiges, F., Tromparent, D. CNC, 2015.
2. Christian Thuderoz, 'Palabre coutumier et négociation collective', conference given at the Tjibaou Centre, Nouméa, May 2011.
3. This figure of the union hero is embodied, for example, in the figure of Etienne Lantier in Emile Zola's famous novel *Germinal*.

4. See endnote 1.
5. Patrice Godin, 2015. 'Les échanges sont le souffle de la coutume : logiques sociales de la "vie" et de la "puissance" en pays hyeehen', Ph.D Dissertation in social and cultural anthropology, defended September 30, 2015, Université de Nouvelle Calédonie.
6. 'Good faith' is used in several articles of the agreement between the union and the company.
7. US Code 1976, Vol.8, Title 29 LABOR, p. 718. §158. D, obligation to bargain collectively.
8. There is a strong contrast with the comments we received, at the same period, from the Industrial Relations Manager of a French–Canadian plant, which was also unionized according to the same legal rules imported from the neighbouring United States. This industrial relations manager, a former trade unionist who had moved to the management side, defined his relations with the new local trade union leader as follows: 'He is not a friend, he is not an enemy, he is someone who can help you' (Segal, 2002: 17–40).
9. Employees and managers, who receive a monthly wage, are called *salaried workers*. The other workers, covered by the agreement between union and management, are called *hourly workers*.
10. This public intervention in France is included in labour laws as explained by French law Professor Alain Supiot: 'In France, the dominant conception of labour law has always been that of legislative interventionism to protect employees. Labour relations continue to be considered as contractual relations but they are subject to rules of public policy designed to protect the weaker party to this contract', Mückenberger, U., Supiot, A., in Zimmerman, B., Didry, C., Wagner, P, (eds.), Editions MSH, Paris, 1999. 'Le travail et la nation : histoire croisée de la France et de l'Allemagne', (p. 88).
11. This symbolic equality described by Tocqueville was not self-evident when it came to the relationship between domestic workers and their employers (Foner, 1998).
12. Once the union has obtained recognition by obtaining a majority of workers' votes, union membership becomes compulsory.
13. In the name of respecting the balance, the Wagner Act was later supplemented—notably in 1947 by the Taft Hartley Act—which prohibited a number of unfair labour practices, either by management or the union, that could alter this balance.
14. ILO Convention 154 on social dialogue.
15. *ILO Declaration on Fundamental Principles and Rights at Work and its Follow-up adopted by the International Labour Conference at its Eighty-sixth Session, Geneva, 18 June 1998 (Annex revised 15 June 2010).*

8
Customer Relations

A Japanese customer recounted her misadventure in a Parisian department store:

> As it is the sales season, large bargain bins are laid out with special offers. I start searching and end up choosing two panties and two bras. Then the saleswoman comes behind my back and grabs the underwear off my hands: 'Not like that!' I don't understand what I did wrong; I apologize and explain to the saleswoman that I must have misunderstood what is written because I speak poor French. 'That's no reason for mixing panties and bras brands.'
>
> (Nakamura, 2012, p. 47)

After such an experience, our Japanese narrator quickly concluded that customers were treated badly in France and that even the employees of the most famous department stores were rude and cavalier. In other circumstances, clients may, however, experience services that far exceed their expectations. An American lady living in Paris recounted her experience in a computer store. She wanted to have an advertising flyer printed so as to launch her new activity. At first, the shopkeeper gave her a sceptical look; printing was not part of the services the shop provided. Although she addressed him in French, he said he did not understand what she wanted. Once she had explained in detail what had brought her to the store manager, conveyed her dismay at not finding a solution, and begged him to do her that favour, he said that he would see what he could do. Thirty minutes later, he looked into her problem and opened the document on his computer. After perusing the leaflet, he told her that it was really ugly and could not be sent out as it was. After listening to her translation of the document, he suggested several changes. Improving the layout took them quite some time. By the time he had finalized a document that looked 'absolutely gorgeous' and printed it, it was one hour past the store closing time. She expected to be charged a lot of money for the work that had finally been much more extensive than what she had first requested, but he refused any payment, wished her good luck with her business and invited her to come back if needed (Platt, 1994: 79–80). These contrasting experiences demonstrate that customer satisfaction is not systematically neglected by French salespeople.

Such a diversity of interactions could suggest that satisfying clients is only a matter of people and moods, that one must find the right person; nice, kind and in

Cross-Cultural Management Revisited: A Qualitative Approach. Philippe d'Iribarne, Sylvie Chevrier, Alain Henry, Jean-Pierre Segal, and Geneviève Tréguer-Felten, Oxford University Press (2020).
DOI: 10.1093/oso/9780198857471.001.0001

a good mood, at the time of the interaction. In fact, satisfying a customer will vary with the situation. Is it a business connection between companies or a transaction between a shopkeeper and an individual? What is the purpose of the transaction? Is it to acquire a product or to obtain a service? Is it an everyday-use object or service? Is it to buy a very sophisticated or tailor-made product, or a product or service endowed with strong emotional dimensions; a scarce product or service; a public service? Depending on these professional contexts, several types of customers will emerge: users, citizens, consumers, patients, etc. who have expectations that will not be met in the same way.

Not only does the desire to satisfy one's customer vary according to individuals and circumstances, but a great variety of business situations entail different ways of obtaining that satisfaction. We will nevertheless show that within a given society, common cultural references give meaning to such contradictory situations as those in which service is abominable, correct, or zealous, because they are all underpinned by a shared understanding of the social relations between suppliers and customers.

The purpose of this chapter is to give examples of the various ways in which customer relations are conceived in different parts of the world so as to understand better what is at stake behind the widely-shared slogan that customer satisfaction is essential. Judging by mission statements and principles of management, customer satisfaction has indeed become one of all organisations' priority objectives; however, the diversity of cultural meanings awarded to the social relation taking place between a customer and his or her supplier is not given enough attention. Using increasingly sophisticated and abundant data, companies strive to get to know their customers better and adjust their offer accordingly; simultaneously, they frame customer service relations through prescriptions conveyed to the staff in contact. They do not, however, pay enough attention to the mental models for social interactions that the person serving the client harbours, models which influence the way he or she follows, or not, the prescribed conduct. Sales relations are not only of an economic nature; they are also social and, as such, are embedded in cultural universes of meaning. Once the social nature of these relations is taken into account, the concrete interactions taking place between a seller and his or her customer can be seen from a new perspective. Whether one considers one's client as a partner, a family member, a friend, or the king in person, one perceives the way to satisfy him or her in a rather different manner.

The first section of the chapter shows to what extent considering the role played by culture in one's model of customer–supplier relations differs from the usual ways of approaching the subject. Three situations located in three different countries are presented in the second part; they reveal how diverse the models of social relations between customers and suppliers can be. The final section exposes the way relationships with customers get influenced by culture, thus putting into perspective the universalist slogan affirming the primacy of customer service in firms.

8.1 Customer Relations Cultural Dimension: a Blind Spot

Customer relations are part of the marketing function, taken in its broadest sense. The challenge is to develop the business by fine-tuning the adaptation of the product or service to the market segment it is targeting. Clients are approached through their needs, which the organization seeks to satisfy. In today's globalized context, international markets are to be approached according to local customers' specific expectations. Hence the interest cross-cultural marketing is showing for clients' cultures, with culture being defined as the usual social practices of a given community (Rugimbana & Nwankwo, 2003). In practice, companies adapt their offers to local customs: for instance, in India, McDonald's, the hamburger specialist, replaces beef with chicken and offers vegetarian sandwiches.

More recently, new technologies and sophisticated data processing have enabled marketing professionals to refine customer information (initially defined by segments) so as to identify customers individually. Customer Relationship Management (CRM) focuses on identifying specific consumption profiles in order to meet or, better still, to anticipate demands by offering products and services tailored to each individual. However, CRM remains within the paradigm of adapting the product to the target without thinking that the very meaning of the customer–supplier relationship can vary from one cultural universe to another. What is being sought is the finest possible understanding of the client. For example, Iyer, Sharma and Bejou, (2005) argue, particularly in relation to transition or developing economies, that national contexts can have an impact on 'the level of service expected by the client' and encourage those responsible for designing relational marketing strategies to 'challenge their personal assumptions and replace their own value and belief systems with real and concrete research about the interpretations of the world around them'. Whenever the cultural issue, which includes many aspects other than national culture, is taken into account, it is only as a feature that characterizes customers' consumption patterns and helps to define their profiles; it is not considered as a factor likely to influence the sales relationship itself.

Customer relations are also addressed in the literature on service management, a sector in which co-producing a service requires a direct interpersonal relationship between producer and consumer. Thus, many authors develop specific principles of management for the front office staff including: designing service scripts that frame the development of the relationship; identifying critical moments that can turn a relationship into either failure or success; managing difficult and deviant clients; managing emotions; ergonomics and line managers' support to the front office staff. They focus on staff management so as to ensure a quality service offer and, in particular, on interaction management, but the universality of good practices in such an area does not get questioned. While differences between types of services are indeed mentioned as elements to be considered when defining appropriate practices, the idea that customer relations could take on different meanings in different cultures is not covered by this literature. Guiding people's behaviours through general prescriptions without seeking to understand the social relationships at stake in customer–supplier in customer-supplier relations is an indisputable possibility.

The topic of negotiation, whether analysed from a comparative or from an intercultural perspective, does not focus on the cultural preferences of consumers but on the relationship between sellers and their customers. Various studies show that the context, the exchange process, as well as the protagonists' profiles, change according to the countries concerned (Usunier, 1992; Faure, 2004). Thus, a distinction is made between cultures in which the relationship takes precedence over the transaction and those in which the object of the transaction comes first and the relationship second. The interaction rituals to be respected are specified, country per country, highlighting, for example, the unavoidable exchanges of gifts or of business cards held with both hands and the bowing to Asian interlocutors. This literature also focuses on the different frameworks that modalities of information exchange and concessions are to follow, depending on the country. Explicit exchanges prevail here while implicit messages are predominant elsewhere. These analyses shed light on many practical aspects of 'trade between cultures' (Usunier, 1992), they do not give access to the meaning of these rituals. Any sales relationship implies, on the one hand, an adjustment between demand and offer and, on the other hand, an interaction between those who formulate them. Understanding the references which give meaning to the interaction goes beyond learning rituals: it makes it possible to avoid misusing them and helps to face hitherto unknown business situations.

Finally, the sociology of work and occupations addresses the different postures assumed by salespeople in different situations. They consider customer–supplier relations from the perspective of the social relations to which the protagonists instinctively refer. For example, Lazarus (2012) shows that, depending on the client's economic resources and their potential value to the banker, different social connections are likely to emerge in their relationship. The banker can turn into a merchant, a judge, an advisor, or a saviour. In general, sociologists tackle the balance between the social connections and power relations that may arise between the protagonists of a service relationship. However, they deem these relations universal; they do not understand to what extent the identified roles and postures may emerge or be declined differently, according to the national contexts concerned; and they rarely compare the latter. For example, the fact that the same relationship is perceived as an oppressive power relation in one cultural context and interpreted as legitimate dependence in another is not really addressed. However, these interpretations play a paramount role in how service providers will interact with their clients. Whoever claims to improve customer satisfaction must therefore not only strive to get to know customers better through in-depth studies of their expectations, they should also be interested in the people serving them and in their universes of meaning concerning service relations.

In the remainder of this chapter, we will not contribute to the already well-documented literature on considering consumer culture when adjusting products and services, or to the literature on the modalities of negotiation in each location. Instead, we will show that, as could be expected in the case of social relationships, customer relations do not have the same meaning in all cultures and that an effective management of service relations requires disclosing these interpretations.

8.2 Three Examples of Customer Relations Bearing the Stamp of Culture

The very way customer relationship is conceived is of major importance insofar as it structures the interpretation that employees make of a large number of situations encountered in organizations. Gaining a new client to build a business relationship, managing risks and disputes in a business relationship, recovering dues from clients or drafting institutional documents about one's offer (see Chapter 11) all constitute situations that make sense in the light of people's cultural perspective of what customer–supplier relationships should be. As will be shown in this section, examples from China, France, and Côte d'Ivoire, illustrate how diverse such representations can be and point to the concrete effects that these representations can have on protagonists' attitudes and behaviours. The chosen examples correspond to different business relationships; yet all of them illustrate the attitude to adopt when dealing with a dissatisfied customer. They were chosen for their ability to reveal the cultural logics that nourish them and underpin all aspects of customer relations in a given society.

8.2.1 Protecting One's Customer in China

From a Western perspective, sales relationships in China are paradoxical. On the one hand, contracts between partners are systematic, very precise, and detailed, with partners insisting on the need to formalize what is being exchanged. Negotiating them takes time, with details being discussed at length. On the other hand, all partners, both foreign and Chinese, agree that contracts are not respected. In addition, they cannot be used as a protection in the context of legal remedies which, first, remain exceptional so as to avoid direct confrontation and, second, are ineffective due to a biased and failing legal system.

To illustrate the relationship between customers and suppliers in China, we use an example from Duan (2010).

> Once, one of my customers with whom we have a long history of cooperation complained about the poor quality of our products and asked me to go on site to solve the problem. I went to the appointment to speak *sincerely* about the problem. First of all, responsibility must be clarified. If it's mine, I'll take all the goods and change them. If it is his, I am also considering compromises. In the end, it was his, that is, he failed to ensure the necessary maintenance. I still decided to change the parts for them. Why? Why? Because I'm considering our *long-term relationship*. If I had revealed that it was because of the maintenance department shortcomings that the spare parts quickly went out of service, the managers who were really liable for the damage would have been blamed by their superiors. In that case, they would have expressed their *dissatisfaction with me*, but it is with them and not (directly) with their hierarchies that I work. If I put them in a very *embarrassing situation*, it will be difficult for me to see them next time: I risk losing them as customers. On the contrary, if I willingly assume responsibility that is not mine, these really liable people will have a very strong *sense of gratitude* towards me because they owe me something. This context is very favourable for *strengthening our relations*, communication will then be easier and we will understand each other better. This *sentimental* attachment will undoubtedly result in more orders afterwards, more *faithfulness*, more *loyalty*. Our *fates will be more closely linked* (Emphasis added). (Chinese sales agent)

This quotation shows first of all that the sales exchange came along with a set of long-term interests. The value of exchanges was not measured instantly in the one-time operation that was to solve the problem of defective parts; the purpose was to ensure customer faithfulness and loyalty for a recurring business flow—*our fates will be more closely linked.*

This was why the seller did not seek to comply scrupulously with the contract which would have led him to refuse the replacement of the defective parts since their maintenance was the customer's responsibility. He preferred to preserve a peaceful relationship—avoid *dissatisfaction*; do not put customers in *a very embarrassing situation*. The vocabulary used in the quotation emphasizes the importance of taking into account the feelings that were intertwined with interests. The supplier was careful not to trigger the negative feelings that might have emerged from this problematic situation. Instead, the favour that he was implicitly granting his customer would trigger positive feelings that could not but serve his interests. By making arrangements that put his client at ease, the seller initiated a cycle of social debt—a *very strong sense of gratitude; they owe me something*. He was willing to go beyond what the contract required him to do, because he hoped to get some return later. He could not be sure he would get it, but he was counting on it because he knew that his gesture would be interpreted as generosity compared to what he could have done, had he been in strict compliance with the contract. In this dialogue, the contract constituted a reference: by specifying what each party owed the other, it made it possible to benchmark debts or gifts, in case the contract implementation did not follow the terms agreed upon. In other words, it set a reference that made the gaps measurable and allowed the partners to become aware of the nature of their debts. Social relations were made up of mutual debts that had to be honoured in the long run. In this perspective, the contract was a benchmark against which to assess the reciprocity of contributions and concessions.

As shown by this author, finding proper solutions, however difficult the situation might have been, was what concerned the partners in this business relation. Discussion enabled them to find arrangements around the contract. What mattered most in this relation was to preserve the customer's loyalty and to keep up the peaceful social partnership that united them.

The following example highlights how social relations are conceived in France. Although it rests on a very different situation, a training session for saleswomen, the cultural logic underpinning the sales relationship clearly appears.

8.2.2 Training for Sales in France

The situation we are going to analyse is taken from the research conducted by Hanique (2004, p. 202) on the transformation of the role of counter tellers at La Poste (the French Post Office). The scene took place during a training session of tellers through role-playing expected to enable them to develop sales. In particular, they had to learn how to deal with a '*grumpy and conservative*' client. The transcribed exchange began when the trainer interrupted one of the tellers as she performed the exercise:

THE TRAINER: You are La Poste [the Post Office]. So, say instead: 'La Poste offers you' or 'La Poste commits itself'. You must think of the best that La Poste can offer.

CORINNE: What's best for them or best for La Poste?

THE TRAINER: It's the same thing. La Poste offers the best for its customers.

[CHUCKLES, MOCKERY . . .]

THE TRAINER: Your job is to satisfy your customers, that is, to respond to their requests and identify their latent needs. For example, if a customer presents himself with a package that he has wrapped up himself, tell him that La Poste offers a range of ready-to-ship products that guarantee a safe delivery.

SANDRA: When I am a customer somewhere, I trust someone when I know that what they are offering me is what they would have chosen for themselves. And at the counter, when I see that customers arrive with a well-made, well-wrapped package, I don't see why I would honestly tell them to unpack their package and pay three times the delivery price to buy a La Poste parcel!

THE TRAINER: Well, that's a mistake! To be confident, customers need to have real professionals in front of them. And real professionals are tellers who know their products. There you go. The clients do not come to see 'any Joe Bloggs', who 'in their place' would do like this or that, but Sandra, Corinne, or Jackie who are professional tellers. You must not put yourself in their shoes.

SANDRA: You're right, if we put ourselves in their shoes, we wouldn't sell much.

During this exchange, the tellers questioned the trainer's advice and, at first sight, the protagonists appeared to have very different visions of customer relations. However, these two visions (whose divergences will be explained further on) both complied with the French conception of proper customer relationships, as we shall see in what follows.

To start with, all the participants in this session agreed on one point: what one *is* determines how one should act. In other words, a person defines what he or she must do, according to his or her status, profession, and position, in the relationship: 'you are the Post Office. So, say…'; 'when I am a customer'. Even if the trainer and the tellers drew different conclusions, they concurred on the challenge that being tellers represented, and on the fact that one's professional posture dictated what one's conduct should be.

Beyond the debate, the protagonists agreed that sellers should be considered as 'professionals' who were to judge what was best for their customers. For the trainer, La Poste had to 'satisfy customers, i.e. respond to their requests and identify their latent needs'; real professionals knew how to detect what these needs were, even if they were not explicitly formulated. Customers were to be satisfied, not simply by responding to their requests but by going beyond them and judging on their behalf what they might need, even though they themselves are unaware of it! Customers had to be advised by professionals, who were familiar with the Post Office services and knowhow so as to identify clients' needs, rather than by Joe Bloggs, a philistine whose opinion was not trustworthy. The trainee tellers were not to be outdone: they declared that they were putting themselves in their clients' shoes—'what they would have chosen for themselves', but they were not doing so only in a personalized empathetic way. They first established themselves as competent evaluators of the technical aspects: 'when I see that customers arrive with a well-made, well-wrapped package, I don't see why I would honestly tell them to unpack their package…'. They, the tellers, were, in the last resort, judges of what a good package looked like and whether it should be undone! The protagonists agreed that they had to 'offer clients what was best for them'. Their opposition did not reside in this common principle, but, more specifically, in how to determine what was 'best for clients'.

Another remarkable point of convergence in this story is that no one used the word 'seller'. The trainer did not use it and insisted on the necessity to be 'real professionals'. The tellers did not use it either, they preferred to say 'someone who offers me what they would have chosen . . . '. All agreed that the function consisted of 'proposing', 'committing', 'guaranteeing', etc. The protagonists obviously concurred on their unwillingness to consider the business through its financial aspects: money, profits, pecuniary interest. At no time did the trainer say that the ready-to-be-shipped parcel would generate more revenue for the company and that the interest of La Poste should have been privileged. The trainer strived to show that it provided customers with professional service. He placed the tellers in the position of expert advisors, not of salespeople trying to increase the company's turnover. When the tellers used the word 'price', it was to discredit the recommended sales approach which, from their point of view, was close to a scam—*pay three times the price*. In the eyes of all the training session participants, professional tellers had to propose, not sell with interest, thus stepping in the tracks of Molière's *Bourgeois Gentilhomme* who stated 'mere interest is something so base that an honest man should never discover an attachment to it'.[1]

The protagonists of this training session used the same reference system to give meaning to the situations: they agreed that they had to rise to the state of 'professionals', and that as such, they were in charge of knowing how to define what was best for their clients, instead of the latter and on their behalf. This model of social relationships based on advisors' expertise allowed the rebalancing of sensitive relations between clients liable to behave in a kingly manner and suppliers potentially succumbing to their whims by their need to sell.

Of course, this common framework for interpreting the social relationships between clients and suppliers did not erase the differences of opinions between the tellers and their trainer. For the trainer, the company had translated what constituted the best service to customers into a range of products that guaranteed sending convenience and content preservation. From his point of view, counter tellers could, by mastering this range, access a new professionalism. Conversely, the tellers, who were experienced in dealing with customers, claimed to know better than their hierarchy what the best offer was for each customer. What caused their chuckles and resistance was that La Poste and its hierarchy were trying to deprive them of their judgement criteria in their interactions with customers. By reducing their personal advisory know-how through the systematic use of standardized services, the trainer meant to deprive them of their ability to offer ad hoc solutions. In addition, the so-called technical expertise linked to their familiarity with the product range did not adequately conceal its financial nature. In other words, the dispute between the trainer and the tellers centred on how best to appear the expert in front of the customer.

Thus, beyond their differences, these two approaches had in common their way of putting at a distance the monetary connection to the client, either by not mentioning it at all or by offering the cheapest service. Both perspectives focused on the product that enabled the service to be delivered. Above all, the protagonists shared their emphasis on professionals' expertise: expertise legitimized the fact that sellers knew better than their customers what the latter needed. It somehow placed professionals 'above' their clients in that they had a better grasp of the possible responses to their needs. It should be noted that highlighting professionals' expertise in a client relationship was a central point for all protagonists, even though tellers' work required neither high qualifications nor sophisticated knowledge. The value of expertise, however modest it might be, made it possible not to grant the client the last word. Satisfying customers meant providing service, not being at their service in the sense of doing everything they requested, which would have meant recognizing a dependence tie that would be difficult to accept (see Chapter 3 p. 64).

This example echoes a myriad of very diverse service situations, all marked in the French context by this prevailing social relationship between sellers who define themselves as experts and clients whose wishes will only be satisfied if the experts consider them to be relevant.

With the next example, we deal, as in the first case, with a situation where a dispute between a customer and a sales representative got settled, but this time in an African context.

8.2.3 Managing a Dispute in Côte d'Ivoire

This case is based on the memoirs of the former CEO of the Ivorian Electricity Company (Zadi Kessy, 1998), who recounted a particularly tense exchange between a customer with several months' unpaid bills and one of the company's sales managers (Henry, 1999).

This case, all the more interesting as it ends with an astonishing 'happy end', highlights the logic underpinning business relations in a West African cultural context.

To start with, the customer—an important political figure—presented himself at the company's offices; he was worried: his electrical connection had just been cut off because his unpaid bills amounted to more than one million West African CFA francs [about €1,500]. The power cut-off was the reason for his visit at the Ivorian Electricity Company. He asked them to restore the power immediately. Faced with this request, the sales manager asked her own manager to let her negotiate payment facilities with the customer.

> With all due respect to his rank, she offered him the possibility to pay half of the outstanding debts immediately, before the power was restored, and the rest in three monthly instalments.

In accordance with the contract, supply could be restored provided that the customer paid off his debts. From the very beginning of the exchange, the sales manager proposed to spread the repayment of arrears. Considering the social position of her interlocutor, she did not even mention the late payment penalties usually applied in such cases. Despite the 'subtlety' and 'all the respect' she seemed to demonstrate, the customer got angry:

> The customer refused the offer in a brutal way. He demanded the restoration of electricity *unconditionally*, especially since he had been made that promise by a company official. He insisted on reminding the sales manager that he was one of the pioneers of the emancipatory struggle in our country and that she owed the political struggle he had waged with all those of his generation the job that she now had and of which she was so proud. When the customer noticed that she did not *obey his threats*, he shouted in a moment of anger: 'In what country are we, where small leaders think they are big and where real leaders have no authority and *are flouted*!' (Emphasis added)

In his anger, the customer made a veiled threat at the sales manager's job. She was the one who should feel personally indebted to those like him who fought for the country's independence. He therefore expected her to 'obey his threats'. But when he saw that she did not submit, he got angry and blamed her for wanting to 'flout' leaders' authority.

> After his tantrum, the sales manager made him a new offer that he accepted and he immediately had a cheque handed over to her.
>
> The sales manager made it a point of honour to restore power immediately. Without any problems, our client respected the payment schedule for the deadlines. He even *honoured* the sector by coming in person to pay one of the bills. During this visit, he left the following message for the sales manager to the litigation agent who greeted him: 'Give her my business card and tell her that *she works well*. I *congratulate* her and *encourage* her.' Flattered by these compliments, our sales manager called him back to thank him. He took the opportunity to give her some *advice*. (Emphasis added)

The oral exchange, violent as it first was, subsided and ended with an arrangement. Then, both parties endeavoured to stick to their commitments to the best of their abilities: the sales manager 'immediately' restored the power, while the customer scrupulously respected his payment schedule. What was most surprising was that an endless succession of courteous exchanges ensued. The customer, who would undoubtedly not be considered by the reader as a model of virtue, even went so far as to 'congratulate' the sales manager for her good work and 'give her advice'.

This reversal, quite enigmatic when seen from the outside, becomes clearer when considering the two underlying interpretative logic lines. The narrator opposed two types of relationships, one characterized by hostility and personal threats, the other in the form of a continuous exchange of kind and friendly gestures.

When at first, the customer appeared tense, one expected him to focus on the reasons that account for the situation—the unpaid invoices and the contract penalties. Instead, he invoked the malevolent behaviour of the sales manager—her insolence towards the authorities. The case analyst (Henry, 1999) was told a similar example by a Togolese company sales manager who explained that, in comparable circumstances, customers 'will not discuss unpaid invoices. They won't say: "I'm ashamed, I didn't pay"'. They will first say: 'Your agents have behaved badly towards my family. They were very, very, very insolent with me. [...] One of your agents made *a derogatory remark in my home.* Damn it! That's *nasty*! Call him up, I want to meet him! He's not thinking about the power cut right now. He wants to meet the agent. It's quite a ceremony!' Such a reaction could be seen as a ploy to divert attention. But testimonies concord: a person faced with negative control—a sanction for example—experiences violent fears, to the point of forgetting the objective reasons for the control and suspecting a premeditated attack on his or her person, or on his or her relatives. The sanction, even if legitimate, is spontaneously perceived as a sign of malicious intent. The sales manager's insistence on charging the customer, even if the debts were spread out, confirmed his fears; hence his apparently disproportionate response to the dispute. The relationship is initially interpreted on the basis of people's supposed behaviour and intentions, rather than on the reality of the facts.

Conversely, once agreement had been reached by the protagonists, the author insisted on the quality of the relationship that developed between them. In contrast to the first reaction, what took place consisted of repeated assaults of kindness, thanks, compliments, flattery, and gestures to honour the other. Now that the customer's positive intentions had been confirmed, Zadi-Kessy seemed to consider that it was legitimate for the authority figure to give advice and encourage the saleswoman. As for the latter, her first move had been to avoid applying the penalties due so as not to be accused of malice and to suffer retaliation from a powerful customer; she managed to turn the situation around thanks to her ability to show kindness. Her 'calm', her 'subtlety', and as the author mentioned elsewhere (pp. 189, 190, 209), her 'smile', her 'extreme courtesy', and her 'respect for procedures' (i.e. who did not let herself be impressed by threats) were the keys that enabled her to turn the situation around. One can, for example, imagine that she managed to gently explain to the angry client that, on the contrary, she was only thinking of kindly helping him but that she had to stick strictly to procedures.

In his concluding comments, the author of this narrative pointed to the relational qualities of the company's sales managers as the precise qualities that enabled the company to achieve its objectives. In this context, the quality of the relationship, friendly or unfriendly, was in some respects more decisive than the very purpose of the commercial transaction, especially if binding rules were to be enforced.

Even if these examples illustrated quite diverse business situations, they showed that cultural logics always underpin the different facets of customer–supplier relationships. Most importantly, these three cases illustrated how the relationship between a service provider and his or her client could be interpreted in very different terms depending on the culture. In each context, the way customer–supplier relationships were conceived needed to be clarified so as to give meaning to what, regardless of the business situation, was at stake.

8.3 The Cultural Embeddedness of Customer Relations

Business relations are not just about exchanging goods for a certain amount of money. They are social relations among people. Even when business is dematerialized, such as in Internet sales, exchanges are possible because stakeholders trust virtual operators. And when buyers do not know the service providers, the presence of a 'trusted third party' is essential to secure the transaction. This extreme case of a sale without direct contact shows that it is the social dimension (reputation, brand, previous experience . . .) that limits risk and creates the proper conditions for an acceptable exchange. All transactions are therefore governed by social relations. And these social relations cannot escape people's cultural references.

As shown in the previous chapters, the management precepts which are taken for granted are rooted in the American culture; they rely upon contract-based transactions. The relationship between sellers and their customers is a relationship of equals bound by a freely defined contract. Both parties' mutual interest is considered and their objective is to find the terms of a win–win agreement. Money is the counterpart for the good(s) provided or the service rendered. What is important is that the terms of the contract are explicit and clear to all parties; they know what they are committing to. The contract is binding and everyone, after having negotiated its clauses more or less fiercely, feels bound by a commitment made with full knowledge of the facts. As contracts are the main regulation instruments of business relations, it makes sense that lawyers get mobilized to check any major contract.

In such relationships, customer satisfaction is achieved by responding as closely as possible to their desires. First, sellers endeavour to literally meet the demand. They have to grasp the problems on their customers' sides, understand their priorities and expectations, and strive to respond to them in order to build customer loyalty. It is also common practice to solicit answers to a customer satisfaction questionnaire so as to demonstrate one's scrupulous desire to meet their expectations and to always serve them better.

Should a dispute with the client arise, parties start discussions to resolve it to the satisfaction of both parties, but if one of them feels aggrieved and does not accept the transaction amicably, they will not hesitate to go to court for non-compliance with the contract so as to enforce its terms. Judicial procedures are perceived as ordinary remedies when direct discussions have not enabled a resolution.

In addition to their contractual nature, business relations in the American context also come along with some seductiveness. Selling implies some seduction to convince and finally win the sale, win over competitors, be the best. Gaining is not perpetrated against one's customer; what is sought is a win–win relationship. In such seductive relationships, sellers' behaviours are decisive: to get the sale, smiles, listening, an ability to put oneself in customers' shoes to understand their needs, and setting aside one's ego to focus on customers' concerns are all recommended. The social relationship is balanced insofar as both parties find some benefit in the deal; if indeed customers come first, sellers are largely rewarded by their interests in the sale. Customers get the service and pay according to its quality; sellers receive the payment. It is a balanced exchange between equal partners.

In the three examples developed earlier on, the conception of a seller–customer relationship based on a contract that formalizes the transaction terms around well-understood mutual interests, does not permit an understanding of what was taking place. Other social relationships were at stake, which gave meaning to the observed exchanges.

In the Chinese context, the relationship between the business partners was already fairly strong; the supplier's behaviour aimed at maintaining it, at linking their respective fates more closely by making the customer benefit from a service that was not strictly due. The social relationship that bound them extended beyond the present transaction; they belonged to the same community, a community bound by flows of debts and repayments. In this *Guan Xi* community, everyone is expected to maintain their reputation by ensuring a long-term equity of business flows. Reciprocity is appreciated, not at each exchange level but in the long run. The concept of *Bao*, which means 'pay back', is at the heart of the networking system. The required fairness between contribution and remuneration creates debt and embarrassment when someone receives favours without having earned them. This causes pressure to pay back (Li, 2015). Members are bound by a moral duty to help and assist each other or risk losing face. They are never even. Everyone is expected to maintain relationships and, in return, benefit from the protection of the network.

Relationships within the network are designed on the model of family solidarity. 'Gifts and exchanges of services must be complemented by regular meetings.

The objective is to demonstrate through personal presence the sense of familiarity [*Qinqie Gan*] that one intends to maintain, and to minimise the distance in order to enter into a somewhat "fusional", intimate relationship, as close as can be to the family relationship model' (Ascencio & Rey, 2004: 59). As the authors suggest, the reference in social relations is the family, and in particular filial piety. 'The Chinese have no society other than their family', according to Liang (2010). It is therefore not surprising that customer–supplier relationships should have a strong emotional dimension. One's customer is like a relative who is granted favours and who shows some loyalty to the supplier in return.

However, fair long-term relationships are not the only types of business relations likely to be established in China. When partners do not know each other well; when their relationship has not yet been put to the test and trust well established; the client–supplier connection essentially relies on power and opportunism. The lesser dependent of the two parties endeavours to negotiate as many short-term benefits as possible, and everything seems to be permissible, there are no moral limits. Even when a contract has been signed, the partner does not feel formally committed by the written document, nor by a still embryonic relationship. Then the relationship is that of two strangers pursuing their respective personal interests without any regard for the other's, or even to his or her possible detriment, and in the short term. Opportunism is the dominant rule of conduct in a relationship that has not been established over time.

For instance, in her investigation work on the transformation of a privatized hospital in China, Li[2] (2015) showed the potential difference in caring for patients who knew the hospital staff and for patients who were considered as strangers. On the one hand, employees' acquaintances and relatives were treated with scrupulous care; some doctors, in defiance of all rules, even granted them reductions in medical expenses or provided them with free treatment. On the other hand, staff denounced the fact that, whenever there were no personal links with patients, the latter were more often than not ripped off; [*Zai*], the word used to describe the fact literally translates as 'have their throats slit', 'are killed' or 'are shot down', suggesting particularly brutal treatment.

These examples extracted from the Chinese scene highlight the limits of a universalist economic conception of customer relations in which the object of the transaction would be clearly regulated by the contract and the relationship would give the exchange a human tone around this common interest. However, the cultural embedding of business relations does not mean that only one form of social relations can exist in a given society. The coexistence in China of long-term customer–supplier relations and short-term relations marked by acute opportunism illustrates the variety of concrete forms service relations can take. In the Chinese context, depending on whether social connections are relations of proximity, such as real or assimilated family ties, or social connections between strangers, business relations take completely different forms.

As exposed in Chapter 3 pp. 65–66, in the French context, being subjected to the power of money is part of the fundamental fear. Yielding to personal interests is perceived as abasement when one should instead act on behalf of great causes and personal convictions. Consequently, business relations cannot but take a delicate turn from the outset, since they involve sellers subjected to buyers' desiderata that they will have to try and satisfy so as to obtain the expected financial counterpart. All sorts of words and phrases reveal an entire universe of meaning that, in the French context, points to a fundamental distrust of financial ties. As d'Iribarne (2009) points out, even when it comes with a financial counterpart, the act of selling is not perceived as worthy.

The very word 'client' is not easily accepted in all contexts. State owned firms, for instance, when they were requested to modernize in the 1990s, as was the case of La Poste, the afore-mentioned organization, encountered a great deal of reluctance on the part of their staff to adopt the term 'customers', in lieu of the 'users', 'subscribers', 'beneficiaries' or others, formerly in use. While it is noble to serve the general public, it is far less so to be at the mercy of specific clients' requirements. Even in other professional contexts, replacing 'customer' with other terms such as 'host', 'guest', 'visitor', 'passenger', etc., is quite common. One could see another sign of such reluctance in the linguistic impossibility to translate literally the 'customer-driven' so regularly applied to organizations in company charters or other reference documents of the kind. A 'customer-oriented organization' [*organisation orientée client*] is the closest translation one can find; being customer-oriented does not however imply that everything starts from clients' will; it clearly nuances the dependency relation.

The devaluation of sales functions which is taking place in France is also reflected in tensions on the labour market: these sectors are not very popular, even in some cases where attractive remunerations are offered. In addition, young people entering the sales function often report that they are only training there with a view to moving on to such professions as marketing, where the connection to customers is not so direct. They consider studying the market and managing the product as more rewarding than selling to a demanding clientele. Finally, France is one of the countries where 'small' jobs, including sales, are often replaced by automatic machines, thus eliminating human sales relations. Companies justify this evolution by stating that counter staff and other gas station attendants are to be trained in more qualified professions that will give them the possibility to free themselves from 'ungrateful tasks'.[3]

In this specific universe of meaning, there are, however, resources to make the sales profession nobler and break what is perceived as position disadvantage in sales relations. It gets done through job titles and contents changes: for instance, salespeople may, depending on the sector, be called customer advisors, hosts, technical sales representatives, etc., all of which evacuate, or limit the scope of, the sales inherent to that profession. This vocabulary change is also intended to promote a new type of relationship. What is at stake is no longer executing requests—not to say orders, if we consider the 'order-giver' ['*donneur d'ordres*' is the French designation for the 'principal'] used in subcontracting relationships—on the grounds that one is paid for it, but of listening to one's client, of displaying one's expertise to make a diagnosis of the client's situation and prescribe an appropriate solution. Such a perspective is perceptible in the description that a career counselling agency proposes for a store salesperson:

> The salesperson welcomes customers in the store or at the shelf. He or she helps them to make their choice by presenting them products likely to suit them. He or she has them try items on (clothing, shoes, etc.) or demonstrates certain devices.[4]

The consulting role is highlighted in all sectors; for example, a steel sales engineer describes his job as follows:

> For our customers, we will have the status of a factory representative: we are the ones who will solve all their problems. With them I feel a little like a general medical practitioner: I listen to them, they confide in me, then I make a diagnosis. Either I'm able to solve their problem by myself, or I direct them to a specialist, a Group colleague with expert knowledge.[5]

Counsellors act the way doctors do with their patients; knowledge is on their side, they solve their clients' problems as partners should or, if necessary, refer them to other experts (d'Iribarne, 2009). In this way, the appalling vision of staff 'at the mercy' of clients whose whims are commensurate with their purses gets replaced by the vision of professionals mastering their art. That posture of advisors taking care of their clients is not only valid for large accounts and technical, or tailor-made, products. For example, a traveller asking Parisian metro tellers for a return trip to a given destination, will, quite often, be offered a cheaper daily package that provides the same service. From the company's point of view, this sale will appear unreasonable since it reduces turnover, but the tellers will claim that such an action provides the customer with better service; it fills the need that they have perceived rather than the client's demand.

That is how the sales function can gain its nobility. Expert professionals systematically will be opposed to 'carpet sellers' ['*marchands de tapis*', that is, those who would place too much emphasis on negotiation in the sales process] and to 'soup sellers' ['*vendeurs de soupe*'—those who would not be attentive enough to product technical qualities]. The function refers instead to experts able to offer their clients more than they have requested. Sellers do their clients services the way they think fit and, by delivering more than is strictly expected, they free themselves from a mere executing task of clients' orders.

The relationship between counsellor and novice can even turn into a teacher–student relationship. When asked about his job, a French translator specified that it took time to provide a quality translation and added: 'Clients must be educated. A good translation can only be done within a reasonable time limit.' By saying so, the translator was referring to his unwillingness to sacrifice the quality of his translation for a busy client. His expertise required him to convince his client to respect the reasonable time frame that he needed to provide work befitting a professional. When a seller's position is fragile, for example because his expertise is objectively very limited, thus making an advisor's posture hardly credible, he or she will be particularly sensitive to the form of customers' requests. If clients formulate what could be assimilated to an unkind order or demanding criticism of the service, they are at risk of being ill-treated. Any request that, in the eyes of the seller, attempts to establish a relationship of servility is likely to generate strong resistance, whether in the form of an open and aggressive response or of a more discreet revenge. The seller will want to show that he or she is not at the customer's beck and call, and that treating him or her in this manner is definitely not the way to obtain quality service. The same resistance may also arise when a client does not conform to the profession best practices; in that case, the seller will not hesitate to snub the customer. This is what happened to the Japanese customer, who opens this chapter, when she unintentionally mixed the panty and bra brands. This is also what happened to the customer cited by Segal (2009) who wanted the cheese-bar saleswoman in a supermarket to start to slice the whole cheese he had selected while a piece of the same cheese, already started, was available. When he took offence at her polite but firm refusal and said: 'I thought the customer was king', she replied, 'Ah, absolutely! The customer is king, but we've never known of what exactly!'. Conversely, once customers recognize the salespersons' expertise, expose their problems and rely on them to find a solution, they are likely to obtain zealous service. The sellers can hasten to provide service that far exceeds customers' expectations and sometimes even for free, as was the case for the American lady who was simply asking for printing and finally benefited from additional free editing expertise. That is, in the French context, what differentiates 'being at somebody's service' which conjures up a resented state of dependency and 'rendering service' of one's own free will by mobilizing one's know-how. Sales force management policies will be all the more effective as they are in harmony with these cultural references.

In the case of Côte d'Ivoire, and more broadly of West Africa, the relationship asymmetry or the fact that sellers are dependent upon clients' wishes is not an issue. In the afore-mentioned example, the sales manager accepted the very unbalanced relationship with a leading political figure, and she willingly emphasized their rank difference in the exchange. What worried the protagonists—and the client in particular—were their respective intentions, in the broadest sense. Intentions go beyond the mere potential desire to cheat in the ongoing transaction; they refer more broadly to the will to harm or on the contrary to help. The fundamental fear of being the victim of hidden interests and of bad hidden feelings is revealed in strong defensive reactions, which go beyond the immediate purpose of the transaction.

As shown in Zadi-Kessy's narrative, social relationships are interpreted in the light of two converse types of relations: those binding friends and those opposing enemies. Depending on which of these interpretations applies, behaviours are just as converse. In a relationship between friends, mutual assistance, advice, and services that go beyond expectations, dominate; while relationships between enemies are marked by immense mistrust, suspicion, threats of serious reprisals, and accusations. The challenge in a business relation is therefore to reassure one's customer of one's good intentions, to build, and to maintain a friendly and personal relationship. Such a friendly relationship makes it possible to lower one's guard and work transparently towards the convergence of both parties' interests. Business is all the more serene when feelings are positive and openly expressed. Rituals that promote relationship reassurance are therefore essential.

If, in the social relationships, the personal relationship is more important than the contract, as is the case in the Chinese context, a different interpretation frame applies. While reference to family and to intergenerational ties prevails in China, in West Africa the reference community is that of a society of friends and kinship. Friendship then becomes the yardstick by which the relation with one's client is to be interpreted.

8.4 Conclusion

'The customer comes first', 'the customer is king', 'customer is at the centre of the organization', 'a customer-driven culture', etc. These are all mottos requiring companies to not only give priority to listening to and satisfying customers, but also to organize their production processes according to the added value they will bring the latter. These injunctions have a universal scope: it is obvious and indisputable that customers give the organization its purpose and provide it with the means for its development or, at least, its sustainability. However, behind this universal truth, different types of social images give meaning to the relations between clients and their service providers.

Undoubtedly, the success of the transaction depends to a large extent on the adjustment of supply and demand, but the social relation at stake also has a role to play. If the business relationship conjures up an awkward social situation, the services on offer will not be enough. This chapter has shown how the cultural universe of meaning frames the forms of acceptable social relationships and therefore the legitimate forms of business relationships, which are only a particular form of social relationships. In other words, sales relationships are interpreted and experienced in the light of the representations of social ties that exist in a society. This cultural interpretation influences both the roles assigned to the protagonists and the tools used, such as the contract, to secure the business relationship. Ignoring these representations is not likely to result in customer satisfaction.

Thus, as will be seen in Chapter 10 p. 193, a French project manager referring to his Chinese client, said: 'An evolution is a cost so we can hope that the customer will think before making too many evolutions…or he will pay. That's the way we proceed in Europe. I know that Chinese customer may have a different way of thinking, but it's our job to "educate" him.' In accordance with the French perspective, the point is to make clients understand that changes in their requests have a cost that will necessarily be passed on to them and that, in their own interests, it is more advantageous not to multiply the changes. After what we have seen on the two universes of meaning, we can guess that this educator's posture, quite natural in the eyes of the French supplier, is very likely to offend the Chinese customer and damage their long-term relationship.

A myriad of exported business strategies fail because of a lack of knowledge of the cultural context of customer relations that exists in the targeted place. Trying to impose strict contractual regulations where the network approach prevails or trying to highlight sellers' expertise in a context dominated by mistrust is, for instance, doomed to fail.

Knowing the cultural context of sales relations is as useful as tracking down customers' slightest desires even before they have become aware of them, or finely analysing their consumption practices through 'Big Data'. Sales managers' prescriptions will only be effectively implemented by their salespeople if their cultural universe of meaning allows them to see these methods in a positive light. While neglecting this point has a more indirect cost than neglecting customers' needs, it is nonetheless an important ingredient for long-term business success.

Notes

1. Molière, *Le Bourgeois gentilhomme* (1670), Act 1/Scene 1.
2. Li, Fang (2015) *Rupture organisationnelle et continuité culturelle : une étude de cas—La privatisation d'un hôpital public d'une région centrale de la Chine*, Doctoral Thesis, (Université Paris Dauphine).
3. 'Rendez-nous les caissiers' (Give us back the cashiers), *Marianne*, May 30–June 5, 2009, p. 68.
4. ONISEP on the job of store salesman: *Professionnel qualifié, le vendeur sait écouter le client, l'informer et le conseiller en fonction de son profil et de ses besoins*, http://www.onisep.fr/Ressources/Univers-Metier/Metiers/vendeur-vendeuse-en-magasin (accessed on 7 June 2019).
5. Cited by d'Iribarne P. (2009), *L'épreuve des différences*, (Seuil)1st ed., p. 24.

9
Ethics and Corporate Social Responsibility

Corporate ethics is a privileged field in which the universal and the local meet. More and more multinational companies are adopting documents under various names (such as code of ethics, code of conduct, or principles of action) to display the guidelines adopted by their managers and to provide a certain number of benchmarks for their staff. They set up ways to ensure that the defined guidelines are respected (through ethics training or monitoring tools). These codes cover many of the firms' everyday efforts to fight corruption, respect the rights of employees, and promote social responsibility. The variety of ways of being, values, and customs strongly influences ethics. This diversity affects the behaviours considered to be (or not to be) morally acceptable as well as the motivations to behave ethically, or the types of control that a company can legitimately exercise over its employees. For a company, developing a common ethic is not without its difficulties.

An important aspect of the issue is that, while companies with ethical concerns have long existed in various parts of the world, the current requirement to formalize such ethics has largely originated in the United States. Spreading such formalization throughout the world often requires considerable adaptations (Palazzo, 2002; Thorne & Saunders, 2002; Helin & Sandström, 2008). Whatever the objective that companies are pursuing by adopting a formalized ethical approach—whether it is to respond to a real ethical concern or simply in an effort to give a good image of themselves—such adaptations are needed. It is common, especially in France, to accuse companies that display their ethics of hardly respecting the corresponding principles. These accusations have not spared some of the companies that have opened up to our investigations. Our purpose in this chapter is not to investigate the extent to which these accusations are wellfounded, as ethical audits might. It is to understand the benchmarks within which ethical approaches make sense, both for company employees and for those who, from the outside, are concerned by their actions.

We will first examine the cultural dimension of social responsibility issues. We will pay attention to the differences between the approaches that prevail in France and in the United States, and will discuss responsibilities towards the surrounding world in Mexico, and towards employees in China. We will focus on the means that the company can use to get its employees to comply with the ethics of the company. In a second part, we will approach the questions of corruption by first

Cross-Cultural Management Revisited: A Qualitative Approach. Philippe d'Iribarne, Sylvie Chevrier, Alain Henry, Jean-Pierre Segal, and Geneviève Tréguer-Felten, Oxford University Press (2020).
DOI: 10.1093/oso/9780198857471.001.0001

considering an Argentinian case, then by focusing on the differences between cultures where an ethic of respect for principles prevails and those where an ethic of loyalty towards friends and relatives prevails.

9.1 The Cultural Dimension of Social Responsibility

As long as corporate social responsibility is considered at a very high level of abstraction, for example, by talking about respecting the dignity of employees or about taking into account the future of the planet, it is possible to make very abstract statements of universal value. But this is not the case when you get down to facts and specify concretely how the company intends to act. The precise expectations of the various stakeholders vary significantly according to the cultural context. Hence the impossibility to ignore the diversity of what good relations between a company and its stakeholders imply in practice.

9.1.1 Responsibility Towards the Surrounding World

The way in which a company that wants to act responsibly towards the surrounding world must act depends, of course, on many material aspects of the societies concerned: the state of their health system, the quality of their education system, that of their infrastructures. It also depends on how the population conceives the company's place in society, and this perception depends on cultural elements.

For instance, to mark the year 2000, Danone, the global food-products company, decided to mobilize its personnel worldwide for a humanitarian cause. To do so, they asked each of their employees to follow the company example and, just as they were doing, give the equivalent of one hour of their pay; the response was extremely variable from one country to another. According to the head of Danone's initiative (Giraud, 2000), 'In France, this operation prompted more rejection than anywhere else, since the company's legitimacy in initiating actions that are usually considered as individual choices is much less accepted than in other societies where the company is seen as a guarantee of seriousness and transparency'. A French manager in Total Group[1], another French-based international company, showed similar reluctance (d'Iribarne, 2002, 2013). When asked about his company's policy towards the surrounding society, he answered: 'Americans (...) contribute a lot to charities of all kinds. That's their involvement in local communities. In their internal letters, we often see the CEO washing cars to raise money for good causes. This is very American. They do it: it's not just words, they actually do it. But here, it wouldn't have any impact; the context isn't the same, the culture isn't the same... Here, it wouldn't work.'

This difference reflects the fact that those who find their references in different cultures do not conceive the relationships that bind the company to the surrounding society in the same way. In the United States, the company is seen as part of a community (or of a set of communities). This implies a kind of diffuse responsibility towards the members of that community. It comes along with an emotional dimension. Conversely, in France this dimension is not well developed. To observe the gap separating them, one only needs to compare the two American and French versions of the values of the same company, Lafarge (d'Iribarne, 2009) : 'Contributing to building a better world for *our communities*'/'*Contribuer* autour de nous *à la construction d'un monde meilleur*' and 'Acting as responsible members of *our communities*'/'*Agir en tant que* citoyen *responsable*'. On the French side, the term *community* has been eliminated. Far from the emotional bonds, diffuse responsibility, and social pressure, that the term *community* evokes, the term *citizen* refers to the belonging to a political group where responsibilities and rights are defined by law. The same text was translated into Arabic in Jordan (d'Iribarne, 2009). It contains a new set of formulations for the same general idea that a company has responsibilities towards the surrounding world: 'initiatives for social and charitable works'; 'helping local communities when unforeseen events occur'. Again, the relationship projected is different. The words *charity* and *unforeseen events* evoke a kind of paternal attention that leads to being attentive to the difficulties that affect everyone's life.

There are countries where the surrounding society has high expectations of companies and where these expectations open up a particularly wide field for the exercise of social responsibility. This became evident, for example, during investigations carried out in Danone's Mexican subsidiary (d'Iribarne, 2003; d'Iribarne & Henry, 2007). The staff enthusiastically evoked a project '*Construyamos sus sueños*' (Let's build their dreams) meant to help children in difficulty. An operator reacted to the project:

> Danone Mexico isn't just concerned with Danone, with Danone's growth in Mexico, but also with the growth of everyone as a worker of the society where the plant is located, of the community in which it lives. In other words, it is not only a question of Danone growing, but of the community also growing along with Danone.

Each employee feels that he or she is personally helping, it is not just the company that is helping.

Not only does culture influence the content of the company's duties to society, it also influences the drivers of the sense of responsibility. For instance, the 'Stewardship' of the original English version of Accenture's corporate values gets translated into French as 'Gestion responsable'. Or, in Jansen's values, the American version 'We must maintain in good order the property we are privileged to use' becomes: '*Nous devons entretenir les terrains, usines, bureaux dont nous avons la jouissance*' (We must maintain the land, factories, offices that we enjoy the use of). The term Stewardship, which evokes the image of the good steward, stems from the biblical context: God has entrusted the world to men and He will hold them accountable for their management. Such a reference is hardly conceivable in France, inducing a much more neutral expression. Similarly, the American 'We are privileged to use' belongs to a very different register from the French *that we enjoy the use of.*

In France, the feeling of responsibility can hardly be linked to a religious register. It is rather based on the obligation to live up to one's place in society, to hold one's rank. This ethic finds an echo in the words of French managers invited to comment on a code-of-conduct draft for Total Group:

> Companies the size of our new group, (...) because they often have powers greater than those of certain countries, will not behave in a purely commercial manner, as our competitors do (...). It is normal that we should have rules that are a little above the rest. We must lead on these kinds of issues, and not follow others.

The *size of our group*, the *powers* it entails, its greatness, come into play. You have to be worthy of it. For another manager, you must avoid 'behaving in a purely commercial [not to say base] way', even if supposedly lesser competitors may do so. Many comments head in the same direction: 'When we arrive somewhere new, we can't content ourselves with simply applying local labour law: we are Total'; 'We have to (...) remember the size of our company, our sense of responsibility'; 'We also have our gentlemen's ethics'.

In the afore-mentioned Mexican case, the basis of the company's responsibility towards the surrounding world was again different. Those who expressed themselves on the subject constantly referred to a form of reciprocity in help (*ayuda*), a form of gift and counter-gift, enacted within a mutual commitment:

> We like belonging to a company that, along with its business goals, feels a responsibility to the community. This isn't being philanthropic, but if the community has given you this much, the least you can do is to return in some way some of what it has given you.

This difference between conceptions of the company's role also concerns its responsibility towards its shareholders.

9.1.2 Responsibility to Shareholders

Where responsibility towards shareholders is concerned, comparing the ways in which it is presented in two versions—French and American—of the principles of action of a multinational company, Total, is again enlightening. 'Delivering the value creation that our shareholders expect' becomes: '*Répondre aux attentes de création de valeur de nos actionnaires*' (Meeting the value creation expectations of our shareholders). In the American version, the company places itself in the position of a supplier responding to a request (delivering). In the French version, a different link is staged. The company asserts its sensitiveness to a call which it will 'meet'. This gives the company much more scope for action and initiative than if it simply has to *provide*. By engaging in a dialogue with its shareholders, it establishes a different relationship with them than if it were to simply execute an order: it draws a veil on the fact that, in practice, the company is largely subject to its shareholders.

The shareholder section of the Principles (*Our guiding principles*) of a leading US company, ExxonMobile, helps to understand the US concept of shareholder responsibility:

> We are committed to enhancing the long-term value of the investment dollars entrusted to us by our shareholders. By running the business profitably and responsibly, we expect our shareholders to be rewarded with superior returns. This commitment drives the management of our Corporation. (ExxonMobile)

The company takes an openly moral perspective: shareholders have *trusted* the company. They deserve to be *rewarded*. It is the *long-term value* of the company that counts and it is not interested in speculators. It seems natural in the United States to closely associate, as ExxonMobile does, a moral approach and a search for high profitability. Anyone who behaves morally deserves to be rewarded with economic success. However, in many places, especially in France, associating these two domains is unacceptable. As a result, companies that have their roots in the country find it difficult to make room for their shareholders in their ethical approach.

We encountered a good illustration of this difficulty as we were working with Total, a multinational company based in France, on the writing of their principles of action. Many of the French managers who were asked to react to a draft of the 'principles' voiced reservations about the very principle of including shareholders in an ethical approach. 'Profitability for shareholders part of ethics?', 'It's rather uncalled for here, it shouldn't appear in a code of conduct'. In addition, managers from many countries, particularly those from Northern Europe, objected to the wording adopted in the draft. The French text went as follows:

> *TotalFinaElf veille à*[2] *la protection des intérêts de ses actionnaires en visant une rentabilité satisfaisante de leur investissement* (TotalFinaElf protects the interests of its shareholders and aims to provide them with a satisfactory return on their investment).

Some found this wording too French: 'I noticed that the wording gives a passive position to shareholders. Here, it is the group that knows what is good for them. From an Anglo-Saxon perspective, it is the shareholders who say what we have to do; it's our job to satisfy their requirements.' As the idea of trust was absent, others were shocked by the lack of an openly ethical dimension to the formulation: 'It is the shareholders who trust the group; we are accountable to the shareholders' or 'The shareholders who invest must be able to trust the group's best practices. Otherwise they are potentially harmed. The shareholders support us. They must be able to rely on a code of good practice.' In response to these reactions, and following our suggestions, the wording was revised. It read:

> *TotalFinaElf veille à mériter la confiance de ses actionnaires avec l'objectif d'assurer la rentabilité de leur investissement* (TotalFinaElf ensures to earn the trust of its shareholders with the objective of ensuring the profitability of their investment).

Thus, *to earn the trust* replaced *protect the interests*. The reference to an actual ethical dimension—the trust that is deserved—avoided the strict introduction of the register of interests which the French perceived as problematic in an ethical statement. The text was eventually slightly modified. The 2019 French version reads:

> *Total s'attache à mériter la confiance de ses actionnaires avec l'objectif d'assurer la rentabilité et la pérennité de leur investissement.* (Total strives to earn the trust of its shareholders with the objective of ensuring the profitability and sustainability of their investment.)

Veiller à (ensure), too French, has been replaced by *s'attache à* (strives to) and the idea of sustainability introduced; the corresponding English version reads: 'We strive to earn the confidence of our shareholders, with the objective of providing them with a profitable and sustainable investment.'

Mentions of their responsibility towards their staff equally show dissimilarities.

9.1.3 Responsibility Towards Staff

Companies must not only provide their employees with a decent wage but also with a sense of being considered, respected, as human beings and as workers. However, if the desire to be considered and respected seems universal, what concretely conveys the feeling is intimately linked with the cultural context.

This issue was addressed with respect to delegation, control, and leadership (in Chapters 1, 2, and 4). We saw, in particular, that what makes one feel respected is significantly different in the United States and France. In the United States, one must feel independent of other people's will, and the appropriate way to achieve this objective is to establish relationships inspired by the image of the freely-entered-into contract between equals. In France, the contractual logic is far from occupying the same place. Working for someone, having to fulfil the objectives set for you, gives the feeling of being in a lower position, even when it comes along with a clear-cut contract. Another way of staging relationships of authority is required to keep the image of servile submission at bay, both in the way they are organized in practice and in the words used to evoke them. The duties associated with the place that each person occupies in society are highlighted. Referring to these duties protects against the arbitrariness of those, superiors or clients, who are in a position to grant you any sort of advantages, provided that you meet their requirements. This is what allows you to escape a supposedly servile way of depending. The reference to one's *métier* (profession), to the person who has a *métier*, to the greatness of the *métier*, plays a decisive role.

As the circle of countries under scrutiny widens, it becomes clear that everywhere the way in which authority gets exercised is an important element of a company's respect for its employees. At the same time, one notes that the ways in which this is done are extremely varied.

The distinction between virtuous and bad authority is predominant in the Chinese culture. But what characterizes virtuous authority and, even more so, what safeguards against power abuse are quite distinct from what, in this domain, seems self-evident in Western countries. The conceptions that prevail in the West are rooted in the Greek experience of the *polis* (Vernant, 1962). This legacy has shaped the way in which the meaning of autocratic power, as opposed to democratic power, has developed. A political regime with no opposition to constantly challenge the actions of those in power is deemed despotic. Modern China has inherited a different history and another world vision. The opposition between good and bad authority has been constructed differently (Jullien & Marchaisse, 2000). It is feared that an overly weak authority figure or vacillating rules might open the gates to disorder, putting society at risk to collapse into anarchy. The strict enforcement of rules is consequently perceived as a necessity, all the more so that compliance cannot be taken for granted in a country where everyday relationships are so characterized by strong individualism. At the same time, the opposition between good and bad authority lies at the heart of Chinese history (Granet, 1994 [1929]). The representation of a good authority is inspired by the image of the virtuous leader devoted to the good of the people and a model of virtue, as described by Confucius (1999):

> The person in authority [*junzi*] . . . pursues what he desires without being covetous . . . is not this to be majestic without being fierce? (20:2).
>
> If a minister makes his own conduct correct, what difficulty will he have in assisting in government? If he cannot rectify himself, what has he to do with rectifying others? (13:13). (Confucius, 1999)

Obviously, the Chinese are not 'Confucian' in the sense that their day-to-day behaviour would necessarily be inspired by the Master's teachings; in any event, cultural context produces no magical effect on behaviour. Yet, Confucius's teachings have helped to construct the interpretive framework used by the Chinese to make sense of daily life and to judge their fellow men. However, his teachings reflect a world vision that to date permeates China's history.

Expectations towards companies in the exercise of their responsibility towards their employees are marked by this Chinese vision of a virtuous authority. They are not expected to establish bodies that allow staff to challenge management's policies and decisions or to avoid being overly directive to their staff. On the other hand, they are expected to exercise over their staff the form of strong, fair, and nurturing authority that corresponds to the ideal image of virtuous authority. For example, in a Chinese subsidiary of a Western company in which we collected employees' reactions to the way in which the company implemented its Principles of Action, a set of policies in line with this Chinese image of virtuous authority was strongly supported. Be it the role given to competence—which combines justice (judging according to competence) and nurturing character (developing competence)—the place of security seen as protecting not only individuals but also their families, or the place given to a long-term perspective (d'Iribarne, 2009).

How do companies ensure that the principles are respected?

9.1.4 A Company's Control Over the Ethics of its Employees

As a legal entity, a company can choose the principles that guide its policies in matters of ethics and social responsibility. However, on a day-to-day basis, its practices are largely determined by the orientations taken by each and every member of its staff. Each company must be organized so as to ensure that its employees act in accordance with its principles. Here again, culture comes into play. The dominant conception of the right way to exercise this control took shape in the United States. But, as we shall see, it is linked to a specific cultural context. Outside the United States, local contexts impact on the way in which companies should proceed to control the ethics of their employees.

If we look at American firms' ethical codes, or those of British firms strongly marked by an American influence, ethics and the pursuit of interests are tied on two accounts. Having a good reputation, founded on strict integrity, is a fundamental element of business success; and this success generates the resources needed to do good. For instance, in its Code of Ethics, ExxonMobil states that: 'A well-founded reputation for scrupulous dealing is in itself a priceless corporate asset.' As, following its merger with Amoco, BP Group's Chief Executive was presenting their business policies, he stated from the outset that 'a good business should be both competitively successful and a force for good'. He also included among the group's fundamental values 'a belief in honest exchange and an awareness that a strong reputation is essential for business success'.

We found this same view in the statements made by the American managers whom we interviewed at Total:

> I think that this code of conduct concept is what you want to promote (. . .). You need to stress integrity and honesty (. . .). Our ability to succeed in business many times relies on our reputation . . . so, I'm particularly sensitive to maintaining a good level of support in terms of requiring our people to be at the required standards.

In such a moral register, the community formed by every member of the staff is collectively responsible. Everyone is concerned: in their personal actions as well as in their ensuring the integrity of them all. This is also reflected in the statements of the Americans interviewed in the same survey:

> It's a collective effort. We are all part of the integrity and honesty; you have to have both of them to be successful. If you don't have any of those standards, with a high standard of integrity, and hopefully we have grown up with that, then you are not going to be successful.

In American codes of conduct or business ethics, and the British ones that they inspire, the pronoun *we* indiscriminately refers to the enterprise as such and to all of its employees:

> ExxonMobil Corporation is committed to be the world's premier petroleum and petrochemical company. To that end, *we* must continuously achieve superior financial and operating results while adhering to the highest standards of business conduct.[3]
>
> At the core of BP is an unshakeable commitment to human progress. *Our* products and services are creating the freedom to move, to be warm, to be cool, to see, and enjoy a better quality of life. *We* believe this freedom is inseparable from the responsibility to produce and consume our products in ways that respect both human rights and natural environments.

In this view, everyone is concerned by everything they know, and mutual control is part of everyone's job: 'I think you have to have a procedure where employees can report unethical issues. I mean you know. It is just to put everything on the table.'

The role of senior executives is twofold. They serve the company by defending ethics as the source of its reputation—*as an asset*—in line with their responsibility to shareholders. They also serve its moral mission in measure with the leadership they exercise in the community; they teach the gospel by setting an example (Peters & Waterman, 1982). Since Americans do not perceive these two roles of defender of the company's interests and of preacher of morality as conflicting in any way, their co-existence bothers no one.

The French do not share Americans' idea that ethics and self-interest naturally go together well. The legitimacy of any company, as a corporate body represented by its management, playing a leading role in ethics seems especially dubious. French employees have difficulty seeing companies as more responsible for supervising ethics than they are themselves; they question the very notion. Isn't the company subject to its economic objectives, a kind of cold monster devoid of honour that clearly situates itself on the side of its own self-interests? Does not management—accountable for these interests—sometimes naturally put pressure on the company's employees to act in unethical ways? Is it not really up to the employees to claim an ethical point of view supported by an elevated vision of their *métier*? 'Today, they [the management] scare you, but then they say business must go on', claimed a French manager who we interviewed. In these conditions, the company seems out of place when claiming to play a role in ethics. Some French managers take a radical stance: 'The company's sphere and the ethics sphere remain two distinct areas; ethics are an individual's personal business. I do not see how a company can have an ethic.'

There is, of course, a basis for ethical conduct in any French firm, but French employees see ethics stemming from the free pursuit of individual notions of duty, rather than from the actions of a community that strictly controls its members, supervises, and sanctions them. This holds whether one speaks of a religious ethic that depends on personal conscience, or an honour ethic, according to which acting under coercion would lead to lowering oneself. The French see individuals as being supported by their own convictions, that is, as the carriers of ethical conduct. 'Everyone talks about ethics. For me, ethics is the way each person perceives things and behaves as best they can.' 'I have my own conscience, that is sufficient.' This emphasis on a personal ethic leads employees to see external pressure, especially from management, as outside of the field of ethics. 'If we make someone else responsible for our responsibilities, we are falling into a deal made by management, the censor, and the others. Ethics is committing oneself.'

While in the United States ethics are generally seen as one entity linking honesty in management, benevolence in the community, and discipline in personal life, the French distinguish between types of ethics. One sphere includes whatever concerns the firm and managerial rectitude. Another sphere covers whatever pertains to 'private' life, an area in which French employees will not tolerate company meddling: 'In the French system, everyone wishes to protect their personal lives and tries to erect a separation between their personal and professional lives. (...) It's not the same for Anglo-Americans.'

Just as the French are reluctant to see the company play a leading role in ethics, they massively reject the means used by American companies to encourage their employees to act ethically: anything coming under the enforcement (the term itself is significant) of an ethical approach is unwelcome. The company's role is at best acceptable to call everyone to a sense of duty. 'The company should make employees aware that there are laws, rules, an ethic that they should adhere to of their own volition', one manager remarked. The idea of a leading role in ethical matters for the company seems questionable, even shocking. French employees find it especially hard to accept the American view that companies have to implement procedures that make every employee 'accountable'—accountability is an American notion—for breaching ethical standards, thereby prodding them into acting correctly. Obviously, on matters of legal compliance, French employees find it natural that the company—responsible for application of the law—should turn to its staff and ask them to answer for their actions, but ethics belong to a different register.

Each and every one is responsible for their own ethics, and deemed the best to assess situations taking into account their complexity, and here again French and American conceptions differ:

> Our company asks senior executives to consider where [in which country] they are located; that's the opposite of American companies who arrive with a doctrinal code, with very little margin for initiative (...). Either you choose the American way, or you have faith in employees' intelligence to apply the rules.

Similarly, the idea of associating sanctions with the violation of a code of ethics arouses great reluctance, again with a rejection of an American way of doing things:

> It is not at all part of our culture to talk about sanctions in writing; we say that we obey laws and regulations, that there are legal sanctions; we do not say that an employee who trespasses the law will be protected. Punishment will come—there's no need to write it out.

This negative attitude towards sanctions sometimes comes along with a sharp critique of what is deemed a tendency of Anglo-American companies to throw their responsibility back onto their employees. 'At Mobil, the charter was used to cover the company: we don't want to know what you are doing. If you get caught, you signed the charter, you will be fired.'

Furthermore, the idea of asking employees to alert management to colleagues' unethical behaviour provokes radically different reactions in France and the United States. While Americans may perceive this as a civic duty, the French view such informing on colleagues as highly condemnable:

> I wondered if they were going to implement what Anglo-Americans call 'whistle-blowing': when an employee notices that ethical standards are breached, he can call a kind of toll-free number to confidentially report it... Here, without talking about whistle-blowing, they say that any employee may ask a question, but they don't say how (...). How can we be sure that it has nothing to do with denunciation, with informing on colleagues? In the United States, there's a toll-free number to denounce people who don't follow ethical standards. That's informing on them.

This gap between these two conceptions of good relationships between a company and its employees is reflected in many ways. One example is the contrast between the ways in which the same company, Lafarge, can express its values depending on whether it does so in English (from an American perspective) or in French (d'Iribarne, 2009). The American version clearly shows the obligations to which its staff members are subject. Each of them is required to apply the rules defined by the company. What is required is part of a contractual relationship and its respect is part of the contract. The company must define precisely the obligations to which those who work for it are subject. By contrast, the French version keeps on treating the matter with kid gloves. It suggests a kind of voluntary membership. The obligation is mitigated by moving from formulas that firmly express the company's will to formulas that leave a lot of room for everyone's goodwill: '*We want* all of our employees to be key players in the formulation of their own personal objective' becomes: '*Nous* attendons de *chaque collaborateur qu'il joue un rôle déterminant dans l'élaboration de ses propres objectifs*' (We *expect* each employee to play a decisive role in developing his or her own objectives). Or 'These rules should be known by everyone in our organization and *implemented* consistently' translated into '*Ces règles doivent être connues*, acceptées *et* appliquées *de façon cohérente*'. (These rules must be known, *accepted and applied* consistently.)

It is because, in a French vision, the fully legitimate source of obligations stems from the conviction that everyone has duties associated with the position they occupy in the company. And everyone tends to consider that they are the sole judge of these duties. Under these conditions, the company can invite, suggest, propose, encourage. It is difficult for it to pretend to impose.

Corruption issues are another aspect of ethics that will be dealt with differently depending on the cultural background.

9.2 Corruption Issues

The excuse of a 'cultural exception', often invoked to dispense with anti-corruption measures, proves increasingly unacceptable in international business circles and elsewhere. However, we see many questions about how anti-corruption efforts should accommodate cultural differences. The World Bank, fully aware of this issue, struggles to provide an adequate response. A note sent out by the Bank in a series 'intended to summarize good practice' (Arvis & Berstein, 2002, p. 2) asserts that 'research does not support claims that US-style compliance systems encounter serious resistance in other cultures'. However, this point of view is immediately qualified:

> The challenge for companies is to formulate core principles and implement credible procedures adapted to local business cultures. In particular, for companies operating in industries with substantial local ownership (as is common in China), the need to adapt training, dissemination, and information systems, to local customs is more than an intellectual exercise.

In fact, the motivations for honest behaviour are not uniform. After examining a successful cultural adaptation in an Argentinean case, we will see in what way this can be done in cultures where either an ethic of purity, or an ethic of fidelity, prevails.

9.2.1 An Effective Approach to Fighting Corruption in Argentina

In Argentina the situation concerning corruption is far from bright, both in terms of the country's political system and its business enterprises. However, some companies have energetically tackled the problem, and not without success. Our study of the policy pursued by one of these companies was conducted in a subsidiary of an international French group (d'Iribarne, 2003; d'Iribarne and Henry, 2007). We were able to assess to what extent its achievements were due to the cultural relevance of the approach used.

The company comprised three branches, two of which had been marked by strong corruption in the more or less recent past. The corporate tools already used or being set up to deal with the issue did not, at first glance, seem out of the ordinary. Great efforts were made to recruit people 'who were upright'. The dismissal of corrupt staff, or of individuals involved in conflicts of interest, gave a clear signal that things had changed, especially as sackings involved important job positions. In the main branch, a 'contract committee' monitored all purchasing decisions over a certain amount of money. A code of ethics was also adopted that was giving a prime place to the question of corruption and conflicts of interest. Furthermore, an 'ethics referent' was appointed. All employees could turn to him and have his help on resolving the questions of interpretation likely to arise concerning values and ethical principles.

On closer inspection, however, many quite uncommon features came to light. Firstly, the ethical referent occupied a unique position. Rather than providing a highly independent ethical counterweight to the company's structure of authority, his role as director of human resources meant that he was an integral part of this structure. In the American model, employees report suspected wrongdoings to a structure that is independent of senior management, and denunciations are sent in anonymously. In the present case, however, the reporting employee was obliged to reveal his identity to the director of human resources. These various elements inspired questions about the way in which a 'universal' approach had been adapted to the specific features of the ethical benchmarks prevailing in Argentine society.

The existence of a plurality of ethical references arouses conflictual feelings within individuals. On the one side, there is an ethic based on religion and honour that draws a distinction between what is good and bad *per se*, and between honesty and dishonesty. Yet, simultaneously, the daily functioning of society is influenced by an ethic of loyalty to friendship-or interest-groupings, where a strong sense of solidarity reigns for better, or sometimes, for worse. Undoubtedly, there is something universal about the coexistence of an attachment to principles and a requirement of loyalty to one's relatives. However, it does cause a particular problem in the Argentinian context.

The question of limits is all the more acute here, as shared concepts of the borderline between good and evil are particularly absent in Argentinian society. 'One thing will appear honest to one person and dishonest to another.' Given the plurality of coexisting interpretations, it is difficult to transform the very general and abstract great principles and ethical references (some speak of philosophy) into a set of rules. Enforcing them by an effective system of social control that draws the line between honesty and dishonesty in a wide variety of concrete situations is just as difficult. Therefore, when leaders set the example of lax interpretations of principles, most employees lack the strongly internalized concepts of these principles which would enable them to resist. Wherever solidarity within a group of 'friends' tends to prevail over respect for principles, the development of an organized system of corruption, based on the formation of networks of complicity, finds favourable soil for growth. Many individuals are fully aware that there are widely varying perceptions of the line separating good and bad. They are ready to believe that they are on the good side, but uneasy about not being entirely certain, so they look to external references that will eliminate their doubts and provide reassurance.

The company did not fight against the networks of corruption simply by using a combination of controls and punishments, as would have been done anywhere else. Rather than ignoring the logic of group solidarity, the company set about mobilizing this same logic to fight against corruption. It thus took measures to ensure that, instead of being tugged in different directions between the conflicting influences of the honesty principle and their belonging to 'friendship-groupings', its personnel would be integrated into a sort of virtuous network led by the company's managers. While largely using the standard tools for fighting corruption, they also adapted them in order to achieve this.

In a context where the practical consequences of grand principles are particularly uncertain, you need 'to constantly define the boundaries of what is good or what is bad', says one Argentinian manager. Generally speaking, promulgating a code of ethics constitutes an effective means of clarifying matters. In the Argentinian context, however, finding an appropriate place for such a code is no easy task. If the code simply exists as a declaration of principle with no detailed content, it will compete with what each individual feels that he has learnt from his upbringing, and the reception will be cool. So, precise limits are needed, which are best set down in writing. By setting practical rules, it is possible to avoid lax interpretations of principles. If all loopholes are to be eliminated, then safeguards will need to be multiplied. This is what the *Principios de ética* of the main branch did with regard to corruption. They included a *Declaración de Valores y Principios Eticos* that summed up corporate values and principles in two short pages. Brief as it was, the declaration rejected corruption in uncommonly thorough terms:

> [The company] prohibits its employees from offering, requesting, or accepting any kind of incentive, present, gift, money, bribe, or compensation (*incentivo, obsequio, dadivo, dinero, soborno o recompensa*) that could be interpreted as a reward for actions related to one's job in the company.

The series of words used to designate the various faces that corruption may assume, finds its sense in such a context. It is good to hunt out any corruption hiding behind the euphemisms serving to conceal it. Is such a radical vision acceptable as standard behaviour? Some people resisted: 'It may be rather difficult to measure what a 'present' (*obsequio*) is; a desk alarm clock can be a present. I don't believe it's an ethical fault to accept a present of this nature from a supplier.' Under these conditions, putting landmarks on paper does not avoid interpretation—a responsibility that leaves employees confronted with their own doubts. That is where the 'ethical referent' plays an essential role. Our interviewees' remarks constantly referred to 'doubts'; to points that were 'not clear'; to things 'which could be interpreted' as a conflict of interests; to what one 'believed'; what 'appeared' good or bad to you; what was 'perhaps' not transparent; what was 'considered' bad, or was 'frowned upon'; indicating a highly subjective vision of ethics. The way in which the ethical referent's activity was referred to, once again showed how applying principles to concrete situations will raise questions. Thanks to him, those who were in doubt about what was good or bad could find an answer to their anxieties and regain their 'peace of mind'. The ethical referent himself relied on a collegial structure. The director of human resources, who was the first in line, might also have doubts, and so landmarks were established collectively. Furthermore, the ethics committee at the group's headquarters constituted a 'supreme court', a 'defining' authority figure, that could be turned to 'so as to resolve questions that might be doubtful to us'. From this perspective, it makes sense for the ethical referent to be part of the company managers. He does not simply stand as a witness of transcendent principles that would be imposed on the company. He expresses the way in which the particular community which constitutes the company, united around its leaders, interprets such principles.

As the company sought to be perceived by its employees as a community building relationship of trust and mutual support, it made an original use of the traditional supervisory bodies. They were presented as bodies that were there to provide help and support to individuals so as to counter external solicitations and internal temptations, almost as much as—if not more than—bodies that would sanction those who went astray. The 'contract committee' is therefore viewed largely as a means of assistance, of 'backing up' those who wish to act in an upright manner. It appears as a source of 'comfort', particularly when the decision that seems best is not underpinned by obvious criteria and might thus be regarded with suspicion. Furthermore, those who work for the company will be proportionately less tempted to deviate if they can rely on internal support to deal with difficulties, rather than feel compelled to seek help from a group of accomplices. That way, everyone is able to understand that showing loyalty to a company ready to help them in the event of hardship is, in effect, the best way for them to ensure that they will be able to fulfil their duties toward their families (whereas, if they tried to get rich at the company's expense, they would risk losing their jobs and would consequently no longer be able to do so). Moreover, when companies are attentive to the difficulties of their members, relationships of 'trust' develop, leading to the feeling of forming a 'team'. Each member feels that the team's interests must be protected, which implies dealing with it honestly.

What is of great interest in this case is the complexity of the cultural context, in which an on-principle commitment to honesty goes hand in hand with an attachment, for better or for worse, to interest and friendship groupings. The instruments that the company used find simultaneous meaning in both registers. Thus, insofar as it helped to resolve cases of conscience, the ethical referent contributed to the proper functioning of an ethics of respect for principles. But, through his duties as director of human resources and the quality of the relationships that he had established with staff members, he was part of a friendship and interest network. In the same way, the control authorities simultaneously found their place in both registers. What may appear to be odd in the policies put in place is in fact a good adaptation to the specific context.

9.2.2 The Ethic of Purity and the Ethic of Loyalty

This Argentinian case illustrates a much more general phenomenon: the contrast, at least as far as ideal types are concerned, between two major families of ethics (d'Iribarne, 2000).

The first type concerns the ideal of the good man. Whether one follows a law promulgated by a great religious founder, obeys a code of honour, or respects principles reputedly consistent with universal reason, one must show oneself to be pure, worthy, and obedient of the requirements of a transcendent ideal (Kant, 1985). Rather than constituting the source of duty, one's relationship with others is the very substance of duty (Aristotle, 1965). Correspondingly, duty binds us to others irrespective of the relationship we have with them, with man in general, with strangers, with enemies even. It is underpinned by a transcendent authority (God, the gods, reason) whose prescriptions will apply even in the absence of external supervision. Conversely, in the second type of ethics, the prime concern is loyalty to the group that one belongs to, be it family, clan, brotherhood, or network of interests. While proof of almost extreme availability—of one's time, possessions, and even one's life—must be shown to the members of such groups, everything is permitted towards outsiders. If an individual neglects his or her duty, he or she does not risk feeling unworthy in the presence of a transcendent authority, he risks suffering the vengeance of the group that he or she has betrayed. The group will not fail to use means of control and retaliation, including obscure means that escape outside observation.

These different ethics can be designated in various ways. The nature of duty contrasts the ethics of purity—or virtue—to the ethics of loyalty; the scope of obligation contrasts universalist ethics with particularistic ethics; and the nature of supervisory authority figures contrasts transcendental ethics with the ethics of immanence. In practice, there is a strong linkage between these three dimensions. Thus, a universalist ethic entailing duties toward those who have no power over you will have trouble functioning in the absence of the control provided by a transcendent authority.

In many of the European-style cultures (in Northern Europe rather than Southern Europe), various forms of ethics based on respect for principles are the norm, but this is much less true in many other societies. The ethic of loyalty to one's relatives holds almost total sway over a good part of sub-Saharan Africa. This largely accounts for the feeling of strangeness that outsiders experience in these societies. They find it disturbing to see tasks, which to their mind come under the strict rule of fulfilling one's professional duties, being interpreted in terms of personal relationships. In Latin America, this ethic of loyalty to one's relatives, tied up with the influence of tightly bonded groups (families or interest groups), is also very important, but it coexists with an ethic of respect for principles (primarily religious). Even though the latter does not really govern life, individuals feel deeply attached to it. This attachment is such that someone endeavouring to comply with this ethic will not be immediately suspected of a hidden agenda, but is more likely to gain true respect, even from those who do not follow the same teachings. Likewise, in the Moroccan case, even though it ordinarily plays only a marginal role in business, a religious ethic of respect for principles exists in that society. Consequently, individuals who, like the managing director of the company we visited (see Chapter 14, pp. 283–4), stand out for their upright behaviour gain respect even from those who act in the opposite way.

Moral condemnation of corruption takes on full meaning in those regions of the world where the ethic of principles prevails. The value accorded to the general precepts of honesty anchors the abidance to the company rules meant to handle all sorts of questions: selecting personnel, choosing suppliers, evaluating subordinates' performance, sanctioning safety violations, and so on. Within this type of ethical framework, it also seems sensible to reject any compromise on precepts or rules which might be made for the sake of personal ties with a relative, friend, or mutual-aid network. Likewise, in this type of ethic, rejecting, in the name of professional duty, the temptations of corruptors offering you the benefit of resources likely to help relatives or friends whom you have a duty to support, is logical.

These kinds of behaviour, which are unquestionably laudable when the prevailing ethic is the respect for principles, become much more questionable when the predominant ethic is loyalty to one's relatives (Banfield, 1958). When group loyalty prevails, adherence to classical standards of 'honesty' can at best be understood as a sign that one prefers loyalty to one's company over loyalty to family or friends. Moreover, as such preference is scarcely credible, one is easily suspected by those who feel betrayed of having inadmissible or secret reasons for acting this way. These can include wanting to keep for oneself what can be taken from the company; not really having the power that one claims (to hire people, for example); being naturally 'mean'; and so on and so forth. It would appear more in keeping with ethical behaviour to accept various forms of 'corruption' than to reject them. Heavy sanctions ranging from ostracism to witchcraft threaten those who betray their own.

These differences strongly affect the way in which companies need to approach the fight against corruption.

Where an ethic based on respect for principles prevails, the personnel have their own motivations to behave honestly. Certainly, to avoid any doubts as to the dividing line between what is licit and what is illicit, and to prevent the less scrupulous from gradually causing the majority of employees to deviate, control mechanisms should be set up. These controls, however, only play a secondary role. Additionally, they must avoid offending the more honest employees; otherwise the effect would be counterproductive. This is the context within which the management tools that serve as a worldwide reference have largely been conceived.

Companies rely on this kind of ethic being internalized by the vast majority of their personnel. Yet where the prevailing ethic is loyalty to one's own, spontaneous respect for some principles cannot be counted on. In extreme cases where the loyalty ethics holds almost total sway, corruption is not even worthy of being named as such in the local culture; its stigmatization comes largely from the outside, or at least, under the influence of an external eye. When ethics are intermingled, the value attached to abidance to principles can be strong enough to prompt discussions on corruption, but not strong enough to build a powerful barrier against it.

Does this amount to saying that the societies where an ethic of loyalty to one's own predominates are invariably condemned to be ruled by corruption? Or that fighting it effectively would require the doubtlessly utopian project of changing the culture itself—by which we do not mean the most common practices, but the universe of meaning that prevails? The situation is not so bleak. In these societies, what is essential is that those in positions exposed to the temptation of corruption be protected from the pressures of close friends and relatives. They must be able to show the latter that refusing their requests is not evidence of disloyalty, but simply means that they cannot act otherwise without incurring serious problems for themselves. This kind of approach is standard in sub-Saharan Africa within the traditional savings institutions known as tontines (Henry et al, 1991). Members of tontines are severely punished if they do not fulfil their obligations towards the group. This allows a tontine member to justify why he is putting aside part of what is at his disposal, instead of giving his relatives or friends the immediate assistance they demand. More generally, this is the broad purpose of establishing strict procedures to frame all acts likely to offer occasions for corruption, and of subjecting their application to very tight controls.

Strict control is not experienced in the same way as in a world dominated by an ethic of purity. When such an ethic prevails, any form of control is perceived as a sign of distrust. Although relatively acceptable within the context of a religious ethic (which regards man as naturally sinful), strict control has a particularly insulting connotation when experienced by individuals that respect an ethic of honour. This is well illustrated by the differences in reactions to control in France and the United States. Conversely, when loyalty to one's own is the dominant ethic, the vigorous control exercised by a group over its members bears no offense. It is all the more acceptable that an individual does not succumb to the forcible solicitations of close relations without reluctance, but resistance is extremely difficult when credible reasons are lacking. As a result, controls that provide the necessary justifications can be experienced in a very positive manner. The same holds true in places where an ethic of loyalty to one's peers exists alongside an ethic of purity. Systematic control stands as a safeguard against the requests of one's close friends and relatives, and helps the individual to avoid 'temptations' and 'internal conflicts'. It is then perceived, as was seen in the Argentinian case, as helpful, as supportive, and as providing some 'comfort'.

In parallel to rigorous controls, a meticulous apportioning of responsibilities (Zadi Kessy, 1998) that prevents individuals from being able to use their authority and grant favours to their friends can also help to protect personnel from pressures that might be difficult to resist (see Chapter 6, p. 119).

When the two kinds of ethics carry significant weight, it is better that their dynamics move in the same direction rather than oppose each other. The more the company will constitute a group whose members share a strong sense of belonging and support, the more that membership will carry obligations that outweigh—or at least balance out—the obligations to other groups. Moreover, the more the company will show solidarity with the communities to which its members belong (families, or local communities), the more the loyalty due to these groups will mix well with loyalty to the company. The Mexican case is an illustration of this kind of reconciliation.

Sometimes, as in the Moroccan (see Chapter 14, pp. 280–5) and Argentinian cases, although the great moral precepts of a religious ethic constitute norms for communal living, they impact business life very unevenly. This gives rise to a kind of ethical hesitancy, combining clear principles and uncertain application. The aim is for the companies who are concerned to bridge principles and practices. This is what happened in these two cases.

9.3 Conclusion

Ethics is a particularly problematic issue in management. The gaps between stated intentions and achievements often seem considerable, in all areas, from respect for the environment to anti-corruption fights. These differences are often interpreted by highlighting the lack of a real ethical will on the part of companies. However, being satisfied with such an explanation requires forgetting that ethics does not only concern the way governing bodies act. It also concerns each individual staff member and their breaches of ethics, whether through corruption, lack of respect for subordinates, or in any other domain. Often, if companies do not implement more effective policies on all these points, it is not because they do not intend to. It is that they do so inefficiently, neglecting the real drivers of ethical conduct in each cultural context.

Taking these factors into account and designing the policies implemented accordingly can therefore lead to great progress in efficiency and, as Americans would point out, to increased profits.

Notes

1. Total Group has over the years changed names several times, so has Exxon also mentioned in this chapter. In each case, the name used is the one valid at the time.

2. The expression '*veiller à*' is very typical of a French approach, as shown by the comparison of the English and the French versions of the Universal Declaration of the Rights of the Child (d'Iribarne, 2017). It places the person who claims to have an ethical position in a dignified position.
3. Throughout this chapter, whenever needed, italics were used for emphasis in interviewees' speech.

PART III
RETHINKING INTERCULTURAL RELATIONS

10
Interpersonal Communication

In a globalized world where people of different languages and cultures live side by side, where projects rely on transnational teams, and where commercial exchanges are no longer hindered by borders, intercultural communication is a recurrent theme, particularly in management manuals. Management relies on good communication between individuals called upon to work together: they have to share data, to agree on the actions to be taken, or the objectives to be achieved. In doing so, they are being encouraged to develop a cultural, intercultural, or multicultural competence (Bartel-Radic, 2009) involving knowledge (linguistic, cultural, and social), strong personal motivation to come into contact with different cultures, and the ability to 'adapt to [their] specificity, in particular through empathy, openness and emotional stability'.[1] This chapter aims to show that things are more complex, and that each case requires special attention.

As was seen with regard to management by objectives (MBO), decision-making, customer relations, and all other managerial acts, communication between colleagues is seldom easy. Even the use of a common language—that is, one that is the native language of neither of the interlocutors—does not always allow them to understand each other. Sometimes neither party has really mastered the common language; in most cases, misunderstanding arises because the structures or words used are rarely unambiguous. The first section of this chapter will present concrete situations in which, depending on the linguistic community to which the speakers belong, different meanings have been attributed to the words used. We will then show how the cultural universe specific to each linguistic community also influences the way in which speakers use the language and how these communication styles can generate friction or misunderstandings. The good and bad fortunes of common corporate languages (CCL) will be the subject of the third part. Indeed, although having a common language is a necessity in today's global world, in itself it cannot suffice. The distinct universes from which speakers draw to make sense of what they are reading or hearing 'colour' the language in different shades, sometimes generating doubt, misunderstanding, or frustration that can disrupt the proper functioning of the organization. This implies both that the very writing of this book by non-native speakers is a challenge and that questionnaire based cross-cultural studies should be approached with caution since the questionnaires were designed in one specific cultural universe, the researcher's, and submitted to numerous back-and-forth translations. We will

Cross-Cultural Management Revisited: A Qualitative Approach. Philippe d'Iribarne, Sylvie Chevrier, Alain Henry, Jean-Pierre Segal, and Geneviève Tréguer-Felten, Oxford University Press (2020).
DOI: 10.1093/oso/9780198857471.001.0001

conclude that to alleviate intercultural communication difficulties close attention should be paid to the context—unique each time—of the exchange.

10.1 Words are Only Signs Which are Open to Interpretation

Whether messages are written in accordance with the lexical and grammatical requirements of a language or, conversely, written by speakers who have not initially mastered it as native speakers, they will only make sense after receivers have used their interpretative ability to extract what they perceive as relevant information. To do so, speakers instinctively transpose the messages into their own linguistic-cultural universes, in short into the universes of meaning that are most immediately accessible to them cognitively (Sperber & Wilson, 1995), a process which may bring about distortions in meaning.

For the following message to make sense, the recipient will only have to guess what lies behind the inadequate words.

Dear Terrysan

I'm staying at warm Orlando/Florida now. It's very comfortable. I do not want retune [sic] to a winter season. By the way, I guess that I had not told you the visit purpose to Ceslup[2] as you say. Having only said that I visited Ceslup simply on March 4th. I think this time that the purpose that I visit is only a short-time greeting simply. It is not a training. Therefore, it [sic] will only talk with the staff off Ceslup for a while.

Unfortunately, I still think that it is difficult to discuss about a product since detailed [sic] are not known about Ceslup products.

I appreciate your advice.

BR/RYO

However, well-written exchanges may be even more difficult to understand. The examples presented below show that, just as a wink—that is, the blinking of an eye—may mean different things depending on the code assigned to it and the context in which it is used (Geertz, 1973), the words used in a message may vary in meaning according to the linguistic and cultural origins of the correspondents. By instinctively assimilating the common language to their respective native languages and simultaneously transposing the message into their own universe of meaning, each of them understands the message differently. Two illustrations set in different contexts, one Franco-American, the other Franco-Chinese, testify to dissimilarities that lead to misunderstandings with consequences that may be difficult to measure on the spot but are very real.

10.1.1 A Misunderstanding of a Linguistic and Contextual Nature

The US senior vice-president of the subsidiary of a French multinational company in the United States remembers:

> On occasion I took requests for information from my French counterparts as quite literal. So, I did them, literally, as requested. For example, once there was a speech on short notice by a key executive in Paris. I asked: 'This is on a very, very tight time scale. Should I come to Paris?' I was told 'Yes, you must come'. I interpreted 'must' as a command—that is 'yes, you are commanded to come'. On reflection it appeared it was a nice request—that is 'Oh, yes: it would be wonderful to have you if you can come'. The result of the misinterpretation of the word *must* was I travelled over and back in 36 hours, never slept, etc. to attend a talk I could easily have missed and no one would have cared.

The difficulties that this US senior manager experiences in his French multinational enterprise (MNE) not only stem, as he believes, from a tendency to take the words read or heard literally, but from his assigning to them a meaning that is based on his own cultural background. His first misapprehension is linguistic: he 'heard' his correspondent's ELF in his native Anglo-American English. In fact, far from consisting of the absolute obligation *must* would have conveyed in his native language, his French correspondent's utterance only amounted to the formula used in France to recommend an action, a restaurant, an outing, considered worth doing or going: *il faut vraiment que tu viennes, que tu ailles*. . . . This American-English speaker might have recognized the similar use of *must* in his native language—that of a *must-see film*—if he had not, at the same time, instinctively mistaken the French context for his native work environment, in which a *must* uttered by one's boss is an indisputable order.

Lack of awareness of possible word-meaning disparities, or of dissimilar managerial contexts, can lead to frustration and discomfort that often remain unspoken, unless they eventually lead to stereotypical generalizations or reappear long after, as in the case of this American senior vice-president. They may also surface when triggered by a linguistic misunderstanding, which is what happens in the next email exchange.

10.1.2 A Cultural Vision that Weighs on the Overall Meaning

François, a French project manager working in France, communicates with Chen, his Chinese counterpart in the Chinese manufacturing plant of their company—an automotive equipment manufacturer. François has established a schedule for the production of the tools required to start the manufacture of a Chinese customer's new car model. The finalization of an electronic component—MASK—is the cornerstone of the project. Once finalized, it can no longer be modified, hence François's email asking Chen to agree on the proposed schedule.

However, Chen wishes to postpone François's deadline:

I have checked your planning; and found that you want to launch MASK in Jan. 06. I think it is impossible, so I want to change MASK time to March 06. Do you agree?

Chen

In his reply, François reviews the necessary steps, each time stipulating the number of weeks needed for each of the various actions required, and he concludes that it would be dangerous to postpone the MASK validation to a date allowing no room for manoeuvre in the event of unforeseen circumstances. Finally, he enquires as to the reason for the requested delay and, attributing his colleague's concern to the time required to validate the software, he reassures him on that matter:

Why do you think it could not be possible? We have enough time to validate the software before end 2005. Please explain.

Chen undeceives him: it has nothing to do with the software but with the client:

I think that the problem will come from customer, not from our software. Customer usually modify requirement after Out Tooling System [the implementation of the tools needed for production to start]. I know that we can ask customer pay for a modification. But we don't like to do some futile work.

Out Tooling System is in August 06. There are 20 Weeks between March and August. We have enough time to launch MASK.

Of course, I will do my best to push customer to confirm before Jan 06.

François's reaction to this message is not long in coming. Clearly triggered by the use of *futile*, his answer is sharp:

Please consider that it is not futile work. Pushing the customer to freeze the software and launch the mask, and then asking him money in case of evolution, is a good way to make the customer more 'responsible'. An evolution is a cost so we can hope that the customer will think before making too many evolutions... or he will pay.

That's the way we proceed in Europe. I know that Chinese customer may have different way of thinking, but it's our job to 'educate' him.

François naturally takes *futile* for the negative value judgement that characterizes the word in French; in other words, he 'hears' Chen say that trying to convince his client to meet deadlines is not worth the effort—an utterly unacceptable statement in a French work environment where one is supposed to position oneself as the expert who guides his clients, determines what is best for them, and helps them to go through the steps that they are strongly advised to take (see pp. 160–162). This mentoring attitude involves strict rules (including penalties for failing to meet deadlines) to which the client must adhere from the outset. It is to this whole normative set that his *it's our job to 'educate' him* refers, an attitude that he presents, in a clearly ethnocentric remark, as European, but which, in fact, characterizes the French conception of what the relationship with customers should be (d'Iribarne, 2006a; Tréguer-Felten, 2012, 2018).

However, Chen's *futile*, in its English sense of pointless (useless), translates one or the other of several Chinese expressions which also refer to the uselessness of the action. In a pragmatic Chinese reading, wasting time on an approach obviously doomed to fail is absolutely unprofessional. Chen knows, as do his colleagues (to whom the first-person pronoun *we* refers) that Chinese customers do not respect deadlines—a *we* which contrasts with the personal pronoun *I* that he uses in his final sentence: *I will do my best to push customer to confirm before Jan 06*. Rather than trying to charge his customer for late changes—a move that cannot have a positive effect and could even lead to the client being lost—he proposes a strategic move: postponing the validation date without letting his client know. Aware of the inevitable and probably tardy requests for modifications, he gives himself time so as to grant his client a favour—that is, the exceptional privilege reserved for the *Lao Pengyou* (old friend) so often mentioned in commercial relations in China! In short, the postponed deadline is meant to allow him a gesture of goodwill likely to foster mutual respect and maintain the harmonious quality that is so essential to a long-term relationship with his client.

Although François and Chen are clearly not on the same wavelength, both are in perfect conformity with their respective professional environments, and each is working for the good of their company. However, the ideas that each has of their own professional conduct—their *métier* (profession)—are evidently not the same and are clearly not transposable into the cultural universe of the other. Not only are the actual words used instinctively invested with the meaning that they convey to speakers in their respective native languages, and transposed into the corresponding cultural context of the person using them, but they have influenced the overall meaning of the exchange, reflecting their different visions of how the task should be accomplished. As was shown in Chapter 8, these visions are intimately linked to the political cultures of their respective countries (Chevrier, 2012a).

Despite their identical functions within the same company, François and Chen cannot fulfil them in the same way. Their common language does not help much, either because their words take on different meanings (known only to them, individually), or because they can, when using emotive words like *futile* or *educate*, convey negative, positive, or neutral value judgements, likewise linked to their cultures. The move, seen as devoid of any hope of success and even as a professional error in Chen's pragmatic universe, becomes, for François, a casual refusal of the responsibilities incumbent upon a *good* professional in charge of mentoring his client—hence his *It's our job to* educate *him*—an attitude which, were it applied to a Chinese customer, would probably be perceived as arrogant and aggressive.

In this case, it is the situation, laden as it is with the positive or negative valences specific to each of the speakers and intricately linked to their respective cultural contexts, that gives meaning to the message; the words used all potentially present a risk not only for the process of communication between them, but also for the action to which it leads. Each of the correspondents has read the situation in the light of his own universe. However, not having access to the worldview in which the other's views are embedded, he then attributes them to other factors. The Frenchman will have at best concluded that Chen is—and perhaps all Chinese are—unprofessional; the Chinese, that this Frenchman is an unbearably arrogant man who thinks he knows everything when in fact he, Chen, risks losing a customer. At worst, this episode will have fuelled Chinese resentment (still alive today) of the country's humiliation during the 'unequal treaties' with the Western powers in the nineteenth century!

These examples are far from unique, and do not only involve individual speakers in geographically distant countries with notoriously different languages and cultures. Management concepts generally have names which can be very similar in many European languages (English, French, Spanish, etc.) because of their Latin or Greek origin. Their users are therefore convinced that they are talking about the same thing, but, over the centuries, the words have taken on meanings that are closely related to the linguistic and cultural communities in which they are used. The resulting misunderstandings, or uneasiness, can remain unheeded for a long time before they suddenly arise, often indirectly.

10.1.3 From Simple 'False Friends' to Differently Connoted Senses

Misunderstandings may be induced by words commonly referred to as 'false friends'—that is, words which look identical in more than one language, but do not have the same meaning. A good example would be the English *partner* which designates an associate rather than the French tennis- or card-game *partenaire*; or *differences*, more often assimilated by the French to simple diverging opinions than to the disputes to which they often refer. However, where concepts are concerned, dissimilarities can be much more profound. This is the case for the concept inherent in the English word *compromise*.

In her book on the British and French companies involved in the construction of the Channel Tunnel, Geoffroy (2001) refers to the different attitudes of the English and French employees towards compromises. For some, a compromise was an achievement, for others a quasi-impossibility. While all meanings inherent in the concept—agreement and promise of agreement, acceptance of undesirable conditions, endangering of one's reputation—are included in the definitions found in English, French, or Spanish dictionaries, the primary associations to which the term refers, in one or the other of these linguistic communities, differ. For the English, finding a compromise (*reaching a compromise*) is a positive way of managing working relationships or the essential step in sealing a trade agreement—a meaning only represented nowadays in the French language in the real-estate *compromis de vente*. For the French, a *compromis* can only be accepted with reluctance because it is associated with a disgraceful retreat. In a society whose members are defined by the status conferred on them by their position—along with its obligations and privileges (see pp. 63–64)—agreeing to a compromise is similar to capitulating either through fear or self-interest, behaviours which are considered as highly contemptible in French society (d'Iribarne, 2006a). This is reflected in the verbs *se compromettre* or *être compromis* of the same semantic family. The connotation dissimilarity is even more striking for the Spanish *compromise*, which neither refers to the English agreement nor to the French unacceptable behaviour, but to a commitment, a promise, as in *un anillo de compromiso* (an engagement ring) or in the slogan launched by this aviation company to celebrate its tenth anniversary:

Boliviana de Aviación: 10 años de trabajo, compromiso y pasión

The same could be said about the issue of control. American subordinates generally view positively the control that their leader exercises over their activities in order to assess how well they have achieved their objectives and consequently calculate their bonus (see Chapter 5 p. 22). The French, on the other hand, would perceive such control as unwelcome surveillance (Kassis-Henderson, 2005), which is not conducive to fostering the cooperation needed for them to achieve their objectives, and as a lack of confidence in their ability to accomplish the assigned task.

In short, apparently similar words can often refer to concepts that may have quite distinct meanings in local cultures. Throughout this book, we have encountered a few such concepts, the universality of which comes down to the English word that refers to them, masking the diversity of their real meanings. This cannot be ignored without putting organizations at risk—see Tietze's demonstration (2008: 40) that 'the use of the Anglicism "management", "to manage" and "manager" do not capture the nuances of meanings attributed to them in different languages'. As stated in the first chapter, management was born and developed in a specific cultural universe, that of the United States. It developed in accordance with the features that underpin the American political culture and became formalized in their tongue, English, the language in which management theories still circulate today throughout the world. By using (almost) identical words, people believe they understand each other. For instance, the notion of trust, that one might deem universal, is conceived on different bases according to the languages and cultures concerned (Usunier & Lee, 2005). Even teamwork may be influenced by the different ways in which teams are perceived. Gibson and Zellmer-Bruhn (2001) noticed that the employees that they interviewed on teamwork were referring to teams through quite distinct metaphors, depending on the culture from which they originated. Some likened them to families, others to communities, to partnerships, to sports organizations, or to military organizations, triggering attitudes and expectations that varied accordingly. Such diversity is worth taking into account when putting together multicultural teams, as it may affect the implementation of any team-building approach.

The use of English titles throughout multinational companies may be just as confusing, as, depending on the country in which they are applied, they may cover different functions. Bargiela-Chiappini (cited in Tietze (2008: 66)) reports on the difficulties encountered by the *middle managers* of an Anglo-Italian joint venture because their English job descriptions were irreconcilable with what their Italian bosses expected from them. Similarly, Chevrier and Segal (2011) noted that among the English native-speakers working in the subsidiaries of a French MNE, the English title *business-owner* that had been adopted throughout the organization aroused expectations of a greater decision-making power than that which the business-owners had actually been granted.

All these examples show the role that culture plays in the way words make sense to those who are using or hearing them. Sometimes, not quite understanding perfectly what has been said or read, speakers themselves inject a meaning—for example, the use in ELF of a *must* not in accordance with English natives' use of the word, which was in turn aggravated by the instinctive 'reading' of the situation in a North-American work environment. The situational context weighed even more heavily on the misunderstanding between the French and the Chinese managers. In all conscience, each of them considered the situation as pertaining to his own business environment, 'colouring' the exchange accordingly. What made things worse is that some of the words used, such as *futile* or *educate*, had a stronger emotional–cultural charge than others, even carrying connotations endowed with opposite valences, the one positive, the other negative. In these two examples, even though the speakers were unaware of it, they were the ones who conferred meaning to the words.

This is not always the case, as differences in meaning may be inherent in the languages themselves—as in the case of the so-called 'false friends'—or arise from different connotations (as for *compromise* or *control*) which, acquired along with the linguistic community's history, may convey positive or negative images directly related to its cultural foundations. Languages may also, independently of their speakers, give very different meanings to seemingly identical words. We will see in the third section that these observations raise questions as to the expected benefit emanating from the generalization of a managerial ELF: why should one expect a *middle management* position to correspond everywhere to the same function, and fit into the same organizational structure everywhere?

Before going any further, we need to consider the manner in which people communicate and get their messages across. Communication does not simply amount to words and structures; whichever language is used (including the speakers' native languages), messages may be stated clearly, buried in a mass of details, or merely hinted at. In other words, communication can be broken down into the propositional content and the manner in which it is conveyed. The latter may vary with individuals, but some ways of communicating are more or less frequent depending on the culture they belong to.

10.2 Cultural Communicative Styles May Hamper Communication

Although most speakers are unaware of it, the manner in which they communicate is a practical application of the social relations prevailing in their culture. As such, it may destabilize the correspondents who are wont to proceed differently, and even, as will be seen, give rise to interpretations far removed from what the communicative style conveys in their original cultures. Language is only one of the constituents of communication: style, explicitness or implicitness, the persuasive organization of speech, etc., are often the cause of disagreement, unease, or even aggression, among those who proceed otherwise and interpret this different communicative style in the light of what, for them, is the norm.

This point is illustrated in the cross-analysis of their different communicative styles that a group of Finns and Swedes made, when asked about their experience of the ELF recently adopted in their organizations (Louhiala-Salminen, 2005: 409). The Finns considered themselves '"factual" and "direct" communicators, implying that they are effective', the Swedes saw the Finns' mode of communication as 'blunt', 'pushy' and 'few-worded'. 'The Swedes, however, saw themselves as '"discussive" and "democratic", again implying that they are effective', while in the eyes of their Finnish partners they were seen as '"wordy" and "talk[ing] endlessly"'.

There is a similar underlying gap within Air France-KLM, a Franco-Dutch company, with Dutch people aware of their 'direct ways' but unaware of the way 'these behaviours are experienced by the French' and convinced that this characteristic, which is related to their culture, is positive, because it allows them to 'discuss things for what they are'.[3]

Such discrepancies are even more frequent in communications between Westerners and Asians. After repeatedly hearing the 'yes, yes' with which Asians punctuate their speech, how could Western businessmen doubt that the contract with their Asian contact is to be signed? Which one of them has not been horrified by the happy face of the announcer of dramatic news—for example, the murder of a politician or the death of a loved person—when in truth, the announcers were only trying to hide their own discomfort or pain in order to avoid making the recipients of the bad news uncomfortable. As will be seen in the misinterpretation by a Frenchman of his communication difficulties with his Japanese counterpart, the manner in which we use a language, even if we master it, is embedded in the way relationships with others make sense, in Japan as in any other culture.

10.2.1 Anything Rather than Uttering an Offensive Rebuttal!

In July, Alain, a French employee in a Franco-Japanese company, questioned his Japanese counterpart about the next biannual seminar which was to be held in Japan. The meeting was to take place during the winter, so he thought that it would be a good idea to hold it in a ski resort in Hokkaido. Wandering together on the slopes during the weekend preceding the meeting could cement the links between them, and actively contribute to team-building! When consulted, Sakurasan seemed to agree in principle; he said that he would ask his boss. Time went by and Alain heard nothing more about the project. Taking advantage of an exchange of emails on another subject, he enquired as to the boss's opinion on his, Alain's, idea for the venue of the meeting. Still no answer! August came, he went on leave, and on his return, enquired again, this time by means of an email exclusively dedicated to the issue. For lack of an answer, he decided to call Sakurasan on the phone; he was then told that the weather forecast predicted that there would not be any snow in Hokkaido next winter. Knowing that this northern Japanese island is one of the most snow-covered areas in winter in the country, he was enraged—and puzzled. How could meteorologists announce such news several months in advance? He finally came up with the only possible conclusion: 'He's making fun of me. He takes me for an idiot. How can he imagine I will believe such a lie? It would have been so easy to say that his boss didn't agree! We would have avoided wasting all that time and our plans to hold the meeting in another location would already be up and running!'[4]

Had this exchange taken place in Japanese or French rather than ELF, it would probably not have turned out any better, because modes of communication are generally too internalized to change with the simple switch to another language. Alain had forced himself to hold back before questioning his colleague, but the refusal which Sakurasan was *shouting* through his persistent silence didn't get across, leading Alain to revert to his normal ways, pick his telephone and ask Sakurasan a direct question which he hoped would lead to a clear answer. Sakurasan, for his part, did everything he could to avoid saying *no* to Alain, because in his culture, any kind of refusal is unacceptable. Seen through his Japanese eyes, saying nothing was the proper respectful behaviour owed to a colleague; whereas telling Alain that he was wrong or that his boss did not support his idea was a really aggressive action. He did know that French people's ways differed, but he could, nonetheless, not force himself to do it. Driven to his limits by Alain's direct question, he was compelled to invent a reason which, he hoped, would finally drive his point home. In short, for Alain, this behaviour was an attack on his intelligence, and a *lie* so huge that only a stupid individual could believe it. To him, telling the truth would have been much easier. For Sakurasan instead, the excuse that there would be no snow was the ultimate retreat after the silence, which was supposed to get the message across, had failed.

This manner of inducing others to proceed by themselves to the necessary deductions is often misunderstood by Western businessmen, yet it is fundamental in the Japanese acceptable way of living together. In Japan, where interactions are a priori based on the establishment of a harmonious relationship that nothing should ever be allowed to disturb, speakers will tend to apply, in their native language as in any other language, a mode of communication consistent with this norm.

10.2.2 A Recommendation that May Not Bring the Expected Result!

It is therefore not surprising that there were dubious reactions to the public announcement made at the turn of the century by the Japanese Prime Minister:

> Those who bear Japanese destiny in the 21st century will see to it that they are able to convey their thoughts and intentions in English, the international community's lingua franca. (Quoted in Kameda (2001: 144))

The Prime Minister was in fact combining two aspects that should not be confused: language (its lexicon, syntax, and fixed expressions) and communicative competence. What is generally problematic for the Japanese, is the latter. Commanding Japanese people to communicate in the way Westerners—and particularly United States nationals (those that the lingua franca of business immediately brings to mind) do—that is, by being direct and explicit, implies that the Japanese should renounce their own idea of proper social relations.

> For Japanese to develop and maintain harmonious relationships, they must be able to accurately 'read' the feelings of others and adjust their own expectations and behavior accordingly. Explicit and precise verbalizations of feelings often are unacceptable. (...) The Japanese standard for communicating with others is expressed in the phrase Ishin-Denshin, which literally means 'from my heart to your heart' or 'heart to heart'. In its Japanese context, it is a kind of cultural telepathy. (Kameda, 2014: 96)

Such *cultural telepathy* is generally expressed in a predilection for tacit communication and a tendency to avoid conflict—severely repressed at certain times in the country's history. 'Dissent always runs the risk of being misrepresented as dissension in Japan' (Kameda, 2001: 146). Japanese speakers prefer never to refuse directly, letting others understand their meaning without having to spell it. Therefore, expecting the acquisition of English to allow them to communicate their thoughts the way their Western partners do and to change their Japanese communicative style is utopian. It is too deeply imbued with the respect for the other (hence the use of implication), the show of humility, and the cautious use of verbal communication that all underpin their view of the proper way of living together (Kameda, 2014: 96–97).

One could wrongly consider the Japanese case as an exception and think that Westerners sharing the same 'global business culture' (Charles, 2007) have no difficulty getting along with each other. However, communicative styles are always rooted in the specific idea that prevails here or there of what interpersonal relationships should be. In some cases, their characteristics, for example, the habit of letting the other person finish his or her sentence before speaking, are attributed to a simple linguistic transfer (for example, the need to wait for the final verb that gives full meaning to a German or Japanese statement). Other characteristics, which are specific to speakers of this or that country, are often misunderstood—for example, the sometimes-insistent way of presenting arguments in favour of one's opinion; the tendency towards explicit and even abrupt discourse, or, conversely, towards an obliqueness which veils one's conclusion.

Few speakers are aware of the specificity of their own communicative style and, even more so, of its potential effect on people who are used to doing things differently. Everyone uses what, for them, is the proper way to proceed, and they may perceive dissimilar communication styles as *deviant*, interpreting them according to their own mode of communication, seeing them as aggressive, arrogant, or even amounting to simplistic or unnecessary (if not irrational or hypocritical) reasoning.

In all the situations mentioned above, only a good understanding of the context in which the exchange takes place, and of the dissimilar cultural backgrounds which it virtually brings together, may shed light on the meaning that the speaker gives to the situation, and on the reasons why it may not correspond to the other speaker's expectations. It is illusory to believe that communication problems can be solved by the mere use of a common language; however, having a language in common is a necessity as increasingly diverse groups of employees are generally unable to communicate with each other in any of their respective native languages. In short, they cannot do without a common language, but so as to avoid the aforementioned difficulties, they should be made aware of the limits accompanying its use.

10.3 Towards a Fully Informed Use of the Common Corporate Language

Defining one (or more) working languages and ensuring that they are best used in the field (Frederikson et al., 2006) is the most commonly recommended method to face the linguistic diversity that MNEs encounter nowadays. In most cases, English—or rather ELF—is the language chosen for this role. It used to be restricted to international trade or foreign operations, but today, it is used on a daily basis by a workforce who, despite their different linguistic and cultural backgrounds, have to work on common projects. One such illustration is the Fiat Palio, assembled from parts manufactured in seven different countries, which involved employees speaking twelve different languages (Feely & Harzing, 2003). Such an undertaking could not have been carried out without a common language, if only at the minimum level that Charles (2007) describes as 'language to get the job done' and Tréguer-Felten (2013) as 'language of *common action*'.

When asked about their experience with ELF, representatives of international companies of various sizes[5] start by saying that ELF is not a problem, before reporting facts that contradict this statement. For example, the managing director of the Toulouse site of a German engineering company noted that, to ensure that the message got across, whenever possible they reverted to their native languages; or that a commercial offer presented in ELF to a potential French customer was only successful after they had switched to the local language. A representative of a joint venture between the European consortium Airbus and an Italian industrial group remarked that ELF is indeed the staff's common language, but that, very often, to move forward, they had to use local languages, hire engineers and technicians who were competent in them, and make efforts to understand the local country's culture.

Such remarks abound. Many ELF users complain that communication is not going well.

10.3.1 Deficiencies Generally Attributed to Poor Control of ELF

After presenting the various measures used to remedy a situation that some consider hopeless, we will see that the main reason for communication difficulties does not reside in people's fluency in ELF, but in their own cultures. We will conclude on the necessity of trying to understand the universe of meaning that influences linguistic interpretation in ELF speakers with different native languages, and their understanding.

ELF appears to be the most commonly used working language in the world (Neeley, 2012), however, its users do not fail to indicate that its use comes with problems which are generally due to linguistic deficiencies.

> The use of English is very convenient and there seems to be no quick way around it. On the other side, *English is misused* by a lot of people. This is mainly due to lack of language skills. In case of lack of skills, native language parts are inserted into the English, leading (in some case) to hardly understandable texts (a German engineer in a MNE, quoted in Lejot).[6]
>
> [Wastes of time in meetings] are not due to people speaking slowly, those make you lose 10% of time, it does not matter. It is due to the fact that some people understand nothing and you have to repeat everything three times, you speak about something for ten minutes and after ten minutes you realize that the person you were speaking to is not at all in phase with what you were saying; this is a real waste of time (the French manager of a transnational project, quoted in Saulière).[7]

Some managers are aware of their difficulties in getting messages across, and strive to find ways to reduce them. The marketing vice-president of an international company—a native English speaker with only basic knowledge of French—who was leading a project team whose members (various native language speakers) worked in France, set up compensatory measures:

I'm presenting on priorities and objectives. That's a pretty important topic. It could really disrupt what people are working on today (. . .). So, I would expect a lot of questions. And if I don't get those questions, it makes me nervous and makes me think that something was lost in translation. (. . .) Um, but then just so nothing is lost in translation, I do like to follow up with written email communication or written document communication, just in case there was something that might have been lost in translation. (. . .) So, if it's really, if it's very serious, I do always follow-up with an email. (Marketing VP & Marketing Team Manager, San Francisco, California.)[8]

Another, noting that the English terms might have different meanings in French and German, endeavours to explain them. The commonest idea is that until everyone has mastered this essential ELF, a few simple instructions will suffice to overcome communication deficiencies. This was exactly the intention of this same project manager:

> Yeah, um, I think we could do... um, I think, I don't know what the phrasing of this is... but sort of language sensitivity training when somebody joins B-Company. You know, just trying to explain that 'You're going to communicate with people who have different levels of capabilities in different languages and what are some of those good practices for making sure that you don't... that you get your point across and can have productive communication' (ibid.).

Similar recommendations are offered to those who really master the language, be they English-natives or not:

> Strong speakers must agree to slow down their speaking pace and use fewer idioms, slang terms, and esoteric cultural references when addressing the group. They should limit the number of comments they make within a set time frame, depending on the pace of the meeting and the subject matter. They should actively seek confirmation that they've been understood, and they should practice active listening by rephrasing others' statements for clarification or emphasis.
>
> (Neeley, 2015)

Everyone is looking for solutions to the so-called 'language barriers', which, according to Harzing and Feely (2008), are linked to various factors articulated in vicious circles:

> Failure to communicate effectively leads to uncertainty, anxiety and mistrust, which produces misattribution, conflict and cognitive distortion, to which the various parties respond by engaging in greater formality in communication, which is less effective... and the circle is completed
>
> (Blenkinsopp & Shademan Pajouh (2010: 40).

In other words, there seems to be very little hope that communication might improve! Yet the observations that come from the field can offer clear hints about what should be examined. For example, one member of a transnational team is quoted as saying: 'Even if we all speak pretty good English, we all speak our kind of English' (Lagerström & Andersson, 2003: 91), thus indicating that what is needed is an analysis of the specific context in which speakers of different native languages and cultures strive to understand one another. The stumbling blocks in situations of intercultural communication are not a matter of language itself; instead, they are linked to the cultural background underpinning the situations experienced.

10.3.2 Language? No, Speakers' Cultural Background

To show that the difficulties are not specific to ELF, the following situations that we will describe (one Franco-Swiss, the other Franco-Canadian) use another common language, namely French. The professional and cultural contexts specific to each of the groups concerned lead to misunderstandings which, although focusing on specific French words, are not strictly linguistic in nature. The border situation which will finally be presented stages French and German professionals who find working side-by-side arduous even though they are all familiar with the others' culture, speak extremely close dialects, and do not necessarily need a common language to understand one another—they practice what is generally called *inter-comprehension*, that is, everyone expresses themselves in their native language and no translation is required. This leads to the conclusion that, whichever language is used, communication cannot be satisfactorily achieved unless speakers on both sides attempt to enter the exact universes of meaning on which their counterparts are drawing to make sense of the ongoing exchange. It appears that, more than simply language, it is culture, as we defined it (see p. 63), that weighs on communication.

Due to the acquisition of part of their company by a large French group, Swiss engineers were required to work on electrical engineering projects along with their French counterparts.[9] Their common objective was to deliver, on a turnkey basis, substations which were built from equipment produced either in the Swiss plant or in any other of the group's plants in Europe—in France or elsewhere. Collaboration proved more difficult than expected. The Swiss and the French complained that communication was poor, and conflicts and tensions kept arising between departments, and between individuals. The situation very soon gave birth to stereotypical judgements. The Swiss complained: 'the French are convinced they know everything better than everyone else', while the French claimed 'the Swiss are self-satisfied; they always consider that they do better'.

What emerged from the comments relating to their dissent was that each party appeared to have a different idea of what quality meant. While everyone agreed on the objective to sell quality substations, the vision they had of *quality* differed, and these divergent ideas were all the more likely to generate intercultural conflicts that the Swiss considered quality to be their national trademark:

We have a quality image because we are based in Switzerland (Swiss secretary).

For the Swiss engineers who were interviewed, quality was associated with the reliability of high-end (but expensive) equipment and reflected in the details:

Swiss technical quality requires the best supply, but also attention to detail and attention to finish. (. . .) Nothing is so insignificant as to deserve to be neglected.

For the Swiss, no detail in the entire process of selling and producing the finished product could be neglected, even in the most insignificant way. This included all aspects of the process, such as the sales presentations and subsequent contacts with the customer, the efficient organization of the production environment, as well as acknowledging the importance of an egalitarian production process in which each individual, with his or her different skill sets, worked in complete autonomy. For them, it was only by strictly adhering to the minute details of these standards of excellence that a 'perfect' product (in their eyes) could be produced.

The French engineers quickly became aware of the differences between their respective ideas of quality. On the one hand, they considered the use of high-end equipment (therefore a priori safe) to be a marketing risk in countries that did not have the means to afford it; on the other hand, to their minds, the quality of a project did not lie in a detailed and standardized production process, but in offering ingenious solutions. Far from this concern for detail, they called for a global approach, using modelling and systems thinking—an approach which aims to integrate all the components of the whole:

In France, we start with the environment, the system. Conversely, the Swiss are pushing very hard on the details. They take care of the particularities, but see very little of the generalities (. . .). The French rather tend to look at the large masses.

Thus, for them, quality could only be conceived in relation to the 'formal technical truth' and presenting a project to a customer consisted in demonstrating the technical validity of the proposed solution:

We assume that customers know what they are talking about, that they are competent. Even at very advanced levels, they are engineers addressing engineers (French project manager).

As can be seen, the notion of quality may be designated by this one and only word for both the Swiss and the French, the manner in which the engineers of each culture conceive it notably modifies its nature. For the Swiss, quality emerged from a universe in which each and every individual, in an autonomous way, played their part in a well-ordered construction process that would give birth to the 'jewel' that would satisfy the customer; for the French, quality required everyone to collaborate on the project, paying great attention to the interfaces between the working units, and less attention to the form in which the finished project would be presented to the customer. What really mattered was the ingenuity of the technical content of the solution to be presented. In short, to them, quality was represented by a solution likely to satisfy a customer seeking expert advice (see pp. 160–162).

Using the same word, in the same language, for a concept does not necessarily make that concept unique. The following example shows that, just like a concept, simple words can refer to concrete realities that can be understood differently by different speakers.

This handover took place in Quebec in the early 1980s; French managers and supervisors had been sent there to start up an aluminium smelter.[10] Once the plant started operating at full capacity, the smelter would be run by local teams. Naturally, the chosen common language was French.

The project managers had spared no effort to promote the best possible understanding and communication between the teams and to ensure a smooth takeover between the French and Quebec teams. Pairs comprising one French expatriate and a Quebec counterpart had been formed well in advance of the plant start-up; they had been encouraged to get to know each other well and to forge close ties. To this end, each Quebec professional had been sent to France to spend several weeks so as to get to know his 'correspondent'. They spoke the same language (at least theoretically), and each of them had had solid experience in the same industry. In short, they had the necessary commonality to get along well. As the rest of the story will show, this prediction did not come true.

After a few weeks, far from working together with the expected symbiosis, the pairs had exploded. It was particularly striking in the case of a French workshop manager and his Canadian counterpart who was, for the time being, his assistant. Every day, the Frenchman went through the work that was being done, taking a demanding look at everything taking place in his department, intervening at once on any subject if his teams seemed to be deviating from what *he* considered the right way to do things. Conversely, the Quebec professional confined himself to administrative tasks: he stayed in his office and tried to plan the work of his team as rationally as possible. The confusion that resulted from these opposing behaviours is rooted in the idea prevailing in their respective cultures of what the role of a workshop leader is.

The Frenchman acted as he would in France, a professional context in which his function is crucial. The workshop manager is the key man: the one who, always in the field, keeps a close watch, moves from one end of the workshop to the other to manage the daily numerous small problems and ensure that the instructions that he is in charge of relaying are properly implemented by his team. It had been his understanding that he was to train his Quebec counterpart for that role of a workshop manager. For him, training his counterpart consisted in taking him into the field to watch how he, as a workshop manager, operated so as to acquire the tips and tricks of the *métier* and be able to take over when the time came. However, his deputy did not see it that way.

The Quebec manager saw his role in a completely different manner and his attitude clearly indicated it. The training that he was receiving was completely at odds with his anticipated future function in the Quebec professional world, once the French expatriates had left. Inspired by the American methods in use in Quebec, the organizational system has a specific task for everyone, assigned by the higher-level manager to whom they report at regular intervals. There is therefore no need for a daily check of tasks, the control of which is handled, according to explicit procedures and rules, by the next level of authority. The function of a workshop manager is more a matter of short-term planning and management. The future Quebec workshop manager was all the more frustrated that his training had nothing to do with what he and his colleagues had expected—that is, a rapid and planned training session that would have progressed according to a well-established formal schedule.

With the creation of such pairings, the people in charge of the general management of the project had thought to protect themselves against the risks of poor interpersonal understanding. In fact, it had had the opposite effect: the French name for the position (*chef d'atelier*) covered divergent concepts of the function. The elevated French notion of one's *métier*, and the proper way to practice it clashed with the American contractual organizational logic from which the Quebec practice was partly inspired—an organizational logic in which each manager comes up with specific objectives for their team members to achieve, and is responsible for ensuring they are achieved (see Chapter 1, pp. 18, 19).

Finally, the linguistic commonality between the French and Quebec professionals had masked differences that might have been noticed more easily in a country whose language was foreign to either of them. However, the parties concerned might just as well have decided, as is often the case with ELF, that the problem was only linguistic and that the difficulties were due to the local population's poor command of that language!

It seems that, even when there is no need for a common language, the risk of divergent understandings persists as demonstrated in the following border situation.

In this case, the co-workers' native languages are intelligible to all, and yet they experience a certain lack of understanding.[11] Allco, headquartered in Saarbrücken (Saarland, Germany), is a joint subsidiary of two state-owned railway companies, the French SNCF and the German Deutsche Bahn AG (DB). Staffed by a Franco-German team, this subsidiary develops cross-border train services and operates the Eastern-Europe high-speed line between France and Germany. As such, it acts as an interface between two parent companies belonging to different countries, both steeped in traditional public service missions, each being integrated into specific institutional and cultural systems.

As a bi-national company, Alleo has made it a point to implement Franco-German parity at all hierarchical levels, and to distribute authority evenly. In Saarbrücken, Alleo employs about ten people, French and German; but it is responsible for about 200 to 300 French and German employees, who, working in Franco-German teams, welcome and accompany travellers throughout their journeys. At the time of the investigation, the majority of employees, and several managers, were from the neighbouring regions—Lorraine in France, Saarland in Germany—and they had few difficulties with the language or languages in which to communicate. In most cases, they had grown up in a bilingual environment and had been exposed to border contacts; some of the French spoke a Germanic dialect in their families and the Saarlanders had learned French at school. The language in which they communicated was therefore not an issue when the two groups had difficulty in reaching an agreement—a fact clearly demonstrated by the bimonthly experts' information meetings which were held in a bilingual format, that is, everyone speaking in their native language or switching from one language to the other, sometimes even using a key concept of the other language or responding quickly to a question in that language.

However, the distribution of tasks and roles within the pairs was not that easy—for example, after signing the regulatory text stipulating that German and French controllers would take charge of the same train *together*, the decision-makers discovered that for the French, *together* meant acting side by side, or even back-to-back (for protection), in the carriages, while for the Germans, it was a matter of being present at both ends of the train to control the maximum number of passengers between stops, which were generally more frequent in their country.

These bicultural teams, who came from organizations set in different cultures, embodied traditions related to their functions that are also quite different. At SNCF, the ticket inspector had, as indicated by the title of *contrôleur* (controller) by which users designated him, the right to require travellers' identity documents to check the authenticity of their tickets, whereas at DB, since the mid-1990s, everything had been done to ensure that, just as their name of *Zugbegleiter* (train attendants) suggested, they made passengers' journeys as pleasant as possible. They wore name tags, which slightly reduced the distance with passengers, they served them coffee—just as is done in airplanes—or sold them underground tickets so that when they got off the train, passengers could reach their final destination more easily.

Cohabitation did finally set in with surprising effects, probably linked to the cultural proximity between these border populations. The working language itself (or, should we say, the working languages: French for some, German for others) had become richer. German DB employees had included French SNCF terms in their exchanges, for example, *Jours particuliers* (special days) and *Feuille de route* (road map) and increasingly used the term REX (for the French *retour d'expérience* (experience feedback)) in lieu of the German term *Erfahrungsrückfluss*.

Simultaneously, the French participants had reviewed their previous judgements, particularly regarding the rigour of their foreign colleagues:

The (French) conductors thought that the Germans would be more rigorous with the regulations and there were some surprises. For example, while in France, 10% of our agents refuse to wear the regulatory cap, in Germany, 90% do. And with the ticket control, a big surprise, we discovered a German word, the word 'Kulanz', the Zugbegleiter were content to gently scold passengers who were not in order, without punishing them (Alleo manager).

They had also put their respective modes of communication into perspective:

The direct side of the Germans is quite surprising, the French are not so harsh, they are at the limit more tortuous.

Clearly, in this case, what was in question was not the language but the cultural context that gave different meanings to concepts, while concrete reality challenged the individuals' previously acquired stereotypes, or simply set them wondering.

Obviously, when individuals from different cultures work together in a professional context differently perceived by each group, the language in which they express themselves cannot play the 'unifying' role generally attributed to CCL. Rather, it tends to cover the expectations of the staff with a thick veil under which their frustrations smoulder, and these ultimately crystallize into negative stereotypes that may leave their mark, unless, as in the border situation above, the familiarity due to the individuals' numerous previous contacts reduces their impact.

This chapter on the comprehension difficulties arising when words or messages get transposed into a new language/culture cannot end without mentioning two specific cases, both connected to possible word- or concept-meaning discrepancies. As non-native English speakers writing in ELF, the authors of this book have repeatedly been confronted with difficulties to convey exactly what they meant. We shall explain some of the concepts that were pondered on, before broaching the topic of questionnaire-based cross-cultural studies in which such difficulties tend to be overlooked.

10.3.3 Conveying One's Ideas in Another Language

Not only did the ELF conveying our ideas and findings risk being perceived by native speakers as not exactly right, but it might also be 'heard' by other readers in their native languages (Tietze, 2008) and instinctively made sense of, based on their specific universes of meaning. In order to avoid what philosophers Quine or

Davidson had only seen as difficult 'interlinguistic synonymy', our response was to ground our interpretations—and their ELF formulations—on convincing empirical examples. However, in some cases, the very description and interpretation of these examples required using expressions that were not immediately translatable into ELF. In some cases, they were rooted in French culture, for example, the concept of *métier* which the reader has encountered several times already. In others, depicting the situations encountered required expressions that did not have perfect English equivalents. Some of these expressions were so central that we felt it preferable to share the thoughts underpinning them, all the more so that these explanations would also provide a concrete illustration of the fully informed use of ELF that we advocate.

One such expression is related to *authority*. As we scrutinized more and more diverse environments, we realized that everywhere people were ready to accept what, following our research in China, we had come to designate as *un bon pouvoir* ('good power' in French)—that is, either an authority figure perceived as legitimate because of the specific talents he or she is endowed with, or the authority itself. We had adopted that expression as we were reporting on our Chinese data. However, we felt that the polysemy of the English word '*power*' might draw attention away from the meaning we wanted to convey. We had to find an English formulation that could similarly convey the more or less general idea that, to be efficient, authority must be acceptable and accepted. As we recalled those times, we remembered that historically, the legitimate Chinese authority figure had to be deemed virtuous and following the so-called rites (see *The Analects* (Confucius, 1999)). These reflections led us to replace the French subjective and vague qualifier *bon* by 'virtuous' and *pouvoir* by 'authority', and to choose the expressions *virtuous authority* and *virtuous authority figure.*

Such expressions would not seem familiar to any of our readers, but they were vague enough to contain the various norms expected of these authority figures according to the specific universes of meaning of those who might be subject to them. For instance, in France, leaders will be expected to be *à la hauteur* (up to the task)—that is, at the same time able to perform their task, and behaving as befits their position. New Caledonians will expect them to provide the protection that they feel in need of, while US nationals will want to be treated fairly without intruding on what they conceive as their lawful rights and property.

Besides, even though the expected behaviours are quite diverse, almost everywhere, the standards required from authority figures could be categorized as *virtue*. In addition to that, the word used for *virtue* in most European languages—Benjamin Whorf's Standard Average European languages (1956)—shares the same Greek and Latin origins. The word is historically connected to religion and/or politics; it commands respect and confers some legitimacy on whoever is considered as virtuous. These are in a nutshell the considerations supporting our choice of *virtuous authority* and *virtuous authority figure.*

Another type of difficulty arose as we tried to convey the French *rapport social.* How could the historical and political references with which the French formula is loaded be transferred into a language developed in communities which do not share such a background? France, where social classes have had clashes so violent as to cause a revolution meant to abolish royalty, nobility, and their privileges, can have tense social relations. This formula encapsulates all that. More than simply referring to social relations, it implies the need to keep a certain balance between the supposedly no longer existing social classes. This is particularly true for industrial relations in which employees and employers have in a way interiorized that necessity and transferred it into what is, or is not, to be done. However, not all cultures share that background. So, we decided to clarify the concept whenever necessary, and in other cases, ignore our conflict-loaded French vision of *social relations* and use it as a more neutral expression.

Other words which would be acceptable in French in most situations had to be translated in various ways according to the situation being described. This was the case for work relations. In France, in China, and presumably in other cultures, hierarchical relations are of a vertical dyadic nature. Descriptions will consequently refer to *superiors* and *subordinates.* In other cultures, these relations may be conceived differently: for example, in the United States, a *leader* will have *followers*, and other titles such as *managers, executives*, etc. will be qualified as *senior* or *junior*, thus referring to their respective experience levels. The German couple *Vorgesetzter/Mitarbeiter* uses another type of contrast. It simply refers to their respective localization: the authority figure ahead of those who work with him or her. These are but a few of the images used for hierarchical relations. As a rule, whenever we were confronted with such occurrences, we endeavoured to find the words that best suited the local and situational context, occasionally reverting to the words *boss* and *employee*, which seemed the least evocative of a specific type of relationship.

It also occurred to us that some of the international management concepts used in their English designations may convey vague notions that no one seems to agree on. An example will illustrate what we mean. Once, in an international team gathering some French, British, and American researchers, *International Business* had to be translated into French. You could have thought that translating these rather simple words would be easy. But it proved impossible: four or five French formulations emerged. None could satisfy everyone, revealing the different ways in which these various native speakers made sense of the term. *International Business* was finally kept as such in the French text. This is the fate of many of the management concepts that travel round the world in their English formulation. It is definitely one of the reasons why adopting what we call a fully informed use of the language is a necessity. One should be fully aware that one and the same ELF word used in any international situation, in any group of people originating from different cultures and speaking different native languages, may be conveying images and representations that, once instinctively transposed in their respective universes of meaning, may be in total disagreement with what they originally referred to.

This kind of awareness is what questionnaire-based cross-cultural studies tend to overlook.

10.3.4 Idols with Feet of Clay?

All over the world, when making judgements about a society, a mode of government, or even behaviour, people regularly use a set of common terms: individualism, collectivism, leadership, visionary, confident, motivated, self-centred, etc. However, this vocabulary is misleading. Whoever uses it associates with each of these terms a set of representations which reflect their own culture, for example, the representation that they have of an authoritarian manager, of a charismatic leader, or what, in their eyes, corresponds to an individualistic attitude. These concrete images nourish the corresponding words and give them meaning. As can be seen throughout this book, the images associated with a word may differ considerably from one culture to another. Moreover, the words used to describe each of these traits in the various languages often match each other only very roughly. Such diversity of individual mental images, and therefore of the meanings that may be associated with the same word, seriously challenges the results of studies based on the responses provided by individuals scattered around the world—often in about fifty or more countries, as in Hofstede's initial study (see p. 62). The meanings associated with the words used and the situational contexts that the questions themselves project are quite different. Besides, the questions, as well as the answers, are subject to a to-and-fro translation process that can only further undermine the reliability of the responses.

The impossibility of associating a consensual set of properties to a given word, and thus of characterizing a culture by a few words in an unambiguous way is particularly striking in the American case. The classic cascade delegation model (discussed in pp. 18–20): with target setting and a posteriori evaluation of results—be it positive or negative—thrives in the United States. It is common to relate this successful modus vivendi to the strong American individualism, which means that everyone is judged on their own performance against previously identified targets. And indeed, if this is the experience which is associated with the word *individualism*, it makes sense to say that the United States is an individualistic country. But, as discussed in p. 175, ethical charters and procedures such as whistleblowing hotlines also flourish in the United States. As such, these procedures imply fairly strict control of each team member's work by fellow workers. One could then conclude that the United States is a communitarian country. The same approach can be applied to France; one will consider the French, always ready to defend their *acquis*[12]—what rights and benefits they have obtained over the years—as individualistic. Or, conversely, as Kramsch does, one can consider their tendency to follow fashion as the antithesis of the label of individualists that they generally claim for themselves (1993: 208), quoted in Katan (1999 : 164).

Depending on the semantic elements associated with a particular word, it may or may not seem appropriate to characterize a culture, or to define a national attitude or character trait. In fact, this remark is, in fact, very general in nature: seeking to characterize anything by a few words supposed to have a common meaning transcending a variety of cultures is a great source of misunderstanding in the relationships between individuals from different cultures. At all times, they decode one another's actions—something which is a natural component of human intercourse. However, since what is associated with a word differs from one culture to another, those who encounter a foreign culture tend to reconstruct it according to their own logic. Based on observed traits, they will tend to describe the culture or person as individualistic, authoritarian, or exceedingly or insufficiently autonomous, insofar as, in their own culture, the association between these words and these traits is relevant. From this point on, they will tend to assume that everything that, in the logic of their own culture, is related to these words is present in the definition in question.

In returning to the attitude scales, we must note the remarkable position occupied by the Scandinavian countries, Denmark, and the Netherlands, on the initial four bases of Hofstede's model: very strong individualism, very weak control of uncertainty, very short hierarchical distance, and very strong femininity. With these characteristics forming the basis of the study, it becomes obvious that the questionnaire on which it is based was constructed on features that contrast the rest of the world with the North European culture in which it was conceived. In p. 54, the description of the way Volvo's Swedes constructed an imaginary representation of French culture illustrated such a cultural interpretation of an 'abstract' term. Representing a culture by the scores obtained on a few attitude scales feeds this type of imaginary reconstruction. Whoever consults the study naturally associates the images that the corresponding words suggest in their own culture with the various scores—images that may unfortunately have nothing to do with the national reality of the country endowed with these scores. To escape the illusory comfort of the transparency of words, one needs to take a very concrete interest in the realities to which they refer. Adopting a phenomenological approach, one has to observe what the terms *customer*, *decision*, *superior*, *honesty*, etc., mean in a given culture, as we are doing throughout this book.

10.4 Conclusion

If we simply define intercultural competence by the qualities generally implied by the term—a dose of tolerance, openness, emotional stability, and empathy—then intercultural communication between people simply endowed with such basic competences is unlikely to work at its best. Admittedly, attitudes such as these will probably make it possible to perceive the discomfort of one's interlocutor, or help to detect expressions which deserve to be clarified, but they can never replace the analysis, linguistic and cultural, of the context of the exchange, and the research necessary to highlight the real meaning of the exchange for the interlocutor of the other culture.

The only way to avoid the misunderstandings that threaten any attempt at intercultural communication is to appreciate the influences exerted by our respective native languages and cultures. Apparent similarities in meaning between words in two different languages can lead to non-native speakers using these words in ELF with the meanings assigned to them in their respective native languages. Remember the French senior correspondent's 'You must come' which did not have the same value for the American manager. These misunderstandings also have their roots in cultural differences, as in the example where the idea of the proper way to maintain social relations is also instinctively invoked when communicating with others, as was illustrated in the Japanese manager's use of an implausible reason to avoid a refusal that he perceived as both equivalent to a lack of respect, and a hostile act, or by the contrasting uses that Swedes and Finns made of the CCL during their meetings.

Being aware of such realities is crucial for intercultural communication—and for intercultural management which, like all human activities, depends on it. It is illusory to believe that certain character traits and mastery of the language of communication are sufficient to communicate successfully; it is also illusory to consider ELF as the necessary and sufficient universal language of business. Speaking English as a lingua franca does help to communicate; however, it will never eliminate communication issues, or, as a manager of a multinational company once said: 'ELF is not the problem, communication is'. This realization implies abandoning the model of communication as a simple coding–decoding process. We must accept the idea that the words said, or heard, may not make sense in the same way for our correspondents, and, at the slightest hint, make the effort to try and understand the meaning they give them, in other words to access their universes of meaning.

Acquiring this awareness will certainly be much more beneficial than deploring the fact that not everyone uses English as native speakers do!

Notes

1. Quoted in Faust-Morel, Catherine (2015) 'Représentations et gestion des compétences interculturelles', Doctoral Thesis, (Université Paris-Est), p. 18.

2. Company name was changed for confidentiality reasons.
3. See d'Iribarne, Philippe, and Noorderhaven, Niels, 'Les rapports entre Air France et KLM dans le vécu du personnel. Une perspective culturelle', *Rapport* mai 2017.
4. Private interview reported by Catherine Faust-Morel.
5. Unless otherwise stated, the following remarks were heard at round-tables in seminars organized by GEM&L, (an association of researchers in language and management) in Marseilles and Toulouse in 2013 and 2014.
6. Quoted in Lejot, Eve (2013) 'Regards croisés sur le multilinguisme en contexte professionnel à Hambourg', Doctoral thesis, (Université Paris), p. 74.
7. Quoted in Saulière, Jérôme (2013) 'Organizational Language Boundaries and the Dynamics of Language Change: Three Case Studies in a French MNC. Working paper', (EGOS colloquium), p. 9.
8. Quoted in Church-Morel, Amy (2016) 'Language Diversity in Team Work', Doctoral Thesis, (Université Grenoble Alpes), p. 158 and 211.
9. This situation is depicted in Chevrier (1998).
10. This situation is depicted in Segal (1990).
11. The Alleo situation presented here was described by Barmeyer, C. and Davoine, E. in 'Culture de travail émergente dans des organisations bi-nationales – une analyse de deux cas franco-allemands', *Atlas Seminar*, 2014.
12. Such a characteristic reference in the sessions of the European Commission that the term (untranslatable in English) has finally been kept as such in *Eurospeak*, the language used within the European Commission (Wagner et al., 2002).

11
Corporate Communication

Acquiring a strong corporate identity has become one of the preoccupations of organizations all over the world. To do so, they rely on various tools, one of which is the self-presentation that conveys their core values to their stakeholders. Formerly included in corporate brochures handed out to visitors, these self-profiles generally constitute one section of organizations' corporate websites. Due to the perceptions of English as *the* business language (Neeley, 2012), even organizations originating from non-native English-speaking countries tend to offer an English version of their home self-presentation. It partakes of their effort to strengthen their visibility. Every organization wishes to establish a worldwide corporate image, seen as its corporate identity in spite of the fact that it is not so much a representation of '*what the organization is*', as '*how it wishes to be seen*' by its stakeholders (Bhatia & Lung, 2006: 267). The 'ideal organization' constructs projected to complete this persuasive enterprise generally proceed from a real mirror game: they are framed so as to satisfy the expectations of the organizations' audience. In other words, they tend to be projections of what, within a given society, is perceived as positive and rewarding, and as such they are embedded in the local culture.

This does not only concern the informative content of the self-presentation, but also the way in which it is communicated. It contributes to the image conveyed, and is just as likely to be rooted in the local culture. In fact, on this point as on many others, corporate communication is hardly different from interpersonal communication. As was seen in Chapter 10, pp. 197–200, some communication modes are favoured here and avoided there, but everywhere they have an impact on the addressee's perception. For instance, those who keep reminding friends or relations of their qualities can pretend that they are modest; no one will take their word for it. The turn of their sentences, the formality of their speech, their tendency to argue or not, all contribute to the speakers' images and modify the way in which they are perceived. The same goes for organizations: the type of information supplied, as well as the way it is put into words, contribute to the picture of themselves that they are projecting.

Hence the question arises as to how well the information and the form of speech conveying it are received when self-presentations initially conceived for home audiences are simply transposed into English as a lingua franca (ELF)[1] to target audiences unknown aside from their ability to understand the language. Are

Cross-Cultural Management Revisited: A Qualitative Approach. Philippe d'Iribarne, Sylvie Chevrier, Alain Henry, Jean-Pierre Segal, and Geneviève Tréguer-Felten, Oxford University Press (2020). © Philippe d'Iribarne, Sylvie Chevrier, Alain Henry, Jean-Pierre Segal, and Geneviève Tréguer-Felten.
DOI: 10.1093/oso/9780198857471.001.0001

these profiles not likely, as happens in interpersonal communication (see Chapter 10), to disturb rather than convince readers used to other modi operandi? In other words, does the ideal image on which these portraits are based cross borders well? And if not, what other options exist for organizations wishing to internationalize their corporate identity? These are the questions that this chapter tackles; to do so it relies on the comparison of self-presentations produced in two countries as distant geographically and linguistically as culturally. As will be shown, the two groups' projected images clearly contrast each other, confirming that the firms are addressing foreign audiences that they cannot imagine different in any way from their respective national audiences, and prompting questions about the appropriateness of such transpositions (Tréguer-Felten, 2014).

The first section of the chapter is dedicated to the data—two corpora of ELF self-presentations (one Chinese, one French)—and to the comparison methodology; the findings are exposed and discussed in the following section; while a few of the other possible options for firms to internationalize their corporate identities occupy the third and final part. We conclude on the generally ignored necessity to fully understand how each specific cultural context will influence the way in which people will make sense of the corporate messages they receive and to tailor communications accordingly.

11.1 A Comparison of Chinese and French ELF Self-presentations

Corporate self-presentations have one specific feature: for the external audience, they are *the* organization's voice; however, far from resulting from a single person's writing, be they produced internally or entrusted to an external agency, they systematically pass through several hands before obtaining top management's approval. Such collective authorship is an interesting feature when comparing speech cross-nationally since it eliminates any risk of attributing to cultural contexts traits which would only be individual idiosyncrasies.

11.1.1 The Data

Whether stemming from Chinese or French organizations (see Table 11.1), the corporate brochures and electronic documents under scrutiny were either gathered in China or from firms having operations there, so as to guarantee that the corporations belonging to either country could have been part of the audience that these corporations had in mind when producing their documents.[2] They were collected in two successive batches: one before China joined the World Trade Organization, the other one some ten years later. In order that no corporation's specificity (such as size or activity sector) might blur the findings, they were

Table 11.1 Chinese and French firms and their respective activity sectors

Ch1	GT LAW OFFICE	Law firm
Ch2	SNERDI	Engineering
Ch3	DBC	Industrial boiler manufacturer
Ch4	LYHCC	Transportation
Ch5	SINOTRUST Research & Consulting	Market studies
Ch6	CZEC	Engineering
Ch7	SDEPDI	Engineering
Ch11	The Creative Life (TCL)	Information technology
Ch12	Huawei	Telecommunication networks
Ch13	ZTE	Telecommunication
Ch14	COSCO	Transportation
Fr1	DS Avocats	Law firm
Fr2	CGEA—ONYX	Industrial services
Fr3	EDF	Electricity producer
Fr4	Bureau Veritas	Quality control, certification
Fr5	Thermocoax	Cable manufacturer
Fr6	Schneider Electric	Electric material manufacturer
Fr7	SGN	Engineering services
Fr11	Veolia	Industrial services
Fr12	Saint Gobain	Various chemicals producers
Fr13	ALSTOM	Power plants, transportation system manufacturers
Fr14	Faurecia	Automotive supplier

collected randomly, apart from their partaking of what is commonly called 'Business-to-Business' (B2B) communication.

Thus assembled, the two corpora are similar in size: a total of 17,342 words for the Chinese corpus and a total of 15,302 words for the French one. Each of them comprises seven paper self-presentations (first batch) and four website *About Us* sections (second batch). Chinese self-presentations are designated as Ch1, Ch2, Ch3, etc., the French ones as Fr1, Fr2, Fr3, etc. However, so that numerical self-presentations are recognizable at first sight, they all bear two-digit numbers: for example, Ch11, Fr11, etc.

Since both the information communicated and the adopted mode of communication contribute their part to the construct, the focus of the analyses does not lie exclusively on the messages issued: in order to include the form of speech, the comparison methodology simultaneously considers the informative content and the grammatical structures summoned to convey it.

11.1.2 A Discourse Analysis that Relies on Linguistic Categories

To highlight all the discursive features, a cross-cultural discourse analysis (CCDA) methodology was used (von Münchow, 2012). Each corpus discourse was 'deconstructed', searching for apparent 'anomalies'—for example, unexpected dissimilarities between the two corpora—which might be of interest in regard to the initial objective—that is, determining if each country's corporations are indeed addressing the foreign audience that their choice of ELF indicates. Hypotheses were formed as to the reason for these so-called anomalies, the viability of which was checked by exploring discourse further, finally retaining only the items which formed coherent and valid systems. In other words, these bottom-up analyses proceeded along an abductive process (Eco, 1992).[3]

Not only was the use of words scrutinized—systematic occurrences or recurrences, preferential lexical registers . . . —but attention was also given to the syntactical frames housing them, to the communicative style adopted or to the enunciators' positioning, all the while assessing their role in supporting the verbal arguments which outline the emerging ideal-organization-construct. The following examples of personal pronouns and verb tenses illustrate in what way grammatical categories help to highlight the dissimilarities.

In both corpora, authors either refer to their organizations by company names—SNERDI, DBC, EDF, Bureau Veritas, etc.—generally followed by impersonal verb forms, or by first person pronouns in the plural (*We*). However, these impersonal or personal stances are not used in similar ways. Relatively infrequent in the French self-presentations, the occasional personal pronoun forms introduce specific verbs; conversely, what characterizes the Chinese uses of *we* pronouns is not so much the nature of the verbs they govern as their greater frequency, and above all, their positioning in specific sections.

The French personal verb forms *we can assist . . .* ; *we are confident . . .* ; *we trust we can help you*, etc. almost always refer to the organization's knowledge or to its aptitudes, denoting the organization's conviction that it is up to the task. Such formulations support a knowledge-holder image supposed to inspire confidence in clients. By saying that they know what to do and how to do it, they are telling their customers: 'Do not worry, you can trust us, you can count on us to do our job for you.' What these same first person pronouns communicate in the Chinese corpus is fundamentally different. Here again, they aim at inspiring customers' trust, but far from relying on knowledge to do so, Chinese companies strive to establish a quality human relationship; this is clearly the purpose of the sections in which these *we* appear. Called *Introduction*, *Chairman's Speech* or *Chairman's Address*, these sections are generally accompanied by a photograph of the organization's top manager/s, clearly designating him/them as the author/s of the text, and encouraging clients to believe that they will not be dealing with a non-human entity but with the real person/s whose face/s and name/s appear on the page.

Similarly, the different verbal tenses that organizations use to define themselves provide indications that, once articulated with other lexical and syntactical features, point to different attitudes towards customers and to dissimilarities in their supposed expectations.

> Since our founding in 1994, GT Law Office has grown into a large-sized[4] [sic] comprehensive, yet specialized, cooperative partnership (Ch1)
>
> DS Avocats, founded in Paris in 1972, is today one of the key European players and a leading law firm in Asia (Fr1)

Quoted from law firms' self-presentations, these two sentences are at the same time very similar—they present the firm and indicate its 'birth date'—and quite different. A metaphorical description will underscore the dissimilarity: due to the progressive verbal tense used, the Chinese firm can be seen running its long-distance race from its birth to its present size; conversely, the present tense of the French sentence evokes snapshots of the firm: one at the time of its birth, and one today, as it appears, along with the other members of the lead group, on the finish line of a race involving several competitors. In other words, while the Chinese law firm draws attention to its internal progression and (using a very clumsy formulation) introduces the notion of partnership (supposedly with its customers), the French firm aligns its past (the historical actor's ranking owed to its 30 years of existence) and its present (the success that ranks it among the Asian key players). Even the narrators' positioning differs: with the introduction of a first person pronoun: 'Since *our* founding', the Chinese firm introduces a subjectivity that strikingly contrasts the French firm's objective tone which, should one stick to the sports metaphor, could have been uttered by the race commentator.

Using such grammatical categories makes it possible to bring to the fore contrasts which might otherwise have been overlooked. In the latter case, the dissimilarities highlighted are an epitome of what distinguishes the Chinese and French self-presentations. Not only does it point to differences in the qualities considered apt to inspire stakeholders' trust, but the subjective or objective discursive modes reveal dissimilar stances towards customers, confirming that the ideal organization represented in each corpus aims to convince audiences that both the Chinese and the French authors assimilate to their audiences at home.

11.2 Trust-inspiring Features that Vary According to the National Culture

Chinese or French, the self-presentations under scrutiny have one thing in common, they reflect organizations' conviction that, in order to inspire trust in their stakeholders, they must show that they are competent, honest, and well disposed towards them (Dietz et al., 2010; Isaksson, Jørgensen, 2010); however, significant differences emerge as to what these qualities cover in practice, leading to the conclusion that the global images conveyed diverge.

As the following examples show, the characteristics related to competence or to companies' good disposition towards stakeholders clearly differ according to the corpus. As for honesty, its manifestations are so integrated to either text that highlighting them has to be done along the way.

11.2.1 Flexibility and Innovation Versus Achievements

Chinese organizations mainly emphasize their flexibility and ability to innovate and the efforts required to achieve this aim. Thus, the terms *effort, difficulties, arduous work, strive, endeavour* or *exert oneself*, or verbs such as *become, improve or strengthen* that integrate change into their semantics, are recurrent. Moreover, when success is reported, the verbs referring to it are not past tenses, the tenses used to refer to a definite time in the past, but perfects—either present- or past-—the tenses used to suggest that the action that started in the past, or at a time further in the past, continues in the present time. In addition, the authors frequently opt to put emphasis on the duration of the action by using perfect progressive tenses (as in the aforementioned self-presentation of the Chinese law firm).

> Sinotrust has offices in Beijing, Shanghai /.../ and *has built* a presence in over 40 cities (Ch5)
>
> Through consistent implementation of management transformation, *we have gradually perfected* our operation and management processes (Ch12)

Such an insistence on the ongoing process rather than on the action itself is similarly reflected in the recurrent references to experience, to its mode of acquisition or its depth—for example, experience is reported to have been *accumulated* or *gained*, to be *extensive* or *rich*.

Highlighted by a figurative language that depicts organizations as determined to achieve their goals whatever the efforts required to do so, the difficulties encountered in the past or likely to appear in the future partake of the dynamism that Chinese organizations attribute to themselves:

> There is *no even path* to development, and there are no limits to *innovation* (Ch11)
>
> Already on the newly-set historical starting line, DBC will *cleave through the waves and brave* all the difficulties so as *to sprint* for new success (Ch3)

Besides, in accordance with the indication provided by the photograph of the leader(s)—included in six out of eleven self-presentations—or by the biography of the senior managers which replaces them in one of the *About Us* sections, the qualities highlighted apply to human beings rather than inanimate professional organizations. Presidents embody the organizations. Hence, the impression that the claims emanate from the persons represented; they are claiming that the organization is reliable and trustworthy—three quarters of the verbs referring to the organization's success are in the first person speech (*we*); while the words used are often borrowed from the lexical register of emotions. Such words as *sincere, sincerity*, or *devotion* appear again and again, along with verbs referring to states of mind: *we hope, we believe*, which introduce wishes or promises regarding future collaborations between the organization and its customers. All these characteristics give speech a very personal tone:

> Huawei's logo... conveys Huawei's *sincere* commitment to helping its customers (Ch12)
>
> *Our ever-lasting promise* is to provide best services to our clients... (Ch14)

Present in both paper brochures and digital documents, these features concur to indicate that, in the eyes of Chinese companies, customers expect flexibility rather than accomplished success and the friendly and personal sort of relationship which the personal style, as well as the focus put on the top managers embodying the organization, point to. This is in stark contrast to the French emphasis on accomplished and proven success, or to the organizations' offers of assistance to their clients.

As the aforementioned French law firm's sentence suggests, French organizations do not place themselves in an interpersonal relationship but rather in a strictly professional relationship. They claim to be successful, a claim justified by their leaders' positions. Had they uttered these statements in first person speech—as corporate documents produced in the United States generally do—and not in that predominantly impersonal style, such claims could have been seen as bearing the brand of American-style communication and marketing. In addition, while readers of Chinese documents are greeted by the top managers' smiling faces, those of French self-presentations are immediately confronted with slogans (presumably borrowed from their advertising campaigns) exhibited in a prominent place, either praising the firms' assets or highlighting the commercial benefits that customers can expect:

> A world *leader* in all its business [sic] (Fr12)
>
> Get more with the world's Power and Control *Specialist* (Fr6)

Such a professional posture is supported by predominantly impersonal speech. As already mentioned, first person pronouns are rare, and, when they occur, they are not conveying top managers' emotions or moods. Instead, they govern verbs meant to restore confidence in potentially doubtful customers and express the firm's self-assurance: the firms affirm that they are equipped to serve their clients and know what the latter need (see p. 157). The impersonal style of most formulations gives speech an appearance of objective truth that is reinforced by various other features. For instance, statistics which prove the veracity of their leadership claims are recurrent either in text or in adjoining graphs. Companies are generally referred to by their names and the verbal tense of most assertions is the present, which, in both French and English, is the grammatical tense used to convey general truths (Riegel et al., 2001; Lapaire & Rotgé, 1991). The resolutely assertive tone that results is further supported by the legal or mathematical lexical registers that the formulations borrow from: *demonstrate, proven, by definition, guarantee*, or *ensure* keep occurring. In addition, the structure [COMPANY NAME + is + x] is used to define firms or to present them as members of predefined categories: *a process-engineering company, a leading law firm*. Finally, the claims meant to convince customers are not simply formulated but systematically justified, either verbally or through numerical evidence.

This impression of verified claims is further reinforced by the repeated mention of the organization's leading position, even if the justification of that qualification requires restricting the size of the market concerned.

> One of the leading French players *in this area* (Fr1)

In the same spirit, the claimed leading positions are presented as resulting from the organization's expertise: the nouns *expertise, know-how* (generally qualified as *unrivalled, unique*), *expert/s*, as well as the verbs *know, specialize*, are omnipresent. In fact, the focal point of the French self-presentations is not the patiently acquired experience—encountered in the Chinese corpus—but the expertise that is claimed and demonstrated. All organizations present themselves as experts in their fields, an affirmation reinforced by the speech assertive tone: they know what is *required, ideal*, or *essential* for their clients—in eight documents out of eleven—and they can solve any problem, in any place, provide tailored, ideal, or optimal solutions, or simply the best solutions:

> Professionals next to you, *wherever* you are (Fr2)

Success, the ultimate proof of their competence, is also reflected in the syntax. Structures linking affirmation of excellence (or success) and actions implemented, or intrinsic qualities and achievements, draw attention to the fact that success owes nothing to chance and that everything, from the number of customers to the firm's reputation or performance..., is quite simply deserved (in sheer contrast with the way the Chinese documents introduce praises of the organizations' activities in the comments of important and recognized institutions or personalities).

> *Our policy* based on client satisfaction *allows Bureau Veritas to count* more than 100,000 clients all over the world, and thousands in China (Fr4)
>
> *The experience and dual culture of the lawyers* running these offices, together with a sound knowledge of local networks, *have earned* DS Avocats *a high reputation* with clients and local authorities (Fr1)
>
> In 2007 we continued to demonstrate improvement (...). *This* performance *is the result of* the strategic choices made by the company in the last several years (Fr11)

In a nutshell, the ideal organization portrayed in the French self-presentations is a successful organization which provides evidence as to why this is so. Customers can therefore trust it—speech that contrasts with the subjectivity of Chinese self-presentations and their insistence on the sincerity of their actions and their dedication to serving their customers.

Whether French or Chinese, the ability that these organizations claim is not the only quality used to inspire trust in their customers; they also want to show their good intentions towards them.

11.2.2 Harmonious Partnership Versus Professional Mentoring

As the photographs of smiling top managers which appear in the Chinese documents suggest, customers are offered to enter a kind of communion based, among other things, on warm human relations. Firms and their customers are to form a partnership and share a harmonious relationship: one third of the sentences referring to clients—generally designated as *friends, colleagues,* or *partners*—mentions the actions that the organizations intend to carry out with them, using such terms as *common, joint(ly), partner(ship), cooperation, hand in hand,* or *together.*

> CZEC (...) engages in (...) *cooperation* in the *sincere* and pragmatic spirit with domestic and foreign colleagues for creating a glorious future *in common effort* (Ch6)

The promised communion extends even more broadly to Chinese society as a whole. Organizations depict themselves playing an active social role which society, in some way, returns in the form of praise. While French companies use impersonal forms to give a semblance of objectivity to the statements that make them appear at their best (*DS Avocats is a leading law firm, SGN has the necessary expertise to meet the needs...*), Chinese firms step back and hand the floor to society. Various institutions or high-ranking personalities testify to the value of this or that organization, sometimes in the form of calligraphies—given ample space in the document—praising its accomplishments; in other cases, it is through certificates and awards which are either mentioned in the texts or used as illustrations.

> The Shanghai municipality recognized SNERDI as *Hi-Tech enterprise* (Ch2)

Society is even present at the heart of writing through formulas known to every Chinese (but appearing here in ELF): quotations from '*centons*'—the term Granet used to designate the proverbs or common sayings that convey millenary wisdom (Granet, 2012[1934]: 58)—or references (rooted in the country's past) which, according to Zhu (1999), are still part of Chinese professional discourse. Such symbolically strong formulas testify to the organization's integration into the societal fabric and contribute to the communion offered. Taken from one of the digital documents, the following excerpt gives an idea of how such references work with an informed audience.

> Over the next decade, aided by the '*east wind*' of China's reform and open-door policy, TCL's corporate culture of dedication... (Ch11)

The formula *East wind* simultaneously refers to the unexpected happy reversal of a battle, narrated in a great Chinese classic; the symbolic meaning of the crucial event that makes success possible; and the speeches delivered by Mao Zedong in 1957 and Deng Xiao Ping in 1992 that have both marked the country's history.[5] These two words are sufficient for China's past to be integrated to the organization's profile as proof of its involvement with society at large and of its dedication to the country's success.

On the French side, no such offer of a harmonious relationship is to be found, but a proposal of professional expertise—that is, organizations are putting their knowledge at their customers' service. Syntax and lexicon highlight the mentoring role that companies attribute to themselves: they are attentive to their customers' needs and will make them benefit from the expertise that the latter are in need of; *assist**,[6] *expert**, *guiding*, *help**, *know**, *special**, *support** represent nearly 1% of the French 15,302 word corpus, while the grammatical functions assigned to the terms designating customers clearly put the latter in beneficiary positions.

> Whatever your needs... Whatever your business sector... Our business is *taking care of yours*... (Fr4)

> Wherever you are in the world, Schneider Electric *is there to listen* and *provide you with* the comprehensive range of products [...] (Fr6)
>
> (...) reflects (...) a corporate culture that focuses on *listening to customers* to *satisfy their needs* (Fr2)

Thus, two thirds of the occurrences of the verb *provide* are not followed by *service* or the names of whatever products, but by *with help, assistance,* or *support*:

> *Providing* clients *with* assistance... (F1)

As a mentor, one organization does not hesitate to suggest that they know better than their client what the company's plants need (see p. 157):

> Cooperation with NPP's operators and design engineers... guarantees you get the system your plant *really* wants (Fr6)

Such expert's positioning[7] is underscored by the logical appearance which the aforementioned structures give to the French firms' speech.

In a nutshell, the three qualities that inspire trust—competence, honesty, and benevolence—are found in both corpora, but in practice, they cover different qualities, both in terms of information content and of discursive features.

Whereas *honesty* translates into sincere and dedicated behaviour in the Chinese documents, in the French self-presentations it resides in the 'justification' which supports most assertions, and in the appearance of truth conferred on them by the impersonal speech equivalent to introducing an external narrator. To testify to the validity of their statements, the former rely on fame (society's testimonials), the latter on proof. Whereas for the Chinese writers, competence consists in being flexible, adaptable, and producing continuous effort; for their French homologues, it consists of expertise and the success that it enables. Chinese companies' goodwill consists in offering to work hand in hand with customers in a harmonious relationship, while the goodwill of French companies consists in making them benefit from their expert guidance and mentoring. Consistent throughout each corpus, these two images definitely contrast each other.

11.2.3 Within Corpus Consistency But Contrast Between Corpora

Since constructing corporate identity aims, among other things, to distinguish an organization from its peers, one would have expected to find, within each corpus, variations in the qualities put forward or in the speech forms preferred to inspire trust, but this is not the case. The foundations of the self-profiles are stable from one self-presentation to another, including between documents gathered before and after a decade rich in geopolitical events that have changed the general context of each of the countries concerned. The same applies to the stylistic processes used—that is, figurative language and personal discourse on the Chinese side; logical argumentation and impersonal formulas on the French side—or the lexical registers used preferentially.

Over a ten-year period—a rather short time-span for linguistic evolutions—stability in the specific discursive features of a language, or dissimilarity between two native languages is to be expected. However, in this particular case, the discursive differences were not picked out in two different languages but in one and the same language, ELF, the so-called common language. In a similar way to what was exposed in Chapter 10 for interpersonal communication, these discrepancies stem from ELF speakers' unconscious transposition of the language into their native languages; and the consequences of such transfers may be just as problematic.

The comparison between these two corpora shows the limits of organizations' most commonly used approach. Having texts, initially written for the organization's national audience, translated into ELF—or, for that matter, into any other lingua franca, such as French in many African countries or Arabic in North-African or Middle East countries—so as to make themselves known beyond their borders is standard practice. However, far from displaying the figure of a universal ideal organization that inspires trust in audiences as culturally diverse as those having access to the Internet, the ideal organization constructs which emerge are deeply embedded in the issuing organizations' national cultures. Confirmation of the fact is to be found in the studies performed by various researchers on native language self-profiles distributed in these same countries. To name but a few: Hardy et al. (2008) report on a similar integration of Chinese companies into the Chinese society. According to the authors, they seem to be doing their utmost to conform to the 'exemplary enterprise' figure that Chinese local governments maintain through their institutional communication and their awarding of 'model/exemplary enterprise' certificates (such as those appearing systematically in the Chinese corpus self-profiles). Similarly, the emphasis on expertise detected in the French corpus is one of the characteristics which Bintz et al.[8] identify as the most striking difference between the *About Us* sections of French and American architectural agencies.

Finally, this comparison shows that while these organizations were convinced that, by transposing into ELF the self-presentations conceived for their national audiences, they were 'internationalizing' their corporate images, they were instead 'projecting' the visions of their own local audiences and of their expectations internationally, at the risk of offending, amusing, or intriguing, rather than convincing, the international audiences that they were trying to reach. The fact that this identical thought process equally underpins all the self-presentations that were examined, be they Chinese or French, written in the organization's first language or in ELF, whatever the organization's size or the sector of activity in which it operates, is instructive. It shows to what extent the ideal organization construct that organizations deploy, as well as the form of the speech adopted to convey it, is not universal but culturally marked.

Translating documents meant to inspire trust in an audience is bound to fail if the translation process does not integrate their specific culture. This is the reason why selecting ELF to make those documents accessible to all readers, regardless of their native languages and of the underpinning cultures, cannot achieve that aim. In addition to the drift that messages in any foreign language generally undergo due to speakers' tendency to 'hear' in their native languages (see p. 200), the fact that a corporate identity cannot but be embedded in the targeted public's cultural context makes ELF an inappropriate choice. Indeed, how could such a condition be fulfilled for audiences of whom one knows nothing other than their ability to understand the language?

11.3 Alternative Moves for Corporate Identity Internationalization

Provided organizations know what specific audience they are targeting, they will fare better having their self-presentations or other corporate documents translated directly into that audience's native language. The move is definitely less economical, but having the local context and expectations integrated in the organization's discourse may prove far more rewarding.

As many researchers have pointed out, concepts generally have a core meaning that is common to most languages but some of their numerous facets may be prominent here, and perceived as not so important there. For instance, according to Usunier and Lee (2005) trust is the most prominent trait which varies with the language spoken: the reliance on, and confidence in, people which is perceptible in the native English-speaking countries is in stark contrast with the sharing of common beliefs that is constitutive of trust in France and other Romance countries, or with the emphasis on sincerity that trust includes in Japanese business. If an organization wishes to make itself known to one of these audiences, the transposition of its corporate identity into their mother tongue makes it possible to adapt its profile so as to highlight the features most compatible with their expectations. Such a move is impossible when ELF is used indifferently to reach any foreign community.

By not adapting their images to local expectations—which can be done while retaining what may be their worldwide recognized feature, for example, Swiss solidity, French luxury, etc.—the companies who choose such a good-for-all ELF version probably deprive themselves of an asset. One can suppose that the most discerning readers, ignoring a rhetoric that falls short of convincing them, will be able to selectively pick, in what they may consider as 'exotic' presentations, the factual information which they are seeking. The greatest risk probably lies with on-the-field inadequate use of such self-presentations, in particular where business prospection is concerned. Rather than using the documents as such, as is often done, business prospectors would be far more efficient if, in such local encounters, they used a short presentation written by the local staff in their native language. Such an adaptation, performed with the help of local contacts, will facilitate speech-form adaptation as well as avoidance of too culturally-marked discourse liable to offend.

Some companies are aware of the necessity of such localization; they strive to conduct communication operations that better integrate the expectations of their various audiences.

11.3.1 Adjusting to Local Publics

Although offering an ELF version of their global website seems to be the most widespread practice, a number of corporations are doing otherwise. For example, for quite some time, the Swedish group Electrolux has been known to limit translation into ELF solely to its annual report, leaving local teams in charge of local communication, in particular concerning products. On the basis of the list of assets received in ELF (the group's common corporate language) for each product, they select those that they deem best suited to their particular context and prepare communication accordingly (Jämtelid, 2002, cited in Gunnarsson (2006: 254)). Brochures, magazines, or other documents are also written in the teams' native languages and distributed in their markets. As for websites conveying the main corporate communication messages, they adopt some local features suggesting that they too are administered locally, which does not prevent them from respecting a certain number of parameters common to all.

Such localization of information is the approach adopted by NGOs such as Greenpeace or WWF. They have regional sites built according to the official criteria specific to each of these organizations, but the messages that they display are designed locally so as to adapt optimally to the region concerned (Guillaume, 2010). This is also the move that is recommended to multinational firms:

> [Adopting] a relatively cultural neutral website template communicating a consistent image across the Internet, but leaving agreed freedom to the local branding team to integrate cultural specificities. (Halliburton & Ziegfeld, 2009: 921)

Not all corporations have yet followed suit, but some world-class groups are showing dynamism in this area: they draw inspiration from the practices of their local competitors (particularly in certain Asian markets) to better meet their customers' expectations.

This is apparently the case for McDonald's. Their sixty-or-so subsidiary websites appear extremely diversified; not only are they translated into local languages, but their content and the rhetoric used also seem to be adapted to their viewers' local contexts. Lee et al. (2006) report on a comparison of the group's global websites: at home; in the UK; in mainland China; in Hong Kong; and in Taiwan. Home messages are obviously adapted to viewers; sometimes the informative content has been modified; for example, collaborative relationships with local communities are stated in Western countries as well as in Hong Kong or Taiwan, but only the relationships with government are mentioned in mainland China. In other cases, specific messages have been added, with the clear intention of meeting the expectations of local customers—for example, in order to respond to the expectations of Chinese mainland customers in hygiene, they report on their insistence on cleanliness. Sometimes, although expressed in the local language, the messages include a few English words—for example, in Taiwan, where it is quite trendy for young people to use such mixed codes.

But changes also involve the stylistic form and rhetoric. For example, messages written in Mandarin slip into stylistic forms that are typical of Chinese discourse, such as repeated parallel structures that highlight important messages:

> (For McDonald's, 'the best' means . . .)
> (For our customers, 'the best' means . . .)
> (For our community, 'the best' means . . .)
> (For our franchiser, 'the best' means . . .)
> (For our employees, 'the best' means . . .)
> (For our suppliers, 'the best' means . . .)
> (For our shareholders, 'the best' means . . .)
> (For our partners, 'the best' means . . .)
> This parallel construction not only reinforces the company's mission of accomplishing 'the best service' but also gives viewers an impression of formality and respect. Parallel construction is one of the most typical rhetorical devices adopted in written Chinese. It is extensively employed on the websites of different industries targeting viewers of Chinese mainland. (ibid.: 279)

Adopting such rhetorical forms, or the formal tone to which the Chinese public is accustomed, indicates efforts to slip into the local fabric and reinforce the impact of the corporate messages. Nonetheless, McDonald's does not distort the foundations of its corporate communication: its corporate values are present, as is a reference to teamwork which the authors deem inadequate because it is poorly adapted to the conception of work that prevails in Chinese culture (ibid.).

As these examples attest, organizations can certainly make themselves better known when they communicate in the local language or in ELF that adopts a somewhat local discursive approach, especially if they take the trouble to understand what differentiates the local clients that they are addressing from those for whom the documents were originally designed.

Indeed, while translating into the audience's native language is important, doing so without adjusting to the specific context of the targeted audience may be completely counterproductive; this is particularly true for the tools that partake as much of corporate communication as of management—for example, corporate values or the codes of conduct that translate the latter into practical instructions to be implemented. Quite a few researchers have reported on the negative impact that translations which do not endeavour to transpose the document content into the local context may have: failing to understand how the local staff make sense of the corporate message endangers its impact (see Barmeyer & Davoine, 2011, 2013; Helin & Sandström, 2008, to name but a few); others insist on the necessity to 'recontextualize' the message if one wants it to be perceived positively and implemented (Brannen, 2004; Björge et al., 2015; d'Iribarne, 2012b; Tréguer Felten, 2017).

11.4 Conclusion

This chapter has been devoted to the limitations of a lingua franca from which neither corporate nor interpersonal communication can escape. By translating almost literally into a language perceived as 'common', or by expressing themselves in it, organizations as well as individuals believe that they are 'on the same wavelength' as their interlocutors, when the latter are, in fact, transposing the words heard or read into their own linguistic and cultural universe. Such a transfer necessarily influences the way in which the represented reality will make sense.

The comparison of self-presentations which companies based in France and in China produced in their common language—that is, ELF—illustrated the limits of an approach which is generally perceived as *the* way to reach any readers, wherever they are in the 'big, wide world'. The comparison of the two corpora has brought out not one but two figures of the ideal trustworthy organization, each of them aiming to inspire confidence in readers whom the Chinese or French authors clearly imagined as 'clones' of their respective compatriots—that is, individuals entertaining the same expectations, sensitive to the same qualities, and familiar with the same discursive modes as the latter. The obvious distance between the audiences embedded in the messages and speech of each corpus is such that one can doubt the effectiveness of the approach, suggesting that corporations should seek other ways to make themselves known internationally. Some organizations already do count on their local teams to relay corporate or marketing messages in their native language; they adapt their corporate websites, not only through translation into local languages but also through messages that adjust to the audience's local context, even when they use a lingua franca such as ELF.

Ignoring the specific cultural context in which corporate messages will make sense is a danger all the more acute that they bear on the personal motivations and behaviours of individuals, as is the case for corporate values and even more so for the codes of conduct that require their implementation. Indeed, how can people be motivated by documents set in an environment so alien that they cannot project themselves into it? Successfully translating a message without altering its persuasive potential requires setting it in a new context, that of the target audience. If such linguistic–cultural transposition is not carried out, as is the case for translations into a language considered to be 'common', the representation of reality proposed in the initial document will take on different colours, depending on the interpretation that the 'new' readers' linguistic and cultural contexts will induce (similar to what was shown for interpersonal communication in Chapter 10).

Notes

1. For English as a Lingua Franca.
2. More information on data collection can be found in Tréguer-Felten, Geneviève, 'Le leurre de l'anglais lingua franca. Une étude comparative de documents professionnels produits en anglais par des locuteurs chinois, français et nord-américains', Doctoral Thesis, Université Paris 3, November 23, 2009, and in Tréguer-Felten (2013).
3. Precisions on the methodology can be found in Tréguer-Felten (ibid.).
4. Apart from italics which may have been added for emphasis to self-presentation quotations, the speech in its original form has systematically been respected.
5. http://english.peopledaily.com.cn/200201/25/eng20020125_89333.shtml (accessed on 10 December 2008) and http://history.cultural-china.com/en/38History1740.html (accessed on 11 September 2010).
6. Word roots followed by asterisks refer to all the different inflected forms of a word: for instance, *assist** refers to: *assists, assisting*, and *assistance.*
7. See Tréguer-Felten (2012).
8. Bintz, Pierre-Alain; Cellier, Laurie; Le Thérisien, Céline; Meunier, Anouck; Thevenet, Marie; 'Le rapport au client dans les agences d'architecture françaises et américaines sur la base de l'étude comparée de leurs sites internet', Master Thesis, Master 2 Management Interculturel, Paris, ISIT (Institut de Management et de Communication Interculturels), September 2012.

12
Intercultural Team Challenges

The globalized economic environment has multiplied multicultural[1] professional contexts and forced many employees to interact, more or less regularly, face-to-face or at a distance, with colleagues, managers, employees, customers, or suppliers from a variety of countries. These work situations are known to be potentially difficult, and require special skills. However, the challenges raised by intercultural teams tend to be underestimated.

In practice, companies quickly train expatriates to develop awareness of cultural differences prior to departure, and rely on managers' determination to succeed and employees' open-mindedness. Indeed, cooperation problems tend to be interpreted in the light of the lack of 'tolerance' or 'openness' of the people. However, the willingness of the members and the warning against national prejudices are not sufficient to overcome the challenges raised by intercultural teams. Seeking to eliminate or nuance stereotypes because they are scientifically unfounded or morally questionable does not solve the problem of coordinating with others. At best, this makes relationships smoother but does not offer a guide to define ways of working together. Cooperating is not straightforward when the premises of cooperation itself are not shared, even though it implies 'open' people. The earlier chapters have shown that, in each place, management practices are rooted in cultures defined as conceptions of acceptable ways of living together or specific interpretations of social relations. In international organizations that require the cooperation of employees from different countries, members do not share the same conception of leadership, control, decision-making, customer satisfaction, or even ethics. As a result, cooperation can rarely be based on work processes that have been accepted by all from the outset. It is as if players around the same table wanted to play together but each with different rules of the game—and worse, play without an awareness of the differences in the rules that guide them. Therefore, we can imagine how surprised they may be with each other's play.

The aim of this chapter is to use comparisons of the cultural conceptions regarding management, in order to understand the dynamics of multicultural working contexts. It shows the effects of the variety of cultural conceptions on international teamwork, drawing upon the approach to culture as a universe of meaning developed in this book.

The chapter is structured as follows. In each of the first two sections, we develop an example of work in an intercultural context and, for each, we show how the

Cross-Cultural Management Revisited: A Qualitative Approach. Philippe d'Iribarne, Sylvie Chevrier, Alain Henry, Jean-Pierre Segal, and Geneviève Tréguer-Felten, Oxford University Press (2020).
DOI: 10.1093/oso/9780198857471.001.0001

interpretative approach to cultures sheds light on the difficulties encountered by the teams. In the third section, we present an overview of the intercultural dynamics in international teams ranging from frontal conflicts to the complementarity of the team members' contributions fed by differences in cultural representations. We conclude with the potential improvements in management in an intercultural context that this new approach to culture brings.

12.1 Agreeing in a Bi-national Team

Let us begin by detailing a case briefly mentioned in Chapter 6 (pp. 111–112). In the 1990s, the car manufacturer Renault entered into an alliance with the Swedish manufacturer Volvo to jointly design a vehicle platform. After a few years of cooperation among engineers and technicians from both companies, the alliance failed and so did the project. A series of interviews with the protagonists, conducted after the project failure, revealed the extent of intercultural misunderstandings, particularly due to different conceptions of decision-making (d'Iribarne, 1998). The global failure of the alliance was not only due to intercultural misunderstandings; the future of these companies, which were perceived as national champions, was under scrutiny and caught up in major political and symbolic issues. Power games and the risk of domination between two uneven-sized companies contributed to the failure of the alliance, but we will demonstrate that cultural differences about the right ways to come to an agreement added to strategic divergences and hastened the failure of the alliance.

12.1.1 Mutual Reproaches

French and Swedish interviewees expressed many mutual criticisms, particularly in regard to the challenges of making effective decisions together. Let us consider again the main recriminations of the Swedes towards the French:

- A significant imbalance in speaking out. The French monopolized the floor at meetings and left little room for their Swedish counterparts to have their say. In addition, they expressed themselves with a vigour which was felt as a will to dominate: 'We were surprised by the strength and willingness of the French people we met. I was shocked. The way they expressed themselves, their willingness to prevail, even in ordinary discussions, their desire to climb up, even at the expense of others.'
- A way of arguing perceived as very aggressive. The Swedes were surprised that the French used the warlike register in which arguments are meant to

beat the opponent, while the Swedish project manager, on the contrary, claimed a peacekeeping role: 'I avoided getting into debates on technical subjects. I was dedicated to keeping the peace.'

- The lack of concessions on the part of the French: 'The French are used to sticking to their guns to get a consensus, not the Swedes. We are flexible enough to be able to keep quiet and listen to each other. The problem is that it has happened too often that Renault representatives have not made compromises, while we have.'

Finally, the Swedes blamed the French managers for not attending the meetings during the deliberations but finally being the ones who made the decisions without respecting the choices discussed at length between experts. They interpreted these practices as abuses of power by the leaders who denied any autonomy to the teams. Consequently, decisions were never definitively made, since leaders, later and at their own discretion, might change a decision that the team thought it had made collectively:

> There were leaders behind the French whom we did not see; we never met them. They originated things but were not visible. We never had access to the people in charge, it was a big cloud. They never participated in the work but influenced it from the outside.

For their part, French engineers and technicians blamed their Swedish counterparts for spending an excessively long time discussing and laboriously reaching compromises. For them, the discussions were not very efficient:

> At Volvo, we meet to understand, then we analyse at length and finally, decisions are made after long and painful iterations.
>
> I was irritated by the difficulty of getting full agreement to make decisions, it takes a lot of time, they hold meetings again and again on the same subject, they are less responsive than Renault.

Moreover, according to the French, during the discussions, the Swedes did not differentiate between essential and less important elements; the hierarchy of priorities was not established:

> The way Volvo works does not allow us to find a sound compromise for an entire vehicle. Everything is viewed in the same way, has the same weight, which does not bring consistency.

Everyone took care of their own scope and each expertise was valued at the same level.

Finally, the French criticized their counterparts for a lack of flexibility. Decisions made were never questioned, which was, they thought, often harmful:

> They propose a release date without necessarily seeking to optimize it, to set ambitious objectives. However, once set, this date is untouchable.
>
> It's a real steamroller, it takes two years to change a trajectory.

12.1.2 The Encounter of Two Cultural Logics

The encounter of two implicit models of appropriate ways to come to an agreement (see p. 109) explained the perceptions of the hurdles and the negative judgements that emerged. Let us briefly summarize these two models, which were more or less consciously used by the partners to assess their cooperation.

On the French side, making the right decision is first and foremost a question of technical optimization. The solution is assessed in terms of performance against prioritized criteria to be met. In real life, the solutions do not satisfy all the criteria and depending on the experts' professional speciality, the hierarchy of technical criteria to be met may be different. This is why experts expect the 'best' technical solution to come out of vigorous debates. In these oratory contests, arguments are prepared to convince the opponent. At the same time, every contestant is looking for the flaw in the reasoning that is opposed to them. The forceful tone of the speaker is a sign of commitment and conviction that reinforces the substance of the argument and contributes to its defence. In practice, the 'best' solution is rarely found because it depends on technical points of view and the argumentation may drag on. Therefore, the hierarchy has often to be called for to arbitrate between points of view or to approve the decision if a solution has been found. Managers are entitled to make the decision for two reasons: their position and their competence. Their position, which is supposed to be above the parties, can give them a cross-sectional and global view; the hierarchy ensures that the view is at the right 'height'. Moreover, they are supposed to owe their position to their technical competence, hence their expert point of view enables them to make technically relevant decisions. In the French context, a leader who has neither the technical competence nor the overarching perspective has no strong legitimacy (see p. 84). Calling upon one's statutory authority is often perceived as a sign of weakness by employees. The precedence of technical considerations also means that each time a solution, which better meets the technical criteria, arises, it is possible, and even desirable, to question the decision, regardless of the hierarchical level of the person who has the idea. Being able to move on quickly to a technically more convincing solution is praised as flexibility and responsiveness.

On the Swedish side, as seen in Chapter 6 p. 113, a right decision is a decision that is acceptable to all, in other words, one that each expert can deal with. To achieve this, participants have to listen at length to everyone's point of view in order to pinpoint the greatest common denominator of these opinions. The core principle of the process is to compromise on what is not initially shared and thus gradually converge towards consensus. Decisions are made as close to the grass-roots as possible, between experts, and the hierarchy is not entitled to question them as they have been constructed by all. Once everyone has had the opportunity to express themselves and take part in the collective decision through a peaceful and courteous exchange, everyone is required to show solidarity and support and implement it without reservation.

12.1.3 From Misunderstandings to Conflicts

Implementing and evaluating a decision-making process from different implicit frames of references, Renault and Volvo staff had a hard time coming to an agreement. Some of them managed to decipher their observations and to understand part of their partners' logic as well as some of the mistakes made. Building on this understanding, they made some efforts to adapt: a Swedish engineer said he had learned 'the French way of arguing' and a Renault employee conceded: 'we don't know how to keep quiet and listen to the other; we have to stop always being right'.

However, in this project team, intercultural learning remained marginal. Some, perceiving differences in behaviours, expected others to adapt: 'At first, we had to tell them: "Cut us off!" because if not, very politely, they let us speak and did not utter a word', said one French interviewee. Above all, most of the protagonists did not understand the logic of their counterparts' universe of meaning. While they were able to accurately describe their partners' behaviours, they used their own interpretation logic to give meaning to these behaviours and almost inevitably ended up criticizing them severely. For example, one Frenchman said: 'At Volvo, once people have been involved in a decision, it becomes a must. Even if someone knows, admits that it is a mistake, they obey.' In the Frenchman's context, implementing a decision when you are not yourself intimately convinced that the technical solution is relevant is a form of cowardice. One should take the floor to defend one's conviction. In this case, instead of acting as his professional conscience indicates, the individual submitted to group pressure without having the courage to stand up for his opinions. Obeying a 'mistake' was a very degrading act of servility. However, for his Swedish counterpart, what was described as a 'mistake' by the Frenchman was certainly not stupid. Just because the Swede admitted that the solution was not the most technically efficient did not mean that it was a 'mistake'. A decision that had the consent of all the experts, because it was a compromise acceptable to all, was a right decision; it ensured effective coordination of everyone's actions. Hence, the Swedish colleague accepted the collective decision and supported it. He did not feel that he was subjugating himself in any way, let alone demeaning himself by allowing the collective to move forward.

Another Swede articulated this same view of individual positions and collective decisions when he said:

> We were talking together [with the Renault employees] and we thought there was an agreement. But then, they would go home and talk to their boss and he would tell them what they should think.

Noting that, at Renault, decisions were systematically submitted, most often validated, but sometimes changed by the hierarchy, this Swede imagined that French employees had no power and could not make a decision. Moreover, in his universe of meaning, deviance from the decision adopted was threatening and therefore avoided. Everyone supported the decision, made democratically, and was expected to work towards its implementation. This was why this Swede assumed that the French had to comply with the opinion of an all-powerful leader making all decisions. He thus misunderstood the French context in which the leader settled debates that could otherwise have dragged on, but this did not prevent the team members who had disagreed from maintaining a critical eye on the decision made by someone 'who did not understand the question at all!' Business deadlines led them to comply with the set direction but 'they thought no less', a phrase that meant that rallying to common action for the general interest did not imply giving up in any way one's own judgement and convictions. It was not uncommon in the French context for criticism to appear again when a decision proved less effective than expected: 'I told you!' or 'I warned you!' Such a lack of support was much more transgressive in the Swedish context; this was why this Swedish protagonist did not imagine it.

Even if cultural differences were not the only cause of the failure of the Renault-Volvo alliance, the fear of being dominated by a more powerful partner had been reinforced by the diverging views on decision-making. During the first months of the project, the Swedes had accumulated concessions but had not been given the reciprocal concessions expected of their French counterparts, anxious to firmly defend their points of view. 'Renault was much better at negotiating', said one Swedish participant who interpreted the numerous endeavours to convince as attempts to impose their solutions. Noting the evolution of the Swedes' positions, the French thought that their counterparts agreed with their arguments and did not often give in return. In their logic of comparing points of view to bring out the most relevant, compromise was an abdication *(une compromission)*; it meant abdicating of points of view that should remain 'whole' as much as possible (see

p. 195). Finally, the alliance was terminated due to considerations unrelated to the platform project; however, working together had raised a lot of misunderstandings.

12.2 Delegating Across Cultures

The second example concerns GRET, a French development aid NGO. At the time we visited it, its large branch (about forty people) in Madagascar was headed by an expatriate French director. A few other French people worked there as managers of the main projects or volunteers. Most of the staff was local. The highly-qualified part of the Malagasy team held project management or staff positions, the others worked at different levels in projects. In line with the spirit of the development aid, expatriates were committed to empowering Malagasy staff as much as possible. Ideally, the Madagascar branch should gradually run without any expatriates and become entirely local: 'I try to empower the teams. I think it is interesting to have a Malagasy organisation', said the French director. Given the level of qualification of some staff, graduates of master's degrees, and the experience they had acquired, the empowerment objectives seemed reasonable. However, when research began in 2009, the French were experiencing challenges in implementing empowerment.

12.2.1 A Very Slow Empowerment

The branch director complained that he was consulted for any decision which should be made by team leaders and that employees did not take initiatives, and feared to take risks:

> They submit ideas and problems rather than solutions. They are looking for us to make the decision for them.
>
> People need to understand a little bit, take responsibility, have a little courage (...) I'm playing the daddy too much.

The Malagasy employees were ambivalent. On the one hand, they asked to be supported by the hierarchy when making decisions:

> People tend, even me, to always refer to the person in charge to validate something.
>
> If someone wants to make a decision, they are afraid of not having the right to do so, so it is better, as a precaution, to always refer to the person in charge.
>
> I go straight to his office, I explain to him: "I sent this...", you still need an opinion or validation.

But on the other hand, Malagasy employees were also ready to evolve towards a wider range of professional responsibilities:

> In fact, my idea is to evolve, to start managing a small project with a suitable budget, to have a little more decision-making power.
>
> In the long term, for example, I plan to create a local NGO and seek funding from donors, set up a project by myself and my team.

These remarks suggested that more far-reaching empowerment was indeed possible, but the persistent challenges also called for a closer examination of the prerequisites for this empowerment. Identifying and implementing them required an understanding of the universes of meaning for *empowerment* among the French and Malagasy protagonists. The method followed to achieve this will be detailed in Chapters 15 and 16, but here we report on the universes of meaning of both parts and on the problems of empowerment raised by their encounter. In the interviews of the organization's French and Malagasy members, several themes emerged that were closely linked to the empowerment process. We will develop two of them in the following sections: the formalization of roles, tasks, and processes on the one hand, and the articulation between individual and collective work on the other.

12.2.2 Diverging Expectations Regarding Formalization

On the French side, the formalization of jobs was certainly a useful clarification of roles and a valuable landmark, particularly for the work assessment, but the most important was to take ownership of your 'general mission' so that you knew the proper way of using your expertise in each situation. However, the formalization of jobs was, as one expatriate put it, 'a score to be interpreted', not a script to be followed literally. As each project was unique, tasks could not be fully defined and structured:

> Everyone would like to have their own strict responsibilities, etc. However, in the project in which we are working, the relationships we have are a little vague.

Understanding your professional role was the key to adapting to circumstances and exercising your responsibilities; the detailed formalization of tasks or procedures was not the major issue. Overall, compliance with procedures was loose on the French side, in the sense that doing a good job—that is obtaining results—was more important than strictly observing procedures, which was only instrumental (see p. 100). In other words, a procedure was not automatically respected just because it existed, but because it was considered relevant. An exemption or exception might occasionally be justified.

On the Malagasy side, the detailed formalization of roles was perceived as a prerequisite for carrying out your job. When employees were certain of their tasks and responsibilities, they could carry them out without fear of infringing on the prerogatives of others and hence creating conflicts:

> I would like to have a job description definition [which specifies] that you should do this, this, and that. To make sure that I am doing my part of my work, as part of the contract we have made, which we have drafted together.

Formalization not only provided clear roles but also security by strictly delimiting the work scope. It referred to a functional division of labour but above all to a social issue; the point was to maintain harmonious relations thanks to the fact that all the employees remained in their assigned place. Paradoxically, in view of the commonly admitted opposition between individualism and collectivism, it was because Malagasy employees were very concerned about their harmonious integration into the community that they had strong expectations with regard to the precise definition of their individual perimeter of accountability. On this point, the interviews clearly revealed a difference in the relations to work. For a large majority of French interviewees, their actual position was the result of their choice and their decision: they seized an opportunity, wanted to work internationally, responded to an interesting job offer, etc. Once in office, they took ownership of their 'mission' and contributed in some cases to the very definition of the position:

> I had a somewhat catch-all job (. . .) my place was progressively defined, as I said, it was not really a position. This job was a new one, there was not really a clearly defined role.

When describing how they obtained their current job, almost all Malagasy interviewees said that they were asked, assigned, or appointed by someone. The desire to take up a new position was not put forward; they emphasized the fact that a community of people or a line manager acknowledged that they would be at the right place in such a position: 'It is also thanks to my supervisor who wanted me to move forward, who felt that I deserved it, that I was capable.' This recognition by their close social environment gave them professional legitimacy and defined the scope of their job.

In the French logic, recognition by an external body (degree, diploma, status) might have been sufficient to feel legitimate in their position. Moreover, as seen in Chapter 4, p. 77, as soon as the employees' skills, that is, mastery of the job (*métier*), were established, managers tended to trust and control at the right distance.

> He has always been very autonomous (...) it's a project, he's the one who really supports it. (...) He told me about the decisions he had made, and thus I had enough confidence in the project.

Empowerment was done by entrusting a broad mission and not a list of specific tasks. This approach was considered in the French context as a sign of respect: it meant that you treated your employee as a skilled, autonomous, and sensible adult who did not need to be 'taken by the hand' or 'infantilized'. In turn, the trusted employees had to be trustworthy; they had to rely on their own ability to judge, based on professional expertise, which allowed them to take risks and be accountable for them. This approach to empowerment was a source of concern for Malagasy people:

> For the moment, I am not going to say that it is difficult, but I see a job description that is not yet well defined, even if we think it is clear—everyone must do this, must do that—there is always overlap in activities between each partner.

The French managers were reluctant to accept the persistent request of Malagasy employees for more formalization, particularly of their role, mission, and tasks. Through this request, the Malagasies were seeking operational and reassuring guidelines, to ensure that they met the manager's expectations on the one hand, and harmonized collective work thanks to a clear distribution of responsibilities on the other hand. From the French perspective, this latter demand was interpreted in terms of power as everyone's desire to have their own territory ('*pré-carré*') a place of their own without interference from others. In fact, several employees had to feel concerned by the same activity in different ways, for instance because they were in charge of the given geographical area, specialized in the subject, or had already been in relation with the partners involved. Consequently, defining strict boundaries seemed inappropriate and people had to be able to figure out their own field and room for manoeuvre, and engage in close coordination with others based on an overall understanding of their professional 'mission'. These representations can explain that the way in which French expatriates 'empowered the teams' was not very successful because it created uncertainty about the tasks to which Malagasy employees were assigned. Although French managers attempted to comfort Malagasy people by repeating that they trusted them, and reasserted that they were given real decision-making power, they could not overcome this insecurity.

In addition to formalization, another point which gave rise to misunderstandings was the articulation of individual and collective work.

12.2.3 Articulating Individual and Collective Work

From the French perspective, work was first and foremost a matter of individual responsibility. Admittedly, the work group was essential to combine expertise, consult members, and foster debate to define the best technical solutions, as seen above in the Renault–Volvo case. Collective work also brought conviviality and contributed to the quality of working conditions, but it had its limitations. On the one hand, discussions could drag on and become non-productive if the debate was not settled, and on the other hand, someone had to take responsibility for the decision at the end. As one French interviewee suggested: 'When there are two leaders, there are two unaccountable ones.'[2]

In the Malagasy world, the individual's inclusion in the community was more important. As seen above with regard to the importance of being appointed to a position, Malagasy employees were very concerned about being acknowledged by their close social environment for the position they were given. Similarly, in a Malagasy resume, the filiation links with the names and professions of the parents might appear in the section concerning civil status. The indissociable link with the community was thus reasserted in many ways. Within their social group, the links were compelling. Preserving community interests and harmony (*fihavanana*) was a major concern and everyone was at high risk of bearing the consequences of their mistakes (Dalh, 1999; Andrianmanjato, 2013). If social obligations happened to be breached, retaliatory measures would certainly be taken against the trouble-maker. Making a mistake that would harm the community meant exposing oneself to wrath, and risking stigmatization and exclusion from the group. From this perspective, the French risk-taking line was difficult to follow. The French interpretation of the error in technical terms made it admissible within certain limits and reversible; it could be corrected or its harmful consequences circumscribed. The Malagasy social interpretation induced a much greater retaliation risk; the cost of repair was likely to be prohibitive for the individual concerned. This explained the quest for reassurance when making a decision and the desire for group approval for decisions that involved the community:

> I didn't take too many risks because if I ever decide and it could have an impact on the project…
>
> For the sake, the complicity of the team or the solidarity of the team, you have to make decisions together.

On the other hand, consulting everyone, seeking the advice of more experienced people or seeking validation from the hierarchy was not perceived as contradictory to taking on individual responsibility, as the following quotations show:

> I talk to them about it, even if they don't answer, they already know. Because if one day it has an effect or impact on the whole program, at least if everyone is already aware of it...but that doesn't take away my responsibility, I am responsible.
>
> I am responsible for this, even if I refer to him *(the boss)* and it is quite natural. (...) I feel that in the end, in any case, the decisions belong to me and that they are there to provide me with guidelines and to advise me, in fact, thanks to their experiences.
>
> Between X and me, it's everyone take responsibility and then there's a little discussion between us and I think that between X and me, it can be fine, it's fine, but you always have to ask for the opinion of an experienced person who has (his or her) view.

The group enabled them to make a sensible decision about the problem, as is generally the case in the French context, but it also protected them against possible repercussions if the choice turned out to be a bad option. Discussing and sharing decisions did not remove the responsibility of the one who ultimately decided. For French protagonists, 'hiding' behind the group for each decision was seen as lacking courage and refusing to assume individually the decisions for which they were committed. For the French, this process amounted to 'opening the umbrella' to protect themselves instead of 'getting wet' ('*se mouiller*') with a choice, and that was interpreted as a sign of cowardice.

This analysis demonstrates how the encounter of the two universes of meaning in this work context precluded the implementation of effective empowerment. While the protagonists from both sides were driven by the best intentions—a sincere desire to empower on the one hand and a genuine desire to take responsibility on the other—their actions were misinterpreted and hindered the empowerment process.

12.3 Contrasting Intercultural Dynamics

The previous sections have shown the nature of the challenges that arise in intercultural encounters in the workplace. Protagonists involved in international cooperation are often able to accurately describe differences in behaviour, but they cannot figure out the logic behind them if it is too far from their own. When no cultural interpreter is available, some adjustments are made but many misunderstandings persist even when the cooperation is sustained. Time alone does not smooth out the obstacles to understanding and working together. In addition, as Carzozi[3] has shown about Italian expatriates in France, previous expatriation experiences, even if successful, cannot predict the success of a manager assigned to a new environment. Without understanding the logic of each cultural context, stakeholders do not have sufficient resources to determine how to interact effectively.

More generally, beyond the aforementioned detailed cases, the research shows a great diversity of intercultural dynamics depending on the teams and their contexts. We provide an overview of the variety of intercultural interactions ranging from blatant conflict to effective intercultural synergy.

12.3.1 Misunderstandings and Conflicts

The most widely publicized dynamic, because it is the most dramatic and visible, though not the most widespread, is intercultural polarization and open conflict. The Renault-Volvo alliance, as well as the merger between Daimler and Chrysler, which led to the radical break-up of the cooperation, are emblematic examples. In such cases, misunderstandings disrupt the dynamics of collaboration to the point that one or even both actors no longer benefit from it and decide to break with the joint project. In most instances, cultural misunderstandings make it impossible to find a way to reconcile divergent interests because efforts to do so are misinterpreted. A spiral of mistrust hence begins, which is difficult to reverse without external mediators.

However, most often, intercultural misunderstandings do not go so far as to lead to a breakdown in joint operation. Rather, they are a nuisance in the cooperation with which the partners cope in different ways. A peaceful coexistence of different ways of doing things can be achieved if the work does not require fine-tuned coordination and strong integration of all the contributions. Coordination is restricted to a few difficult periods of time when differences resurface but most people show patience in looking for arrangements. Daily work remains compartmentalized enough not to create strong frictions.

When a high degree of work integration is required, such as in the case of projects, there are necessarily many interactions and differences which pose greater challenges. The case of a Lebanese-French cooperation provides a good illustration.[4] The cooperation took place between the Tripoli Water Office and a French service provider in charge of setting up water management for the city. Both partners were determined to make this contract a success and they were highly committed to this cooperation. The French partner was committed to doing a professional job and asked for autonomy. The Lebanese partner wished to engage in cooperation to actively help find solutions to possible problems. To this end, the latter wished to have access to information that they did not spontaneously obtain from the French who felt accountable for the results, but who were determined to use their own working methods. On the Lebanese side, the protagonists acknowledged the technical skills of the French teams but, noting that the French did not share much, they suspected hidden issues and strategies. When they sought information from the service provider, the latter interpreted this as an attempt to control and a lack of trust. From then on, the French service provider hid behind the formal distribution of responsibilities to claim their professional autonomy and be able to work according to the requirements of their profession. Faced with this attitude of information retention, the Lebanese partner was confirmed in their interpretation that the provider was trying to hide things and deceive the client. Due to different cultural representations of what good cooperation should be, which had not been made explicit, mistrust escalated although the partners were initially united with the best intentions towards each other.

Problems can also be experienced in an asymmetric way. Because they have various strategic—expertise, financial resources, close relationship with the client, etc.—or symbolic assets—being from economically dominant countries or representatives of the parent company—, some sub-groups impose their way of working and the dominated groups do not rebel. However, through the lens of their cultural references, the latter do not necessarily give a positive meaning to their work; they disengage through passivity or withdrawal. This may result in contributions that fall short of expectations, requiring considerable energy from the international project manager to compensate for low member engagement (Chevrier & Segal, 2011). It can also take the form of the sudden and unexpected resignation of a local employee, following an appraisal interview with an expatriate which has gone very well from the latter's point of view (Chevrier, 2016). In these frequent cases, the silence of the dominated responds to the blindness of the dominant. In other words, the elements of cultural frictions remain unnoticed and therefore not addressed.

12.3.2 Successful Intercultural Cooperation

Nevertheless, intercultural dynamics can spontaneously turn out well. A favourable situation and a few leaders with good intuitions may fortunately combine so as to make intercultural work situations truly successful. The case of a French-owned perfume company in Miami employing South American employees is an illustration of such a successful combination (Sauvage, 2018). First, the distribution of roles between nationalities served the success of the company. The image of the firm was enhanced by the presence of French designers who enjoy a solid international reputation in the luxury sector in general and perfume in particular. South American employees were developing sales effectively, while this role would have been more difficult for French employees who avoided being dependent on the power of money (see p. 160). Second, the functions were sufficiently compartmentalized that the majority of decisions were made within each department or by management and few of them required a truly intercultural discussion. Consequently, the decision-makers' cultural references were relatively homogeneous for each decision made within a specific unit (a department or the management team). Finally, although they did not give them the same meaning, the company members celebrated some characteristics that ensured the success of their business, as they were convinced of their mutual understanding (see p. 194). For example, all employees used the word 'openness' when describing how their company operated, but on closer inspection, this word did not refer to the same meaning on each side. When they talked about openness, South Americans meant the consideration for personal life, even at work, or the efforts made by the French to cross the language barrier by speaking Spanish. 'Openness' was relational, it referred to the inclusion of staff in a community. What the French had in mind about 'openness' was related to an intellectual dimension: an open mind, a diversity of ideas that facilitated the functioning of a diverse group and allowed them to play the role of mentor to which they were dedicated. Thus, there was productive cooperation despite misunderstandings, insofar as the employees were not really aware of the differences in representations that separated them, but their diverging interpretations stemming from their respective cultural references were positive enough to maintain an excellent working climate and effective cooperation where it was essential.

Another form of cultural synergy based on a hybridization of practices has also been observed. In such cases, conscious and pragmatic efforts lead the employees to find arrangements that meet the expectations of the different sub-groups. One example was Alleo, a joint subsidiary of the French and German incumbent railway companies, which operated on the cross-border Franco-German railway lines.[5] As seen in Chapter 10 pp. 207–9, the merger between the two companies revealed differences in the role of the agents circulating on the train. In the French company, agents identified themselves as controllers whereas in the German company, the train attendants [*Zugbegleiter*] were service-oriented. When extending these service-oriented practices to French staff had been considered, they refused. The assimilation to commercial staff was strongly rejected because it profoundly transformed professional identity from an authority figure entitled to control passengers to a customer-service provider. The French employees also resisted the name tag. Like police officers, they claimed for a badge number so as not to be at risk of being stalked by a caught fraudster looking for retaliation at their private address. Similarly, the French employees were surprised that the Germans, driven by a service-oriented logic, did not always comply with the rules:

> And with the ticket control, big surprise, we discovered a German word, the word "*Kulanz*", the *Zugbegleiter* were only gently scolding passengers who broke the rule, without disciplining them. (Manager, Alleo)

> In both companies, the core of the business is about the 3 S's: Security, Revenue Protection [*Sauvegarde*] and Service, but the priorities are different. At SNCF, it will be in this order, but at DB, it will be Service, Revenue Protection and Security. (Manager, Alleo)

Finally, in order to meet the expectations of both national staffs, comply with the French and German statutory constraints, and avoid undermining the professional identity of the employees, the company proposed a bi-national team of controllers in each cross-border train. After some adjustments in the distribution of roles and the way the work was done in the train, this combination was implemented to achieve the objectives.

12.4 Towards a New Approach to the Management of Multicultural Teams

In order for the rare cases of intercultural situations, in which the protagonists manage to overcome, and also take advantage of their differences, to become the rule, a new approach to the management of multicultural teams must be followed. Such an approach requires an understanding of what is at stake in interactions.

12.4.1 Intercultural Problems are Not What We Think They Are

Paradoxically, when cultural differences are highlighted by the protagonists, they are not necessarily acute. Such differences can be constructed and instrumentalized by employees to resist globalization (Ybema & Byun, 2009; van Marrewijk, 2010; van den Ende & van Marrewijk, 2015). For example, in contexts of hostile or at least unpopular takeovers, the staff of the acquired entity may produce or endorse stereotypes or cultural identities as a pretext for claiming autonomy from a distant new power or for keeping control of their market. Thus, arguing that they were more familiar with Indian-style time management than their European partner, Indian staff claimed to maintain an interface with a customer who, according to the company's standards, should have dealt with the European teams directly (Ailon-Souday & Kunda, 2003). In other circumstances, power issues are disguised as intercultural misunderstandings to justify a cooperation failure. Here again, differences are instrumentalized to achieve strategic purposes.

But more often than not, the differences are not well understood. It is not uncommon for employees to emphasize differences in corporate cultures or professions and to underestimate differences in national or societal cultures. Obviously, international encounters reveal divergences and the interviewed participants express national stereotypes more or less cautiously. However, apart from a few smart observers who finely grasp the implicit cultural representations playing a role in their business world, most are not fully aware of the logics at work, whether it is their own or that of others.[6] Using common words when speaking the same *lingua franca* further deludes them on their points of divergence (see p. 204) as seen above with the word 'openness' in the perfumery company in Florida and the word 'empowerment' (*délégation*) in the French-Malagasy organization.

When difficulties arise, they are frequently attributed to other causes. For example, when a French director did not obtain the commitment he expected from his American manager, he tended to question his skills and motivation without realizing that he had not been clear enough about his own expectations, which, according to his manager, should have been explicit and formalized (Dupriez & Simons, 2002). Sometimes, difficult personalities, a hidden agenda, a lack of engagement and rigour, are summoned to account for unsuccessful cooperations. Participants do not realize that major differences in cultural representations are at work both in creating and giving meaning to these challenges. For instance, the French are quick to blame their foreign colleagues for a lack of skills because their own reference to the *métier* is not shared but they consider the situation in relation to these professional requirements. Those who think of business relations as a continuous flow of reciprocal services, as is the case in China, rather assess the actions of their partners in terms of loyalty. Finally, in West Africa, the challenges encountered tend to be attributed to the malicious intents of one partner or another.

In a nutshell, invisible cultural conceptions, as well as their consequences on work in intercultural situations, are poorly identified and most often underestimated.

12.4.2 The Shortcomings of Traditional Approaches

Intercultural management research has developed considerably over the past thirty years to support the internationalization of firms. Today, three approaches are prevailing. The first is focused on intercultural communication, the second on cultural distance, and the third on corporate culture.

The literature in intercultural communication emphasizes the adjustment of the individuals involved in interactions. Intercultural competence develops gradually as the individual moves through a learning process (Bennett, 1986). People must be aware that communication codes and usual behaviours are varied in order to overcome their stereotypes and prejudices. This perspective is based on the assumption that, if intercultural work is approached with an awareness of the existence of differences (cognitive dimension), with a caring attitude towards others (affective dimension), and with a determination to achieve objectives (motivational dimension), interactions will be effective. However, as aforementioned examples and Chapter 10 have shown, the best intentions and efforts to be 'tolerant' are not sufficient to find common ground and work together efficiently. Trapped in their own cultural universe of meaning, the participants tend to misinterpret the behaviours of others, even though they are based on good intentions, and the initial climate of trust quickly dissipates. Instead of being deconstructed and discarded with greater intercultural practice, stereotypes become stronger or even emerge as collaboration goes on. For example, in the case of the merger between a French company and a Dutch company[7] (see Chapter 6), seven years after the merger, the partners had still not reached the level of integration that would have allowed them to make the most of it. Moreover, the mutual stereotypes were more entrenched than at the outset when optimism prevailed in regard to the opportunities offered by the merger. Being aware of the existence of differences and of the relativity of cultures is not sufficient. Being able to decipher the meaning of the actions of others, based on a more in-depth understanding of the cultural logics involved, is required.

Another part of the literature in intercultural management details the functioning of teams through a series of variables in a model that links the characteristics of the teams (size, degree of diversity, etc.), the operating processes (coordination, communication, etc.), and the results obtained (goal achievements, member satisfaction, intercultural learning, etc.). Such research tries to contribute to optimize the global dynamics by working variable by variable. In this perspective, the cultures of the team members are grasped through cultural distance (Shenkar, 2012). The distance is calculated from the respective coordinates identified for each culture by the psychosocial approach of Hofstede (1980). However, while distant coordinates do indicate cultural differences, a quantitative approach says nothing about the nature of differences, that is, cultural conceptions that are qualitatively distinct. While the assessment of 'cultural distance' can warn about possible challenges, it does not help to understand them in any detail. For example, the Chinese company Cosco (China Ocean Shipping Company) obtained two concessions to operate two of the three terminals at the port of Piraeus in Greece between 2008 and 2010. After a few years of operation, relations between Greek employees and Chinese management got very tense. While the management claimed that Cosco's priority was to create jobs in Greece and provide employee benefits, employee turnover was high and so were workers' and unions' grievances. To understand how culture could play a role in these managerial problems or why Greek employees criticized the 'authoritarianism of Chinese managers', calculations of cultural distance did not help. The two countries do not score the same on Hofstede's attitude and value scales, but they are on the same side of the continuum for power distance (high in both cases: 60 and 80) or individualism (low in both cases: 35 and 20). A closer look at work relations is required to understand how cultural differences may account for the Greek employees' reluctance in accepting Chinese management style. Similarly, the very same power-distance indexes of France, Poland, and Hong Kong (68) conceal the different conceptions of power relations and 'virtuous authority' in these countries.

Popular stereotypes, likewise scientific attitude scales, are used by people immersed in intercultural situations to give meaning to the differences they observe or the behaviours that surprise them. However, in both cases, people interpret social situations in their pre-existing categories. For instance, when non-Chinese people consider that the Chinese are 'very hierarchical' because of their high power-distance score, they refer to their own vision of hierarchy, applying references that are not those of Chinese employees. They imagine a difference in degree (more or less hierarchical, more or less authoritarian, etc.) but still think about power relations with their categories without understanding that the very figures of a respected authority are qualitatively different and do not rely on the same sources of legitimacy (see Chapters 4 and 10). Thus, in the first example in this chapter, the Swedes clearly perceived the role of the French hierarchy as that of decision-makers, but they did not see them as the experts who had opinions based on their technical knowledge, and who wanted to convince others. Therefore, they perceived them as autocrats who imposed their views. Without understanding the cultural logic, the partners did not have the resources to find out how to interact effectively.

The last approach to intercultural management relies on corporate culture to overcome national differences through shared values and standardized practices across the organization. Some research has argued that a strong corporate culture is likely to bring people together regardless of their national affiliations (Karjalainen, 2010). Specifically, the corporate culture would provide two distinct levers. On the one hand, a strong corporate culture is reflected in values formalized in codes and principles, and claimed during rituals bringing people together (corporate ceremonials, team-building seminars, and other social events). Identification and a strong sense of belonging to the organization are fostered by such managerial practices, and in turn, they reinforce the commitment of employees from all origins. Some major corporations even claim that a strong socialization to corporate values produces 'corporate' employees who can be called 'IBMers' or 'Samsung Men and Women' after the name of the company. On the other hand, the corporate culture is epitomized in professional practices, tools, and methods that are intended to unify practices, enhance coordination, and guide employees' actions towards the company's strategic objectives. Integrated information systems are good examples of process standardization within multinational companies. For instance, methods designed by and diffused from the headquarters allow any expert from a large consulting firm in a given country to join a consulting team in another country; that expert will know exactly what steps will be taken throughout the consulting process.

Field observations show that efforts to create a common culture are not in vain. Firstly, promoted principles and values do, to some extent, succeed in generating employee commitment. The values displayed, whether very general such as integrity, respect, or trust, or more specific to the organizations, such as continuous innovation or talent development, are welcomed everywhere. Secondly, standardized procedures operate as a ritual in which every stakeholder's expected action is explicit, thus providing guidelines for work coordination.

However, empirical research within a large multinational company (d'Iribarne, 2012b), has shown that when employees came to giving content to stated principles and translating values into action, differentiated cultural interpretations persisted. Large corporations themselves might not necessarily be aware that the very way they formulate their principles conveys particular conceptions of authority, cooperation and, more broadly, work relations, as seen in Chapter 11. Thus, the same mottoes could generate more or less enthusiasm depending on the context. For instance, being entitled to 'challenge' one's manager could be exciting for Western employees who value professional autonomy, or who see this principle as a protection against power abuse. It made little sense in Jordan, where the principle itself had not been translated into the local version of the company's principles of action, nor in China, where the principle had been translated but was not likely to be implemented. In addition, in France, employees appeared to be somewhat reluctant with regard to the whole code. The very notion of corporate culture tended to be considered as a management manoeuvre to build an ideal image that did not necessarily reflect daily reality. In this context, any discrepancy between the stated principle and managerial actions tended to undermine the credibility of the corporate culture.

In addition, although standardized practices of large corporations can provide shared landmarks for the coordination of members of international teams, the examination of their implementation reveals shortcomings and bypasses, when the major cultural references underlying them are not those of the employees concerned (see Chapter 5). The ritualization of collective work in intercultural environments is effective as long as it takes on a positive meaning in the members' universes of meaning. It means that the potential for social integration across national cultures of corporate cultures remains limited. As soon as practices promoted through the corporate culture clash with some implicit but crucial conceptions of proper ways to agree, exercise authority, and resolve conflicts, they are no longer unifying, and do not help intercultural teams to cooperate.

12.5 Conclusion

This chapter has shown that the effects of cultural differences on intercultural cooperation are still poorly understood. While managers are less inclined to simply deny the question than they used to, they do not necessarily understand the very nature of the intercultural hurdles and do not use appropriate theoretical frameworks and practical tools to deal with them effectively. The approach to cultures as universes of meaning invites us to overcome such limitations. Without claiming that the categories of interpretation of other cultures can be intimately understood, at least this approach gives access to the key references of cultural contexts, which makes it possible to significantly improve intercultural cooperation. We shall see in Chapter 15 how this more in-depth understanding of cultural references paves the way for more effective international teams. In particular, it makes it possible to discern the good intentions behind what is initially shocking, to recognize the points that cannot be negotiated nor changed and those on which managers can rely to find acceptable and effective practices. Indeed, the mere international characteristic of teams does not determine their dynamics and successes. While in some favourable configurations, international teams are fortunately effective, many are penalized by misunderstandings, latent or open conflicts, and all kinds of hurdles whose cultural nature is not acknowledged. Coaching based upon the detailed understanding of the universes of meaning involved would be useful to improve their performance.

Notes

1. In this chapter, 'intercultural' and 'multicultural' will be used interchangeably to designate teams that include members from diverse national cultures.
2. [*'quand il y a deux responsables, il y a deux irresponsables'*]. The play on words is not translatable.
3. Carzozi, Cristina (2018) 'Mobiliser le personnel local et réussir son intégration en France: la stratégie des expatriés italiens d'une multinationale. Le cas INDESIT', Doctoral thesis, (Université Paris Dauphine), Paris Sciences Lettres.
4. Yousfi, Hèla (2006) 'Le contrat dans une coopération internationale: la rencontre des intérêts à l'épreuve de la rencontre des cultures: cas du contrat de gestion déléguée de l'alimentation en eau potable de la communauté urbaine de Tripoli (Liban)', Doctoral thesis, (Université Paris X-Nanterre). https://www.theses.fr/2006PA100039.
5. Barmeyer, Christoph and Davoine, Eric (2014), 'Culture de travail émergente dans des organisations bi-nationales—une analyse de deux cas franco-allemands', *Atlas-AFMI* (IAE Aix en Provence (CERGAM, Aix-Marseille Université)/Kedge Business School, Aix-Marseille).
6. This unawareness explains why surveys based on direct questions to international team members or expatriates fail to uncover the cultural universes of meaning at play and mainly bring out stereotypes and good intentions to make the most of cultural diversity. Chapter 16 will detail an analytical method of interviews which enables the underlying cultural frames of references to be figured out.
7. Iribarne, Philippe d', and Noorderhaven, Niels (2017), 'Les rapports entre Air France et KLM dans le vécu du personnel. Une perspective culturelle', *Rapport* mai 2017.

PART IV

FOR A PRODUCTIVE USE OF THE INTERPRETATIVE APPROACH

13
A Company Odyssey in the South

In 1988, the Société Nationale d'Électricité du Cameroun (SONEL)[1] was subject to hyper-centralization. It hindered the development of the company, which has since been struggling to recover from its centralization process. At the time, the CEO attributed part of the cause to Cameroonian cultural traits. According to him, his employees tended to avoid their responsibilities through fear of being called a 'nasty guy' and having to suffer accusations or retaliation 'even within their family'. In 2016, twenty-eight years later, a new CEO recently appointed to manage the same company explained at a conference that this culture is a 'burden' which he considered to be a strategic issue. He successively referred to bureaucratic habits, fear of assuming responsibility, 'risk of retaliations', and pressure of 'family and friends'. Such similarities between statements—which we will examine later in detail—raise questions about the existence of a cultural obstacle to modernizing management in this emerging country. Has no progress been made between these two testimonies? During all these years, the company has undergone many changes, including two privatizations, several successive CEOs, reorganizations, the introduction of numerous management methods... which apparently did not have any lasting effects. Should we conclude that there is a cultural fatality, as some people think, particularly in Cameroon? Should we just wait and hope that one day, perhaps, behaviours will change?

Unlike the previous chapters—each focused on a management issue—this chapter aims to describe the trials and tribulations of a company over almost thirty years, swung between the winds of globalization and the currents of its cultural universe. Rather than seeking to demonstrate a particular point, the story intertwines the several emblematic questions faced by companies in emerging countries, and serves as an introduction to the last part of the book. This case first illustrates the remarkable permanence over a long duration of a set of Cameroonian cultural traits. Secondly, it shows that these specificities have only rarely been taken into consideration in modernization attempts—if only by chance. However, we note the poor success of some international panaceas such as privatization, which is advocated everywhere by the World Bank. Finally, this story shows that changes are possible if management approaches consider cultural constants.

The value of this case lies in the historical depth of our observations.[2] These began in 1988 when the company was suffering from a high degree of

Cross-Cultural Management Revisited: A Qualitative Approach. Philippe d'Iribarne, Sylvie Chevrier, Alain Henry, Jean-Pierre Segal, and Geneviève Tréguer-Felten, Oxford University Press (2020).
DOI: 10.1093/oso/9780198857471.001.0001

centralization. We have already presented (see Chapter 5, p. 94) the ways in which the cultural traits that mark Cameroonian society render efforts to implement an MBO (management by objectives) unsuccessful. A few years later (1992–1994), a second survey accompanied the creation of a procedures manual whose consistency with the local cultural universe was demonstrated. In 2001, the government judged the company's progress insufficient and, on the recommendation of the World Bank, it was privatized.[3] The appointment of a new CEO, from Washington D.C., marked the beginning of a series of setbacks and advances. These were detailed in a survey conducted between 2006 and 2008 for a doctoral thesis on 'the effectiveness of privatisations' (Godong, 2011). However, in 2014, the American shareholder threw in the towel. The government signed a new privatization contract with a British investor.[4] A different approach was adopted by a CEO who, this time, decided to consider cultural specificities. The changes in the company then shed light on the relationship between what was or was not evolving in the company's culture.

This odyssey is also that of an implicit struggle, almost invisible, between two approaches (Hernandez, 2007): one bet on a programmed disappearance of cultural specificities under the unavoidable influence of universal management practices—whose advent is still awaited; the other approach concerned itself with taking into consideration what Cameroonians call 'local realities', from which it cleverly took advantage.

13.1 From First Attempts at Modernization to the Implementation of Procedures

At the end of the 1980s, the SONEL—with about 3,000 employees—had been suffering for several years from a high degree of centralization, which had become incompatible with the size and complexity of its operations.

Despite the repeated exhortations of the CEO to his employees to accept their responsibilities, and notwithstanding several reports from external consultants called on to help the company, the situation did not evolve. The blockages were such that the company could no longer meet its public service obligations. Its technical and financial results were deteriorating. Some people saw it as a consequence of irreducible 'cultural resistances', but without identifying where they were coming from: colonial archaic habits which were perpetuated beyond independence; a 'French bureaucratic disease' transmitted through public organization pattern; or the legacy of African cultural behaviours unsuited to the modern business world? Other observers saw this as the result of a skills gap, which is common in developing countries. However, since the 1980s, the electricity company had had a particularly well-qualified staff.

Initial research was conducted, at the company's request, in order to try to identify the difficulties and suggest likely solutions. When we first met the company, its excessive centralization processes were denounced by all the staff, for which they gave many examples. Any request—for example, to purchase a ticket on an internal flight—was subject to a multitude of cascading visas, before requiring the approval of the CEO. The complexity of the procedures and the congestion at the top resulted in a slow running of operations. Decisions were delayed in coming back down, or they were simply lost along the way. As a result, the staff's motivation plunged.

The delays in decision-making and the incoherencies and dilution of responsibilities contributed to the staff's low morale and motivation, because they aspired to a less centralized management. As for the CEO, he asserted: 'decentralisation is inevitable', stressing something he saw as necessary, regardless of anyone's will. But despite these unanimous expectations, nothing changed. Invited to propose remedies, international consultants recommended implementing an MBO. It was intended to introduce more objectivity into hierarchical relationships and break the spiral of mistrust and centralization. However, after a pilot test carried out on a number of units, the CEO quickly abandoned it (see Chapter 5, p. 99).

The CEO particularly complained about the behaviour of heads of departments and directors, who were afraid to shoulder their responsibilities. They preferred to send upwards all the decisions that were having negative impacts on people, so that they would eventually be left up to the CEO. During the meeting we had with him, he was interrupted by a manager's phone call, asking for his approval to lend a company vehicle to an employee who asked for it in order to bring his dead wife's body back to the village. The demand was critical, according to the cultural context where funerals play a major role and where no one escapes the obligation to bring the deceased person back to the village. If the manager refused the vehicle—on the basis that this courtesy is not part of the established rights—he faced the worst charges of 'nastiness'. But if he took it upon himself to lend a vehicle, it could have prejudiced him. When asked about the reason for not deciding by himself, the manager replied that, in the event of an accident, he risked an unpredictable negative reaction from the CEO: 'He could say nothing', he answered, 'if he has *any affection* for me, or he could say: "Hold on, I'm going to use this opportunity to settle a score with him." (...) Let's suppose that the CEO is in a *bad mood*. He says: "This is extremely serious (...) I'm going to report it to the Chairman of the Board of Directors and, if needs be, suggest you be replaced".' There is a feeling of insecurity in reporting relationships. 'Even if a manager takes some initiatives', one manager complained, 'there's *always a tendency* to tell him: "It's no good! It's no good!" And *no one explains why*. That causes some frustration.'

The present case illustrates the singularities of the context of interpretation in which it is embedded—of which we already presented major rationales in

Chapter 5 (pp. 97–100). In this context, it seems extremely difficult to admit that when a decision affects a person, it has been taken on a justifiable and objective basis. There is a conviction that a decisive role has been played by the more or less friendly relations that people have with each other. Thus, if a classical system of delegation and control by objectives is put in place, the actors tend to think that if someone is judged positively, it is because his superior is in favour of him and has even been able to set objectives that are easy to achieve; whereas if he is judged negatively, it is conversely that his superior has set objectives that are too difficult for him to achieve.

The report we submitted to the company, after highlighting some features of the interpretation framework, mainly proposed to set up procedures likely to protect those who must make decisions which were most directly implicating individuals (d'Iribarne, 1990). Then a few years later, having analysed the case of a Togolese company that had achieved good performance thanks to the use of a detailed procedures manual (Henry, 1991),[5] we informed the Cameroonian company's CEO—who had been replaced in the meantime—about the results of the research carried out in the Togolese company. Our analysis was showing that the difficulties it had had to overcome were very similar to those encountered at SONEL, in terms of behavioural problems and also in the way to interpret them. The CEO—although sceptical about the idea of any cultural approach—was immediately convinced: 'This is exactly what I wanted to do,' he told us, 'even though I hadn't been able to formulate it clearly.' He asked us to test the perspective of writing detailed procedures with the company's managers and employees.

A new survey conducted to this end showed respondents' enthusiasm concerning the idea of developing and publishing similar manuals. Most of the interviewees considered it as a self-evident matter, which corresponded to their idea of modern management. A supervisor, inspired by his enthusiasm, described the future manuals as 'true democracy'.

In the basic outline, the project launch phase took up the usual steps for introducing a new management tool: recruitment of a consultant, preliminary study, opening seminar, appointment of a project team, training of the writers, etc. More specifically, the central challenge of this phase was to answer questions in which local fears could be identified: why had such manuals never been produced until now even though they were useful—that is, who took advantage of the lack of manuals? Was there not a risk that those whose interests would be threatened would sabotage the project? Why did the management suddenly have an interest in change? Was there not a risk that the process would be taken over by a particular department? A regular employee, convinced of the value of written procedures, expressed his scepticism about the idea that leaders agree to make procedures available to all: 'Frankly [i.e. it is obvious],' he explained, '[the superior] has to be generous to scuttle his own ship [i.e. to renounce power] because in fact, people like to make themselves indispensable.'

A few months later, the company had produced a dozen large binders containing its detailed procedures (see Chapter 5, pp. 94–96). These manuals were unanimously welcomed. Once they had been distributed, some managers organized a collective reading of their team's files. The managers invited their colleagues to read them and 'to stick to the letter and spirit of the text'.

We could have thought that this management method, taking advantage of the cultural context and welcomed with such enthusiasm, would lead to a sustainable appropriation—as happened, for example, in a case in Morocco that will be presented in Chapter 14 (p. 280). But practically, this did not happen: the new approach started declining a few years later, before being abandoned.

The use of detailed procedure manuals, compliance with which needs to be ensured by a rigorous audit, is likely to lead to the development of more trustworthy relationships between superiors and subordinates and to better cooperation among the colleagues. However, it may be a matter of concern in the relations between the latter and the surrounding context. By allowing strict control over each agent's actions, it protects them from outside pressure to obtain multiple favours, such as, for those who have the support of a 'well-placed' person, not having to pay their electricity bill, or obtaining a right-of-way on a company vehicle. However, the application of the audited procedures is likely to generate strong resistance in the social environment and in particular among political personalities. To resist these pressures, it is necessary for the CEO to have a solid personal situation—such was not the case at that particular moment. The CEO who had decided to have the procedures drafted had a strong internal standing in the company: he had already managed it a few years earlier, but his political position was shaky: he had been suspected in some recent political troubles and was expected to participate in the national redistributing 'system'. His recent appointment had been the result of a subtle balance. But, the management was not strong enough to resist external pressures. Consequently, they didn't lead the reform to its end which included the establishment of a strong internal audit. As a result, the files gradually lost their credibility and were hardly ever updated. For a while the company remained in an uncertain situation, with these files still benefiting from some consideration. One could have hoped that the initial impetus provided by this successful experiment would be renewed.

Though . . . at the end of the 1990s, under the leadership of the World Bank, with which the government had been negotiating investments for the sector, a completely different debate took centre stage. For the bank, a few principles of 'good governance' prevail: public management cannot be effective; management is a private leaders' competence; consequently, privatization is seen as the sovereign and universal medicine against public companies' mismanagement. Conversely, cultural aspects, which need to be corrected if they introduce economic biases, are considered as a secondary factor (Iribarne, 2015).

New tribulations then led therefore to a radical challenge to what might have seemed established: the benefits of the procedure manuals were forgotten and, through its privatization, the company came under the control of a foreign group.

13.2 A 'US-made' Privatization

In 2001, a privatization contract was signed with an American group which was specialized in energy but deprived of any actual experience in Sub-Saharan Africa. The electricity company underwent a series of deep transformations.

A new CEO from Arlington (USA) was appointed. Within a few days, he reorganized everything and introduced methods 'made in the USA'—what, he rightly believed, he had precisely been appointed to do. He appointed a team of new directors whose actions were evaluated on the basis of quantified objectives and were directly accountable to him—in line with his American management logics (see Chapter 1, p. 17). Moreover, he considered that the local use of procedures was a symptom of bureaucratic mismanagement which went against his own vision of governance. He decided to abandon the manuals—especially since, from his perspective, the cost of rewriting them, made necessary by the reorganization, would have been too high in view of the expected benefits. He decided to emphasize the directors' personal accountability for their objectives. Recruitment and internal promotion procedures were streamlined and left to the directors' discretion. They were supposed to follow the same contractual logic as the one he, the CEO, had with his directors.

But these changes were not having the expected effects. At the end of the first year, managers were far from achieving their objectives, which were proving to be unrealistic. The directors had accepted them out of a spirit of goodwill and loyalty. As for the freedoms given to them for recruitment and promotion so that they could surround themselves with high-performing colleagues, they led to a 'totally reversed perception' (Godong, 2011: 186–194): employees were convinced that recruitment and promotions were made, more than ever, 'on a clientelist basis' and 'regionalist' logic. Finally, without a clear definition of the new procedures, teams could hardly find their way around. The general atmosphere was characterized by mistrust and traps (including against directors). The company's results were deteriorating: it encountered an increase in breakdowns on the national grid, a decrease in invoiced volumes, and a decline in the rate of invoice collection.

After one year, the group decided to replace the CEO. His successor, more open to dialogue, continued to promote the management methods defined by the head office. Over the next two years, the results showed some slow improvements. Once again, the group decided to change the CEO, and this time it appointed someone selected among the company's Cameroonian engineers.

This new CEO, who a few years earlier had been part of the experience of the procedures, decided to have the manuals gradually rewritten and to consolidate the 'audit and control unit'. However, at the same time, a new collateral constraint emerged, from abroad, which diverted his priorities. As the electricity company was now governed by US law, it was subject to the brand-new Sarbanes–Oxley Law on financial transparency—enacted in the aftermath of the Enron financial scandal. The procedure files were therefore written first and foremost to meet this purpose. The audit unit—renamed SOX, according to the acronym of the law—was fully dedicated to the application of American regulations.

The field survey conducted by Godong between 2006 and 2008 showed that the cultural logics had not faded (Godong, 2011). On the contrary, employees were still asking for 'clear' procedures (p. 175) to 'fight against elusive behaviour' (p. 192) or to 'reduce—if not eradicate—the suspicion, mistrust, and fear that individuals usually have about others' individual actions' (p. 203). The procedures manuals were considered by the staff as an 'absolute reference' in terms of organization (p. 201). 'It is necessary to state precisely', the author writes (p. 174), 'what must be done. And do everything to (. . .) reassure the other persons about the control of procedures. It is necessary to describe in a very specific and schematised way what [employees] have to do, in what order they have to do it, and for what purpose.' The difficulties encountered inside the company reflected the same fears as those observed fifteen years earlier (p. 146): 'I have often received people here,' explained an HR manager, 'who come to tell me: "I was told that *it is you who are personally blocking* my promotion" and I answer: "No, I am not the one working against your employment!".' True, this HR manager strongly rejected the charges brought against him, but he was not surprised at all that they might exist.

In the following years, the American company tried to modernize management by introducing several successive methods, but none of them was very successful.

A first attempt aimed to change the 'corporate culture' by relying on the internal dissemination of a 'good governance' charter. The charter required staff to adhere to six 'collective values', chosen locally so as to be relevant to the context (p. 105): 'safety, integrity, commitment, excellence, equity, and fun (sic!)'. But the charter soon aroused 'mockery, disbelief, and distrust' (p. 112). People considered it 'imprecise', not enabling people to know what ensured the application of values, nor to understand the activities that were actually covered. One manager, giving the example of a meeting on the theme of 'safety' held in a room undergoing restoration work, highlighted these inconsistencies. Other interviewees believed that this policy document covered the general management's hidden agendas—that is, making it easier to criticize agents.

Management also attempted to introduce a so-called '360-degree feedback'—that is, feedback based on several evaluators' comments for each employee[6]—which was supposed to provide an answer to the old quest for objectivity. But after one year, management remarked: '75% of the staff are rated between 92 and 100 points'—i.e. excellent (p. 124). According to the interviewees, this result was explained by (a) a propensity to be 'kind' and to avoid too precise criticism; (b) the fear that the names of those who misjudged their colleagues would quickly be known (entailing a risk of retaliation); and (c) the well understood self-interest of staff who expected to increase the volume of bonuses distributed. 'In any case,' Godong noted (p. 144), 'everyone feels it is worthwhile to avoid for themselves and their family the "suffering" and "annoyances" that Americans put on everywhere.'

Another attempt was done using the KPI (Key Performance Indicators) method, but the result measurement was considered too uncertain, and the emphasis was placed on how the results had been achieved. Once again, it became obvious that what is at stake is (pp. 119–120) 'the search for a break with a managerial past in which the measurement of performance [...had] been overshadowed by all kinds of subjective variables: tribalism, clientelism, friendship'. After a few months, the process, which aimed to indefinitely pursue this objectivity, became trapped under a huge paperwork production.

Finally, American shareholders renounced and negotiated their withdrawal.

13.3 A Resolutely New Approach

In mid-2014, the government signed a new contract with a British investor. A Cameroonian engineer who had spent most of his career abroad was appointed at the head of the company. In the following years, the social climate within the company as well as its public image improved. The main indicators were progressing, although difficulties remained due to accumulated backlogs.[7] Nevertheless, the company continued to depend heavily on State governance, both for the future of its concession agreement renewals and because public non-payments jeopardized its cash flow.[8]

The new CEO considered culture as a strategic issue[9]: 'A cultural insight is really at the core of the integrated leadership model', he explained in a lecture delivered in the USA to an audience of Cameroonian professionals (emphasis added):

> Now I am talking to you about that *stone we have at the bottom*, that lay *the burden*, and [that] is *the culture*. We have to understand that great strategy can be destroyed by aggressive enterprise culture, (...) I mean the country culture as well. (...) As management guru Peter Drucker said, 'The culture *would eat* your strategy for breakfast'. (...) Without cultural insight your vision will just fall flat. So, at ENEO, we did a couple of *transformations of culture, because that is the key problem*. (...) So, by addressing these cultural issues, then we start moving.

He felt it necessary to have a deep understanding—'*insight*'—of the impact of culture—'*cultural issues*'—and to strive to change it—'*transformations*'. At this point, his speech referred indistinctly to the corporate culture and to the country's culture, since it seemed difficult for him to dissociate them. As will be seen, in the discussion that followed the lecture, the author showed that he was trying to modify the former, without considering modifying the latter.

In concrete terms, the CEO presented four priorities aimed at changing the behaviours he had found when he arrived. The first two respectively encompassed the writing of the 'first company Code of Ethics' and the creation of a 'compliance and audit control unit'. The following two seemed more traditional, 'exemplary leadership' and 'over-communication'—that is, 'conferences, forums, brochures, posters, online training and seminars, rewards, *whatever you have, every time you can*'.

Read closely, the company Code of Ethics revealed formulations similar to those used several years before about the use of procedure manuals. The text emphasized the obligation to apply 'strictly', 'scrupulously', 'all' the procedures issued by the company: 'All employees are required to comply with all approved internal policies and procedures.' As stipulated in the Code introduction, this observance 'must prevail *over all other professional* considerations'. And to reassure those who would hesitate because of human nature and feelings, it also said: '*even well-intentioned actions* [but not in compliance with the Code], may have negative consequences for the Company and [for] the persons concerned'. For this reason, everyone is invited to respect them in 'letter and spirit'.

If we compare the Code of Ethics[10] with a fairly close French equivalent, the Cameroonian text appears more precise and imperative. For example, the ban on taking advantage of one's professional position for personal benefit—common in this type of text—specifies that it also encompasses the interests of 'family members' and 'friends'. Another illustration concerns the 'denunciation of breaches'—which in the Cameroonian version becomes 'denunciation of violations' (see Box 13.1). The two texts, which are very similar, are nevertheless different in style. While the French version tends to depersonalize and objectify, the Cameroonian one points to individuals and to their feelings and will: the French text mentions 'the identity of the employee', what 'the situation requires', and 'reporting'; the other refers to '*your* identity', 'not being *afraid*', 'good faith' and '*those who denounce*'. The French text states principles—identity is 'kept confidential', 'no entity is allowed'—while the Cameroonian wording includes concrete commitments—your identity will 'be held secret', '*we* do not *tolerate* any form of *retaliation*'. According to the CEO's own words, the challenge was to actually convince people that they could act without fear of 'retaliation'.

Several elements show how consistent the policies stated by the CEO and the content of the Code of Ethics are with the cultural interpretation context. This coherence seemed to account for the reputation that the company was enjoying at the time, among both its employees and its customers.

Box 13.1 Comparing Lafarge and ENEO Codes of Conduct

Code of Business Conduct Lafarge	Code of Ethics and Business Conduct ENEO Cameroon
When the situation so requires, the *identity of the employee* who *has reported a breach* will *be kept confidential.* No Group entity may take any sanction measures against an employee who has reported a breach of the rules of conduct in good faith.	You can report unethical behaviour in all confidence and *without fear of retaliation.* If your situation requires that your identity *be held secret,* your anonymity will be preserved. We do not tolerate any form of retaliation against employees who, in good faith, report wrongdoing.

However, the CEO underlined how difficult it was to reduce the contradictions between the national culture and the new behaviours that he was trying to obtain in the company. To understand the scope and sustainability of the changes, we will look at the persistence of some cultural traits and at the way in which they serve the new approach to management.

13.4 Epilogue: Permanencies and Changes

The elements successively collected between 1988 and 2016 (Iribarne, 1990; Henry, 1998; Godong, 2011; CEO J.N. Kontchou[11]) not only show real continuity over time but can also be cross-checked in other social contexts throughout the country.

This last section will provide an opportunity to review the elements of cultural persistency and then to show how these traits can be used to achieve change.

13.4.1 The Permanence of the Cultural Frame of References

The similar comments that the two CEOs made thirty years apart draw upon the same structuring image, the emotional force of which accounts for the persistence of culture.

During his presentation, the new CEO described in a few words some of the 'key cultural elements' he had found in the company when he arrived (emphasis added):

> The first one is a *kingdom* mentality. How do you make a company work and break down the barrier, when your managers are behaving like *village chiefs*, have their little *chefferie* [chiefdom], and they do *whatever they want* there. (. . .) We found a tower of paper work; very silo, departmental silo; a lot of management by committee, committee to build a feeder or committee to change a lightbulb; lack of time consciousness, that is very, very sad; multiple informal networks; decision-making based on a set of unwritten unspoken rules, so they have rules that people know but nobody talks about. People realise that information is power, so keep it for yourself, don't share it with people. In a lot of ethics problems, they say: '*la chèvre broute là où elle est attachée*' [the goat grazes where it is tethered]. Always have excuses for not meeting the commitment, always excuses; high risk of retaliation; tricky to manage stakeholders, especially government officials and the press. Time and energy-consuming relatives and friends, and there you have to say 'God save me from my friends, because I'm taking care of my enemies'.

Beyond a recall of the '*administrative and bureaucratic culture*'—piles of paperwork, silo functioning, indifference to deadlines, committees for changing a light bulb—the assessment presents no less than eight points of convergence with his predecessor's speech. It refers to directors who '*behave like village chiefs*' doing '*whatever they want*', echoing those who formerly did '*each their own little rule*' and, according to a manager, could thus 'do whatever they wanted'. He also mentions a management by committees, to enable directors to '*be covered at any cost, i.e. the management meeting or letting* [the CEO decide]'. The new CEO also mentions '*a high risk of retaliation*' reflecting the former fear that it '*might bring trouble down on their own head*'. He also talks about '*political authorities tricky to manage*', echoing the previous '*high-ranking acquaintance in the capital city*'. He speaks of '*unwritten unspoken rules*', which, as in the past, he explains by *a will not to share* information. Finally, both CEOs referred to the '*multiple informal networks*', and so cumbersome '*relatives and friends*'. And again and again, there is that mention of '*the goat which is grazing*'.

These convergences, several years apart, are like as many outcrops of a deep geological basement. The first research showed a set of features that referred, more or less directly, to the *feared perils of machinations invisibly orchestrated by a close relative showing only his or her good face* and, by contrast, to *the glowing image of help from sincere friends* (Iribarne, 2014). A few years later, Godong (2011: 98) highlights the distressing figure of 'the person—hidden in the shadows—who conspires in a "selfish" or "malevolent" intent, in order to enjoy alone' and, on the contrary, the salvation offered 'by "the friend", "brother", "knowledge", or "relationship" with whom he or she finds shelter, security, portection and the promotion of his or her interests'. The peril figure is metaphorically depicted by an interviewee as the evil spell operated by an invisible willingness that leads the country to be subjugated to its animal appetites (ibid.: 162–163):

> Look into the jungle, there are animals that can't be easily changed. This meant that one [i.e. the action of an invisible hand] has rendered the Cameroonian animal. So, it can no longer be changed easily: the one who is well placed to eat does not want to do anything to lose his grip. When things can be arranged, he's not happy. (Godong, 2011)

Ten years later, the CEO uses a similar metaphor to condemn the destructive appetites that operate under the polished appearance of the local culture. However, this time, quoting a management guru, he intends to argue the absence of fatality: 'A culture can be a *powerful animal* that counteracts and [makes an] attempt to change, no matter how good the strategy is. As management guru Peter Drucker said, "culture would *eat* your strategy for breakfast"'[12] (emphasis added). This 'master's' quotation—with an anthropophagous connotation—is all the more meaningful as it is apocryphal, obtained by distorting the authentic wording.[13] To promote his vision of change, the CEO relies on local representations of a destructive appetite that have to be combated.

This central and constantly repeated figure of greed is associated with a series of elements, each one with its own strength: the focus on individuals; the sensitivity to their feelings, and the appetites that motivate their behaviour; the fear that greed and nastiness may lie behind nice-looking words; the concern triggered by a series of unfortunate coincidences; the unbreakable obligation to help friends and family, etc. These various elements are constantly recomposed in new formulations, as in a recent popular expression reminding that 'someone is always someone behind someone' (Nne'e Onna, 2016). This expression, in its own way, elaborates on the elements of the framework of interpretation: individuals and what they are hiding; the inevitable mutual help between friends; the underpinning appetites and ambitions at work; and so forth. The power of these images and of the elements they encompass, which are mentioned over and over in social discourse, testify to the permanence of the cultural reference system.

However, we still need to see how this framework was used to change the culture of the company.

13.4.2 A Cultural Framework Instrumental in Achieving Changes

The CEO's comments and their consistency with the Code of Ethics do not allow us to conclude that it is effective or sustainable over time. Both their discourses are of course consistent with the common way of speaking. But most of all, as we will see, their logics are used to bring about the longed-for change.

In the debate following his presentation, the CEO made a clear distinction between the company's culture and the country's culture: 'The question is how do you change the culture in ENEO, when out of ENEO, nobody believes in that culture. The problem is even deeper. [...] You can change the people in the company, but when they step out of the company, they find something different.' To address this issue, the CEO set out three seemingly simple statements: 'training, communication, and sanctions'. In fact, the change he wanted to achieve in the company did not imply attempting to wipe out Cameroonian's culture but rather integrating its cultural rationale and using it for a renewed management.

The accusation of nastiness—directed against anyone who refuses to satisfy an undue request (see Chapter 5, p. 97)—can then be overturned against whoever tries to exert excessive pressure—would they seek to endanger the person whose assistance they are requesting? We already underlined that the procedures were presumed to be applied to all and followed to the letter, so that their enforcement could protect employees from pressures, feelings, or appetites. The CEO took advantage of the conference to publicly declare that he himself was under good surveillance: 'They [the audit unit] can audit me as well and control me.' In doing so, he publicly announces that he cannot escape from the rule. The credibility of the approach depends on the fact that procedures are regularly controlled. Under this condition, all members of the company can argue that they would endure sanctions if they succumbed to pressure or gave in to any undue interest. As an additional guarantee, the Code of Ethics also covered the need to protect anyone whose action could have negative consequences towards colleagues, or who was called upon to denounce their actions.

Precise and strictly applied procedures reassure those who, concerned about the judgement that will be given on their work, want to know what their superior expects from them. They aspire to express their 'good will' to respond to requests contained in the procedures. As the Code of Ethics recommends to make the procedures the primary criterion for judgement—'*even well-intentioned actions* [but taken outside the procedural limitations] may have negative consequences for people' (emphasis added)—it is also echoing the obligation to be benevolent to others.

From a more general perspective, the CEO's speech relies on the cultural repertoire to fight established bad habits, by explaining that the public service must not be abandoned to the appetites of those eager to take advantage of it. He communicates straightforwardly about the sanctions applied to employees who succumbed to the sirens of appetites and good feelings. Thus, he is returning the self-evident need to fight against destructive appetites in such a way that the company can benefit from it. Overall, the approach is based on the importance given, in this cultural context, to the value of relationships and accordingly to the obscure fear that one experiences against individualistic and antisocial actions (Balandier, Sauvy, 1961; Erny, 1987; Warnier, 1993; Marie et al, 2008; Geshiere, 2013).

In Cameroon, there is great cultural diversity between regions and social groups. This diversity is also visible within the Electricity company, not to mention other influences such as inherited colonial practices, or French bureaucratic model. At the same time, the Cameroonian mosaic is continually evolving under the combined effect of the renewal of generations, globalization influences, the economic context, or political motions. Yet no colonial or African determinism was to be seen here.

A twofold statement should be made. On the one hand, certain interpretative logics are singularly stable over a long duration and common to the various national components, imprinting their mark on multiple social traits. On the other hand, this framework of interpretation has received little attention from the reformers, even though it contains forces on which management can rely, at least to limit the abuses which it too permits.

13.5 Conclusion

All along this odyssey, the company experienced many transformations. It was subjected to two successive privatizations, a succession of eight CEOs, and several reorganizations. Technologies and the economic context changed. After all this time, even the members of staff were completely renewed. Many management methods, supposedly universal, were tested, with more or less rigidity and with relative success. However, we were able to establish the great consistency of a particular cultural universe. Despite the importance of what Cameroonians themselves call 'the country's realities', the management of cultural aspects rarely entered the agenda…it only did when the circumstances were favourable but no lessons were drawn from repeated experience.

The most recent achievement opens an interesting perspective for anyone who is not resigned to the idea that, because of culture, companies and administrations in Sub-Saharan Africa would be condemned to poor governance. Policies that address cultural concerns are more effective than those simply reproducing allegedly universal policies. However, while one might have expected actors to learn from the early progress made in the first phase of the drafting of procedures, the lessons of this experience were swept away by the vicissitudes of history. Awareness that progress can be achieved through an understanding of cultural aspects is not very common.

When this awareness prevails, it remains fragile and is easily overcome by the multiple assaults of universalist visions that are carried out by dominant actors.

The adoption of a particular management method often depends on the whims of the latest management fashion and of the particular interests of the day: the arrival of a consultant who advocates a particular solution; the disbelief of another who just 'can't believe' that a method could work here when it does not in his own country; the vulnerability of a CEO deprived of the political weight necessary to impose an audit system; the national economic situation that forces the government to comply with the World Bank's recommendations; the parachuting of an American citizen convinced that he must sweep the past aside; a redrafting of procedures reoriented to comply with US law; and of course, as Cameroonian wisdom says, 'the grabbing of those who have a strong interest in the status quo', and so on. The fact that the latest CEO tackles cultural issues is only a fortunate coincidence... twenty-five years after the first steps were taken in that direction.

As in many emerging countries, the World Bank has invested considerable energy and resources in 'demonstrating' that 'privatization' is the first of the explanatory variables of development. However, as this Cameroonian story shows, this postulate is too general to be relevant. Private management certainly has the advantage of prioritizing economic objectives over social or political considerations, but this does not mean that it will achieve them. The governance of newly privatized companies does not occur in weightlessness, but within a societal context that shapes practices.

Neither will the very understandable—and often mentioned—idea that it is up to the 'local' to adapt 'global' methods be easily verified. Adaptations are generally made by approximations more than by rational thinking. In practice, there is little chance that coherence will spontaneously emerge at the heart of governance. This is all the truer since it is still necessary to deal with the predominance of the universalist doxa and the multiplication of seminars for 'high-level managers', reproduced at great expense around the world in order to popularize 'good practices', with no concern for the way in which they are received in the field. One must also recognize that few methods are available to help actors shed light on the cultural features of a context so that they may take them into account in an operational way.

One of the final lessons of this Cameroonian odyssey concerns the still present vulnerability of its achievements. Progress has, of course, been made in the name of a strategy that puts 'culture' at the forefront. However, what will happen when the streams of history turn again and a change of direction leads to the adoption of another strategy? Will the lessons of the latest improvements be swept away again? The actors involved in the field—the local economic community, the administration, companies in the sub-region, the World Bank, etc.—do not necessarily perceive that there is much more here than simple strategy: there is a method that could be useful to other local companies in order to improve their managerial effectiveness.

Based on the interpretation of cultures presented throughout this book, it is possible to propose methods that take cultural dimensions into consideration with operational purposes. The following chapters open avenues to address these kinds of situations.

Notes

1. At this time, the company was called Société Nationale d'Électricité du Cameroun (SONEL). Subsequently, it changed its name twice: AES-SONEL from 2001, then ENEO after 2014. In the rest of this text, we will mention it under its name at the time under consideration.
2. The results of the first three investigations have been published (successively Iribarne, 1990; Henry, 2002; Godong, 2011). For the last period, we rely on a presentation by the CEO at a professional conference in the USA (Kontchou, https://www.youtube.com/watch?v=41hE3COlOaQ&t=2413s accessed 22 April 2019) and on the company's 'Code of Ethics and Business Conduct'.
3. The company was taken over in 2000 by the American energy group AES, which at the time wanted to expand to the African continent.
4. Actis is a financial institution created by splitting up the CDC (Commonwealth Development Corporation)—i.e. the main British aid funding agency.
5. Observed at the RNET (Régie Nationale des Eaux du Togo).
6. According to a common international procedure, everyone may know the names of their evaluators but not the individual appraisals made by each of them. The appraisee is only informed of his or her average scores. However, there is still the possibility for his or her evaluators—especially if the relationships are good—to make strictly favourable assessments both in the hope of improving the appraisee's satisfaction and in the fear of being suspected if he or she obtains poor scores.
7. See https://www.eneocameroon.cm/index.php/fr/actualite-nouvelles-deneo/actualite-eneo-eneo-inside/2790-1er-mai-2019-discours-de-joel-nana-kontchou (accessed 5 May 2019).
8. See https://www.jeuneafrique.com/mag/519521/economie/energie-le-camerounais-eneo-sur-courant-alternatif/ (accessed 5 May 2019).
9. The excerpts are from a lecture given in English by the CEO Joel Nana Kontchou at the 2016 Cameroon Professional Society Congress at Price University (Houston, Texas). We made the transcription. The context of the conference—a professional debate in an American university, but a mostly Cameroonian audience—allows us to consider that the content is closer to the author's thoughts than to an official kind of communication. The overlap we were able to make with the company's Code of Ethics tends to confirm his message, https://www.youtube.com/watch?v=41hE3COlOaQ&t=2413s (accessed 22 April 2019).
10. The ENEO Code of Ethics and Business Conduct (communicated to the authors by the company) comprises eleven chapters and is twenty-eight pages long. Lafarge Group's Code of Business Conduct, published a few years before, which was very similar, contained ten chapters and twelve pages. The two documents address, in often similar

or even identical formulations, the same issues: compliance with laws, respect for persons and the environment; information protection; financial transparency; conflicts of interests; prevention against corruption; disclosure of breaches, etc. Their comparison shows both similarities and significant differences. For this type of comparison, see d'Iribarne (2012b).

11. https://www.youtube.com/watch?v=41hE3COlOaQ&t=2413s.
12. This passage is not fully covered in the recorded conference, but it is mentioned in the written version of the speech which is available on the website https://issuu.com/cpsociety/docs/cps_2016_-_joel_nana_kontchou (accessed 22 April 2019).
13. The original quote would be 'culture beats strategy' https://www.quora.com/Did-Peter-Drucker-actually-say-culture-eats-strategy-for-breakfast-and-if-so-where-when (accessed 22 April 2019).

14
Transferring Management Practices

With globalization, companies are faced on a daily basis with the difficulty of transferring their management practices to culturally different countries.

Existing research clearly shows the diversity of situations of transfers (Harzing, 2014; Vo, 2008). They can concern the local subsidiary of an international group—whether or not in an industrialized country—an SME set up by a foreign entrepreneur, a private or public company wishing to apply a new management method with support from a consultant, etc. Situations also differ depending on the size of companies, the business strategies, the level of development of the host country, the respective industrial and administrative traditions, the institutional frameworks, the cultural differences between countries, the dominant positions of a partner over another, etc. A great deal of research concerning the influence that cultures have on management transfers has focused on human resources management (HRM), in particular on employment policies, skills and compensation management, training, or the role of social partners (Waxin & Barmeyer, 2008). However, there has been little research on the impact that cultures have on the functioning of organizations.

Cultural differences can be clearly seen in the different visions of the organization between expatriate managers and local staff. But they also come into play more indirectly *via* management procedures and 'tools'[1] which formalize the organization. Over the last decades, the proliferation of these 'tools'—which are also called 'management instruments'—has accompanied efforts to streamline and optimize companies. Research on this field shows, through different approaches, the two inseparable technical and social sides of these tools (Chiapello & Gilbert, 2013). When one focuses on the existence of their social side—the coordination and empowerment of people—it is also necessary to take into account the influence that cultures have on their content and implementation. The previous chapters give a number of examples of this. In a similar way, Bourguignon et al. (2002) compare the content and practice of American Balanced Scorecards and French Scorecards.[2] However, most current research focuses more on a universal reading, analysing the relations of interests and underlying powers, or the interpretation of tools but confined to the contingent aspects of the organization concerned (David et al., 2012). Little research focuses on the broad cultural roots of organization procedures and the corresponding management tools.

Cross-Cultural Management Revisited: A Qualitative Approach. Philippe d'Iribarne, Sylvie Chevrier, Alain Henry, Jean-Pierre Segal, and Geneviève Tréguer-Felten, Oxford University Press (2020).
DOI: 10.1093/oso/9780198857471.001.0001

In practice, many managers are aware of the potential cultural pitfalls in the transfer of management practices, but they are poorly equipped to prevent them. On the one hand, it seems to them that the methods and tools they must establish are inseparable from the rational and universal aspects that they are responsible for introducing, despite sometimes local incomprehension. On the other hand, they find that the cultural traits that need to be taken into account are constantly changing and quite difficult to characterize. In addition, the most prevalent psychosociological approaches—based on measurable indicators (see Chapter 3, p. 52)—do not make it possible to find indications that are sufficient to allow them to adapt practices to a specific cultural context.

Because companies do not have operational cultural approaches, the prevailing idea is that it is better to consider each case as being specific, act pragmatically, and adapt to the circumstances. Each company tries to adjust its methods in an empirical manner. These pragmatic concoctions—as we have seen in terms of delegation, monitoring, procedures manuals, ethical charters, etc.—produce extremely variable results. Some attempts end up in 'graft rejections', others in remarkable successes—we shall see an example of this in this chapter. Between these two extremes, the vast majority of companies navigate in intermediate channels, very partially applying the imported practices, which produces often poor results, as with the odyssey recounted in Chapter 13 (p. 257).

The objective of this chapter is to put forward methodical approaches that can improve the way in which management practices and their tools may be adapted to new cultural contexts, by relying on an at least partial decoding of the latter. Shedding light on both what works and what does not work using a cultural analysis calls for some caution with respect to widespread dissemination of 'good practices'. This especially points the way towards practical adaptations which have a rather broad scope within a cultural area. Rather than devising methods from outside, efforts should be made to identify examples of sound management in each culture and to understand them from the inside, in the light of their local logics. Each cultural context appears as a reservoir—explored little to date—of approaches that can be replicated locally within the same area.

The issue of adapting management practices to each culture is raised everywhere. It is a particularly crucial issue in emerging and developing countries, which do not have such longstanding experience in adapting practices.

In the first part, we will address the difficulties of a Japanese transplant in the USA, showing how cultural misunderstandings interfere with the application of technical aspects. In the second part, we will, in contrast, describe the success in Morocco of a quality approach which is especially vitalized by local cultural logics. To conclude, we will come back to the cultural aspects of the transfer of management methods and we will propose possible avenues for improving and speeding up the adaptation process.

The proposed approach opens up new promising prospects, particularly for companies in developing and emerging countries.

14.1 The Partial Achievement of a Japanese-American Transfer

As related by two American journalists (Fucini & Fucini, 1990),[3] the establishment of the Mazda automotive plant in the Detroit region in the USA (Flat Rock) provides a symbolic illustration of the difficulties occasioned by an ignorance of the cultural roots of a management method. The story has a particularly general scope as the partners are from industrialized countries and because both of them, at the beginning, are just as motivated by the prospect of a transfer of Japanese management methods.

However, the enthusiasm of American staff for the new management model announced by the Japanese management will not avoid the emergence of increasingly bitter conflicts between the management and staff. We will see how the transfer of Japanese practices comes up against cultural misunderstandings between partners. Everyone's good will and pragmatism are not sufficient to resolve the contradictions between two conceptions of the organization of work.

14.1.1 An Unexpected Turnaround

The project to set up a Japanese plant at Flat Rock aimed to establish methods that had made the reputation and success of Japanese companies in an American context.

At the beginning, the project benefited from near ideal conditions supposed to ensure its success, thereby giving it an exemplary value. The two partners came from highly industrialized countries, with what this implied in terms of skills. Given the industrial reputation of each country, there was little reason to suppose that there would be a sense of cultural domination or the implicit questioning of the partner's management capacities. The plant was located in a region renowned for automotive production with a wealth of experienced staff. The project was based on a common will to adopt Japanese methods, which at the time had gained an international reputation. As the plant was new, the management would not have to tackle pre-existing bad habits. It was obvious that the Japanese management intended to transfer both industrial methods and its vision of a management based on a 'family' spirit. During the recruitment campaigns, it had taken the precaution of giving preference to candidates who showed a clear motivation for the model announced by the Japanese. It would not have been possible to imagine better conditions for a transfer of management methods.

At the beginning, the American staff showed a real enthusiasm for the new 'philosophy' of the proposed management, which was less hierarchical and more respectful of everyone's contributions, focusing on the integration of teams, transparency, and good communication between everyone. Indeed, in Flat Rock, the management introduced the practices commonly used in Japanese companies: elimination of the symbolic distances between managers and the managed, reduction in the number of categories of workers, flexible use of blue-collar workers, elimination of rigid American job descriptions and work rules, an organization promoting group work, use of peer pressure, in particular to reduce absenteeism, consensus-based decisions—that is, imposing listening to everyone, while leaving the decision to the superior. The company applied a set of methods inspired by JIT (Just in Time) and *Kaisen* (continuous improvement of quality).

The application of procedures carefully developed in Japan and established under the management of the Japanese led to clear productivity gains—compared to the averages obtained by American companies. Great efficiency was achieved by strictly respecting operating methods—which could not be departed from as long as they had not been officially revised—and rigorously hunting down wasted time. The Mazda plant thereby provided a good illustration of the gains in productivity and reliability obtained as a result of Japanese organizational innovations—thus leading certain authors to celebrate the advent of a new universal model (Roos et al., 1990; Shimada & MacDuffie, 1986).

However, after a promising start, relations became strained between the management and staff. Recurrent conflicts arose, which eventually led to hard clashes, moving away from the usual procedures for conflicts between the management and trade unions in the USA. The first trade union which had been established at the start-up of the plant had played the game of cooperation with the management—adopting a surprising line compared to American trade unionism, rather close to what could be encountered in Japan—going as far as lobbying against absenteeism. It was subsequently rejected by the staff, which elected a new representation with a mandate to take a less conciliatory line with the company's management.

The group's management, for its part, decided to replace part of the management and, in particular, to appoint Japanese people to replace the two American vice presidents for manufacturing and personnel.

Such a turnaround prompted a questioning over the nature of the conflicts, which in particular concerned more flexible work rules the management had, however, made them the focus of its innovative approach.

14.1.2 A Clash Between Two Political Cultures

When we look closely at the conflicts which opposed the staff and the management, a point keeps cropping up regularly about the boundary between what is 'mandatory' and what is 'voluntary'. While for the Americans, the boundary was both very clear and evident, it seemed much vaguer for the Japanese, who appeared to see in it an indication of showing everyone's attachment to the company.

Two examples clearly illustrate this: it was mandatory to wear the company's uniform—which the managers also wore—but wearing the cap which was, however, provided free of charge, was voluntary. It was mandatory to work some overtime, clearly defined in the agreement between the management and the trade union, but voluntary to do overtime requested without notice by the team leader. For the Americans, things were clear, they had to do what was mandatory, but no form of obligation, even moral, could influence what was 'voluntary'. Many of them considered they were free not to wear the cap; many of them refused to do the overtime requested without notice, arguing, rightfully so from an American perspective, their freedom, as well as personal obligations, family obligations, for example. In their view, asking them for more constituted abusive pressure from a management which was overstepping its rights. The Japanese management was extremely disappointed by this attitude. It recognized the 'voluntary' nature of these special requests. But it felt that doing what was mandatory was a matter of course and if employees were concerned about showing their commitment to the company, they would specifically seek to do what goes beyond this.

The disagreement touches on a critical aspect of each of the political cultures. For the Americans, the boundary is central between what, on the one hand, is mandatory and on which you can be held to account and, on the other hand, what you can do voluntarily without anyone being able to hold you to account. By arguing 'what employees should want to do', the management was intruding on everyone's freedom. It was committing an 'abuse of power'. This way of acting offended the conception of fundamental freedoms related to the ideals of democracy. On the management side, this diffuse boundary indicated rather a minimum based on which everyone should make efforts to demonstrate their willingness to belong to the group, from which the duties and rights of its members stemmed. By refusing to commit to this, the American employees showed that it really did not mean a lot to them to be part of the 'family community' which the company was seeking to build. They were behaving like kinds of mercenaries.

We see the emergence of two conceptions of belonging to the organization, with some considering that they work 'for' the company on the basis of clearly defined commitments and others considering that they fully 'belong to it'. From the Japanese perspective, loyalty towards the company must take precedence over compliance with rules and, beyond this, over the separation between work life and personal life.

The American difficulty of entering into this political culture was shown by a number of other examples in the life of the organization.

The American employees considered that the pressure put on them to improve productivity posed risks for their safety, which was one of the rights they were particularly attached to. The American team leaders, for their part, were frustrated by the fact that they could not make any decision alone and that they therefore did not have the authority that an American supervisor usually has. At the same time, bearing in mind that decisions had sometimes already been taken by the higher levels, they saw the consultation system for people as pure hypocrisy—while for the Japanese, it was a principle of courtesy.

The difficulties of mutual adaptation had negative consequences. The American managers, who were under strong pressure to achieve high outputs, deprived of their usual points of reference—in this case the work rules which govern the limits of the hierarchical power—adopted practices which their team members deemed unfair: arbitrary decisions, favouritism towards more complacent subordinates, or also 'witch hunts'. The Japanese, for their part, had little consideration for partners who, in their view, did not show real loyalty towards the company. Little account was taken of the Americans' opinions compared to those of their Japanese colleagues.

At the end of the day, the 'Japanization' of the organization remained partial both due to institutional constraints—the Japanese could not reproduce in the USA certain employment conditions that were applicable in Japan—and cultural misunderstandings. The productivity gains—achieved in a poor climate of trust and without the American staff's support for the management principles—remained below expectations. The Japanese management, feeling betrayed over its expectations, implicitly abandoned its good practices and the idea of making their American employees fully-fledged members of the company.

A few years later, the project ended as a failure: the American minority partner purchased the shares of the Japanese, who eventually left the Flat Rock site.[4]

14.1.3 Lessons Learned From a Japanese-American Collision

The clash between these differing conceptions of rules and the meaning of the term 'voluntary' is not specific to the case studied. This case is quite representative of the situation of Japanese transplants in the USA.

In a jointly owned subsidiary of Suzuki and General Motors, the president of the trade union complained in similar terms about a risk of abuse by the management (Pinto, 1992): 'Unless you have dotted all the i's in black and white, everything is open to interpretation and management abuse. It just leaves the field free for them to do what the hell they like.' The individual stresses the obvious need for him for clear rules—*dotted i's in black and white*—to oppose a tyrannical power—*do what the hell they like*. On the Japanese side, the position of the Flat Rock management echoes the remarks quoted by Ouchi (1981) of a Japanese chairman of a bank (see Chapter 1, p. 28), explaining that if his employees 'understood [its] philosophy of banking' and the nature of the 'relationships' it wants to forge with the various 'communities', they could 'figure out for themselves' what they must do.

In Flat Rock, the transfer did not allow the methods to achieve their full potential. While the initial conditions seemed particularly ideal, despite the staff's support for the company's values of transparency and equality, despite the rigour of the technical tools and in-house training, the project failed over a cultural misunderstanding, the scale and consequences of which had not been anticipated. The staff found it difficult to appropriate imported practices, at least to reinterpret them from inside their own cultural context. Beyond this Japanese-American encounter, the misunderstanding between two cultural universes, the difficulty in applying tools from elsewhere, and the lesser confidence given to local managers are far from being a unique case.

While we sometimes believe that these difficulties are related to transfers towards emerging or developing countries, they also appear in cooperation actions between industrialized countries. In any case, companies, without necessarily having to face failure, content themselves with a lower productivity and reliability than expected. There is, however, nothing inevitable in this. This is what is shown by the success of a quality approach established by an international group in its subsidiary in an emerging country, Morocco.

14.2 The Moral Reading of a Quality Approach in Morocco

At the time when we contacted the SGS-Thomson plant in Casablanca (now STMicroelectronics), it was experiencing a real cultural revolution. The implementation of a TQM (Total Quality Management) approach brought about a deep transformation in internal relations and a dramatic improvement in its performance (d'Iribarne, 2007a, 2007b).

As with the previous case, the method had been imported by foreign managers—in this case the CEO was French. The cultural issue had not been anticipated either. However, due to a set of conditions which we will discover, the quality approach found a deep consistency with the cultural frame of references and led to good results.

14.2.1 An Application Seemingly Consistent with the Principles

Within a few years, the plant rose to become one of the group's top four units in the world, which led to the decision to double the size of the plant.

The approach, which had been disseminated throughout the group, aimed to organize each unit on the basis of an objective of waste reduction and total quality (hence the term TQM). It comprised several aspects of management, including the strategy, organization, methods, and human dimension. It was conventionally based on a set of tools, including technical procedures ('specifications'), results measurement methods, and self-checking. The group's TQM Handbook stressed that the effectiveness of tools was not independent of human aspects. It consequently called for a change in behaviour. The staff were invited to see 'the analysis of errors as a learning process'. In an even less self-evident register, subordinates were supposed to be able to 'challenge their superior with success (and without risk)'. In the introduction, the CEO called for the 'creation of a TQM culture' which should be based on 'transparency', 'the acceptance of criticism' and 'the ability to call oneself into question'. The company had implemented an extensive training programme to support the approach. It had also introduced incentive rewards and disseminated a sort of TQM myth, celebrating the 'TQM company'.

When we interviewed the staff, they were all unanimous in attributing the changes experienced by the company to the application of the new approach. We will measure the progress achieved through a comparison between the enthusiasm shown and the still recent past, which many described as being full of mistrust. Several observers referred to this past in terms of 'police' management. The slightest criticism was perceived as being a personal accusation, full of undertones and manipulations: 'Everyone passed the buck, like at the police station.' The basic operators reacted with 'mistrust', 'fear', or 'timidity'.

All the difficulties did not disappear as if by magic: 'The ground is starting to be fertile', cautiously observed a head of department, mentioning certain departments which were experiencing difficulty in complying with the procedures. Operators also voiced criticism about superiors who 'are still slightly authoritarian'. However, there were visible changes at all levels. A supervisor expressed his enthusiasm with regard to the new behaviour observed: 'It's wonderful. This behaviour is needed not only in SGS Thomson, we need it everywhere, it's a life.' An executive explained: 'People will pass on this culture in their families, among their brothers, their friends.' The basic operators showed a new sense of responsibility, concerned about aspects that went beyond the quality requested of them. 'Before,' recounts an executive, 'only the management was concerned. [Today] when you are late, there are women who organise themselves to do overtime. When the woman takes up [her station], she asks how late we are.'

Here, we clearly see the dual aspect indicated by the TQM Handbook, concerning both the application of technical procedures and the behavioural change. Some talk about 'TQM behaviour' and 'TQM person', with what that implies in terms of honesty, responsiveness, transparency, etc. A head of department even speaks about a 'moral code of conduct', which therefore serves to draw a distinction between good ('what is TQM') and bad ('what is not TQM'): 'You say to an operator: "Do this or that", she replies: "It's not TQM". [. . .] Someone can come to see me to violate a rule, I reply to them that "It's not TQM" and it's accepted.' At the same time, the people concerned express a great interest in TQM tools: the methods to analyse processes, the 5S rule,[5] self-checking, the suggestions procedure, the reporting of errors, the results indicators. They see a twofold interest in this, considering that their technical requirements also have a moral connotation which is intrinsic to them.

A superficial reading could conclude that the range of 'good practices' has simply been applied. But judging by the company's past, these aspects appear to be far from being sufficient. There is nothing self-evident about the transformation made. In fact, the former way of operating corresponds to a reality that largely prevails in companies in Morocco. A supervisor explains:

> In other [companies], you do not even have the right to demand certain things. Even in others which are slightly advanced and where you have the right to say things, you say them, but *you are spotted*, you are in the bad books. (...) A worker like that, when you see the boss who passes from time to time, she *starts to tremble* (...). And then, when the boss arrives, *everyone must applaud.*

An attempt at a quality approach had moreover already been made and it had failed, as a head of department explains: 'Nothing was done, the engineer was not prepared to listen to the operator.'

We therefore need to seek to understand how such a transformation could take place, especially as it did not involve creating a sort of bubble outside Moroccan culture. Certain signs of individualism, which are usual in social life, persist without them being subject to disapproval—concerning, for example, the diversity of clothing or the stated preference for individual rather than collective bonuses.

14.2.2 The Unforeseen Resources of a Culture

One of the radically new aspects concerns the moral interpretation of the TQM, which allows everyone—and not only those who are in a position of authority—to put pressure on those who deviate from the straight and narrow, on the basis of a rule perceived as objective. Unlike the previous period, criticisms are no longer systematically perceived as a personal accusation or a manipulation. At the same time, everyone feels responsible for examining themselves and, if necessary, for correcting themselves, as this operator explains: 'Each person, each specialised worker must control themselves, she *must control her work alone.*'

In reality, the values applied in the context of the approach were not interpreted as new values—as we often tend to suppose each time we speak about changing the corporate culture. On the contrary, many people stressed that they were precisely the traditional values of Islam and of Moroccan culture. The company's 'TQM' champion made an explicit link—taken up by others—with the values of Islam: 'The culture I saw in the *Kaisen* book,' he explained, 'we have that *in our culture as Muslims*; work in transparency, in cleanliness, help others to succeed; to succeed, you must believe in the thing, it's in the Koran.' This interpretation tends to assimilate TQM to a moral and religious rule of life, giving meaning to one's way of acting.

However, one can wonder why such a moral vision, associated with the values of Islam, is not applied more often in Moroccan companies—and even in the company's past. According to Geertz (1968: 112–113), Moroccan society is based on the juxtaposition of two registers, one concerning a secular world devoted to fiercely defending one's interests, the other marked by a strong attachment to a moral and religious ideal. He writes:

> In Morocco, the bulk of ordinary life is secular enough to suit the most dedicated rationalist, and religious considerations, for all their intensity, are operative over only a few, fairly well demarcated regions of behaviour, so that one gets a ruthlessness in, for example, commercial and political affairs which, at its most egregious, reminds one of the piquant combination of professional brutality and personal pity one finds in some American racketeers. (Geertz, 1968)

In social life, the two registers exist side by side without really merging: while the first dominates secularized life, the second is confined to fewer moral areas. According to the first register, which is largely present in companies, individual actions are interpreted *via* a multitude of interests, games of power and influence, manipulations, also calling on 'police' controls.

In this case, the TQM approach brought about several connections with a world devoted to a moral and religious rectitude. In this field, three aspects particularly left their mark: the operational precision of TQM procedures, the rigorous conduct of the CEO, and the both moral and technical content of training.

The considerable precision of the specifications is regularly commented on. '[They] make it possible,' explains an executive, 'to say "what TQM is". Otherwise we could use the argument one way or the other.' Their formal respect—'to the letter'—matches the image of ritual obligations which the 'good Muslim' abides by. 'We can all the same find operators who apply the work to the letter', a supervisor is pleased to say. In this religious conception, the formal and moralizing interpretation of requirements is seen as being fully respectable—whereas in other cultures, it would give rise to mixed reactions (see Chapter 5, pp. 105–106). This reading interprets criticisms in a register of objectivity. These criticisms escape the profane world of manipulations: 'We are well within our rights', explains an executive. 'It's not *a person-to-person relationship* between [the operator] and me, *we are introducing a system.*'

A number of comments also highlight the rigour of the CEO, in particular the 'transparency' and 'seriousness' with which he complies with the rules. 'The queue in the restaurant,' says an operator, 'even A. [the CEO] queues up, even A. He clocks in. He sets an example.' While being an exemplary manager is a leitmotif of management, it does not refer to the same qualities everywhere. In this case, rather than mentioning the qualities of strategic vision, responsiveness, experience, or personal charisma, the Moroccan staff highlight the simplicity and rectitude with which the director complies with common rules. His attitude seems all the more symbolic as one might have believed he was exempt from them: 'queuing up' in the restaurant, 'clocking in', 'doing the 5S' (i.e. tidying up his workstation), etc. His attitude contrasts with the usual practice of companies in Morocco. Without the usual signs of inequality and respect for hierarchy being removed, the person in question gives the signal of his singular equality with regard to the TQM rules. He demonstrates the equality of all—from the director to the operator—with regard to these rules, giving them the sense of a moral and religious rule of life. It becomes possible to criticize anyone, whatever their position: 'When you come to SGS-Thomson,' says a supervisor, 'and you have the right to say to, I don't know who, to the CEO, for example, Mr Georges A. [the name of the CEO]: "You need to leave [the queue] because you don't have the change", well, it's, *there's no comparison.* (...) These are things which don't exist in the other [companies].' Serving as an example must inspire the entire management: '[Anyone who does not set] the example of an irreproachable TQM conduct,' explains a head of department, '*alters the image of a TQM person.*' Such a combination of rectitude and simplicity evokes—in Morocco's cultural background, prior to Islam and which Moroccan Islam slipped into (Geertz, 1968: 112–113)—the figure of the 'holy warrior'. From a religious perspective, he is an equal at the same time as a revered master. He embodies the figure of the leader, bearing a mystic enthusiasm and a moral rectitude at the service of a conquering dynamism.

Finally, the image of school is often used. 'There has been a radical change,' explains a supervisor, 'before, it was a military barracks, now it's a good school.' The TQM training sessions—combining educational behaviour and a practical intelligence of things—also generate real enthusiasm. 'It's a factory and school at the same time, it's a factory-school', says an operator. We find the image of a community led by a both spiritual and temporal authority, invested with a mission of prophetic preaching. The approach again echoes a Moroccan Islam tradition.

The conversion observed—bringing about a shift from fear of police accusations to accepted criticisms and to a personal rigour of self-checking—is not the result of a 'corporate culture' that would act as a *deus ex machina.* It draws its particular strength from Moroccan cultural traditions.

The cultural interpretation provides an important key to understanding the enigma of a behavioural change. The TQM does indeed draw on universal elements: use of effective technical tools; dissemination of values of transparency, equality, and responsibility; intensive training. However, the way in which the interested parties speak about it has nothing universal—speaking about it in terms of 'values of Islam', 'TQM person', 'moral code', rule 'for life'. Several tangible elements appear to be a necessary condition to echo local figures who give their meaning to the approach: the precise nature of the specifications; the modest rigour of the CEO; and the training seen as a moral and religious school of life.

Corporate culture is sometimes seen as something that should provide added soul, based on a celebration of strong values—devoted to innovation, customer service, concern for performance, etc.—even going against extreme rationalism and the rigidity of procedures. Yet in this company, the practical precision of TQM procedures is itself perceived as contributing to their moral interpretation. It fosters a closer connection with Islam, or at least with Moroccan Islam, which plays a decisive role in the effectiveness of the approach.

The 'TQM culture' does not replace Moroccan culture; on the contrary, it finds unforeseen resources in it. It gives it its coherence and its vitality, *via* a number of tangible aspects which echo it and give it its meaning.

14.3 Paving the Way for a Methodical Approach

In the two accounts of Flat Rock and Casablanca, the cultural roots of management practices and their tools play a decisive role. At the beginning, the question was not raised. However, these examples show, for the first case, a certain need to understand the cultural logics present and, for the second, the interest there can be in resonating with them. In both cases, the results—disappointments or successes—are unexpected. There are, however, methodical approaches to give the best chances of success.

We will start by showing the limits of the approaches that companies generally use to transfer management practices. Then we will propose an original approach consisting in identifying local cultural resources and learning to take advantage of them.

14.3.1 The Limits of Standard Practices for Transfers

What the two previous examples have in common is that they demonstrate the existence of a close link between the effectiveness of technical procedures and the cultural universe in which they are implemented. With no operational cultural approaches to grasp this link, international groups experience difficulties in understanding the realities in the field in order to adapt their management practices to them. The question is largely abandoned on the intuition of managers in the field, who are poorly equipped to resolve it.

The idea largely prevails that the influence of cultures in companies is fundamentally concerned by the 'human' aspects and that it does not really focus on the 'hard core' of management constituted by procedures and tools. Experience has shown us that when we propose to address the issue of national cultures, we are referred to the HR services—responsible for 'values' and 'beliefs'. However, management tools, whatever they may be, contribute to the operation of organizations—for the sharing of information, the coordination of actors and the collective management of processes, individual responsibility, the control of costs and risks, training, etc. The idea of their technical neutrality often has the force of myths (Riveline, 1995). However, the previous chapters have shown that the technical side of management instruments and their social, and therefore cultural, sides are inseparable. The tools and procedures which materialize them bear the imprint of the political culture which saw them come into being. They do not travel without the need to undergo adaptations.

The belief of the universality of management methods is even more important in transfers towards emerging or developing countries. The lack of local skills sometimes, the absence of industrial culture, the prejudice often shared by local partners of a superiority of Western methods, and the rational aspects which the management tools support, overshadow the idea of their cultural roots. There is a great temptation to proceed by duplication, which can lead to absurd situations, as recounted by this director of the subsidiary of a French group in Vietnam:

> [I noticed at the beginning] that they don't measure anything. I say to myself: We are going to implement KPI![6] (...) It was done in two months! But that doesn't mean that they understood. They measured but they didn't understand. People did not see the purpose. (...) The Group is really happy: 'Vietnam is under control!' (...) You just need to enter the figures for everyone to be happy. No one checks what is behind. (...) My failure lies in the fact that I didn't manage to get them to switch from execution to interpretation. [When you look at] a KPI, everything is at 100%. (...). It was nonsense! I said to them: 'It is better to put nothing rather than put things we haven't done.' (...) In fact, it was not integrated.

In practice, companies mainly proceed with empirical adjustments, consisting more in adapting to circumstances than to the cultural specificities identified (Kedia & Bhagat, 1988; Pakdil & Leonard, 2017). While multinational firms are concerned about 'capitalization' (knowledge management) at global level, they have difficulty focusing their attention on the 'cultural adaptations' of management (Gupta & Govindarajan, 2000; Kostova, 1999): managers in the field do not easily report information, fearing that local setbacks or arrangements may be misinterpreted at headquarters (Villette & Fourcade, 2017). They also have the legitimate concern of not too hastily attributing a given failure or even a given success to a cultural influence, as they have few analysis tools in this respect. Finally, it is equally difficult for the management of groups to communicate on local singularities, whereas they ensure that they highlight the success of synergies obtained in their subsidiaries.

At the level of headquarters, three types of response predominate, which, if they have any use, tend more to bypass the question of cultures rather than taking an interest in it.

An initial response consists in promoting strong corporate values. By repeating 'I am a Danoner', it is hoped that local attachments will end up disappearing behind the new values of the company. We have seen the limits of this approach (see Chapter 12, pp. 251–2), whose impact on national cultures, beyond the effect of mobilization, must be seriously relativized.[7]

A second response consists of the widespread dissemination of 'good practices' and the tools which go with them. Entire libraries are built—with the contribution of international organizations, consultants, and researchers—to collect and disseminate the lessons of Success Stories. These successes are explained based on the 'proper' application of tools—that is, compliant with the original specifications—and a contractual conception of relations between people.

Finally, training and communication are seen as the supreme remedies to develop values and practices. Training seminars are produced all over the world to convert managers from all countries to the adoption of 'good methods', without showing concern for the way in which the mechanisms are received and interpreted in the field. In New Caledonia (see Chapter 7, p. 126), managers came up with the idea of training local trade union members in French labour law, without even seeing that this response was way off the logics of action of those concerned.

While Success Stories have the interest of presenting the most widespread methods and tools, they also maintain the idea of a standardization of management models. It is firstly in the interest of business leaders to ensure that their company has a reputation of complying with international standards, such as MBO, KPI, ethics charters, etc. As for the Success Stories,[8] they look at the explanations from rather far away: the good results of companies 'are due to' the fact that they apply the 'good rules'—which does not appear to be questionable. The conditions that enable management to succeed in one company when it does not work elsewhere in the same area are not tackled. However, as will be seen further, a few companies have already asked us to help them understand 'what works' and for what reasons, so that these cases could be generalized.

Great efforts are made in management publications to describe the subtleties of each management tool, however without focusing on the practices relating to their cultural context. We find little insight in them on the way in which each universe of meaning imprints its own logics in these practices.

In the event of failure in applying the 'good' method, experts tend to state that there is a need to do more... of the same actions. In Cameroon, faced with the rejection of an attempted MBO (see Chapter 5, p. 99), a consultant report indicated that 'A malicious suspicion *must not be seen* [in the resistance encountered], but a concern which probably stems from a lack of exchanges'. Hence the author deduced that it was necessary to further strengthen the dialogue and... that managers must demonstrate an unwavering resolve. The best way to brush aside the local logic of the fear of 'malevolence' was to ignore it. It is particularly difficult for a foreign manager or consultant to read local situations without referring to their own framework of interpretation (see Chapter 6, p. 116). They will consequently react without having assessed the importance taken in the local universe of meaning of a particular measure that, according to them, is to have a positive impact.

Most research swings between two extreme purposes, adopting either a view mainly attentive to interests and power relations, but too distantly to discern the cultural facts that are more complex to interpret, or a very close view seeking to specify the peculiarities of a specific organization or the portrait of its manager. Very little research focuses its attention between these two angles, to understand the way in which management situations reveal the general characteristics of a cultural universe.

A more effective adaptation of management procedures and tools to their cultural context is one of the challenges of the globalization of companies.

14.3.2 An Ignored Source of Solutions

In the example of the Moroccan TQM, the effectiveness of the approach is, however, due to a set of elements which may seem disparate or even insignificant to someone outside the culture, yet, put together, they make sense: the precise and practical specifications, the rectitude of the manager in terms of the rules, the moral and practical content of the training. This coherence—echoing a figure of the Moroccan proper way of living together, but not common in companies—could not be projected from outside. It emerged here following a favourable combination of circumstances, bringing together an international method, the beneficial—but more intuitive than conscious—action of a foreign manager, and an appropriate practical adaptation by the local staff.

Management methods and tools are like local plants: their transplantation into another type of cultivation requires an acclimatization process (Lunnan et al, 2005). It may prove difficult and lead to rejections, as with the application of an MBO in Japan, Vietnam, and Cameroon (see Chapters 1 p. 26, 2 p. 41, and 5 p. 99). Many aspects may take on different or even opposite meanings, depending on cultures, as shown with the example of detailed operating manuals, in France—where application without any room for interpretation soon takes on a not so honourable meaning—and in Cameroon where strict respect is a sign of goodwill (see Chapters 5, p. 106). The universe of meaning in which a tool is introduced tends to mark its actual use with its own logics, which are more powerful than the principles initially attached to it.

It is possible to innovate by adapting without ignoring the international standards.

One of the ways which are already used consists in recruiting managers, trained in the two cultures present. But, their role as 'cultural interpreter', while being useful to highlight the meaning given to a situation, is no longer sufficient when the issue comes to adjusting organization and procedures.

When a tool is plunged into another cultural universe, the interpretation given to it is transformed. But its alignment can take time and we will see that it is not enough to wait and insist, as one might be tempted to think. The Moroccan example with its rapid adaptation is an exception here. A successful approach does, however, involve observing the practices within a culture, understanding their coherences, and learning operational lessons from them. Its aim is not to build theoretical models from the outside, but to accelerate the adaptation of tools to a new context.

The approach to cultures which we adopt in this publication opens up the possibility of outlining general characteristics within a cultural area, making it possible to account for varied social facts. It clarifies the meaning of situations, whether it involves recurrent resistance or, on the contrary, management procedures that achieve good results.

In practice, the adaptation approach consists in focusing on difficulties encountered by companies in the context of the transfer of a tool—based on limited practical questions—and, symmetrically, on examples of what, in this same context, appears to work. *The objective is to shed insight into existing practices, what works, and what does not work so well, the meaning given to the resistance or enthusiasm from within their context of interpretation.* It involves showing how—within the same universe of meaning and due to certain organizational arrangements—actors succeed in resolving common management difficulties which, in this context, often seem difficult to resolve. It appears that successes make sense according to the same logics as the situations that pose problems.

This type of analysis, taking the cultural interpretation framework into account, sometimes highlights the considerable effects of 'details'—known to all but deemed insignificant—in management practices. The solutions it involves highlighting are above all local—home-made—as shown by the Malagasy case (see Chapter 15, p. 293). The framework of interpretation which ensures the effectiveness of a local approach remains hardly perceptible from outside—unless it is submitted to a specific analysis.

For example, one often hears expatriates, who are placed in another cultural universe than theirs, say that they are surprised not to find a conception of duty there which, however, seems 'natural' to them. They may sometimes conclude that there is a 'lack of the sense of responsibility' (see Chapter 12, p. 239). In fact, the conception of responsibilities, specific to each culture, is not exercised there in either the way or circumstances which one expects from outside. Yet each conception of responsibilities corresponds to duties that can play an important role in the operation of organizations.

The understanding of certain aspects of a culture makes it possible to avoid an approach which, otherwise, is limited to a succession of fruitless trials and errors and innovations. The cultural interpretations that can be highlighted based on a specific tool or procedure are generally to be found, in a crosscutting manner, with great consistency, in other management situations and in other types of activities.

The issue is to provide insight into the specific logics of a local approach, to understand their conditions of replicability, and to accelerate their dissemination within a given cultural area. The story of the Electricity Company of Cameroon provides a dual illustration of this type of approach. The presentation of the study conducted in a Togolese company immediately gave rise to the drafting of detailed procedures manuals and their local ownership. Conversely, as the new American management failed to learn lessons from this first experience, it abandoned this mechanism (see Chapter 13, respectively p. 260 and p. 262). It took over fifteen years for the approach to be taken up again. Several examples cited in this publication—concerning Tunisia, Madagascar, and Morocco—should have a general scope within their cultural area. We could have cited others in Peru (Sauvage, 2018), New Caledonia (Segal, 2013), China (d'Iribarne, 2012b), or in Mexico and Argentina (d'Iribarne, 2007).

A reading of the cultural logics at work in management practices that appear to succeed provides a significant source for improving the management of companies. It highlights the resources offered by each culture and they are likely to inspire other approaches within the same cultural area.

14.4 Conclusion

The two examples of transfers that we have seen—purposefully chosen—both show the decisive nature of cultures in the dissemination of management practices. The first highlights a cultural divide, which stands in the way of the reproduction of an imported model. In contrast, the second shows the role played by Moroccan culture in the successful implementation of an imported approach, *via* a group of interpretations and tangible traits that are more significant than one could have imagined from outside.

Multinational companies still have considerable room for progress in terms of taking the diversity of cultural realities into account. One finds a great nebula of companies whose management practices have trouble rising to the level of performance that could legitimately be expected. Managers note the existence of a great diversity of cultural behaviours, which have an impact on the operation of organizations, without knowing how to limit their excesses or, on the contrary, take advantage of them. At the same time, this issue of transfers suffers from a lack of capitalization on the successes, apart from a literature that commends managers who apply known standards—without looking at what makes success possible.

We situate ourselves on the side of pragmatic observers, without a universalist or culturalist a priori. The adaptation 'from global to local' seldom takes place spontaneously, or otherwise it occurs through unpredictable coincidences. It is not a question of imposing a dominant vision—ignorant of local cultures—or of resorting to a sort of relativism, abandoning all hope of efficiency to an improbable future. Our approach aims to be empirical, based on both the observation of approaches that work and on a decoding of their cultural context. The most effective practices generally stem from an ad hoc assembly between principles of universal management and local ways of implementing them.

The proposed approach opens quite broad and relatively new prospects for the international subsidiaries of global groups. There is room for improvement by focusing efforts on capitalizing on experiences of implementing a given management method. Managers should probably be trained in how to report on these positive or negative situations encountered, not from a perspective of evaluation, but to give an empirical description of the positive or negative reactions observed. Finally, generally speaking, each company could undertake the inventory, in this same spirit of learning, of the more or less efficient functioning they observe. While the role of managers in these situations is undeniable, such situations do nevertheless reveal what makes sense or not in their context. A methodical taking into account of cultural aspects would significantly accelerate the adaptation of management methods to their context.

In the specific case of emerging and developing countries, there is significant room for improvement by seeking to gain a better understanding of the way in which management procedures and tools come up against difficulties or, on the contrary, take advantage of resources from their cultural context. In all contexts, one finds more effective approaches where others fail, which would deserve attention. Donors, in particular the World Bank—which has an important capitalization role—should put these inventories of successful companies or institutions on their agenda for the purpose of interpretative surveys.

A wide array of studies still needs to be conducted in order to identify the practices that work and throw light on the reasons, not on the grounds that they demonstrate the merits of universal rules, but *to highlight what is specific about these effective practices* and by comparison with what poses problems in the same cultural context (see Chapter 16, p. 306). *It is possible everywhere to better understand the general characteristics specific to a culture which, while allowing a multiplicity of behaviours, sheds light on the ways of acting and replicating efficient practices, in cultural areas that are sufficiently broad to have an operational impact.* Highlighting these characteristics, even limiting oneself in each case to a few practical aspects, can have an operational impact, at the level of an entire cultural area, sufficient to warrant giving them attention.

A realistic approach, based on an understanding of cultures and the resources they hold opens up new prospects for management. The examples cited in this publication show that effective corporate cultures can rely on local cultural logics which have a more constant force. An understanding of these cultural continuities may highlight approaches which can be effectively replicated in the whole area.

Notes

1. The term 'tools' and also 'instruments' refers to all sorts of formalisms—tables, indicators, operational guides, evaluation methods, electronic agendas, databases, etc.—which are omnipresent in organizations, to the extent that we do not always pay attention to them anymore.
2. Beyond more or less common principles—conduct a regular monitoring of individual and collective performances—a number of aspects differ. On the American side, the purpose fits in with the contractual commitment accepted by the CEO and set out among managers; the formalism comprises a common table for the entire company, set out hierarchically; the statistical data have an almost legal value, including an evaluation stage whose methods are closely monitored. On the French side, the purpose responds to an objective of having a strategic vision, in which each department must devise the way in which it contributes to it; one finds a proliferation of tables, which are more or less consistent with each other, allowing everyone to put forward their contribution; the statistical data have an indicative value, it may seem pusillanimous to control the results achieved too closely. There are such great differences given to the meaning of tools that various attempts to unify the two tools have not succeeded.
3. The publication is the result of a specific investigation, like American-style investigative journalism. It is based on a factual investigation which followed the start-up of the Mazda plant in Flat Rock for three years. It provides a very vibrant and precise view of the encounter between Japanese and American people in this plant. The construction of the Mazda plant started in 1985 and the first cars were assembled starting in 1987.
4. In 1992, Ford, which had until then been a minor partner, increased its shares by 50% in a new joint venture which took the name of AutoAlliance International. In 2012, Ford bought the entire plant to take over its management.
5. The 5S method was created in Japan in Toyota factories. It optimizes working conditions and working time by ensuring the organization, hygiene, and safety of a work plan.
6. Key Performance Indicator (KPI).
7. See, for example, the website of Danone Group where the reference to a citizen identity of 'Danoner' is supposed to transcend national distinctiveness. However, the corresponding comments are inserted into hundreds of pages which place great emphasis on the diversity of local projects and cultures. See https://www.danone.com/stories/articles-list/eureka-how-danoners-light-bulb-moments-drive-our-vision.html (accessed 11 May 2019).
8. See, by way of illustration, the website of Princeton University, Innovations for Successful Societies, which is entirely dedicated to the production and dissemination of such success stories. https://successfulsocieties.princeton.edu/. The World Bank is alone an enormous publisher of accounts of international good practices.

15
Efficient Multicultural Teams

The examples of the Franco-Swedish alliance and the Franco-Malagasy NGO detailed in Chapter 12 showed the nature of the difficulties that work poses in an intercultural context. When a bi-national team wants to design a new product and its members do not share the same conception of what making a decision means, reaching an agreement can become a challenge. First, team members may support different views on the subject, as may also be the case in a culturally homogeneous team. Second, they may find it difficult to come to an agreement without one or the other being destabilized and frustrated by a chaotic decision-making process that borrows from diverging logics. Similarly, in an organization where expatriates wish to empower local staff, the transfer of responsibilities is slow to occur, if at all, because the protagonists do not share the same view of effective empowerment and, more generally, of social relations at work.

This chapter proposes an approach to improve intercultural team efficiency. It is based on a detailed understanding of cultures and specifies the conditions for its implementation. The point is not to claim a universal recipe of intercultural management but to show how understanding cultures as a universe of meaning can improve team efficiency and members' experience. In the first part, we introduce an approach meant to support intercultural teams that is conducive to building legitimate and effective ways of working for all members. In the second part, we examine the possibilities for generalizing the approach and propose alternative means when such coaching is not possible.

15.1 An Approach Focused on the Deciphering of Universes of Meaning

In this first part, we describe the support provided to the Franco-Malagasy team of the NGO that wished to develop employee empowerment (see p. 239) and we summarize the coaching process steps.

15.1.1 Close-up Support Based on Mutual Understanding

Our intervention research has enabled us to experiment with a coaching approach that aims to define and implement more effective cooperation practices insofar as

Cross-Cultural Management Revisited: A Qualitative Approach. Philippe d'Iribarne, Sylvie Chevrier, Alain Henry, Jean-Pierre Segal, and Geneviève Tréguer-Felten, Oxford University Press (2020).
DOI: 10.1093/oso/9780198857471.001.0001

they are co-constructed on the basis of a better mutual understanding of what all of the members value (Chevrier, 2012b). The case we describe was introduced in Chapter 12, p. 239, and the aim is now to detail how both expatriates and local staff were supported in the empowerment process.

We had been approached initially by some of the leaders of that NGO—headquartered in Paris—which operates in the field of development, and which has an office in Madagascar. From the point of view of the French managers at headquarters and of the expatriate leader of the NGO in Madagascar, a recurrent problem for the management of the Malagasy local office was to achieve the empowerment of local staff who appeared fearful and reluctant to assume their responsibilities.

After this problem had been defined, we conducted a series of interviews with the entire team. In these interviews, the point was not to ask people about their perceptions of the other cultural group, even though they were sometimes spontaneously mentioned. The purpose was to capture how they understood the relationship to work in general, to hierarchical relationships and to responsibilities in particular. Some forty interviews were conducted in two weeks with French (eight) and Malagasy (about thirty) staff.

The analysis of the interviews (see method in Chapter 16) allowed us to identify that the exercise of responsibility was connected to several issues: the formalization of individual attributions and procedures, training, decision-making, and collective work. However, in these four domains, the universes of meaning of the two cultural groups were largely different. For more details on the differences, we refer the reader to Chapter 12, p. 239. Only the major oppositions already highlighted around formalization are mentioned here. On the French side, the formalization of jobs is certainly a useful reference, so as to clarify roles and assess work, but overly precise definitions are not sought because they stifle the organization. Everyone strives for a high degree of autonomy within a roughly defined area of responsibility. Understanding their professional role allows everyone to adapt to circumstances and fulfil their responsibilities. On the Malagasy side, the quest for social harmony requires that everyone does only what they have been explicitly appointed to do and individual initiatives are regarded as likely to cause serious collective disorders. Consequently, the detailed formalization of roles is considered as a safeguard against disorder by strictly delimiting each person's domain.

After an initial comparative analysis of the universes of meaning regarding hierarchical relationships and the exercise of responsibilities, we shared these results with the protagonists. The feedback on both universes of meaning took place during a plenary session with all the Madagascar office staff present so that everyone could ask questions or discuss the different results.

Time was given to staff to 'digest' this feedback. Employees are often not totally aware of their own references; therefore explanation sessions allow having access to the relativity of these conceptions. This exchange was an opportunity to validate our analysis and possibly enrich it; the analysis of a cultural universe of meaning is never complete, so sharing can be an opportunity to refine or adjust it depending on whether the actors recognize themselves in it or question it. This initial deciphering enabled the actors to better understand the behaviours observed and, above all, to show how what seemed incomprehensible or contradictory made sense in the other cultural universe. This step was intended to defuse some negative stereotypes by giving meaning to observations that no longer amounted to transgressions against one's own implicit references (cowardice, lack of courage or vice versa, lack of seriousness, and approximate organizing). Should we use the metaphor of games, this step would consist in clarifying the rules of the different games played, making it possible to understand the players' intentions and strategies rather than disqualifying these moves from the outset because they seem unsuitable. At that stage, some protagonists may have already taken advantage of this new understanding to change their ways of doing things, but any adjustments remained individual and unilateral.

A few months after the field survey and the first feedback session, we returned to Madagascar with the NGO's head of human resources. The next step was to draw on this new understanding to discuss ways of organizing work and assignments that would be acceptable to all. The aim was for everyone to specify what they really cared about and why, and to define empowerment practices that would respect what mattered most to each party. We organized and led three working groups, each on a specific theme—formalization, skills-building, decision-making processes—bringing together French and Malagasy representatives. Discussions in each group resulted in proposals to improve collective functioning and in particular to achieve greater empowerment of local staff. For example, French managers committed themselves to formalizing job descriptions more systematically, updating the organization chart, and giving more details about the tasks. However, this was a compromise because the desire to maintain flexibility led French officials not to commit themselves to an exhaustive formalization but to propose an update of the tasks during the annual evaluation interviews so as not to 'disconnect' from the actual situation. In addition, they stressed that formalization is 'a reference point but not a barrier'. In other words, they advocated informal discussions to address tasks that had not been anticipated and were not included in any job description, although they were essential for the smooth running of projects. Many other recommendations, which we will not develop here, were made in the three groups.

Once management practices were negotiated, they were tested by the protagonists. Given the geographical distance from the French headquarters, the monitoring of the implementation was carried out by the actors themselves without the help of an external mediator. However, discussions with the Malagasy branch manager, six months after the group work, revealed that real progress had been made in terms of formalization, while other projects, such as training, remained to be implemented. The new formalization practices had actually helped to promote employees' empowerment.

15.1.2 Overview of the Coaching Process

The approach we have just described suggests a way to improve the functioning of intercultural teams by focusing on a better understanding of the members' cultural universes of meaning.

In a nutshell, the process includes the following steps:

1. Identifying problems.
2. Deciphering the cultural universes of meaning that frame their interpretation.
3. Giving feedback to the actors.
4. Setting up and leading mixed working groups to identify ways of working.
5. Experimenting them.
6. Adjusting the ways of working.

The first step, which consists in identifying the problems, is carried out by the organization members themselves; these problems are formulated in terms of management. They can be broad, such as the team's difficulties to achieve its objectives, or much more specific, such as the difficulty in empowering employees. The way the problem is defined will determine the main themes of the interviews, which are always linked to the forms of social relations prevailing in the organizational contexts. Interviews constitute good material for deciphering the cultural universes of meaning. The method will be thoroughly discussed in Chapter 16, but the emphasis can already be put on letting people express themselves in their own terms so as not to impose the interviewer's categories. Ideally, the interview is conducted in the team members' own language, but in practice, it can be done differently when language skills are lacking.

The filter of a lingua franca is misleading, but it nevertheless reveals the speaker's universe of meaning (see Chapters 10 and 11) and can be fruitfully used in field surveys. Content analysis of interviews aims to identify the key references used in the justification of acts or opinions. While lexical analysis and the recurrence of certain words can give good insights, the terms underlying the same references can be very diverse. As detailed in Chapter 16, the analysis focuses on the units of meaning and not on single words. For example, in the aforementioned Franco-Malagasy case, the expression 'mastering your area' (*maîtriser son domaine*) was often used to emphasize the importance of having a clear scope of responsibility, but many other wordings conveyed a desire for formalization: 'I would like to have a job description [that specifies] that you should do this,

this, and that'; 'we must clearly define the frameworks for each person's actions', etc. This analytical work is lengthy but all the more effective when the analyst has experience in many cultural universes and thus identifies more easily, by explicit or implicit comparison, the salient features of a new universe. It is this essential deciphering step that most often justifies the intervention of a cultural analyst in the team. Highly constrained by operational requirements, team members rarely have the opportunity to engage in an in-depth exercise of reflective analysis of their practices.

Using an external expert could also be justified to give feedback to stakeholders while maintaining neutrality to facilitate the process of co-construction of solutions. However, it may happen that cultural deciphering is carried out on the initiative of only one of the parties involved. Consequently, the feedback may not be general but only for the sponsor of the research who decides whether or not to implement the results delivered. Obviously, a collaborative intervention involving all parties and led by an analyst up to the end of the process is more likely to have an impact. In particular, the expert's skills and external position are invaluable when leading working groups to help build solutions that are acceptable to all.

In practice, solutions negotiated in groups can take different forms: a compromise between two practices, the choice of one practice with significant or marginal adjustments to satisfy the other party, or the creation of new practices. The participants engage in discussion to define their working processes, taking account of the specificities of the cultures involved, of which they are now aware. Having a fairly clear vision of the partners' fundamental expectations allows them to open up the door for possible operating modes while being aware of what is not negotiable.

Testing new management processes can be unexpectedly challenging and require adjustments or improvements, so follow-up meetings are useful to monitor the implementation of new practices and agree on adjustments. The objective is for successful practices to be institutionalized so that they persist even if the people who initiated them leave. This makes it possible to go beyond mutual adjustments and to embed intercultural practices in the organization.

This approach may seem cumbersome, but in the context of a permanent team that is essentially bi- or tri-cultural, the long-term benefits are worth the investment. As with learning a new language, sustained effort is required but not always undertaken by expatriates appointed for short periods of time. Nevertheless, this can be very productive, resulting in improved mutual understanding for people who work in another country for a longer period. Like language learning, cultural learning contributes to better cooperation. It helps to resolve recurring conflicts and misunderstandings and to prevent the good intentions of the people involved in cooperation from being misinterpreted, as illustrated in Chapter 12.

Without external intervention, mistrust develops because actors misunderstand the meaning of their partners' actions. The relationship deteriorates and it becomes very difficult to reverse this downward spiral. Conversely, the learning of a culture, like that of a language, can reach different degrees of mastery, making it possible to gradually enter into the 'folds of its thought' (Jullien, 1997). This in turn enables the understanding of another logic beyond a simple glossary which would be limited to establishing more or less approximate word-to-word correspondences. Let us add that, even though it is demanding, learning a new cultural universe is all the easier when one already knows several of them. Similarities and singularities appear more easily. An essential difference between languages and cultures, however, is that a foreign language is immediately perceived as different, while the strangeness of other cultures is not always immediately discernible. There are kinds of cultural 'deceptive cognates'—that is, identical behaviours that hide different interpretations that go unnoticed at first sight—which also explains why efforts to learn a culture are made less often than to learn a language.

15.2 How Can Intercultural Coaching be Adapted to Each Situation?

In this second part, we first examine the conditions for the success and the limitations of the intercultural coaching approach that we have presented. We then propose ways to improve the efficiency of the teams when these conditions are not met. In this chapter, we will not elaborate on the language issues that are essential in intercultural teamwork: they were addressed in Chapter 10.

15.2.1 Conditions for the Success and Limitations of Intercultural Coaching

The approach described above requires a number of conditions to be met. The first is for the actors to be willing to cooperate. Teams are embedded in specific organizational contexts. Intercultural management cannot be considered as a pure encounter of cultures in a vacuum, in other words, without taking into account the institutional context of the people involved. This means, for example, that when there are many conflicts of interest, as is the case with hostile international acquisition, working on intercultural understanding alone may well be to no avail. Employees may be reluctant to work towards a common goal and some may resist integration into a new multinational group for the economic purposes of maintaining local jobs or business activities. Zimmerman & Ravishankar (2016) provide an example of how on-shore members of a team working in the IT field purposely withheld information from off-shore members, because they perceived that the latter would be likely to replace them in the near future.

In such conflict-of-interest contexts, cultural differences may be used to argue that the observed inability to cooperate cannot be overcome since it is based on both deep and unalterable cultural foundations. This does not mean, however, that when power relations are prominent, cultural differences become peripheral. The two dimensions are articulated in the way power games are interpreted depending on the cultural universes of meaning. For example, we have shown that in the context of a transportation infrastructure building project in Algeria, the relations between French expatriates and Algerian engineers on site were first interpreted in terms of expertise by the former and in terms of the desire for domination by the latter. The power based on expertise, claimed and perceived as legitimate by the French, who were very much attached to the notion of *métier* (profession), was contested by their Algerian counterparts, who saw behind the technical arguments the attempt to establish a neo-colonial relationship (Chevrier & Khalfaoui, 2018). Taking into account the interplay of interests and power, on the one hand, and cultural differences, on the other hand, requires working towards the convergence of interests without neglecting the cultural interpretations of these interests by the protagonists.

The context to be considered also includes the teams' tasks. Within the same international group, various situations can be encountered. Depending on the departments and activities, international cooperation may be a simple matter of information exchange and loose coordination between entities that remain independent or it may require further integration of contributions. The stronger the common challenges the more crucial intercultural understanding becomes.

The second condition for success is linked to the stability of international cooperation. Providing support to teams to develop suitable methods requires long-term cooperation and limited member turnover. Investing in refined intercultural understanding will be all the more profitable if teams experiment with operating methods over the long term, have time for members to adjust to each other, enabling them to become aware of their differences. Temporary intercultural teams are less likely to succeed because they lack time for learning and adapting. There is also the problem of space. International teams increasingly work remotely. The globalization of firms, the search for transportation cost savings, and the opportunities provided by communication technologies have increased the number of situations where people work in scattered multicultural teams (Jimenez et al., 2017). In this case, intercultural challenges are combined with those related to geographical distance but also to organizational differences between the entities involved. Team dynamics not only involve differences in cultural understandings, competing interests, and power games, but also a lack of knowledge of colleagues' work environments and constraints (Barmeyer & Davoine, 2019). For example, how might the lack of response to a request be explained: misunderstanding? Deliberate dodging? Temporary unavailability of the contact person assigned to another priority? Not being able to reach this person to clarify the situation face-to-face adds to the complexity of intercultural work. Consequently, when working at a distance, knowledge of the partners' organization and of their culture must both be developed.

In principle, similar coaching to that of co-located teams is possible for dispersed teams. In the same way, a series of interviews with the protagonists can be conducted, either at each site or remotely, and the cultural representations can be analysed and reported back to them. In practice, technology-mediated feedback makes explanations less easy and the exchanges it generates are limited. In addition, the analyst who is geographically located elsewhere—usually on the side of the organizational entity that requested the assistance—is more likely to be perceived as biased, in favour of the commissioning entity, than when working in the workplace shared by a team. Issues of time difference, availability of the team members, and quality of the technical communication systems affect both the team's daily work and the coaching for better intercultural understanding. If it is possible for teams to take advantage of a physical meeting to organize the feedback and especially the work groups, the coaching tips are more or less the same as in the previous case. Otherwise, the analyst can introduce the different interpretations and expectations that might have created tensions in the different teams and sites, and help everyone to think about adaptations that fall within their field of action. An even better solution is to work with several analysts from the cultures concerned, one on each site, as was done in the case of the company Air-France KLM (see Chapter 6).

Finally, the coaching approach is more effective when the number of cultures present is limited. Whether co-located or dispersed, international teams are increasingly diversified. Initially, the internationalization of business was based on the penetration of new markets by companies that were rooted in their home countries. This process has mainly resulted in bi-national teams composed of staff from the parent company and from one subsidiary or, in the case of joint ventures or alliances, staff from two countries. Internationalization is now taking the form of a globalization of activities, embodied in the distribution of the value chain in business networks spread over several countries and organizations (Bartlett & Ghoshal, 2002). Internationalization does not only concern markets but all stages from research and development and product design to retailing, including production generally split between multiple suppliers and subcontractors, and outsourced support functions (accounting or IT systems). Intercultural teams are therefore very diverse in terms of nationalities. It is becoming more and more difficult to gain a detailed understanding of each of the cultural universes of meaning represented in the team; the coaching approach must therefore be adapted.

15.2.2 Pleading for Intercultural Understanding

When the full coaching process is not applicable for the aforementioned reasons, its key principles can generally be adapted. In all cases, the intervention research starts from the practical management difficulties faced by the teams. This is not a team-building exercise meant to oil social mechanisms. The intention is to remedy the inefficiency of management practices thanks to the stakeholders' understanding of their respective interpretations. Regardless of the team's configuration, the objective is to address recurring problematic situations. The point is not to deal with minor frustrations related to particular traditions that are upsetting to those who have to comply with these. The intercultural issues to be addressed are those that raise persistent objections and trigger strong emotions because they relate to the fundamental fears of the cultures involved. It is precisely these points of contention, rooted in fundamental fears, that intercultural coaching seeks to resolve as a matter of priority.

These problematic situations concern all aspects of management the cultural roots of which have been highlighted in the previous chapters. These may include leadership practices that upset employees or fail to achieve results, conflicts in how to deal with a client, difficulties in making and implementing a decision, or relationships that deteriorate during control operations. Once the situation has been identified, the cultural dimensions of conflicts can be explained by an analyst using the aforementioned method. A kind of cultural audit, based on interviews with each of the protagonists, makes it possible to give feedback to the actors on the logics and expectations that frame the interpretations of regular disputes. This enables them to define ways to overcome these disputes by being aware of the resources at their disposal. In a context of great cultural diversity, it will not be possible to achieve a mutual understanding equivalent to that which can be expected in a bi-national context. However, the explanation of the logic underlying the conflict will enable decisive steps to be taken towards the discussion of acceptable solutions and towards resolving conflicts over the main areas of friction.

Our approach differs from the usual methods of intercultural management in several respects. First, traditional approaches focus on selecting employees who can manage intercultural situations because of their initial awareness of cultural differences. Although choosing 'open and flexible' people to work in an international environment is certainly wise, the technical skills required for positions reduce the pool of candidates. Companies do not always have at their disposal these 'global leaders' with great adaptation skills to build teams. During our research, we have also observed that the training generally provided to expatriates before departure has the virtue of making them aware of cultural differences.

However, this is not sufficient for solving teams' intercultural problems. On the one hand, before leaving, expatriates have practical concerns they focus on during their training. As they await practical advice on their place of residence, the schools for their children, or the organizational context in which they will arrive, they are less sensitive to intercultural analyses, the explanatory scope of which they do not yet grasp. Moreover, once the protagonists are in the host country, interactions that unconsciously refer to the most feared social situations are likely to generate visceral reactions of rejection or resistance. It may be the case even if the training brings about a cognitive change in the participants, if the goodwill of the parties is sincerely displayed, and if the protagonists are very 'open'. Emotions may hinder the efforts of discernment. Intercultural training sometimes provides expatriates with a basic knowledge that contributes to reinforcing their stereotypes rather than preparing them for careful observation of their working environment. Finally, in international remote teams, people working in intercultural environments without expatriation are rarely trained.

Considering all these limitations, we rather recommend coaching after the intercultural experience of the people has started; when difficulties arise and must be resolved to ensure collective effectiveness. The approach should focus on specific managerial difficulties and be rooted in the needs identified by the teams.

Furthermore, our approach focuses on 'specific' cultural competence (Livian, 2012), that is, knowledge of the specific cultural contexts (country, region) to which people are exposed. This specific cultural competence differs from generic intercultural competences such as intercultural communication skills or cultural intelligence (Earley & Ang, 2003). These generic competences are defined with a psychosocial perspective and mainly refer to personal qualities such as empathy, openness, tolerance towards ambiguity, and flexibility, among others. The approach developed in this book emphasizes the fact that understanding the cultural logic of partners is one of the keys to collective effectiveness. Beyond the relevant insights observed in some cases, the approach enables engagement with a systematic and conscious process of developing collectively accepted and effective operating modes. While knowing the partners' interpretation frameworks does not directly provide intercultural management solutions, it allows for informed collective action, as long as the protagonists share the same objectives, and it prevents misinterpretations of the partners' good intentions as encountered in Chapter 12 pp. 245–6 with the Franco-Lebanese example.

Finally, this approach, which advocates the informed development of solutions tailored to each team's needs, differs from a normative managerial stream which, as discussed in previous chapters, praises standardized ways of doing things that are supposedly universal but in fact rooted in the dominant American model. Azevedo studied a case of cooperation between two companies, one Brazilian and one Chinese, in which the protagonists claim that such internationalization is an opportunity to 'Westernize' their management practices when neither company is strictly-speaking Western[1]. This shows the strength and extension well beyond the national boundaries of the American benchmark.

Beyond the success of the model, which gives it a strong credibility, American management also enjoys intrinsic qualities of readability. Objective-based contracts and accountability are based on explicit rules that are easy to share, even for people who are unfamiliar with this model. Management methods, such as those used by the Japanese in which the community's rules are implicit, or the French ones in which the reference to the habits and customs of professions is just as implicit, are much more difficult to decipher. Therefore, in intercultural encounters, embracing a game whose rules are clearly codified is easier than embracing one whose participants have internalized the rules but do not express them verbally. Some even consider that the clarification of rules and their strict enforcement is a form of social regulation that has developed in the United States because it was particularly suited to a nation that had built itself precisely on the basis of a diversity of cultural origins.

The American model of management is no better than any other: each culture has its own resources, with its own specific fears (see p. 62), and exporting the American model in a context where very different representations of social life prevail has little chance of being successful (see Chapters 2 and 14). However, in intercultural encounters, the clarity and readability of the model gives it a kind of dominant gene, while very implicit models would be recessive, unless their logics are also made explicit, as this approach does. Indeed, even though the members of international teams are able to explain the basics of American-style management—formalization of the goals and contributions expected from each person, explicit communication to deal with unforeseen circumstances, and accountability—they have not given up on their own cultural references. As seen in Chapter 10 p. 209 with the use of any *lingua franca*, similar terms have different connotations in different cultural contexts. In other words, formalizing, contracting, or articulating values in a common corporate culture is quite effective in guiding the collective work. However, it does not erase the differences in representations of what is, or is not, legitimate in day-to-day management practices. Difficulties and conflicts remain behind the ceremonial adoption of standardized practices (Meyer & Rowan, 1977). The initially perceived richness of individual points of view may open onto an impossibility to agree on any common actions.

In short, a very explicit management style is certainly a resource in a highly intercultural context, but given the diverse persisting ways of interpreting, it is insufficient to overcome all the difficulties. Therefore, the process of analysing cultural differences is a better tool. However, even with close coaching, in highly diverse teams, the variety of viewpoints, expectations, and non-negotiable issues is sometimes such that the patient elaboration of acceptable management practices is unsuccessful or too costly. During the wave of globalization in the 1990s and

2000s, companies underwent international restructuring to target configurations that reflected an optimistic belief in the potentialities of cultural diversity. Airbus, with the distribution of its manufacturing sites in four European countries, was emblematic of this relocation of activities. Faced with implementation difficulties, prohibitive coordination costs, and long lead times, some companies such as Renault, Schneider, or Areva, to name but a few multinational companies of French origin, are gradually reducing the scope of global teams. The projects maintain their international scale but the organization relies more on local teams responsible for specific task-batches which are loosely connected. It is too early to say whether this is a general trend or whether this evolution concerns only a few companies made cautious by experiences of projects led by highly diversified teams that have failed to succeed. However, it seems that, in very complex professional environments, working in parallel on local sites is a more effective way than seeking intercultural synergies to supposedly benefit from cultural diversity. Transaction costs and interfaces are reduced by the coexistence of local operations.

15.3 Conclusion

In some extreme cases, ignoring cultural differences leads to blatant failures and breakdowns in collaboration, the costs of which are clearly visible. However, more often than not, the costs of intercultural misunderstanding are difficult to estimate. These costs are hidden, like a significant friction force that hinders the proper running of a mechanism but is neglected to simplify calculations. There are also invisible social and human costs, as Scola (2005)[2] showed in his study of the health of migrants and people immersed in intercultural environments. Companies these days are frequently relying on the relational and adaptability qualities of their staff or offering cultural diversity awareness training to expatriates. Psycho-social approaches to culture can be useful, but they are rarely sufficient to unravel the cultural roots of recurring frictions that are usually attributed to other problems.

This is why we advocate other, more or less elaborate approaches, depending on the situation. In cases of high organizational and cultural complexity, it may be more appropriate to split the work, work side by side, or limit integrating the work packages so as to reduce the required coordination. If companies are to make the most of diversity, they must set up intercultural work teams in activities where creativity is crucial. Conversely, when the tasks require agreement on specific choices and fine-tuned joint actions, properly allocating different parts of the work to local entities, according to their particular strengths, may be a reasonable method. This way of organizing the work requires only a minimal level of coordination and integration of work packages, and takes advantage of cultural diversity in other ways. In this case, instead of compelling teams to comply with standardized American-inspired management, each of them can capitalize on their own cultural resources.

When bringing together a highly-integrated team with many cultures and remote interactions, coaching can fruitfully focus on key frictional points. The aim is to clarify the actors' differences in interpretation about recurring issues of tension and inefficiency. The intervention of an analyst aims to provide the keys to understanding problematic intercultural situations. This helps participants to decipher the cultural universes of meaning involved. Finally, in situations of lasting intercultural cooperation with a limited number of cultures, the coaching approach that was described using the example of the Franco-Malagasy NGO can be entirely implemented for a significant long-term benefit. The support of an analyst is an investment for effective long-term intercultural cooperation. Protagonists can acquire cultural skills concerning the specific cultures of their counterparts just as they can, at the same time, learn the language to move towards a better mutual understanding. This long-term learning seems more promising than the dissemination of a global corporate culture, which promotes surface uniformity while significant, less visible, differences remain ignored.

Notes

1. Azevedo, G. (2014) 'The cultural hybridization of organizations' (14th Annual Conference EURAM, Warsaw).
2. Scola, F. (2005) *Couverture santé des Français expatriés: enquête auprès d'un échantillon de la communauté française résidente à Rio de Janeiro* (Université de la Méditerranée doctoral dissertation).

16
Guidelines for Deciphering Cultures

The purpose of this chapter is to expound on how to apply our approach practically as one encounters new management situations and/or cultural grounds. For a broader methodological presentation, readers may refer to the different methods used in sociological analysis (Boudon, 2002); in ethnographic description (Agar, 1996; Laplantine, 2015); or for anthropological interpretations (Geertz, 1973; Caratini, 2012). Only the issues specific to the particular sociological object that we seek to bring out (see Chapter 3, p. 50) are developed in this chapter.

We will firstly discuss the specificities of field surveys for such analyses. Secondly, we will see how the interpretative process aims to gradually allow us to enter the universe of a culture. This second step is the most complex and critical to the whole process. However, the quality of interpretation and the facility with which it will be performed is highly dependent upon the materials collected during the survey. The method presented here closely follows the principles developed by d'Iribarne (2011). However, in order to facilitate their implementation, they have been turned into a set of steps and practical criteria.[1]

Before going any further, one point must be highlighted as it bears to such a great extent on the whole process and on the survey in particular. It concerns the nature of the quotations which our analyses use so frequently. Rather than being demonstrative, our approach to analysis is essentially comparative and interpretative. The excerpts from the interviews that are used—expressions, metaphors, short stories, sometimes simple words—are not meant to convey representative opinions, but to gradually take us into the specificities of a cultural universe of meaning. They are meant to illustrate the ways in which members of a society think and feel, and, beyond what separates or opposes them, how they make sense of the social situations that they experience (see Chapter 3, p. 59). What makes quotations so convincing is the coherence of the categories of interpretation in the comments that members of a particular culture make, regardless of their social positions, differences of opinion, interests, or the values they believe in.

16.1 The Field Survey

The objective, through each particular survey, is to highlight the structuring aspects of a *political culture*—taken in its broadest sense as the way in which the

Cross-Cultural Management Revisited: A Qualitative Approach. Philippe d'Iribarne, Sylvie Chevrier, Alain Henry, Jean-Pierre Segal, and Geneviève Tréguer-Felten, Oxford University Press (2020).
DOI: 10.1093/oso/9780198857471.001.0001

relationships between an individual and all others are conceived in a given culture—and to show how this culture changes the way in which organizations operate. We seek to understand the vision that people in that culture have of the *proper way* of living and working together, be it agreeing, cooperating, lobbying, opposing, commanding, controlling, or sanctioning.

16.1.1 Focusing on the Investigation Object

The survey should shed light on the way in which different management situations make sense in the eyes of the interested parties; it does not consist in producing a sociological description of the company under scrutiny—which would then be considered as a case typical of the surrounding culture—but in seeing how, within a given organization, this culture is expressed through concrete relationships and management situations.

Hence, a first rule: only focus on a limited number of questions that are as factual as possible, for example, 'What prevents the implementation of a reform that many consider useful?'; 'How are we to understand such resistance to the introduction of a new management tool?'; 'How can we improve the empowerment of local managers?', 'How could we adapt a procedure imported from another cultural context?', etc. The clearer the stakes, the more concerned managers and respondents will feel, and the richer the interviews will be.

The field survey aims at understanding the context and the issues related to these initial questions. More specifically, it consists in observing work situations, in conducting recorded interviews, and collecting written documents—leaders' speeches, trade union documents, ethics charters, procedures, etc. While the investigation system is in many respects similar to that applied in the sociology of organizations (Crozier & Friedberg, 1977)—that is, identifying groups of actors, analysing their conflicts, their arrangements, the interplay of interests and power—cultural studies are clearly different in that they do not stop at this result. They go beyond, considering that the stakes, far from being universal, depend on the meaning that the very actors attribute to the different situations.

Once transcribed, interviews are the essential material from which one can gradually identify the representations that, within a culture, will, unawares but consistently, structure the various interlocutors' statements. We shall see that a lot of information can be drawn from a limited number of particularly expressive interviews which exhibit varied and even opposing reactions to concrete organizational problems.

16.1.2 Ensuring a Heterogeneity of Points of View

A second rule is to gather the most diverse points of view possible, which does not necessarily mean that the survey should be extended to more and more sectors of the company under scrutiny.

Interviewees should be diverse, including both workers and engineers, trade unionists and leaders, men and women, young and old employees of diverse social or regional origins, etc., so as to ensure that the image brought to the fore does not only reflect a sub-group. However, the objective is not simply to build a *representative* image of the company but to gather different ways of thinking from people endowed with different perspectives, issues, or values.

Such diversity of points of view is essential to support the analysis. It is useful, for example, to compare, on the same practical issue, the reading of people with structurally different positions—internal customers and suppliers; workers in production and in maintenance; employees with monthly and with hourly wages; or subcontracted employees, etc. Different or even opposing positions may reveal common underlying logics and categories. The example of employees of the French post office—introduced in Chapter 8 (p. 151) and proposed as an exercise at the end of this chapter (p. 328)—clearly illustrates what we mean. While employees and their trainers fiercely confront one another on customer service, they all share the same self-evidence: they are the ones who can judge what their customers need; they know better than the interested parties themselves.

In order to distinguish between what is more specifically related to their company's culture, it is necessary to ask respondents to compare the current functioning with their former experiences, either in an earlier period with a different management team or in other companies. These comparisons also reveal the yardstick according to which stakeholders judge different situations or other local forms of management.

Indefinitely multiplying the company sectors under scrutiny is not necessary: choosing them in relation to the issues addressed will suffice. Interviewing people from departments that achieve contrasting results—in terms of internal cooperation and performance—will be useful. Whatever the causes invoked for success or for difficulties, such a comparison will shed light on what, in a given cultural context, corresponds to the positive or negative images of the way to work. Sometimes, apparently trivial practical details emerge which are in reality quite decisive.

Regarding the number of interviews, there is no absolute standard—three to four dozen are generally more than sufficient to address a management issue. Beyond this number, their productivity in new information decreases, characterizing what is called a 'saturation point' (Sardan, 1995; Glaser & Strauss, 1973). When you are dealing with interpretation, the expressiveness of the interviews—the strength of the arguments and images—is more decisive than their number.

16.1.3 Creating a Close Yet Distant Relationship

In spite of an aspiration to objectivity, social sciences cannot entirely avoid interpretation and subjectivity. Researchers' general posture could be compared to that often described in thrillers, where police officers feel the atmosphere and try to understand who they are talking to, what that person does, what he or she is thinking and feeling.

Investigators must be both *familiar and distant*, as befits an ethnographic posture. The quality of the interviews depends on investigators' ability to establish trust in the relationship, by the way they position themselves and show empathy. The ability to understand their concerns, to pass on their expectations, and to influence management views which interviewees will perceive in them is more decisive for the quality of the interviews than precautions that might be taken to optimize the objectivity of their remarks.

It is essential that investigators suspend their judgement and understanding. They must be on the look-out, take nothing for granted, guard themselves against their own self-evidences, or against providing any too-quickly-projected external explanation. They must demonstrate a mix of complicity—through their understanding of the human and professional aspects—and of ingenuity so as to prompt the interviewees to provide circumstantial explanations.

Some researchers, in their attempt to establish detailed descriptions of a situation, strive to measure the effects of subjectivity (Zhang & Guttormsen, 2016). In our case, although facts are important for our global understanding, we do not aim at establishing the truth, we try to assess how people, because they belong to this or that culture, proffer their points of view—whatever the points of view may be. The way in which they may *rewrite* history is less important than the logics according to which they proffer their arguments. In other words, what is important is to understand *what really matters* for the people concerned, and the reasons why it does.

One may wonder about the risk that recording the interviews might make interviewees censor themselves, entailing a bias in their statements. However, note-taking will never be so reliable: investigators are in no way capable of writing down every single word of formulations that are alien to them. Besides, these formulations may subsequently provide valuable clues. Before starting the interview, it is therefore crucial for investigators to explain that it will remain confidential and to underline the possibility for the interviewee of suspending the recording at any time. Experience shows that many interlocutors end up even forgetting the presence of the recorder.

If the interview is perceived as factual, most people will take advantage of the opportunity they are given to make their ideas and their concerns known and to have them forwarded to the management.

16.1.4 Conducting the Interviews

The interviews, which are semi-directive in nature, should remain focused on factual questions related to the survey issues. You may start by asking everyone about the content of their tasks and responsibilities. The answers will often reveal how people relate to their organization. For example, long after we had finished our interviews, we discovered that American interlocutors tended to indicate who they worked for, while French people soon specified who they were and the role that was theirs (see Chapter 4, p. 85).

The questions can then focus on what works well and what does not; on possible obstructions; on objectives that are more or less easy to achieve; on the reasons for conflicts and the possibilities of resolving them; on the quality of mutual understanding between colleagues or with hierarchy; on any practical solutions that might be suggested for the organization; etc. Sometimes respondents need to be drawn back to more specific questions to prevent their comments diluting into abstract or normative considerations. The more factual you keep the topics, the more revealing the interviewees' statements will be as to what matters to them.

In some cases, it may be interesting to ask people to report from a factual point of view on their intercultural experiences. However, asking them to characterize a particular culture—their own or that of a colleague—as is sometimes done, serves no purpose. This type of question leads to clichés that mix identity traits and hasty generalizations, while real cultural particularities escape investigators' attention (see Chapter 3, p. 59). Employees sometimes make fairly precise observations on their foreign colleagues, but experience shows that the way they interpret them is in line with their own cultural grid and that they do not understand how the reported facts make sense for those concerned. In the Air France-KLM alliance (see Chapter 6, p. 116), several French and Dutch interviewees were well aware of their respective correspondents' behaviours and tried to adapt to them. However, they misunderstood their meanings, leaving the door wide open for great misunderstandings.

Reformulations during interviews enable investigators to verify if they understood *correctly*. They also constitute an opportunity to encourage their interlocutors to explain their comments in relation to any objections that they may have, or to highlight points to which they are strongly attached.

The main challenge of the survey is to highlight the way in which interviewees make sense of the situations; how they contrast what they deem legitimate with what they deem illegitimate; what is worthwhile with what is worthless; and, beyond that, how they defend their position on what is worthwhile.

16.1.5 Moving on to Interpretation

Before we move on to the interpretation stage, it should be noted that no preconceived boundaries are attributed to any cultural area: they emerge empirically from the existence of characteristics that are common to a social block—a country, a region, several countries, etc.—and by contrast with others. For instance, the hypothesis of a cultural space specific to France, which the long history of its political space suggested, was confirmed by the permanence of the features observed. They may, however, need to be nuanced in peripheral regions such as the Basque country, Alsace, Corsica (Thomasset & d'Iribarne, 2002), etc. Conversely, in West Africa, we observed features that are common to several countries of a sub-region—Côte d'Ivoire, Burkina Faso, Togo, Benin, Cameroon—even though they may come along with local particularities, for example, in Cameroon, hierarchical forms often vary from one region to another. The inhabitants of this vast West African region, while admitting the existence of local particularities and antagonisms, acknowledge nonetheless that there exists a socio-cultural stratum—just as you can speak of a common geological stratum—that distinguishes them from other cultural areas—American, French, South African, Chinese, etc.

Language borders do not necessarily coincide with cultural borders. However, mastery of the language practiced locally—understanding the intimate meaning of words, knowing idioms, proverbial expressions, having literary or historical references—gives better access to the cultural universe of meaning. However, seeing the local language from a certain distance may sometimes help to perceive the strangeness of a formulation. Even if you do not master the language, experience shows that the translation filter is not insuperable. It allows a lot of interesting representations and formulations to pass through, as was shown with the use of ELF (see Chapter 10, p. 189). Images rarely lose their expressiveness. For instance, a strictly literal translation of corporate documents may turn out to be very instructive. When the opportunity arises, using a back-translation of corporate texts that were translated locally and comparing it with the source text can equally shed light on significant local reformulations.

The interpretation stage which follows is the longest and most delicate step. It is meant to highlight the representations which are specific to a culture, that is, the taken-for-granted elements, underlying categories, structuring oppositions, and constructs from which the members of that culture make sense of ways of acting and evaluate them. Interviews need to be read time and again so as to gradually identify their internal logics. This step requires a familiarization time, comparable to that of immersion in ethnography. Being able to rely on an accurate transcript of the interviews is crucial. A simple quotation which had for a long time not drawn attention may suddenly become enlightening after multiple readings. Finally, to facilitate the process, sessions where interviews are read and discussed collectively can be organized among researchers.

Interpretation mainly relies on a set of principles which we shall now review.

16.2 Interpreting the Data

We shall now present a series of criteria that include, in a form meant to facilitate their use, several principles useful for deciphering a culture.

Generally, researchers are at first somewhat perplexed by the materials that they have collected. If they are approaching a culture other than their own, the logics to be discovered are unfamiliar, hence not immediately visible. If they are deciphering their own culture—whose uses hold no secrets for them—the difficulty is no less, since they have no hindsight to perceive its logic: they see only banalities and self-evidences. In either case, care should be taken not to project interpretations that might be inspired by the extant literature: it would bias their own interpretation. The main difficulty with interpreting is the need to enter the unknown hermeneutical circle of a culture that will make the texts and interviews collected meaningful.

It is as though, in order to fully understand the meaning of each of the statements, you needed to have read and decoded all the texts beforehand—obviously an impossible task: how could you have already done so, when, precisely, you are in the process of approaching them? 'The clues that have been assembled can only take on their full meaning when they fall into place in the overall picture, and this big picture is in turn built up from these clues' (d'Iribarne, 2011). You need to adopt a trial-and-error approach, with an eye on what is particularly meaningful for the speakers, on what they seem unconsciously attached to and which differs from other cultures. The first clues enable you to construct provisional images; starting from these images, reading can resume, while looking back with a sharpened eye; all in all, moving along in a succession of such back-and-forth moves (d'Iribarne, 2011). The material gradually becomes familiar: previously invisible lines of force appear which run through all the texts, giving relief to speech and behaviours.

To help researchers in their progression, we suggest applying seven criteria regrouped in three successive levels—level 1: *redundancy, strangeness, embarrassment*; level 2: *self-evidence, opposition*; level 3: *coherence, horizontality*. Far from being exclusive of one another, these criteria complement and tend to reinforce one another. The three grouping levels are akin to the main excavation stages of an archaeological site: the first level would correspond to the clearing of a few outcrops and the delimitation of working areas; the second to the meticulous clearing of concrete objects; while the third would consist in designing a narrative able to give these elements an overall coherence. Here, the first level consists in detecting specific clues such as recurring expressions or words which bear a 'family resemblance' between them. Then, the task at hand is to connect one to the other and inscribe them in more general images; finally, this will lead to assumptions which should regularly be challenged. Throughout this progression, the convergence of several criteria around the same image can be considered as a reinforcement of its explanatory power. We are now going to illustrate the process.

16.2.1 Level One: Redundancy, Strangeness, Embarrassment

The examples used to illustrate the criteria are taken from fieldwork in France, the USA, Cameroon, and Tunisia.[2]

Redundancy criterion

A first criterion—both the most accessible but also the most nebulous—consists in identifying words or groups of words that revolve around the same semantic field and keep appearing in all interviews. Their frequency may come along with concomitant aspects: (i) some of them convey a wide range of meanings; (ii) the semantic family under consideration is divided into many different terms; (iii) one or the other of them has a huge explanatory power: the mere mentioning of it holds the power to close any discussion; (iv) they are spontaneously associated with ways of acting; and (v) one particular word is central in an institution or a rite.

Such is the case for the word *friend* in Cameroon: it is omnipresent in social intercourse. It occurs in a wide variety of situations with distended meanings: it may refer to a person with whom one has a strong personal bond—a bosom friend; to someone that one has just met; or simply to someone with whom one has common interests. The word polysemy is also reflected in its declinations: *sincere and faithful friend*, *acquaintance*, *brother* (as an equivalent to friend, it loses its biological meaning), etc. Designating someone as a *friend* is enough to justify many situations and behaviours, as in the statement of this worker: 'People who get along well outside work better together. When they have a problem, they *talk as friends* do.'[3] Finally, this word is the central motif of very lively traditional institutions, such as the 'tontines' whose 'main purpose is to gather among friends' (Henry et al., 1991: 124).

Lexical search software can help to bring out important words, but it is far from sufficient as researchers are looking for words which may only be loosely related semantically, or even equivalent formulations that no software can detect. In France, it is easy to verify that *what one is*—followed by one's profession, social position, function, seniority level, grade, etc.—is very frequently invoked to justify the manner according to which one is supposed to act. But no word-frequency list will reveal this trait since it is expressed in extremely varied forms: *For me, a supervisor must*...; *We, manufacturers, we* do not like...; I accomplish *my task as normal*; *as a technician*, I consider; etc. Once we had discovered this trait, it played a major role in understanding the relationships at play within companies in France (see further on the *self-evidence* and *consistency* criteria). Researchers' familiarization with people's ways of expressing themselves is essential, much more than word frequencies, just as it would be if they were in the process of learning a foreign language.

Before you can obtain such clear constructs, you will have to content yourself with collecting the quotes that revolve around the same semantic field, as was done in the following example (it is based on the survey conducted by Yousfi (2017) on the role of the Tunisian General Labour Union (UGTT) during the 2011 revolution (see Box 16.1)).

Symmetrical to the criterion of redundancy, and complementing it, we have the so-called criterion of silence, when—consciously or unconsciously—the

Box 16.1 The Tunisian revolution: an endless negotiation

From the very first cursive reading of the interviews, the frequency with which *negotiation* is mentioned—sometimes implicitly—allows us to glimpse the central place that negotiation holds in human relations. We quote the following excerpts in the order in which they appear:

'tacit *compromise*'; 'precarious *balance*'; 'combining *pressure and negotiation*'; 'there was *consultation for everything*'; 'police officers *asked* union activists to call a truce'; 'the executive board tried to place the Centrale [the union leadership] *as usual in a logic of mediation*'; 'finally *gave in to popular pressure*'; 'promises *to resolve issues by negotiating*'; 'it *has to come to terms* with power'; 'it *must* participate in social *dialogue*'; 'it therefore requires *a lot of acrobatics* to maintain a *balance*'; '[it] must take precautions to *always* have *the flexibility* to intervene (...), *to arrange* the situation, or *to exercise the role of mediation*'; 'to help manage *the dialogue* between partners'; 'its role in *finding solutions* to problems *by negotiating*'; 'It is *necessary* to react with *a logic of dialogue* to find practical solutions'; or finally '[it] must ensure *a difficult equation*'.

Before considering this as a 'Tunisian' trait, one would have to check whether the emphasis on negotiation might not be exclusive to the subject of the survey and to political contexts, and to look for further additional evidence. However, our familiarity with other cultural fields attracted our attention to a possible pre-eminence of human relationships over reference to an abstract common good. In the present case, a trade union official clearly stated the need to sacrifice particular interests to *the saving of* the group: 'Protecting the boat (*chqaf*) from the elements means that *to save the boat, you have to sacrifice things*, you *have to unload* the boat'. Renouncing individual interests (*sacrificing things*) does not refer to a few major principles, but to a common interest (*protecting against the elements*), or even to survival. Another witness reported an agreement between people that referred to the adjustment of personal feelings and interests. He recounted that, at the height of the events, the police chief had met demonstrators in a café to ask them to withdraw slogans that were hostile to the president: 'You are *trade unionists, I love you and I respect you* but here we do not agree, *I did not attack you, I respected you* but I do not want this slogan, leave me alone, *I do not want to have any problems*'.

Other fields would be necessary to confirm the hypothesis of a transverse cultural trait. But the systematic reference to negotiation and compromise deserves to be considered in view of the inevitable, never questioned, and repeated self-evidence: *for everything*; *it has to*; *obligatory*; *a lot of acrobatics*; *always*; *to find solutions*; or *the promises to settle by negotiating*. Their importance is consistent with the concomitant focus on particular interests, be they specific to a person, to a group, or to any entity.

interviewees seem unable to use terms which would be expected either in other cultures or from a universal economics point of view. An emblematic example could be seen in the French general avoidance of words that refer too closely to either a self-seeking or a profit-making act, and in their almost systematic replacement of them by words referring to the more generous image of the one who *offers, proposes, commits himself, advises*, etc. (see the illustration exercise at the end of the chapter). Such surprising silence is the sign of a rather deep aversion.

Strangeness criterion (or reverse criterion)

The idea of strangeness has been conceived since antiquity as an 'inversion'. In 1585, the Reverend Father Froïs reported: 'The Japanese do many things in ways that are exactly contrary to what Europeans consider natural and appropriate', a remark leading to acceptance according to Lévi-Strauss (1998): 'When the traveler convinces himself that practices in complete opposition to his own (...) are in reality identical to them when viewed in reverse, he provides himself with the means to domesticate strangeness, to make it familiar to himself.' This is what underpins our second criterion. It is directly related to comparison, as it identifies arguments or behaviours that are not easily understood by a foreign observer or that contrast with supposedly rational management standards.

A vivid example appears in the case of Malians who give one of their French colleagues the kindly critical nickname of *waraba* (the lion). The interested party understands it as a public recognition of his leadership. What he does not know is that, in Bambara culture, the lion is renowned for being both brave and... stupid. The French colleague hardly imagines that these two qualifications could go hand in hand. His misunderstanding is emblematic of intercultural relations: he perceives a tone of friendly teasing, but, ignoring everything about its logic, he interprets it in his own frame of mind. In the French universe of meaning, courage and intelligence are two virtues that, together, constitute the basic quality of nobility. Such a hybrid figure as this lion's—both noble and stupid—is problematic and even unthinkable (whereas, in Bambara literature, there exists another lion (*jara*) who indeed is the king of animals). Intercultural relations are regularly undermined by such misunderstandings, without anyone even suspecting the reversal due to their respective frameworks of interpretation.

We encountered another kind of inversion, during an investigation in an American factory, when a department head underlined his colleagues' wish to organize their work freely:

> Most people, the American people, don't like to be told how to do this job, what I do first and what I do second. Most of the people feel they have to be somewhat of a master of their own destiny by determining how they accomplish their job (in d'Iribarne, 1989).

The link between a grandiose ideal of freedom, that is, *to be a master of their destiny*, and such a minimal cause, that is, *by determining* (...) *what I do first and what I do second*, quite obvious to the speaker, arouses a certain perplexity from a foreigner (at least, a non-native English speaker). Although this is not an overt inversion, seen from another culture, this American interpretation seems excessive, out of context (d'Iribarne, 2011). What appears to be self-evident to this American speaker seems paradoxical elsewhere. When as an outsider, you experience this kind of astonishment; you can consider the fact as pointing to an interesting research avenue.

Another type of discrepancy may appear when one considers a corporate text that has been translated for distribution in a new context. Writers/translators often make more or less conscious adaptations that stand out in the resulting apparently similar versions. Comparing two versions of a major international group's code of conduct—one American, the other one French—highlighted the quite distinct formulations used to report on commercial relationships. While the American version used vocabulary in line with what can be considered as the classical approach to customer relations—'provide the construction industry'; 'delivering the products'—the French version operated a curious shift—'offrir au secteur de la construction' (offering the construction sector); *'proposer des produits'* (proposing products) (d'Iribarne, 2011). When the recurring differences between the two texts were considered, it became obvious that the wording differences had nothing to do with any linguistic constraint—the French writer could have used the corresponding words *fournir* (provide) and *livrer* (deliver)—but that his avoiding them was consistent with the way the social relations underpinning sales are staged in the French cultural context. In cases where key corporate documents have been translated into a language which is not accessible to the researcher, a literal translation—as close as possible to the source text—may highlight similar discrepancies.

Combining several criteria will always reinforce the interest in a given element. In the afore-mentioned Tunisian example (Box 16.1), the redundancy criterion is coupled with a strangeness criterion. It is detectable in the rather unusual way in which a police chief concomitantly stresses his feeling of affection—I love you and I respect you—and his own self-interest—I don't want to have any problems. It suggests that if negotiation is given so much space, it is because of the need to accommodate both parties' interests: those of the trade unionists present and those of the local police chief.

Embarrassment criterion

The criterion of embarrassment consists in identifying a contradiction, be it subtle or covert, between a theoretically accepted principle—a so-called universal management rule—and the cultural context. In the Chinese subsidiary of a French international group, agents welcomed the new entrepreneurial spirit that allowed them to question their superiors. When asked if people might henceforth question superiors, a Chinese manager answered '*Yes!*' and laughed. And when the investigator's questions became more probing—'Does it happen?'; 'Do you question them?'—his answers became realistic: 'I've never seen anyone do so'; 'It's very rare, I've never heard of it'; or even, as in the spontaneous cris de coeur of a manager who had been rather critical of his managers: 'No, no, no, no, I couldn't do it'.

This criterion, like that of strangeness, points to a gap, no longer between foreign colleagues, but between a stated principle and actual practice. It is usually expressed in the form of a more or less embarrassed admission when the respondent is confronted with an insistent question. A supposedly legitimate way of acting is in fact not quite acceptable and entails informal adjustments.

Such acceptance of rules which are idealized because they are deemed universal will particularly occur in emerging countries. However, similar situations are also to be found in so-called *modern* countries. A foreman in a French factory provided the following comments about the sanctions that were to be applied in case employees were late for work (d'Iribarne, 1989): 'Everyone says that it [applying them] should be done, but we'll never do it here, it's *unthinkable*, it's *impossible*.' Interiorized management standards—which refer to exogenous logics—are bypassed, and contradiction remains in a blind spot. 'There are no sanctions', one of his colleagues explained (Ibid.), 'It's not done here. If the guy doesn't want to understand, we can always find him a crappier job. It may not be very fair, but [laughs] (...) It's not an openly admitted kind of sanction [laughs]'. Wherever you are, some international practices may be difficult to import (d'Iribarne, 2011). In the face of such contradictions, reality is painstakingly dressed, or discreet adjustments made, so as to comply with the ideal images that constitute the reference.

Embarrassment can be detected in awkward laughter and confessions of impossibility, suggesting the existence of taboos or unspoken words: *this is not our style*; *impossible*, *unthinkable*; *never heard of it*; *we just can't*; *it's crazy*; *ultimately*, etc. Such formulations refer to feared or desired behaviours, although their meaning is not always clear. In the previous example, it took a long thinking process for us to understand that this broad-mindedness was in fact connected to a principle of moderation vis-à-vis a rule that they considered too brutal, so much so that it led to unconfessed practices.

Once this first level is completed, you have a series of observations—recurring themes, surprising images, astonishing quotations, the meaning of which is not always clear—which you are going to try to bridge, while striving to keep an open mind so as to avoid hastily projecting outer logics onto the context. Many scattered elements have to be kept on hold, as would the pieces of a puzzle before they eventually find their due place.

16.2.2 Level Two: Self-evidence, Opposition

Just as one needs to be familiar with dictionaries to clearly understand their definitions, one needs to carefully read the interviews so as to gradually determine, according to the situations in which they are used, the actual meaning of the words—at least those that were singled out for their importance or peculiarity—to grasp their positive or negative connotations; to determine the images to which they are associated or opposed.

Two new criteria will help to clarify how situations make sense: the *self-evidence* criterion, pointing in particular to what interviewees consider as normality, and the *opposition* criterion, which makes it possible to deepen the implicit contrasts that structure their cultural universes of meaning.

Self-evidence (or association) criterion

This criterion aims to identify how words make sense owing to the terms and situations with which they are associated. These associations are regularly presented in the form of self-evidence of which, by definition, speakers can hardly be aware.

When a Cameroonian executive mentions 'promotions that are decided in a discretionary way, in a tribal way or through acquaintances', he juxtaposes—as an explanatory equality—the arbitrary appearance of a decision and a reason that would be based on a regional or personal link. The equivalence thus formulated is sometimes discreetly underlined by a formula of the type 'that is to say'. Another states: 'We realise [that at the bank] you have to have pressure, *that is*, a personal relationship', thus underscoring the logical equality of these two terms.

The self-evidence which guides people's interpretations is sometimes identifiable through innocuous tags such as *it means, it is obvious, of course, isn't it, constantly, anybody*, etc. Judgements qualified as *natural* often cover cultural presuppositions. In the same vein as before, a Cameroonian small and medium-sized enterprise (SME) owner explains:

> Theoretically, [the bank] doesn't need to know if you are the brother of the grandmother of the uncle of the aunt of the little sister of the great-grandfather of so and so. That has nothing to do with it. Or if we lived together in high school, if we went to eat the little corn porridge doughnuts next door together. The bank doesn't need any of that! In principle. However, it is true that if the banker is Dad's friend, we stand a better chance to have credit [laughs] (in Henry and al., 1991).

Several inclusions—*theoretically, in principle, it is true*—underline the obvious strength of personal ties which eventually prevail over management rules. If the bank wants to ignore them, it cannot completely ignore their richness and complexity (*the brother of the grandmother of... the great-grandfather*), which is summarized in a simplified formula (*he is dad's friend*) and which finally prevails (*it is true that... we stand a better chance*). Several of our criteria support this reasoning. The self-evidence criterion is reinforced both by *redundancy* (friendship, kinship) and *embarrassment* (the laughter that underlines the contrast between the official rules and the real criteria). Several criteria confirm the idea that personal relationships play a powerful role or, at least, that they are an obvious explanation for any decision for which the reason is unknown.

The particular self-evidences of a culture form a pair of glasses through which the members of that culture interpret life in society. Seen from outside this culture, they either attract attention by their strangeness or simply go unnoticed: what is self-evident for some people will escape others' eyes. Detecting nothing strange could point to the self-evidence criterion, or indicate a criterion of *invisibility* (or *non significance*).

One's '*métier*' (profession)—an unquestioned self-evidence in the French culture—has little resonance in many cultures. We saw earlier that, in the French context, the reference to 'what you are'—your profession and its various incarnations—keeps appearing (*redundancy*). One's classification in a certain professional position comes along with the mention of the corresponding duties and rights: '*Engineers* in France,' explains a plant manager, 'tend to [think]: well, it's *quite obvious* that *I have to* run my own thing.' In this remark, being an engineer evidently entails: a) a compelling self-obligation—*tend to [think] I have to...*—b) the borders of which are rather blurred—*I have to run...*—and, c) which is attached to a strong sense of appropriation—*my own thing*. One's '*métier*'—whatever profession the word may refer to—implies a whole set of rights and obligations. In other French-speaking cultures, the word loses this semantic density. It is rarely used in Tunisia, and when it appears in Franco-Tunisian projects it does not carry the same semantic depth. In Cameroon, where its use is more frequent, a complementary study would show that it refers more to the existence of technical procedures. When a Cameroonian executive explains: 'Relationships count, living together with people has an influence, even on the *métier*', he underlines the objective nature—that is, not connected to people—of the rules of a '*métier*'. Such muted insensibility to the vision of personal and extended obligations attached to one's professional status is to be found in most cultures. While, in France, it is the backdrop of such simple sentences as *it is my job* or *it is not my job*, it will remain invisible to many other cultures.

In conclusion, the self-evidence criterion highlights logics that lie hidden under a double layer of invisibility: one internal so obvious that interested parties are unable to discern it clearly; the other external which observers find difficult to perceive, because it is unknown and means nothing to them. Analysis makes it possible to gradually dissociate the interwoven meanings and extract their signification from the different social situations with which the words are associated.

Opposition criterion

This criterion aims to identify a peculiar type of evidence, consisting of oppositions—positive vs. negative—that structure social representations, and with which members of a culture associate aspects that they consider respectable or desirable or, conversely, detestable or intolerable (see Chapter 3, p. 59).

In the French context, there is a series of such recurring oppositions (d'Iribarne, 1989): great/small, high/low, intelligent/stupid, generous/self-interested, free/submissive, doing a service/being at the service, noble/vile. While there may be quite a few such pairs within a given culture, their number is not indefinite. They do not come in perfect and repetitive forms (as was the case for redundancy): some of their terms are interchangeable, for example, on the positive side, *large* may be replaced by *high*, *generous*, etc. Sometimes, other rarer words are quite revealing, for example, on the negative side, *petty*, *kneeling down*, *bowing to*, etc. However, their connotations may vary, even be just the opposite, depending on the context of use. Whereas *bowing to others* is despicable—and even more so to someone who is greater than oneself—*bowing to reason* is respectable: it shows one's intelligence. The corresponding images strongly structure the cultural universe of meaning.

It is therefore not simply a question of identifying the multiple oppositions—particularly of values—that permeate social life, but of distinguishing the common rationale, based itself on a deeper opposition, underpinning the superficial oppositions. The reading of an article published by five French intellectuals will illustrate the analysis process. The text aims to alert policy-makers to the threat that secondary school teachers may be devaluated and to the urgent need to address the issue (Box 16.2, p. 321). Firstly, we will show how, under a controversial staging, the features opposing what is acceptable or unacceptable in the eyes of the authors appear. We will then consider the emergence of an image of decline in which these traits take on meaning.

To highlight the seriousness of the situation, the authors contrast the eminent image of the role of teachers with that of *socio-cultural animators*, which is not very bright—or perhaps even despicable. If we examine the above extract, we can draw up a list of positive and negative traits which reveals the implicit hierarchy underpinning the authors' comments. At the top of the scale (Table 16.1, p. 322), you find the teachers (left column) characterized as *good teachers*, endowed with a *mission*, *pedagogy* and located in *schools*. At the other end, the animators (right-hand column) are labelled *subcontractors* deprived of specific places (*living spaces*), likely to use *demagogy*, and subordinated to the *media system*.

Box 16.2 The mission of teachers: excerpt

High school students' sudden burst of protest is legitimate. At first somewhat confused, the government seems, all things considered, to see in it an opportunity to accelerate a reform aimed at *impeaching* teachers [*'professeurs'*, the word used in French is not neutral] and *challenging* their discipline. (...) *Disregarded, humiliated,* teachers are tired of having to appear every day before the social success and media system *tribunals.* They are *not just service providers.* They have *a mission* that it is high time for the highest officials of the Republic *to recognize and honour*: they are not only supposed to train skilled workers likely to find employment, they must also open up future citizens to *the intelligibility of the world....*

Pedagogy is no *demagogy.* Public education *must not* become *a subcontracting* of social communication (...) In any case, to make them good teachers, *disqualifying* future teachers *has to stop.*

True, the high school population has changed (...) Does this mean that in order to raise 80% of an age group to the baccalaureate level, it was necessary to *complete the transformation of teachers into socio-cultural animators* and schools into *'living spaces'*?

Élisabeth Badinter, Régis Debray, Alain Finkielkraut, Élisabeth de Fontenay, Catherine Kintzler, 'Souvenez-vous des professeurs' ('Remember Teachers'), *Le Monde*, 25–26 November 1990.

The disqualifying of teachers is represented in the descent from an elevated to a lower position (reading the table columns from left to right). It appears in the underpinning registers of the *noble* and *non-noble* recurrent categories in the French culture—on the positive side: *mission, public education, the intelligibility of the world* and on the negative side: *simple, providers, social communication,* and *training workers.* The argument draws its strength from the echo of what for French readers is a violent opposition. Beyond this opposition, the authors shed further light on the deeper mechanism underpinning it: on the one hand, socio-cultural animators are only executors, reduced to applying what they are dictated to do, and dedicated to frivolous tasks such as games and entertainments. On the other hand, teachers are the owners of their own thinking (*their pedagogy*), which they seem to have inherited, through their predecessors (*the discipline*), from the philosophers of the Enlightenment (*opening up future citizens to the intelligibility of the world*).

Under a succession of plans—teachers/animators; high/low; noble/non-noble—the key to the teachers' *'impeachment'* emerges, making the underpinnings of their nobility and the way in which it may be recovered appear (see middle column, top

Table 16.1 The mission of teachers: analysis

The teachers (*professeurs*)	***impeached*, challenged disregarded, humiliated, tired, [compelled to] appear before the media system court, disqualified, i.e. *to complete transformation* of teachers**	**Socio-cultural animators**
Pedagogy Schools Good teachers Discipline [endowed with] a mission Public instruction Open up future citizens to the intelligibility of the world	*A mission* that it *is high time* the *highest officials* (...) should recognize and *honour*	Demagogy Living spaces Just service providers Subcontracting Social communication The tribunal of success

to bottom). Indeed, teachers do not seem to be compelled to obey any authority other than that of their discipline: *the highest officials of the Republic*, who, according to a managerial logic, might be expected to set their objectives, are not invited to do so. Conversely, they are called upon to *recognize* and *honour* the mission that has been bequeathed upon teachers by those who preceded them, and which, as such, is their property. Teachers perceive the denial of their heritage as a forfeiture aimed at subordinating them to the *social success tribunal*; it fully justifies their urgent appeal: *it is high time that...* they be restored in their greatness.

The mission, which was bequeathed upon them, is the source of their nobility, especially since, in this case, it bears the unalterable mark of the Enlightenment. Hence, respecting it is the key to the salvation of teachers and beyond, that of their students and of society at large.

Conflicts and antagonisms between members of a society are generally underpinned by the specific logics of their culture. Their clashes do not reveal the culture directly but indirectly in the way they oppose each other, as they point to what is, and what is not, of value for all. Highlighting these oppositions is the way to proceed and it is only by connecting them to more general images that their full meaning emerges.

16.2.3 Level Three: Coherence, Horizontality

The objective of the third level criteria is, on the basis of the already identified clues, to infer images in which these indications make sense; this is probably the level that best characterizes our approach. It consists in moving from a collection of clues to a structured and coherent representation of a culture (d'Iribarne, 2011).

Analyses are conducted on a trial and error basis, so as to grasp the global images that feed the social representations which implicitly serve to qualify what to reject or to desire. Entering the specific hermeneutical circle of the culture under scrutiny is the way to decipher it (it has nothing to do with measuring its values on a universal grid). Analysis does not rely on *deductions*—property A presupposing and consequently leading to B—or *inductions*—property A being generalizable to set of A elements. Reasoning proceeds by *abductions*, that is, constructing images within which scattered elements find coherence—just as what is done in criminal investigations, or by assembling the pieces of a puzzle. These images must then be checked to see if indeed they are the backdrop which, beyond what separates the interviewees, inspires their way of perceiving and thinking. The last two criteria—coherence and horizontality—are meant to help in this process.

Coherence criterion

The aim is to bring together the various clues—heterogeneous or contradictory as they may appear—in order to compose overall images likely to give the clues some coherence.

Researchers must imagine pictures similar to those which guide the gathering together of jigsaw puzzle pieces, or to the myth narratives which, in a given society, convey meaning and coherence to a variety of practices or representations. To do so, one has to use one's imagination, experience, and insight. However, it takes time. It requires a lot of going back-and-forth between the materials and the overall images that one is trying to sketch: examining the interviewees' formulations; discovering the logics underpinning their judgement; searching for the possible 'family likeness' between them likely to inspire more general figures; or assessing the vigour with which they underline what they value. Only by dint of such immersion in the material may the underpinning tonalities, the repeatedly-encountered distaste, or the underlying oppositions gradually emerge.

Interviewees invent formulas or sketch imaginary pictures, whose instrumental role for decoding is only understood afterwards. Let us return to the maintenance foreman's words in Saint-Jean-de-Maurienne (analysed retrospectively by d'Iribarne (1989, 2011)). Although remarkable, their profound logic was not clear from the outset. He had invented a narrative whose epic tone was conveying something essential:

> I started from the principle, and that's what I'm trying to ensure . . . that we have the full decision and responsibility when it comes to people's safety. I will give the order or I will personally cut the power myself, I would say at the limit for the whole plant, if I believe that at some point somebody is in danger. So, I admit that I won't feel embarrassed at all to do it [hesitation] without asking for anyone's opinion [hesitation]; immediately I will cut the power. I'll report back later. After that, other responsibilities will be taken on at other levels. I will not hesitate to

> instantly black out the factory if I feel that . . . it is part of my job as a technician, if I judge that there is danger and that we should not endanger anyone in any way (Foreman, in d'Iribarne, 1989).

The agent stages himself alone in a quasi-mythical narrative in order to avert what would represent a deadly danger for somebody. It compels him to take an immediate decision which will have considerable consequences—*to instantly black out the factory*—but which he takes without fear—*I won't feel embarrassed*—and in a sovereign way—*without asking for anyone's opinion*. The demonstration is intended to be representative of a fundamental principle in his eyes—*I started from the principle (. . .) I'm trying to ensure.*

As long as they deal with concrete subjects that concern them, interviewees can be very creative, using poetic expressions—metaphors, parables, or epic stories. It is no longer a question, as was the case with the previous criteria, of focusing one's attention on unusual turns of phrases in a local language, and on the logic that goes with them. When a Cameroonian interviewee talks about the influence of *Daddy's friend*, even if the expression conveys something interesting about the local social logic, it is only a popular language flourish. Conversely, when another speaks of the 'corridor of seriousness', he is inventing an image—it does not belong to the common language—in order to express the extreme rigour necessary for someone not to be influenced by their feelings, their interests, or personal relationships. Similarly, when a Frenchman speaks of 'the notion of overflow at the interfaces', he is trying to dress the frequent conflicts of sovereignty caused by a rather fuzzy reading of one's role in a more respectable conceptual form. Similarly, in Quebec, using the formulation 'the brother displaces the brother' is meant to emphasize the brutality of American-inspired rules for the allocation of positions (Segal, 2002). In Mexico, an interviewee praises their '[working] like *little ants* (. . .) carrying the same *small loads* (parejitos) that together build a *large and solid fortress*'. It conveys these workers' perception of being fragile individuals that have become efficient by acting together in an egalitarian and supportive manner (d'Iribarne, 2007a). Many formulas, which had been spotted in the interviews and made sense of afterwards, were finally acknowledged as emblematic of the culture under scrutiny.

Escaping the straitjacket of language, the expressiveness of such formulas sheds light on an essential mechanism: poetic expression. It is not directly related to language[4] and will easily filter through translation. Poetic surge tends to evoke 'direct emotion/language contact' to bring out 'the imprint of reality', to convey 'the live' and 'the fear emerging from no specific cause [that is its] driving force' (Emaz, 2009). It is a telling sign of a conviction that strives to be heard, the sign of a profound coherence. Highlighting the force which outcrops in these words remains to be done.

Some quotations are presented as the miniature of a 'central figure' (see Chapter 3, p. 59), which imprints its logic and provides coherence to the whole. To return to the

French foreman's quotation, not only did its theatrical form signal its importance, but the author was interconnecting several of the logics that we had already identified: a) the decisive reference to his professional position—*as a technician*; b) the self-prescription of obligations and powers that a given position entails—*if I feel that* (...) *it is part of my job, if I judge* (...) *that we should not*; c) the rather vague boundaries of one's domain—*full and complete responsibility for the whole plant*—and finally; d) his feeling of being the only one in charge, at the time under consideration—*after that, other responsibilities will be taken.*

This speech is not proffered by a great medical professor, but by a modest factory foreman. Nonetheless, it implicitly sketches the glorious figure of the *technician* who identifies with his role—a role from which he draws both the duties and the prerogatives to which he feels bound, and over which others (colleagues or superiors) have little control. This case bears a family resemblance with the aforementioned secondary school teachers' figure (Table 16.1). It completes its logic with its darker side: the instinctive fear that for lack of recognition one's professional status—whatever its 'greatness'—will lead to degeneration and servitude. The contrasts of this twofold narrative, its twofold power of attraction and repulsion, are what made the various statements collected in the Saint-Jean-de-Maurienne plant coherent (d'Iribarne, 1989).

The foreman's narrative contributed by highlighting the way in which French people conceive 'the manner in which an organization should function, attributing considerable significance to each métier, to its traditions, its status, the duties attached to it—to everything that sums up the honour of a *métier*' (d'Iribarne, 2011). Its coherence effect is apparent on two counts, through its poetic form which suggests a mix of self-evidences, judgements, emotions, and compelling reasons, and through the sharpness of a central image which gives unity to many remarks that at first looked rather disparate.

Finally, as we will see, logics such as those of the foreman's narrative are highly repetitive.

Horizontality criterion

A final criterion of horizontality makes it possible to verify both the representativeness of the previous features in various sectors and domains of social life, as well as on a national or regional scale, and their relative persistence over a long historical period.

Specific features, which were not obvious during the first readings, will stand out, appearing almost conspicuous and astonishingly frequent. We saw how the French figure of a professional haunted by the greatness of his or her '*métier*' highlighted the unity underpinning the diverse comments collected within the same plant (d'Iribarne, 1989). Other fields then complemented these initial observations and their permanence was verified in many managerial areas. In this book alone, the primacy given to the obligations dictated by 'what you are', rather than by the instructions you receive, has successively emerged in connection with management by objectives (Chapter 2, p. 36), leadership (Chapter 4, p. 89), safety procedures in nuclear power plants (Chapter 5, p. 103), customer relations at the post office (Chapter 8, p. 151), codes of ethics at Total (Chapter 9, p. 174), and with a cooperation project in Madagascar (Chapter 12, p. 240). Their profound similarity with the secondary school teachers is obvious: they, teachers, consider that the traditions which they have inherited dictate their objectives. The same logic appears again and again, be it to defend major causes—teachers' role in society—or to determine more modest details, for example, the department assistant's remark about the monitoring of fuel consumption which has *always* been monitored, followed by his 'it's not because we are told to do so' (d'Iribarne, 1989). He feels the need to remind the interviewer of what to him is self-evident: the traditions of his service will always be better than any hierarchical instruction.

Some features, once exposed, keep appearing, so much so that they provide a simple answer to the often-asked question of the statistical representativeness of the number of interviews. Obviously, a plant foreman's statement cannot be deemed representative of a global culture, nor of a corporate culture—nobody else reported such a way of operating—or of an informal rule. It emerged from its author's imagination alone. However, its underlying logics appear, more or less evidently, in almost all the interviews. Considering the probability that the same peculiar element—of the *as a technician* kind—should appear in almost all of your thirty interviews is sufficient to indicate that you are dealing with a characteristic trait (d'Iribarne, 2012a).[5] Not all the elements that constitute the coherence figure will systematically be repeated in every interview transcript, but the presence of one only echoes the others. In the story of the post office tellers (see Chapter 8, p. 151 and the exercise at the end of the chapter, p. 328) in less than one page, justifying one's way of acting according to *what one is* appears five times—not because actors disagree on the fact, but as a self-evidence on which they all draw.

Going back in history, not specifically looking for the origins of a cultural trait, but tracking the ancient embodiments of your central figures may occasionally highlight some of their characteristic features in a particularly raw light. While social forms, language, or institutions keep changing, their underpinning logics repeat themselves. 'The bringing together of materials stemming from very diverse epochs and very different contexts multiplies the chances of revealing clues about what is specific to a culture' (d'Iribarne, 2011). If you go back to the French Revolution, Emmanuel Sieyès, a member of the National Convention, provided a striking expression of the horror that those who bend to higher forces out of fear or self-interest should inspire. Going back even further, Montesquieu's statement clearly spelt out the duties that honour dictates to every single person according to their social position (see Chapter 3, p. 64).

The texts that allowed us to cross reference the deep logics of this or that culture belong to a wide variety of literary genres. We used the writings of the great political founders (The Federalist in the USA; Montesquieu, Sieyès, Tocqueville, in France); as well as works on history and social anthropology (Jacques Duby, William H. Sewell, for France; Clifford Geertz for Morocco); fiction (Marcel Proust in France; Octavio Paz in Mexico); epics and popular stories (Kim-Vân-Kiêu in Vietnam; and in Cameroon traditional tales that all showed the unfathomable duties of friendship—liable to even lead to sacrificing one's life—present in all the West African traditions explored); to name but a few.

16.3 Conclusion

Understanding the logics at work takes you from a position where nothing engages your attention—'The stranger', says an African proverb, 'has big eyes but sees nothing'—to that of someone able to perceive the underpinning salient features in ever new formulations. Reality does not necessarily match the images that people have of their own culture or that they seek to convey. But these images influence the way in which management situations make sense for them as well as their way of acting.

The knowledge you acquire about a culture becomes richer with the exploration of each new field or social issue. It does not reduce itself to a few objective and solidified logics. You keep entering their reinterpretations, similarly to what takes place when you are acquiring the subtleties of a foreign language. By multiplying the cases we scrutinized in France, not only did we find everywhere the same readiness to introduce *what one is* to explain one's words and acts, but we enriched our understanding of the diversity of organizational settings that were compatible with the French culture (Segal, 2009).

The interpretation of a culture is, for one part, a subjective process. One's reading will inevitably be influenced by one's pair of glasses—hence the detectable French imprint in the writing of this book, particularly in the conviction that one must first assess a situation and understand it before acting, rather than directly provide empirical solutions. For another part, interpretation relies on experimental verification, as illustrated in the various criteria presented. Sometimes, additional verification intervenes through comments proffered by members of a culture exclaiming: 'When I read you, I figured that you could have been describing my own factory, my own office, my own hospital, my own organisation' (d'Iribarne, 2011).

This kind of understanding makes it possible to get past a flat and oversimplified—even erroneous—vision of a culture, and perceive the logics that give new relief and colours to the ways in which the members of that culture conceive human intercourse. To date, only a limited number of descriptions exist that highlight the functioning of businesses and economic policies. Shedding light more systematically on the way in which innovations can be conducted based on an understanding of the major properties that characterize a given cultural area will be beneficial. Just as one does not have to immediately grasp all the subtleties of the language one is acquiring, one does not need to master all the subtleties of a culture to better understand what its members deem proper. One can start by discerning the general regularities that are essential to a better understanding of the way in which the members of a society think and act together.

16.4 Illustrative Exercise: The Training Session for Post Office Tellers

The training session for the French post office tellers reported in Hanique (2004: 202), stages tellers and a trainer as they strongly confront one another. It provides a good illustration of how the 'criteria' can be applied.

16.4.1 Training for sales in France

The scene takes place during a training session of tellers through role-playing expected to enable them to develop sales. In particular, they have to learn how to deal with a 'grumpy and conservative' client. The transcribed exchange begins when the trainer interrupts one of the tellers as she performs the exercise:

THE TRAINER: *You are La Poste [the Post Office]. So, say instead: 'La Poste offers you' or 'La Poste commits itself'. You must think of the best that La Poste can offer.*

CORINNE: *What's better for them or better for La Poste?*

THE TRAINER: *It's the same thing. La Poste offers the best for its customers.*

[Chuckles, mockery...]

THE TRAINER: *Your job is to satisfy your customers, that is, to respond to their requests and identify their latent needs. For example, if a customer presents himself with a package that he has made himself, tell him that La Poste offers a range of ready-to-ship products that guarantee a safe delivery.*

SANDRA: *When I am a customer somewhere, I trust someone when I know that what they are offering me is what they would have chosen for themselves. And at the counter, when I see that customers arrive with a well-made, well-wrapped package, I don't see why I would honestly tell them to unpack their package and pay three times the delivery price to buy a La Poste parcel!*

THE TRAINER: *Well, that's a mistake! To be confident, customers need to have real professionals in front of them. And real professionals are tellers who know their products. There you go. The client does not come to see 'any Joe Bloggs', who 'in their place' would do like this or that, but Sandra,*

Corinne or Jackie who are professional tellers. You must not put yourself in their shoes.

SANDRA: *That's for sure, if we put ourselves in their shoes, we wouldn't sell much.*

The exercise consists in carrying out the following analyses, all the time remaining as close as possible to the text:

1. Underline what opposes the protagonists of this scene, in order to gradually identify the logics on which they deeply agree and on which precisely they ground their opposed points of views.
2. Identify the elements of the story that correspond to each of the seven criteria (redundancy, strangeness, embarrassment, self-evidence, opposition, coherence, horizontality). If necessary, make a note of the elements of the text that fall under several criteria at once.
3. Highlight the broader images from which the different elements draw to make sense.
4. Finally, with the help of this interpretation framework, reread the scene and show how the divergences between the actors take on even greater importance.

16.4.2 Sequence analysis

The trainer and the tellers clash on two conceptions of customer service. For the trainer, it is a matter of getting closer to the market—*satisfying one's customer*, considered as a statistical category—by providing streamlined product *ranges*, a guarantee of *safe* delivery, and *professional* information at the counter. This development is linked to a general context—not described in the text—of competitive tendering of public services, of searching for greater efficiency and greater profitability of the services. For their part, the tellers criticize this new orientation, which they consider too commercial. They defend the idea of a more personalized service—*putting themselves in the customer's shoes*—and less directly subject to profitability requirements. This debate, which seems standard on the surface, appears to be fraught with deep resentment, as can be guessed from the mentioned *giggles* and *mockery* (embarrassment criterion). The cultural analysis will show that, behind this conflict between two traditional visions of customer service, the debate actually rests on the sensitive issue of the dignity of a teller's job. However, to grasp this, you must start by uncovering the interpretation framework which is common to the protagonists of the scene.

All the actors (trainer and tellers) refer, as an essential reference point, to the various roles encountered at a counter—*you are the post office*; *when I am a customer, [When] at the counter, I see; real professionals are*...; and even *any Joe Bloggs who* (redundancy criterion). And in the minds of the interlocutors, each of these *roles* automatically comes along with certain types of behaviours: *you are the post office, so, say; [as] a customer (...) I trust someone who...; at the counter (...), I don't see why...; [as] a real professional (...) you must not put yourself in their shoes*; and also *any Joe Bloggs (...) would do like this or like that.* In the minds of all these actors, *what one is* implicitly determines the way in which one is supposed to act (self-evidence criterion).

In another register, the word *seller*—and all the words evoking sales: *sale, trade* or *profit*—the use of which would be logical concerning a post office counter—are absent from this exchange (the silence criterion (symmetrical to the redundancy criterion)). The teller replaces it by the circumlocution: *someone who proposes.* And the trainer prefers the words *professional* and *teller.* Seen from a purely economic perspective—here the commercial act strangely consists of *proposing, committing, guaranteeing,* etc. (strangeness criterion). This strangeness phenomenon also applies to the elements previously identified as redundant and self-evident, thus reinforcing their cultural singularity.

According to the tellers, the company's and its customers' interests would be mutually exclusive, or even conflicting—*Better for [customers] or better for the Post Office?* Their question casts doubt by insinuating that such an interest would be unacceptable, fundamentally illegitimate. For both the trainer and the tellers, the words *trade, profit,* worse even *interest* or *money* are naughty words. For all of them, the figure of the *professionals who propose* (the trainer) is the positive opposite of the shameful image of *selling a lot* (a teller). The protagonists in this debate may confront each other, but their arguments are based on a common opposition structure (opposition criterion): proposing vs. selling; free vs. interest. Everyone implicitly agrees that a post office agent should offer and not sell out of interest, in the same way that, even in Molière's time (horizontality criterion), Mr Jourdain's father *was not a merchant* but '*he had a good knowledge of fabrics*' and '*he gave some to his friends for money*'.[6]

The participants in this training session all assume that you must offer clients what is best for them. Their conflict is not about that, but about who should define what is best. Further along, they agree on the fact that it is not up to customers to decide on the subject. The tellers highlight their ability to substitute themselves to them—*what [I] would have chosen for [myself]*—and it is not dictated by empathy. They assume that it is up to them to decide on the technical aspects: *When I see that customers arrive with a well-made, well-wrapped package, I don't see why I would tell them to undo it.* They consider themselves in charge of judging what a *good* package is and of deciding to have it undone! The trainer is in line with the same logic. If he denies the tellers the power to put themselves in the shoes of a particular customer, he considers that the company has that power, according to an obvious principle: 'Satisfying customers', *that is*, 'responding to their requests and identifying their *latent* needs.' Responding to clients' requests is not enough, they are supposed to appreciate their *latent* needs better than the clients themselves can. When the trainer invites the tellers to apply the procedures for the new products—to no avail—he is only following that principle. The figure of professionals acting according to their own judgement and not because they submit to clients' requirements echoes many other observations gathered in French companies (horizontality criterion). In this exchange, it is again shared here by all the participants.

Starting from the internal logic of the story, one discovers the fear at the heart of the tellers' revolt. Postal workers do not fear competition, the productivity requirement, or the evolution of the public service; they are worried that their job might be devaluated. The trainer incidentally lifted the veil on the risk of forfeiture that they are facing. The post office management seems to be ignoring their competence. It is taking over the tellers' competence by pretending to reduce their role to the sale of standard products. Deprived of their ability to place themselves as advisors or judges above their customers, they fear that they will from now on be perceived as low-quality saleswomen, at the mercy of an already capricious clientele quick to show disrespect. The mere sale of a range of predefined products that their trainer is promoting seems very thin to give back some lustre to their already weakened position. For complementary readings, see the reference images specific to the French context in Chapter 3 (p. 64) and the interpretation of this case in Chapter 8 (p. 151).

Several years have passed since that session. The economic, social, and technical problems have obviously evolved, as tellers' roles and mentalities have. However, while the precise terms of this debate may have changed considerably, it is clear that the central fear expressed during this dispute—that of being deprived of one's professional position as a result of the commodification of public services—persists. There is little doubt that this deep fear continues to refract in French social and professional relations, underlining the coherence and permanence of the logics observed.

Notes

1. We borrow several of his formulations. However, for a more complete presentation of the theoretical principles underpinning this approach, the reader may read d'Iribarne (2011, pp. 51–79, 2012).
2. For France, the reader may turn to d'Iribarne (1989, 2008) and Segal (2009), for the USA to d'Iribarne (1989), for Cameroon to Henry (2002), for Tunisia to Yousfi (2017).
3. Whenever we felt it necessary, we added emphasis to the interview transcripts.
4. While this kind of poetry stems from individual creativity, other researchers consider the way in which the logic of a given language may shape the social representations of the

corresponding culture, e.g. François Jullien's work on the 'folds of thought' imposed by the Chinese language.

5. When drawing lots, the probability in a thirty-trial-set that the same side of the coin should turn up—for instance thirty times heads—is higher than one out of a billion $(1/2)^{30}$. An experience that would have reached that score would be deemed sufficient to demonstrate that the coin used is endowed with a special property... or has been tampered with.
6. Molière, *Le Bourgeois gentilhomme* (1670), Act 4/Scene 3.

Conclusion

Making the Most of Culture Understanding

Management sciences have long ignored the cultural embedding of organizations. They consider that economic globalization brings a powerful dynamic of standardization that marginalizes cultural differences in the business world. Sometimes, these differences are seen as being reduced to habits and customs that affect the life of firms or international organizations only on minor points such as respecting punctuality in appointments or expressing straightforward criticism. They consider that the core of management—organizing activities to best serve the interests of stakeholders—will not be affected. Sometimes, too, these differences are perceived as survivors of traditions that will have to be eradicated if modernity and efficiency are to finally triumph. Consequently, best practices, presumably universal, should be established throughout the world. However, in real life, cultures resist.

Established Theories are Inadequate

A great deal of the research carried out over the past forty years has led to a change of perspective and to taking this resistance of cultures seriously. It has mainly sought to characterize each culture by a few scores as more or less hierarchical, individualistic, masculine, and open to uncertainty, as was done by Geert Hofstede (1980), whose research represented a decisive breakthrough. These first studies (Hampden-Turner et al, 1993; Schwartz, 1994; Trompenaars et al., 2011) were very valuable in showing the business world that it is unrealistic to ignore cultural diversity. However, their contributions show limits that cannot be overcome by simply enriching the set of indexes that are used. That approach is both misleading and enlightening. It tends to suggest that there is a mechanical link between the cultural context and people's ways of acting. It does not illuminate the processes through which culture deeply influences these ways of acting without determining them. At the same time, the attempt to reduce cultures to a few scores leads you to imagine that comparing the respective scores of these cultures makes it possible to understand the relationships between those who have different cultural references. Here again, it is highly tempting to see these relationships as

Cross-Cultural Management Revisited: A Qualitative Approach. Philippe d'Iribarne, Sylvie Chevrier, Alain Henry, Jean-Pierre Segal, and Geneviève Tréguer-Felten, Oxford University Press (2020).
DOI: 10.1093/oso/9780198857471.001.0001

shaped by a kind of fatality, ignoring the room for manoeuvre from which the protagonists can draw to find appropriate operating modes.

From a business perspective, there are, within each cultural context, a number of ways of doing things that are more or less effective. Therefore, in situations where inefficiency persists, one would be condemned to choose between two equally problematic options. You either give up and sadly say that culture is responsible and that there is nothing you can do about it; or you face an impossible task of trying to bend that culture in order to comply with international standards. The critical search for management practices, which, in each location, would make efficiency possible, is neglected.

In contrast to this deterministic vision, a post-modern school of thought emphasizes protagonists' autonomy and agency. For its supporters, there may, at some point, exist usual ways of doing things, dominant representations, within a given social group, but they are only local and transitional. Swift social change and the fragmentation of contemporary societies are incompatible with the vision of an overarching national culture. This is a move from one extreme to the other. An analogy between language and culture helps to clarify this point. Everyone's speech can be creative; it will occasionally introduce new words, and a community often develops its own jargon. Nevertheless, these inventions are grafted onto a pre-existing language. Speech, even if its style appears new and singular, always borrows from the substratum of the language in which it is delivered, even though it may transgress certain rules and innovate. As translators know well, language offers very wide possibilities of expression but it also constrains. It may compel speakers to provide some information and restrict expression in other cases. Similarly, a matrix of cultural references is compatible with a wide range of social practices, albeit with limitations. Not everything is possible. By focusing on the inventiveness of each discourse, post-modern analysis somehow neglects the shared language which allows that specific discourse to exist and be understood by others while framing the possibilities of expression. Whereas employees constantly renew their practices through interactions which combine negotiations and power relations, they cannot create them from scratch. Ignoring this fact suggests that any practice could be adopted in any context, provided that one knows how to successfully play a game of negotiation and power. This is illusionary.

This book opens a path that bypasses the aforementioned theoretical deadlocks. It provides an alternative approach which allows people to draw creatively on the resources of each culture while being aware that some practices will not be acceptable. We did not start with a preconceived approach to cultures, trying at all costs to use them to address concrete management issues. On the contrary, we began by examining management issues in some fifty countries and territories across all five continents. These issues involved cultural aspects, ranging from the difficulties in implementing so-called 'universal' management tools to the problematic functioning of intercultural teams. We witnessed the pivotal role played by the ways social relations are conceived, a role that management sciences tend to neglect. Any act of management, any implementation of a procedure or a rule, of a way of deciding, of controlling, or of managing a relation with a client, is inseparable from the social relation connecting those involved. It inevitably implies exercising power, arbitrating between persons whose interests and opinions are in conflict, or serving someone else. These social relations are the source of emotions and reactions that may be very strong. This is one of the reasons why the 'human dimension' is a recurrent issue in the management of organizations, including in its apparently most rational aspects. It is through these social relationships that the cultural context intervenes. The manner in which each way of acting, in companies and in social life in general, makes sense for the employees, and the reactions it provokes, depend closely on the meaning of the social relations at stake in that cultural context.

This is true for a way of giving instructions or evaluating an employee; for being flexible or rigid in the implementation of a contract; for dealing with a customer, etc. When you observe different situations in the same cultural context, different firms, different departments within a company, different dimensions of management, you encounter extremely diverse practices, and these practices change over time. Hence, practices cannot be used to characterize a culture. There is much more unity in the way in which people give meaning to the situations that they experience and in the kind of questions that they ask about them. For instance, in the United States: 'Am I in a position to control my destiny?'; in France: 'Is what I am asked to do worthy of me?'; in Cameroon: 'Are those who present themselves as my friends really my friends?' We have shown in this book that the fundamental management issues are all deeply influenced by the interpretation framework that prevails in a particular cultural area. The further you advance in the research, the more you find, in each context, a common denominator for a whole series of elements that did not seem related at first. As you proceed in your investigations, you uncover the consistency of a set of behaviours and statements that initially seemed to have no common ground.

When we initiated our research, cultures—elements of unity and stability in modern societies, but at the same time very diverse socially and shaped by history—were not accounted for. Culture was an unidentified sociological object. From our observational data, we gradually constructed a theoretical framework to conceptualize this object, making it a grounded theory. The early inspiration, which owed much to Montesquieu and Tocqueville, was based on the idea of a correspondence, in each society, between the universe of rules—the institutions, the result of a desire to organize—and that of a largely unconscious cultural framework, a 'spirit of the laws' (see Montesquieu, *L'esprit des lois*). As research progressed, we benefited from various schools of thought, including the interpretative approach to cultures which was particularly valuable, even if applying such an approach to modern societies required significant innovation.

Listen to Stakeholders and Decipher their Speech!

The reason why this interpretative approach, based on the observation of management situations, had not yet been explored was probably linked to the fact that the approach to cultures referring to the attitude scales model had become obvious to most people. It may also be because the approach we followed requires direct access to companies and organizations; these companies, eager to control their image, are often reluctant to welcome researchers. Moreover, faced with pressing operational priorities, they are generally not ready to tackle complex sociological questions. Hence, researchers usually opt for easier questionnaire-based surveys. But the practitioners who called on us to help them analyse in depth the difficulties they were encountering, or to better understand unexpected successes and find ways to generalize them, concluded that the requirements of the approach were largely offset by its results, not only in terms of understanding what was happening but also in identifying leverages for action.

A prime way to capture the cultural context prevailing in a given country consists in listening to the employees and taking an interest in the prism through which they perceive the situations in which they live, in other words, their framework of interpretation. As was shown chapter after chapter, this prism is reflected in their words, in the phrases they use to talk about their experience. Where we progressed the most in the understanding of the cultural context, we discovered that the way in which employees give meaning to their experience and evoke it in their discourse echoes an element that permeates their existence in all its dimensions. That element is a concern, an existential anxiety, associated with a burning question, a sensation that there is a threat which it is vital to overcome, in words and actions. For instance, in the American context, the fear of not being in control of one's destiny is part of this type of anxiety. Our research has shown that the objects that crystallize anxiety vary from one cultural area to another. It is a central element of a culture that seems capable of surviving through the greatest economic, social, and political upheavals. The dominant fears that are at the heart of a universe of meaning play a major role in the forms of collective life regulation that have taken shape over time in the context under scrutiny. This is because a major objective of this regulation is to protect the people from what they fear most.

Practices Change, but References Remain

The endless debates between those who invoke the unity and stability of cultures and those who oppose them with the diversity and instability of practices stems from the misleading identification of cultures with practices. Even though, in a given cultural area, the fundamental features of a universe of meaning seem to defy time, this cultural context leaves the door wide open for the workforce to make their own choices and be creative. For example, whereas each culture has an image of what virtuous authority should be—a central reference in the judgement that employees make about how they are governed—it does not mean that leaders act in accordance with this image on a daily basis. For instance, in French companies, there may be leaders who do not have the expected vision ('*hauteur de vue*') or settle certain decisions that are long in being taken, but this seriously compromises their credibility and legitimacy within their teams. Conversely, as was seen in some chapters, particularly concerning Morocco and Tunisia, some managers will find innovative ways to embody the virtuous authority figure. Their practices differ from those that typically prevail around them, but they are well appreciated by employees.

The challenge for management is not to modernize against tradition. What is at stake is changing practices so that they serve the organizational objectives and take on a positive meaning in the given cultural universe of meaning. The point is to innovate by making the most of cultures; the required congruence with the interpretation framework does not imply inertia, quite the contrary. In many places, the gap between usual management practices and the employees' cultural references means that there is considerable room for developing more suitable practices. Whenever imported management methods are not well received, explicitly rejected, or generating silent resistance, they disappoint their advocates. Often, the next reform leads to their being abandoned. In such situations, the approach developed in this book helps to analyse the failures and understand what motivates the employees. Then, with full awareness of the context, it makes it possible to correct the situation. Managers can imagine practices which employees will heartily adopt because of their positive meaning. This similarly applies to international transfers of management tools or to business partnerships, regardless of their legal status (acquisition, merger, alliance, consortium, etc.).

Our research began in the 1980s, just before globalization emerged as a major topic for social sciences. Since then, societies have become increasingly multicultural, and highly internationalized organizations are emblematic of this diversity. More and more mobile individuals were born in one country and educated in another by parents who may have different cultural backgrounds. In this context of cultural interbreeding and heterogeneity, do cultural logics, most often associated with countries, still exist? Experience shows that these logics do not disappear. Just as there are bilingual individuals, there are bicultural individuals, capable of passing, depending on the circumstances, from one set of cultural references to another. But these references are still very much present.

Initially inspired by approaches that concerned political institutions rather than companies (d'Iribarne 1996, 2003), our field work has mainly focused on the latter. However, this new approach to cultures does not only concern them; the influence of these cultural logics extends to all institutions.

Launching Further Research

At this stage of our research programme, the theoretical framework is consolidated and has been tested on all continents. The universe of meaning of large cultural areas has progressively been revealed. France, the starting point of the research, is now extensively documented, as are the United States, the Netherlands, and part of West Africa. However, there are still many countries in which the work we have already carried out can be extended. In some of them, our understanding of fundamental fears has started, but remains fragmented. In some other cultural areas, such as Russia, we have not yet carried out any investigation. Besides, the research undertaken on how to support the implementation of management methods must also be pursued.

Based on the theoretical and methodological approach presented in this book and on existing work in many geographical areas, tremendous improvements can be made in the cultural contextualization of management practices. The scope of application is very broad. Whether firms are being transformed with the implementation of new tools or managerial methods, or whether they are becoming more international, the managers of these changes have a vested interest in questioning the meaning that employees give to the changes. As was demonstrated throughout this book, while practitioners are often good observers of the behaviours of their peers from other cultures, they spontaneously project their own cultural interpretations on these behaviours. If they do not decipher the meaning from the point of view of the employee or partner, there is a strong risk of entering a spiral of misunderstandings, disengagement, and even resistance. This results in tensions, delays in processes, poor productivity, and quality concerns. Consequently, significant human and financial costs emerged that are difficult to assess precisely because they are spread over time, distributed among the entities involved, and therefore less easily measurable. If, instead, business leaders stopped downplaying the difficulties they are facing as they attempt to protect their organization's reputation, and took the time to explore staff's cultural interpretations, then the improvements in commitment, engagement, loyalty, and ultimately social performance could be significant.

The cultural roots of the social worlds are deep and cannot be tackled by simply raising awareness of what can be considered as 'folklore' differences. Economic organizations, which are the main focus of this book, are not the only ones concerned. International institutions are also primarily concerned. However, as the authors have experimented, the denial of cultural differences prevails in both the World Bank and the European Commission. The universalist economic perspective, which ignores cultural frameworks, entails serious implications for the development of international institutions, and serious consequences both for the development of the poorest countries and for European integration. When cultural differences are mentioned they are assimilated to superficial habits, which does not allow a thorough understanding of the cultural dynamics at work. An approach that seeks to disseminate good practices without focusing on their meaning for the workforce does not have any significant long-term effectiveness. Instead, the approach to culture as a universe of meaning opens up a wide range of opportunities for aligning social practices with interpretation systems. This is the path that has yet to be taken.

Bibliography

Aeschylus (1981), *The Persiansin Tragedies* (Oxford University Press).

Agar, Michael H. (1996), *The Professional Stranger: An Informal Introduction to Ethnography* (Academic Press).

Ailon-Souday, Galit and Kunda, Gideon (2003), 'The Local Selves of Global Workers: The Social Construction of National Identity in the Face of Organizational Globalization', *Organization Studies*, 24 (7), pp. 1073–96.

Alexander, Jeffrey C. (2005), *The Meaning of Social Life. A Cultural Sociology* (Oxford University Press).

Alexander, Jeffrey C. and Seidman, Steven (eds.) (1990), *Culture and Society: Contemporary Debates* (Cambridge University Press).

Alvesson, Mats (2002), *Understanding Organizational Culture* (Sage Publications).

Anderson, Benedict (1983), *Imagined Communities: Reflections on the Origin and Spread of Nationalism* (Verso).

Andriamanjato, Richard (2013), *Le Tsiny et le Tody dans la pensée malgache* (L'Herne).

Aristotle (2004), *The Nicomachean Ethics* (Penguin Books).

Arvis, Jean-François and Berstein, Ronald E. (2002), *Implementing Anticorruption Programs in the Private Sector: Lessons from East Asia* (The World Bank).

Ascencio, Chloé and Rey, Dominique (2004), *Etre efficace en Chine. Le management à l'épreuve de la culture chinoise* (Pearson).

Balandier, Georges and Sauvy, Alfred (1961), *Le Tiers-monde, sous-développement et développement (réédition augmentée d'une mise à jour par Alfred Sauvy)* (Travaux et documents, cahier n°39: PUF).

Bamber, Greg, et al. (2016), *International and Comparative Employment Relations: Globalisation, Regulation and Change* (Sage Publications).

Banfield, Edward C. (1958), *The Moral Basis of a Backward Society* (The Free Press).

Baremberg, Mark (1993), 'The Political Economy of the Wagner Act: Power Symbol and Workforce Cooperation', *Harvard Law Review*, 106, pp. 1379–450.

Barmeyer, Christoph and Davoine, Eric (2008), 'Ch. V 3. Culture et gestion en Allemagne: la "machine bien huilée"', in Eduardo Davel, Jean-Pierre Dupuis, and Jean-François Chanlat (eds.), *Gestion en contexte interculturel: approches, problématiques, pratiques et plongées* (Presses de l'Université Laval et Télé-Université (UQAM)).

Barmeyer, Christoph and Davoine, Eric (2011), 'The Intercultural Challenges of the Transfer of Codes of Conduct from the USA to Europe', in Henriet Primecz, Laurence Romani, and Sonja Sackmann (eds.), *Cross-cultural Management in Practice: Negotiated Meanings* (Edward Elgar), pp. 53–63.

Barmeyer, Christoph and Davoine, Eric (2013), '"Traduttore, Traditore"? La réception contextualisée des valeurs d'entreprise dans les filiales françaises et allemandes d'une entreprise multinationale américaine', *Management International/Gestiòn Internacional/International Management* 18 (1 Autumn), pp. 26–39.

Barmeyer, Christophand Davoine, Eric (2019), 'Facilitating intercultural negotiated practices in joint ventures: The case of a French–German railway organization'.*International Business Review*,28, (1) pp. 1–11.

Bartel-Radic, Anne (2009), 'La compétence interculturelle: état de l'art et perspectives', *Management International/Gestiòn Internacional/International Management*, 13 (4 Eté), pp. 11–26.

Bartlett, Christopher A. and Ghoshal, Sumantra (2002), *Managing Across Borders: The Transnational Solution* (Harvard Business Press).

Bazin, Laurent (1998), *Entreprise, Politique, Parenté, une perspective anthropologique sur la Côte d'Ivoire dans le monde actuel* (L'Harmattan).

Bellah, Robert N., et al. (1985), *Habits of the Heart, Individualism and Commitment in American Life* (University of California Press).

Bennett, Milton J. (1986), 'A Developmental Approach to Training for Intercultural Sensitivity', *International Journal of Intercultural Relations*, 10 (2), pp. 179–96.

Berger, Peter and Luckmann, Thomas (1989 [1966]), *The Social Construction of Reality* (Penguin Books).

Bhatia, Vijay K. and Lung, Jane (2006), 'Corporate Identity and Generic Integrity in Business Discourse', in Juan Carlos Palmer-Silveira, Miguel F. Ruiz-Garrido, and Immaculada Fortanet-Gómez (eds.), *Intercultural and International Business Communication* (Peter Lang), pp. 265–85.

Biernacki, Richard (1995), 'The Fabrication of Labor, Germany and Britain, 1640–1914', University of California Press.

Birkinshaw, Julian (2013), 'Management Ideology: The Last Bastion of American Hegemony'(The British Library).

Bjørge, Anne K. and Whittaker, Sunniva (2015), 'Corporate Values: A Linguistic Approach', *International Journal of Cross Cultural Management*, 15 (3), pp. 347–62.

Blenkinsopp, John and Shademan Pajouh, Maryam (2010), 'Lost in Translation? Culture, Language and the Role of the Translator in International Business', *Critical Perspectives on International Business*, 6 (1), pp. 38–52.

Bony, Jacqueline (de) (2007), 'Le consensus aux Pays-Bas, autonomie individuelle et coopération', *La Revue Française de Gestion*, 170, pp. 45–58.

Boudon, Raymond (2002), *Les méthodes en sociologie* (PUF). (English version: Boudon, R. (1981). *The logic of social action: An introduction to sociological analysis*, (Taylor & Francis)).

Bourguignon, Annick, Malleret, Véronique, and Norrekelit, Hanne (2002), 'L'irréductible dimension culturelle des instruments de gestion: l'exemple du tableau de bord et du *balanced scorecard*', *Comptabilité-Contrôle-Audit*, numéro spécial(Mai), pp. 7–32.

Bourrier, Mathilde (1999), *Le nucléaire à l'épreuve de l'organisation* (coll. Le travail humain, vol. 294: PUF).

Boyacigiller, Nakiye A., Kleinberg, Jill, Phillips, Margaret E., and Sackmann, Sonja A. (2004), 'Conceptualizing Culture: Elucidating the Streams of Research in International Cross-Cultural Management', in B.J. Punnet and O. Shenkar (eds.), *Handbook for International Management Research* (University of Michigan Press), pp. 99–167.

Brannen, Mary Yoko (2004), 'When Mickey Loses Face: Recontextualization, Semantic Fit, and the Semiotics of Foreignness', *Academy of Management Review*, 29 (4), pp. 593–616.

Bureau, René (1979), 'L'insertion des Africains dans l'industrie', *Revue Projet*, 139 (Novembre), pp. 1069–89.

Caratini, Sophie (2012), *Les non-dits de l'anthropologie* (Éditions Thierry Marchaisse).

Castel, Robert (1995), *Les métamorphoses de la question sociale* (Fayard).

Champy, James, and Cohen, Lawrence (1995), *Reengineering Management* (Dunod).

Chanlat, Jean-François and Pierre, Philippe (2018). *Le management interculturel: évolution, tendances et critiques* (Éditions ems).

Chanlat, Jean-François, Davel, Eduardo,Dupuis, Jean-Pierre (eds.) (2013), *Cross-Cultural Management: Culture and Management across the World* (Routledge).

Chapman, Malcolm (1996), 'Social Anthropology, Business Studies, and Cultural Issues', *International Studies of Management & Organization*, 26(4), pp. 3–29.

Charles, Mirjaliisa (2007), 'Language Matters in Global Communication', *Journal of Business Communication*, 44 (July), pp. 260–82.

Chevrier, Sylvie (1998), 'Le solide contre l'ingénieux : malentendus dans la gestion de projets franco-suisses', in Philipped'Iribarneet al. (eds.), Cultures et mondialisation. Gérer par-delà les frontières(Seuil), pp. 137–61.

Chevrier, Sylvie (2009), 'Empowerment: A Practice Embedded in Cultural Contexts. A Comparison Between the United States and France', in Carol D. Hansen and Yih-Teen Lee (eds.), *The Cultural Context of Human Resource Development* (Palgrave Macmillan), pp. 77–89.

Chevrier, Sylvie (2012a), *Gérer des équipes internationales. Tirer parti de la rencontre des cultures dans les organisations* (Presses de l'Université Laval).

Chevrier, Sylvie (2012b), 'Transfert de responsabilités dans les projets de coopération au développement: le cas d'une ONG franco-malgache', *Management International/Gestiòn Internacional/International Management*, 17 (1), pp. 103–16.

Chevrier, Sylvie (2016), 'Ch. 17 A Tough Day for a French Expatriate in Vietnam: the Management of a Large International Infrastructure Project', in Christoph Barmeyer and Peter Franklin (eds.), *Intercultural Management. A Case-Based Approach in Achieving Complementarity and Synergy* (Palgrave-Macmillan), pp. 228–39.

Chevrier, Sylvie and Segal, Jean-Pierre (2011), 'Coordination des équipes multiculturelles au sein des multinationales. Des acteurs en quête de modes d'emploi', *Revue Française de Gestion*, 212, pp. 145–56.

Chevrier, Sylvie and Khalfaoui, Liece (2018), 'Diversité culturelle et relations de pouvoir au coeur de l'innovation ordinaire', in Nadine Tournois and Philippe Véry (eds.), *Internationalisation ouverte* (Vuibert), pp. 65–88.

Chiapello, Eve and Gilbert, Patrick (2013), *Sociologie des outils de gestion. Introduction à l'analyse sociale de l'instrumentation de gestion* (La Découverte).

Confucius (1999), *The Analects* (Library of Chinese Classics: Hunan People's Publishing House—Foreign Languages Press).

Crozier, M. (1964), *The Bureaucratic Phenomenon.* (University of Chicago Press).

Crozier, Michel and Friedberg, Erhard (1977), *L'acteur et le système, les contraintes de l'action collective* (Seuil).

Dahl, Øyvind (1999), *Meanings in Madagascar: Cases of Intercultural Communication* (Greenwood Publishing Group).

David, Albert (en collaboration avec Hatchuel A. and Laufer, R.) (ed.), (2012), *Les nouvelles fondations des sciences de gestion* (Presse des Mines de Paris https://www.pressesdesmines.com/produit/les-nouvelles-fondations-des-sciences-de-gestion/).

Deal, Terrence E. and Kennedy, Allan A. (1982), *Corporate Cultures. The Rites and Rituals of Corporate Life* (Addison-Wesley Publishing Company).

Deguy, Michel (1985), *Définition de fonctions, évaluation des emplois* (Éditions d'Organisation).

Dickson, Marcus, et al. (2012), 'Conceptualizing Leadership Across Cultures', *Journal of World Business*, 47 (1), pp. 483–92.

Dietz, Graham, Gillespie, Nicole, and Chao, Georgia T. (2010), 'Unravelling the Complexities of Trust and Culture', in Mark N. K.Saunders, et al. (eds.), *Organizational Trust. A Cultural Perspective* (Cambridge University Press), pp. 3–41.

Dobbin, Frank (1994), *Forging Industrial Policy. The United States, Britain and France in the Railway Age* (University of California Press).

Drucker, Peter (1998), *Peter Drucker on the Profession of Management* (Harvard Business School Press).

Duan, Mingming (2010), 'Contrat et culture dans les relations interentreprises en Chine', *Management International/Gestiòn Internacional/International Management*, 14 (2), pp. 121–9.

Dupuis, Jean-Pierre (2013), 'Intercultural Analysis in Management: Decompartmentalizing the Classical approach', in Jean-François Chanlat, Eduardo Davel, Jean-PierreDupuis (eds.), *Cross-Cultural Management: Culture and Management Across the World* (Routledge), pp. 41–70.

Dupriez, Pierre and Simons, Solange (2002), *La résistance culturelle: fondements, applications et implications du management interculturel* (De Boeck Supérieur).

Dupuy, François (2005), La fatigue des élites (Seuil).

Earley, P. Christopher and Ang, Soon (2003), *Cultural Intelligence: Individual Interactions across Cultures* (Stanford University Press).

Eco, Umberto (1992), *Les limites de l'interprétation (I limiti dell' interpretazione [1990])*, trans. Myriem Bouzaher (Grasset).

Eisenberg, Eric M. (2006), 'Karl Weick and the Aesthetics of Contingency', *Organization Studies*, 27 (11), pp. 1693–707.

Emaz, Antoine (2009), *Cambouis* (Seuil).

Ende, Leonor van den and Marrewijk, Alfons van (2015), 'The Social Construction of Cultural Differences in a Siberian Joint-Venture Megaproject', *Journal of Strategic Contracting and Negotiation*, I (2), pp. 168–85.

Erny, Pierre (1987), *L'enfant et son milieu en Afrique noire* (L'Harmattan).

Faure, Guy-Olivier (2004), 'Approcher la dimension interculturelle en négociation internationale', *Revue française de gestion*, 6, pp. 187–99.

Feely, Alan J. and Harzing, Anne-Wil (2003), 'Language Management in Multinational Companies', *Cross-Cultural Management*, 10 (2), pp. 37–52.

Foner, Eric (1998), *The Story of American Freedom* (WW Norton & Company).

Fourquet, Jérôme, Mergier, Alain, and Morin, Chloé (2018), 'Inutilité ou absence de reconnaissance: de quoi souffrent les salariés français?', *Fondation Jean Jaurès*, 3 (10).

Frederiksson, Riikka, Barner-Rasmussen, Wilhelm, and Piekkari, Rebecca (2006), 'The Multinational Corporation as a Multilingual Organization: The Notion of a Common Corporate Language', *Corporate Communications: An International Journal*, 11 (4), pp. 406–23.

Frois, Luis R. P. (1998 [1985]), *Européens et Japonais. Traité sur les contradictions et différences de mœurs. Préface: Claude Lévi-Strauss* (Chandeigne).

Fucini, Joseph J. and Fucini, Suzy (1990), *Working for the Japanese: Inside Mazda's American Auto Plant* (Free Press).

Garfinkel, Harold (1973), *Studies in Ethnomethodology* (Polity Press).

Geertz, Clifford (1968), *Islam Observed: Religious Development in Morocco and Indonesia* (The University of Chicago Press).

Geertz, Clifford (1973), *The Interpretation of Cultures:Selected Essays* (Basic Books).

Geertz, Clifford (1983), *Local Knowledge. Further Essays in Interpretative Anthropology* (Basic Books).

Geoffroy, Christine (2001), *La mésentente cordiale* (Grasset).

Geshiere, Peter (2013), *Witchcraft, Intimacy, and Trust, Africa in Comparison* (University Press of Chicago).

Gibson, Cristina B. and Zellmer-Bruhn, Mary E. (2001), 'Metaphors and Meaning: An Intercultural Analysis of the Concept of Teamwork', *Administrative Science Quarterly*, 46 (2001), pp. 274–303.

Giddens, Anthony (1984), The Constitution of Society: Outline of the Theory of Structuration (University of California Press).

Giraud, Bernard (2000), 'L'entreprise confrontée à sa responsabilité sociale', *Le Journal de l'Ecole de Paris du management*, (juillet-août), pp. 1–9.

Glaser, Barney G.and Strauss, Anselm L. (1973), *The Discovery of Grounded Theory: Strategies for Qualitative Research* (Aldine).

Godin, P. (2009), 'Préface', in Jean-Pierre Segal (ed.), *Le monde du travail au cœur du destin commun* (No. halshs-00666396: Editions de la direction du travail et de l'emploi).

Godong, Serge-Alain (2011), *Implanter le capitalisme en Afrique, bonne gouvernance et meilleures pratiques de gestion face aux cultures locales* (Karthala).

Granet, Marcel (1994 [1929]), *La civilisation chinoise: la vie publique et la vie privée* (Albin Michel).

Granet, Marcel (2012 [1934]), *La pensée chinoise* (Albin Michel).

Greenwood, Ronald C. (1981), 'Management by Objectives: as Developed by Peter Aeschylus, assisted by Harold Smiddy', *The Academy of Management Review*, 6 (2), pp. 225–30.

Guillaume, Astrid (2010), 'La traduction au service des ONG', *Hermès*, 56 (Traduction et mondialisation. Cognition, Communication, Politique), pp. 83–9.

Gunnarsson, Britt-Louise (2006), 'Swedish Companies and their Multilingual Practices', in Juan Carlos Palmer-Silveira, Miguel F. Ruiz-Garrido, and Immaculada Fortanet-Gómez (eds.), *Intercultural and International Business Communication* (Peter Lang), pp. 243–63.

Gupta, Anil KumarandGovindarajan,Vijay (2000), 'Knowledge Flows within the Multinational Corporation' *Strategic Management Journal*, 21(4), pp. 473–96.

Halliburton, Chris and Ziegfeld, Agnes (2009), 'How Do Major European Companies Communicate Their Corporate Identity Across Countries? An Empirical Investigation of Corporate Internet Communications', *Journal of Marketing Management*, 25 (9–10), pp. 909–25.

Hamel, Gary (2007), *The Future of Management* (Harvard Business School Press).

Hamilton, Alexander, Madison, James, and Jay, John (1992), *The Federalist or the New Constitution (1787, 1788)* (Everyman's library).

Hampden-Turner, C. and Trompenaars, A. (1993). *The Seven Cultures of Capitalism: Value Systems for Creating Wealth in the United States, Japan, Germany, France, Britain, Sweden, and the Netherlands* (Doubleday).

Hanique, Fabienne (2004), *Le sens du travail. Chronique de la modernisation au guichet* (Erès).

Hardy, Mylène, Wen, Hongjian, and Ma, Fengsu (2008), 'L'image de l'« entreprise exemplaire » en Chine', *Communication et organisation*, 34, pp. 68–83.

Harzing, A.W.K., and Feely, A.J. (2008), 'The Language Barrier and its Implications for HQ-Subsidiary Relationships', *Cross Cultural Management: An International Journal*, 15(1), pp. 49–60.

Harzing, Ann-Wil and Pinnington, Ashly (eds.) (2014), *International Human Resource Management* (Sage Publications).

Helin, Sven and Sandström, Johan (2008), 'Codes, Ethics and Cross-Cultural Differences: Stories From the Implementation of a Corporate Code of Ethics in a MNC Subsidiary', *Journal of Business Ethics*, 82 (2), pp. 281–91.

Henry, Alain (1991), 'Vers un modèle du management africain', *Cahiers d' Études Africaines*, 124, pp. 447–73.

Henry, Alain (1995), 'Quand donc les experts partiront-ils?', *Gérer et Comprendre*,39(Juin), pp. 71–81.

Henry, Alain (1998), 'Les experts et la décentralisation, effets d'illusion au Cameroun', in Philippe d'Iribarne, et al. (eds.), *Cultures et mondialisation. Gérer par-delà les frontières* (Seuil).

Henry, Alain (1999), 'Chroniques d'un management fricain', *Annales des Mines:Gérer et Comprendre*, 56 (Juin), pp. 51–60.

Henry, Alainand Monkam-Daverat, Ignace (2001), *Rédiger les procédures de l'entreprise, guide pratique*(Editions d'Organisation).

Henry, Alain (2002), 'Les experts et la décentralisaton; effets d'illusion au Cameroun', in Philipped'Iribarne, et al. (eds.), *Cultures et mondialisation. Gérer par-delà les frontières* (Seuil), pp. 193–222.

Henry, Alain (2011), 'Les traductions vietnamiennes d'un code d'éthique français', *Annales des Mines—Gérer et Comprendre*, 104 (Juin), pp. 48–60.

Henry, Alain, Tchente, Guy, and Guillerme-Dieumegard, Philippe (1991), *Tontines et Banques au Cameroun, les principes de la société des amis* (Karthala).

Hernandez, Émile-Michel (2007), 'DOSSIER: Le management Africain: pratiques...et théories—Entre tradition et modernitě, proposition d'un modèle de management Africain', *Gestion*, 2000, (1), p. 24.

Hersey, Paul, Blanchard, Kenneth H., and Johnson, Dewey E. (2007), *Management of Organizational Behavior: Leadership Human Resources* (Prentice Hall).

Heusch, Luc de (1981), 'Préface', *De la Souillure* (Translated from *Purity and Danger* 1967 edn:François Maspero), pp. 18–19.

Hobsbawm, Eric and Ranger, Terence (1983), *The Invention of Tradition* (Cambridge University Press).

Hofstede, Geert (1980), *Culture's Consequences* (Sage Publications).

Hofstede, Geert (1991), *Cultures and Organizations: Software of the Mind* (McGraw-Hill).

Hofstede, Geert (2001), *Culture's Consequences: Comparing Values, Behaviors, Institutions and Organizations Across Nations* (Sage Publications).

House, Robert J., et al. (eds.) (2004), *Culture, Leadership, and Organizations: The GLOBE Study of 62 Societies* (Sage Publications).

Howell, Jane M. and Avolio, Bruce J. (2004), 'Transformational Leadership, Transactional Leadership, Locus of Control, and Support for Innovation: Key Predictors of Consolidated Business-Unit Performance', *Journal of Applied Psychology*, 78 (6), pp. 891–902.

Humboldt, Wilhelm von (2000 [1822]), *Sur le caractère national des langues et autres écrits sur le langage*, ed. Denis Thouard (Seuil).

Iribarne, Philippe d' (1989), *La logique de l'honneur, gestion des entreprises et traditions nationales* (Seuil).

Iribarne, Philippe d' (1990), 'Face à l'impossible décentralisation des entreprises africaines', *Revue française de gestion*, 80 (Septembre), pp. 28–39.

Iribarne, Philippe d' (1996), *Vous serez tous des maîtres: la grande illusion des temps modernes* (Seuil).

Iribarne, Philippe d' (1997), 'Les dysfonctionnements des démarches de qualité totale dans l'industrie manufacturière : une étude de cas', *Annales des Mines—Réalités industrielles*, 2 (Février), pp. 17–21.

Iribarne, Philippe d' (1998), 'Comment s'accorder: une rencontre franco-suédoise', in Philippe d'Iribarne, et al. (eds.), *Cultures et mondialisation* (Seuil), pp. 89–115.

Iribarne, Philippe d' (2000), 'Éthiques d'entreprise et mondialisation', in Monique Canto-Sperber (ed.), *Dictionnaire d'éthique et de philosophie morale.* (3rd edn: PUF).

Iribarne, Philippe d' (2002), 'La légitimité de l'entreprise comme acteur éthique en France et aux Etats-Unis', *Revue française de gestion*, 28 (140), pp. 23–39.

Iribarne, Philippe d' (2003), 'Trois figures de la liberté', *Annales. Histoire, sciences sociales*, 58 (5Octobre), pp. 951–78.

Iribarne, Philippe d' (2006a), *L'étrangeté française* (Seuil).

Iribarne, Philippe d' (2006b), 'L'AFD et ses partenaires: la dimension culturelle', *AFD*, Document de travail n°23.

Iribarne, Philippe d'and Henry, Alain (2007), *Successful Companies in the Developing World* (Agence Française de Développement (AFD), Research Department).

Iribarne, Philippe d' (2009), *L'épreuve des différences* (Seuil).

Iribarne, Philippe d' (2011), 'How to Use Ethnographical Case Studies to Decipher National Cultures', in Rebecca Piekkari and Catherine Welch (eds.), *Rethinking the Case Study in International Business and Management Research* (Edward Edgar).

Iribarne, Philippe d' (2012a), *L'envers du moderne, Conversations avec Julien Charnay* (CNRS éditions).

Iribarne, Philippe d' (2012b), *Managing Corporate Values in Diverse National Cultures* (1st edition, 2009: 'L'épreuve des différences', Seuil) (Routledge).

Iribarne, Philippe d' (2013), 'The Effect of Culture on Business ethics', in Jean-François Chanlat, Eduardo Davel, and Jean-Pierre Dupuis (eds.), *Cross Cultural Management: Culture and Management Across the World* (Routledge).

Iribarne, Philippe d' (2014) *Theorizing National Cultures* [online text], Agence Française de Développement (1st edn,2008,*Penser la diversité du monde*,Seuil)(AFD)https://www.afd.fr/sites/afd/files/imported-files/Theorising_National_Cultures.pdf.

Iribarne, Philippe d' (2017), 'Entre droits et mise en scène des rapports sociaux: l'influence des cultures', in Marie-Christine Jullion, Geneviève Tréguer-Felten, and Christian Tremblay (eds.), *L'enfant et ses droits. La Convention internationale des droits de l'enfant à travers les langues et les cultures* (LED).

Iribarne, Philippe (d') and Henry, Alain (2007), *Successful Companies in the Developing World. Managing in Synergy with Cultures* (Agence Française de Développement, Research Department).

Iribarne, Philippe d', Henry, Alain, Segal, Jean-Pierre, Chevrier, Sylvie and Globokar, Tatjana. (eds.) (1998), *Cultures et mondialisation* (Seuil).

Isaksson, Maria and Jørgensen, P. E. Flyvholm (2010), 'Communicating Corporate Ethos on the Web', *Journal of Business Communication*, 47 (2), pp. 119–40.

Iyer, Gopalkrishnan, Sharma, Arun, and Bejou, David (2005), 'Une analyse du processus relationnel sur les marchés internationaux', *Revue française du marketing*202 (2/5 Mai), pp. 99–115.

Jämtelid, Kristina (2002), *Texterochskrivandeieninternationaliseradaffärsvärld. Flerspråkigtextproduktion vid ettsvensktstorföretag.* (Almqvist & Wiksell International).

Jimenez, Alfredo, Boehe, Dirk M., Taras, Vasyl and Caprar, Dan (2017), 'Working Across Boundaries: Current and Future Perspectives on Global Virtual Teams', *Journal of International Management*, 23 (4), pp. 341–9.

Jones, Alexander (1966), 'Genesis', in *The Jerusalem Bible* (Darton, Longman & Todd).

Jullien, François (1997), *Traité de l'efficacité* (Grasset) English translation: Jullien, Francois. *A treatise on efficacy: Between Western and Chinese thinking*, (University of Hawaii Press, 2004).

Jullien, François and Marchaisse, Thierry (2000), *Penser d'un dehors (la Chine). Entretiens d'Extrême Occident* (Seuil).

Kameda, Naoki (2001), 'The Implication of Language Style in Business Communication: Focus on English versus Japanese', *Corporate Communications: An International Journal*, 6 (3), pp. 144–9.

Kameda, Naoki (2014), 'Japanese Business Discourse of Oneness: A Personal Perspective', *International Journal of Business Communication*, 51 (1), pp. 93–113.

Kant, Emmanuel (1985 [1785]), *Fondements de la métaphysique des moeurs* (Bibliothèque de la Pléiade).

Kant, Immanuel (1991), *Kant Political Writings*, ed. H. S. Reiss, trans. H. B. Nisbet (2nd enlarged ed. Cambridge University Press).

Karjalainen, Helena (2010), 'Can Multicultural Human Resources Management Problems Be Solved by an Organisational Culture?', *Management International/ Gestiòn Internacional/International Management*14 (4), pp. 99–114.

Kassis-Henderson, Jane (2005), 'Language Diversity in International Management Teams', *International Studies of Management & Organization*, 35 (1), pp. 66–82.

Katan, David (1999), *Translating Cultures. An Introduction for Translators, Interpreters and Mediators* (St. Jerome Publishing).

Kedia, Ben L. and Bhagat, Rabi S. (1988), 'Cultural Constraints on Transfer of Technology Across Nations: Implications for Research in International and Comparative Management', *Academy of Management Review*, 13 (4), pp. 559–71.

Kim, Uicho, Triandis, Harry C., Kâgitçibasi, Çigdem, Choi, Sang-Chin and Yoon, Gene (1994), *Individualism and Collectivism: Theory, Method, and Applications* (Cross cultural research and methodology series, Vol. 18.: Sage Publications).

Kostova, Tatiana (1999), 'Transnational Transfer of Strategic Organizational Practices: A Contextual Perspective', *Academy of Management Review*, 24 (2), pp. 308–24.

Lafarge (2004), *Rapport annuel*, p. 23: https://www.lafargeholcim.com/sites/lafargeholcim.com/files/atoms/files/05242005-press_finance_Annual_report_2004-uk.pdf (accessed 29 June 2019).

Lagerström, Katarina and Andersson, Maria (2003), 'Creating and Sharing Knowledge Within a Transnational Team—The Development of a Global Business System', *Journal of World Business*, 38 (2), pp. 84–95.

Laloux, Frédéric (2014), *Reinventing Organizations* (Nelson Parker).

Lapaire, Jean-Rémi and Rotgé, Wilfrid (1991), *Linguistique et grammaire de l'anglais* (2nd edn: Presses universitaires du Mirail).

Laplantine, François (2015), *La description ethnographique* (Tout le savoir, n°128: Armand Colin).

Lazarus, Jeanne (2012), *L'épreuve de l'argent. Banques, banquiers, clients* (Calmann-Lévy).

Lee, Miranda Y.P., So, Daniel W.C., and Wong, Lornita Y.F. (2006), 'An Inter-linguistic and Inter-cultural Analysis of Global Corporate Web Sites', *Corporate Communications: An International Journal*, 11 (3), pp. 275–87.

Lévi-Strauss, Claude (1998), 'Préface', in R. P. Luis Frois (ed.), *Européens et Japonais. Traité sur les contradictions et différences de mœurs* (Chandeigne).

Li, Fang (2015), *Rupture organisationnelle et continuité culturelle: une étude de cas - la privatisation d'un hôpital public d'une région centrale de la Chine*(supervised by Jean-Pierre Segal)(Université Paris Dauphine thesis).

Liang, Shuming, Masson, Michel, and Zhao, Xiaoqin (2010), *Les idées maîtresses de la culture chinoise* (Editions du Cerf.Institut Ricci).

Livian, Yves-Frédéric (2012), 'Le concept de compétence interculturelle est-il un concept utile ?', *Annales des Mines—Gérer et Comprendre. ESKA*,2012(1) pp. 87–94.

Locke, John (1960), *Two treatises of government: A critical edition with an introduction and notes by Peter Laslett* (Cambridge University Press).

Louhiala-Salminen, Leena, Charles, Mirjaliisa, and Kankaanranta, Anne (2005), 'English as a Lingua Franca in Nordic Corporate Mergers', *English for Specific Purposes*, 24 (4), pp. 401–21.

Luneau, René (2004), *Comprendre l'Afrique: Évangile, modernité, mangeurs d'âmes* (Karthala).

Lunnan, Randi, et al. (2005), 'CULTURAL COUNTERPOINTS: Global Transfer of Management Practices Across Nations and MNC Subcultures', *Academy of Management Executive*, 19 (2), pp. 77–80.

Lunnan, Randi and Traavik, Laura E. (2009), 'Is the Standardization of Human Resource Practices Perceived as Fair Across National Cultures? The Case of China, Lithuania and Norway'. *Baltic Journal of Management*, 4 (2), pp 127–48.

March, James G. and Simon, Herbert A. (1958), *Organizations* (Wiley).

March, James G., Cohen, Michael D., and Olsen, Johan P. (1972), 'A Garbage Can Model of Organizational Choice', *Administrative Science Quarterly*, 17 (1), pp. 1–25.

Marie, Alain, et al. (2008), *L'Afrique des individus: Itinéraires citadins dans l'Afrique contemporaine (Abidjan, Bamako, Dakar, Niamey)* (Karthala).

Marrewijk, Alfons van (2010), 'Situational Construction of Dutch-Indian Cultural Differences in Global IT Projects', *Scandinavian Journal of Management*, 26 (4), pp. 368–80.

Maurice, Marc, Sellier, François, and Silvestre, Jean-Jacques (1982), *Politique d'éducation et organisation industrielle en France et en Allemagne. Essai d'analyse sociétale* (PUF).

Merton, Robert K. (1952), *Bureaucracy* (The Free Press).

Meyer, John W. and Rowan, Brian (1977), 'Formal Structure as Myth and Ceremony', *American Journal of Sociology* 83 (2 September), pp. 340–63.

Montesquieu, Charles de Secondat (1748), *The Spirit of Laws* (https://archive.org/stream/MontesquieuTheSpiritOfLawsCambridgeIntegral/Montesquieu%20-20%27%27The%20Spirit%20of%20Laws%27%27%20%5BCambridge%2C%20integral%5D_djvu.txt), accessed 15 May 2019.

Morgan, Gareth (1988), *Images of Organizations* (Sage Publications).

Münchow (von), Patricia (2012), 'Cross-Cultural Discourse Analysis and Intercultural Education in Foreign Language Teaching and Learning', *Journal of Intercultural Communication*, 29 (August), http://immi.se/intercultural (accessed on 20 February 2015).

Nakamura, Eriko (2012), *NÂÂÂNDE?! Les tribulations d'une Japonaise à Paris*(NIL).

Neeley, Tsedal (2012), 'Global Business Speaks English', *Harvard Business Review*, 90 (5 May), pp. 116–24.

Neeley, Tsedal (2015), 'Global Teams That Work', *Harvard Business Review*, (October).

Nguyen, Viet Long (2015), *Enjeux managériaux des entreprises internationales dans le contexte vietnamien*(supervised by Jean-Pierre Segal)(Université Paris Dauphine thesis).

Nne'e Onna, Valérie (2016), *Croyances magico-religieuses, imaginaire collectif et commerce, itinéraires de petits commerçants à Yaoundé*(supervised by Jean-Paul Colleyn and Yvan Droz)(EHESS Paris thesis).

Ouchi, William G. (1981), *Theory Z. How American Business Can Meet the Japanese Challenge* (Addison-Wesley).

Pakdil, Fatma and Leonard, Karen Moustafa (2017), 'Implementing and Sustaining Lean Processes: The Dilemma of Societal Culture Effects', *International Journal of Production Research*, 55 (3), pp. 700–17.

Palazzo, Bettina (2002), 'U.S. American and German Business Ethics: An Intercultural Comparison', *Journal of Business Ethics* 41, pp. 195–216.

Parlement français, Auditions, Présidente Odile Saugues (2004), *Rapport sur la sécurité du transport aérien de voyageurs, Tome II* (1717: Assemblée Nationale).

Peters, Thomas J. and Waterman, Robert H. (1982), *In Search of Excellence: Lessons from America's Best-Run Companies* (Collins Business Essentials).

Pinto, Liz (1992), 'Japanese Labor Ideals Don't Fly: Transplant Workers are Disillusioned', *Automotive News*, 9.

Platt, Polly (1994), *French or Foe. Getting the Most out of Living and Working in France* (Culture Crossings Ltd).

Primecz, Henriett, Romani, Laurenceand Sackmann, Sonja (eds.) (2014), *Cross-cultural Management in Practice: Negotiated Meanings* (Edward Elgar).

Riegel, Martin, Pellat, Jean-Christophe, and Riou, René (2001 [1994]), *Grammaire méthodique du français* (PUF).

Riveline, Claude (1995), *Evaluation des coûts, éléments d'une théorie de gestion*, (Presses de l'Ecole des Mines).

Roos, Daniel, Womack, James, and Jones, Daniel (1990), *The Machine That Changed the World* (Rawson Associates).

Rosanvallon, Pierre (2011), *La société des égaux* (Seuil).

Rosny, Eric de (1996), *La nuit, les yeux ouverts* (Seuil).

Rugimbana, Robert and Nwankwo, Sonny (eds.) (2003), *Cross-cultural Marketing* (Cengage Learning EMEA).

Sardan, Jean-Pierre O. de (1995), 'La politique du terrain. Sur la production des données en anthropologie', *Revue Enquête*, 1 (Les terrains de l'enquête), pp. 71–109.

Sauvage, Emmanuelle (2018), 'The Hidden Dimension of Happy Cultural Cooperation', *Management International/Gestiòn Internacional/International Management*, 23 (1), pp. 91–152.

Schell, David W. (1993), *Forgiveness Therapy* (Abbey Press).

Shenkar, Oded (2012), 'Cultural Distance Revisited: Towards a More Rigorous Conceptualization and Measurement of Cultural Differences', *Journal of International Business Studies*, 43 (1), pp. 1–11.

Schwartz, S. H. (1994), 'Beyond Individualism/Collectivism: New Cultural Dimensions of Values', in Uichol Kim, et al. (eds.), *Individualism and Collectivism* (Sage publications).

Scola, Franck (2005). *Couverture santé des Français expatriés: enquête auprès d'un échantillon de la communauté française résidente à Rio de Janeiro* (Université de la Méditerranéedoctoral dissertation).

Segal, Jean-Pierre (1987), 'Le prix de la légitimité hiérarchique. Une comparaison franco-américaine', *Annales des Mines—Gérer et Comprendre*,7, pp. 66–7.

Segal, Jean-Pierre (1990), 'Les pièges du management interculturel. Une aventure franco-québécoise', *Annales des Mines—Gérer et Comprendre*, (Décembre), pp. 47–58.

Segal, Jean-Pierre (2002), 'Le frère déplace le frère; un épisode de la vie d'une usine québécoise', in Philippe d'Iribarne, et al. (eds.), *Cultures et mondialisation. Gérer par-delà les frontières* (Seuil), pp. 19–42.

Segal, Jean-Pierre (2009), *Efficaces ensemble: un défi français* (Seuil).

Segal, Jean-Pierre (2009), *Le monde du travail au coeur du destin commun* (No. halshs-00666396: Editions de la direction du travail et de l'emploi).

Segal, Jean-Pierre (2011), 'Management international au Vietnam', inA. Florin and S.Guillonnet (eds.), *Les apports des sciences humaines et sociales, Actes du colloque international de Hanoi 2011* (Université de Nantes), pp.69–75.

Segal, Jean-Pierre (2011), 'Transférer un cadre institutionnel métropolitain est-il raisonnable? Application à la régulation du travail en Nouvelle Calédonie', in Danielle Leeman, et al. (eds.), *L'interculturel en entreprise: aspects civilisationnels, économiques, historiques, juridiques, linguistiques* (Lambert Lucas), pp. 51–62.

Segal, Jean-Pierre (2013), 'Ruptures organisationnelles et continuité culturelle', in Ulrike Mayrofer and Philippe Very (eds.), *Le management international à l'écoute du local* (Editions Gualino), pp. 231–49.

Segal, Jean-Pierre (2013), 'Les bonnes surprises du management interculturel: le redressement spectaculaire d'une entreprise de transport public en Nouvelle-Calédonie', *Annales des Mines—Gérer et Comprendre*, 114 (4), pp. 61–72.

Segal, Jean-Pierre (2014), 'Gestion & Société's Approach to Cooperation of French Firms', *International Journal of Organization Analysis*,22 (4), pp. 470–85.

Sewell, William H. (1983), *Gens de métier et révolutions: langage du travail de l'Ancien Régime à 1848 (Vol. 23)* (Editions Aubier).

Shenkar, Oded (2012), 'Cultural Distance Revisited: Towards a More Rigorous Conceptualization and Measurement of Cultural Differences', *Journal of International Business Studies*, 43(1), pp. 1–11.

Shimada, Haruo and MacDuffie, John Paul (1986), 'Industrial Relations and "Humanware"—Japanese Investments in Automobile Manufacturing in the United States', (School of Management, Massachusetts Institute of Technology).

Sieyès, Emmanuel (1988 [1789]), *Qu'est-ce que le Tiers-Etat ?* (Champs Flammarion).

Sinha, Durganand and TripathiI, Rama Charan (1994), 'Individualism in a Collectivist Culture: A Case of Coexistence of Opposites', in Harry C. Triandis (ed.), *Individualism and Collectivism; Theory, Methods and Applications* (Sage Pubications).

Soderberg, Anne-Marie and Holden, Nigel (2002), 'Rethinking Cross Cultural Management in a Globalising Business World', *International Journal of Cross Cultural Management*, 2 (1), pp. 103–21.

Spears, Larryand Lawrence, Michele (ed.)(2002), *Focus on leadership. Servant Leadership for the Twenty-First Century.* (John Wiley & Sons).

Sperber, Dan and Wilson, Deirdre (1995 [1986]), *Relevance: Communication and Cognition* (2nd edn: Wiley-Blackwell).

Staber, Udo (2006), 'Social Capital Processes in Cross Cultural Management', *International Journal of Cross-Cultural Management*, 6 (2), pp. 189–203.

Swidler, Ann (1986), 'Culture in Action: Symbols and Strategies', *American Sociological Review*, 51 (April), pp. 273–86.

Thomasset, Alain and d'Iribarne, Philippe (2002), Culture de la relation et rapports de travail dans l'entreprise en Corse(INTEFP).

Thorne, Linda and Saunders, Susan B. (2002), 'The Socio-Cultural Embeddness of Individuals' Ethical Reasoning in Organizations (Cross-Cultural Ethics)', *Journal of Business Ethics*, 35 (1), pp. 1–14.

Tietze, Susanne (2008), *International Management and Language*(Routledge).

Tocqueville, Alexis de (2002 [1840]), *Democracy in America Vol.2*, trans. H. Reeve (University of Pennsylvania https://www.academia.edu/4780188/Democracy_in America By_Alexis_de_Tocqueville_A_Penn State Electronic Classics Series_Publication).

Tréguer-Felten, Geneviève (2012), 'La 'relation client' à la lueur d'une analyse de discours comparative', *Management et Avenir*, 55 (Juillet-Août 2012. Cahier spécial: La question du langage et de la communication dans le management international: un défi pour les hommes et les organisations), pp. 105–26.

Tréguer-Felten, Geneviève (2013), 'Can a Lingua Franca Bridge the Communication Gap between Corporations Set in Different Cultures?', in I. Kecskes and J. Romero-Trillo (eds.), *Research Trends in Intercultural Pragmatics* (Mouton Series in Pragmatics: Mouton de Gruyter), pp. 263–82.

Tréguer-Felten, Geneviève (2013), '"Commun'action" ou "commun'entente"? Un défi linguistique pour les entreprises', *Synergies Italie*, 9, pp. 47–58.

Tréguer-Felten, Geneviève (2014), 'Rhétorique et traduction des discours de communication *corporate*', in Marie-Christine Jullion and Paola Cattani (eds.), *Le Lingue, le culture e la traduzione per la mediazione: Prospettive didattiche e di ricerca/Les langues, les cultures et la traduction pour la médiation: perspectives d'enseignement et de recherche* (L'Harmattan Italia, L'Harmattan), pp. 48–63.

Tréguer-Felten, Geneviève (2017), 'The Role of Translation in the Cross-cultural Transferability of Corporate Codes of Conduct', *International Journal of Cross Cultural Management*, 17 (1), pp. 137–49.

Tréguer-Felten, Geneviève (2018), *Langue commune, cultures distinctes. Les illusions du Globish* (Presses de l'Université de Laval).

Triandis, Harry C. (1995), *Individualism and Collectivism* (Westview Press).

Trompenaars, Fons and Hampden-Turner, Charles (2011), *Riding the Waves of Culture: Understanding Diversity in Global Business* (Nicholas Brealey International).

Usunier, Jean-Claude (1992), *Commerce entre cultures* (PUF).

Usunier, Jean-Claude and Lee, Julie Anne (2005 [1992]), *Marketing Across Cultures* (4th edn: Pearson Education Limited (1st edition Prentice Hall Europe)).

Vernant, Jean-Pierre (2007 [1962]), *Les origines de la pensée grecque* (10th edn: Quadrige/PUf).

Villette, Michel and Fourcade, François (2017 [2016]), 'The incompatibility of worlds within a multinational corporation: The experience of a French expat in a Mexican factory (French version: sept. 2016, n°126)', *Annales des Mines—Gérer et Comprendre*, 2: http://www.annales.org/gc/GC-english-language-online-edition/2017/VILLETTE-FOURCADE.pdf (accessed June 11 2019).

Vinel, Jean-Christian (2006), 'La naissance de la liberté syndicale aux Etats-Unis: Commonwealth c. Hunt (1842), les sociétés de compagnonnage et la liberté d'association', *Cahiers d'histoire, revue d'histoire critique*, 98(janvier-mars), pp. 93–108.

Vo, Anne N. (2008), 'Ch. 10. Le Transfert des politiques et des pratiques de GRH dans les entreprises multinationales', in Marie-France Waxin and Christoph Barmeyer (eds.), *Gestion des Ressources Humaines Internationales* (Editions Liaisons), pp. 415–59.

Wagner, Emma, Bech, Svend, and Martinez, Jesus M. (2002), *Translating for the European Union Institutions* (St Jerome Publishing).

Warnier, Jean-Pierre (1993), *L'esprit d'entreprise au Cameroun*, (Karthala).

Waxin, Marie-France and Barmeyer, Christoph (eds.) (2008), *Gestion des Ressources Humaines Internationales* (Editions Liaisons).

Weber, Max (1978 [1922]), *Economy and Society: An Outline of Interpretive Sociology* (University of California Press).

Weber, Max (1992 [1905]), *The Protestant Ethic and the Spirit of Capitalism* (Routledge).

Weber, Klauss and Glynn, Mary Ann (2006), 'Making Sense with Institutions: Context, Thought and Action in Karl Weick's Theory', *Organizational Studies*27 (11), pp. 1639–60.

Whorf, Benjamin Lee (1956), *Language, Thought and Reality. Essay, Collection of Texts* (The MIT Press).

Wilkinson, Adrian, Wood, Geoffrey, and Deeg, Richard (eds.) (2014), *The Oxford Handbook of Employment Relations: Comparative Employment Systems* (Oxford University Press).

Willis, Paul (1979), *Masculinity and Factory Labor*, reprint in Jeffrey C. Alexander and Steven Seidman, *Culture and Society; contemporary debates*, (Cambridge University Press), 1990, pp. 183–4.

Wittgenstein, Ludwig (1958 [1953]), *Philosophical Investigations*, trans. G. E. M. Anscombe (2nd edn. Blackwell Publishing).

Womack, James. P., and Jones, Daniel T. (1997), 'Lean Thinking—Banish Waste and Create Wealth in your Corporation'. *Journal of the Operational Research Society*, 48(11).

Wuthnow, Robert (1987), *Meaning and Moral Order* (University of California Press).

Ybema, Sierk and Byun, Hyunghae (2009), 'Cultivating Cultural Differences in Asymmetric Power Relations', *International Journal of Cross Cultural Management*, 9 (3), pp. 339–58.

Yousfi, Hèla (2005), *Poulina, un management tunisien* (Agence Française de Développement).

Yousfi, Hèla (2014), 'Rethinking Hybridity in Postcolonial Contexts: What Changes and What Persists? The Tunisian Case of Poulina's Managers', *Organization Studies*, 35 (3), pp. 393–421.

Yousfi, Hèla (2017 [2015]), *Trade Unions and Arab Revolutions: The Tunisian Case of UGTT* (1st edn:Karthala) (Routledge).

Zadi Kessy Marcel (1998), *Culture africaine et gestion de l'entreprise moderne* (Editions Ceda).

Zhang, Ling Eleanor and Guttormsen, David S. A. (2016), '"Multiculturality" as a Key Methodological Challenge during In-depth Interviewing in International Business Research', *Cross Cultural & Strategic Management*, 23 (2), pp. 232–56.

Zhu, Yunxia (1999), *Business Communication in China* (China in the 21st Century: Economy, Society and Politics) (Nova Science Publishers, Inc.).

Zimmerman, Angelika and Ravishankar, M. N. (2016), 'A Systems Perspective On Off-shoring Strategy and Motivational Drivers Amongst On-shore and Off-shore Employees', *Journal of World Business*, 51 (4), pp. 548–67.

Index

Note: Boxes are indicated by an italic '*b*' following the page number.

For the benefit of digital users, indexed terms that span two pages (e.g., 52–53) may, on occasion, appear on only one of those pages.

www.ingramcontent.com/pod-product-compliance
Lightning Source LLC
Chambersburg PA
CBHW071200260726
48726CB00020B/57
* 9 7 8 0 1 9 8 8 5 7 4 7 1 *